Political Campaign Communication

Principles and Practices
Fourth Edition

Judith S. Trent and
Robert V. Friedenberg

Praeger Series in Political Communication

PRAEGER
Westport, Connecticut
London

Library of Congress Cataloging-in-Publication Data

Trent, Judith S.
  Political campaign communication : principles and practices /
Judith S. Trent and Robert V. Friedenberg.—4th ed.
    p.   cm.—(Praeger series in political communication, ISSN
1062–5623)
  Includes bibliographical references.
  ISBN 0–275–96404–3 (alk. paper).—ISBN 0–275–96405–1 (pbk. :
alk. paper)
  1. Electioneering. 2. Communication in politics.
I. Friedenberg, Robert V. II. Title. III. Series.
JF1001.T73   2000
324.7—dc21   99–14854

British Library Cataloguing in Publication Data is available.

Library of Congress Catalog Card Number: 99–14854
ISBN: 0–275–96404–3
     0–275–96405–1 (pbk.)
ISSN: 1062–5623

First published in 2000

Praeger Publishers, 88 Post Road West, Westport, CT 06881
An imprint of Greenwood Publishing Group, Inc.
www.praeger.com

Printed in the United States of America

The paper used in this book complies with the
Permanent Paper Standard issued by the National
Information Standards Organization (Z39.48–1984).

10 9 8 7 6 5 4 3 2 1

To Evelyn Crothers
and the memory of
Aaron Friedenberg

Contents

Series Foreword   xi
  Robert E. Denton, Jr.

Preface   xv

I. Principles of Political Campaign Communication   **1**

1. Communication and Political Campaigns: A Prologue   3
   Importance of Political Campaigns   3
   Changes in the Political Campaign   5
   Technology in the 1996 Presidential Campaign   12
   Communication and Political Campaigns   14
   Organization and Preview of Chapters   15

2. Communicative Functions of Political Campaigns   19
   First Political Stage: Surfacing   19
   Second Political Stage: Primaries   31
   Third Political Stage: Nominating Conventions   43
   Fourth Political Stage: The General Election   55
   Conclusions   57

3. Communicative Styles and Strategies of Political Campaigns   63
   Preliminary Considerations   64
   Styles and Strategies of Campaigns   76
   Conclusions   104

4. Communicative Mass Channels of Political Campaigning   109
   Early Studies   112
   Contemporary Studies   119
   Conclusions   131

5. Communicative Types and Functions of Televised Political
   Advertising   139
   Historical Development   140
   Types and Functions of Political Ads   145
   Televised Attack Advertising When the Candidate Is a Woman 156
   A Final Question   164
   Conclusions   165

II. Practices of Political Campaign Communication   **171**

6. Public Speaking in Political Campaigns   173
   The Decision to Speak   173
   The Speech   181
   Political Speechwriting   189
   Surrogate Speakers   198
   Conclusions   202

7. Recurring Forms of Political Campaign Communication   207
   Announcement Speeches   208
   Acceptance Addresses   216
   News Conferences   225
   Apologias   235
   Conclusions   242

8. Debates in Political Campaigns   249
   History of Political Debates   252
   Deciding Whether to Debate   256
   Applying the Conditions Requisite for Political Debates 259
   Political Debate Strategies   265
   Effects of Political Debates   274
   Conclusions   282

  9. Interpersonal Communication in Political Campaigns   293

     Interpersonal Communication between Candidates and Voters   294

     *Interpersonal Communication between the Candidate and
     Prospective Financial Contributors*   302

     Interpersonal Communication between Voters   311

     Conclusions   314

 10. Advertising in Political Campaigns   319

     Developing a Master Plan for Political Advertising   322

     *Basic Considerations in the Selection of Political Advertising
     Media*   326

     Campaign Advertising Strategies   345

     Media and Other Types of Political Consultants   349

     Functions of Political Consultants   353

     Conclusions   357

 11. Political Campaign Communication: An Epilogue   367

     Selected Bibliography   375

     Index   379

Series Foreword

Those of us from the discipline of communication studies have long believed that communication is prior to all other fields of inquiry. In several other forums I have argued that the essence of politics is "talk" or human interaction.[1] Such interaction may be formal or informal, verbal or nonverbal, public or private, but it is always persuasive, forcing us consciously or subconsciously to interpret, to evaluate, and to act. Communication is the vehicle for human action.

From this perspective, it is not surprising that Aristotle recognized the natural kinship of politics and communication in his writings *Politics* and *Rhetoric*. In the former, he established that humans are "political beings [who] alone of the animals [are] furnished with the faculty of language."[2] In the latter, he began his systematic analysis of discourse by proclaiming that "rhetorical study, in its strict sense, is concerned with the modes of persuasion."[3] Thus, it was recognized over twenty-three hundred years ago that politics and communication go hand in hand because they are essential parts of human nature.

In 1981, Dan Nimmo and Keith Sanders proclaimed that political communication was an emerging field.[4] Although its origin, as noted, dates back centuries, a "self-consciously cross-disciplinary" focus began in the late 1950s. Thousands of books and articles later, colleges and universities offer a variety of graduate and undergraduate coursework in the area in such diverse departments as communication, mass communication, journalism, political science, and sociology.[5] In Nimmo and Sanders's early assessment, the "key areas of inquiry" included rhetorical analysis, propaganda analysis, attitude change studies, voting studies, government and the news media, functional and systems analyses, tech-

nological changes, media technologies, campaign techniques, and research techniques.[6] In a survey of the state of the field in 1983, the same
authors and Lynda Kaid found additional, more specific areas of concerns such as the presidency, political polls, public opinion, debates, and
advertising.[7] Since the first study, they have also noted a shift away from
the rather strict behavioral approach.

A decade later, Dan Nimmo and David Swanson argued that "political
communication has developed some identity as a more or less distinct
domain of scholarly work."[8] The scope and concerns of the area have
further expanded to include critical theories and cultural studies. Although there is no precise definition, method, or disciplinary home of
the area of inquiry, its primary domain comprises the role, processes,
and effects of communication within the context of politics broadly defined.

In 1985, the editors of *Political Communication Yearbook: 1984* noted that
"more things are happening in the study, teaching, and practice of political communication than can be captured within the space limitations
of the relatively few publications available."[9] In addition, they argued
that the backgrounds of "those involved in the field [are] so varied and
pluralist in outlook and approach, . . . it [is] a mistake to adhere slavishly
to any set format in shaping the content."[10] More recently, Swanson and
Nimmo have called for "ways of overcoming the unhappy consequences
of fragmentation within a framework that respects, encourages, and benefits from diverse scholarly commitments, agendas, and approaches."[11]

In agreement with these assessments of the area and with gentle en-
couragement, in 1988 Praeger established the series entitled "Praeger Series in Political Communication." The series is open to all qualitative and
quantitative methodologies as well as contemporary and historical studies. The key to characterizing the studies in the series is the focus on
communication variables or activities within a political context or dimension. As of this writing, over 70 volumes have been published and
numerous impressive works are forthcoming. Scholars from the disciplines of communication, history, journalism, political science, and sociology have participated in the series.

I am, without shame or modesty, a fan of the series. The joy of serving
as its editor is in participating in the dialogue of the field of political
communication and in reading the contributors' works. I invite you to
join me.

                                              Robert E. Denton, Jr.

NOTES

    1. See Robert E. Denton, Jr., *The Symbolic Dimensions of the American Presidency*
(Prospect Heights, Ill.: Waveland Press, 1982); Robert E. Denton, Jr., and Gary

Woodward, *Political Communication in America* (New York: Praeger, 1985; 2d ed., 1990); Robert E. Denton, Jr., and Dan Hahn, *Presidential Communication* (New York: Praeger, 1986); and Robert E. Denton, Jr., *The Primetime Presidency of Ronald Reagan* (New York: Praeger, 1988).

2. Aristotle, *The Politics of Aristotle*, trans. Ernest Barker (New York: Oxford University Press, 1970), p. 5.

3. Aristotle, *Rhetoric*, trans. W. Rhys Roberts (New York: The Modern Library, 1954), p. 22.

4. Dan D. Nimmo and Keith R. Sanders, "Introduction: The Emergence of Political Communication as a Field," in *Handbook of Political Communication*, ed. Dan D. Nimmo and Keith R. Sanders (Beverly Hills, Calif.: Sage, 1981), pp. 11–36.

5. Ibid., p. 15.

6. Ibid., pp. 17–27.

7. Keith Sanders, Lynda Kaid, and Dan Nimmo, eds., *Political Communication Yearbook: 1984* (Carbondale: Southern Illinois University, 1985), pp. 283–308.

8. Dan Nimmo and David Swanson, "The Field of Political Communication: Beyond the Voter Persuasion Paradigm," in *New Directions in Political Communication*, ed. David Swanson and Dan Nimmo (Beverly Hills, Calif.: Sage, 1990), p. 8.

9. Sanders, Kaid, and Nimmo, *Political Communication Yearbook: 1984*, p. xiv.

10. Ibid.

11. Nimmo and Swanson, "The Field of Political Communication," p. 11.

Preface

When the first edition of this book was published in 1983, it was the first book-length study of election campaigns that utilized the principles and practices of speech communication to examine elective politics. While we certainly drew on other disciplines and acknowledged the merit of much of the material they contributed to the study of election campaigns, we argued that communication was the epistemological base of political campaigns. Consequently we wrote from a speech communication perspective. We have been extremely gratified by the reception that our first three editions received. We continue to believe the utilization of the principles and practices of speech communication as a means of examining elective politics contributes appreciably to our knowledge of the electoral process.

If there is any one theme of this book, it is that we view political campaigns as communication phenomena and in the following pages have examined those communication principles and practices central to election campaigns. We have sought to offer readers a realistic understanding of the strategic and tactical communication choices candidates and their managers must make as they wage the campaign. To that end the five chapters in Part I have been edited and updated to reflect what occurred in the 1996 and 1998 election campaigns as well as to consider the early stage of the 2000 campaign. Similarly, all of the five chapters in Part II have been edited and updated to reflect recent election campaigns and any changes resulting from them.

This was a collaborative effort. We examined drafts of each chapter, shared equally in the writing of the epilogue and various editing chores. Chapters 1–5 were written primarily by Juddi, and Chapters 6–10 were written primarily by Bob. Both share any of the successes or shortcomings of this volume.

We wish to acknowledge many people for their aid in producing this book. Particularly helpful to both authors were our colleagues, students, staffs, and libraries of our home institutions, the University of Cincinnati and Miami (Ohio) University. The staff at Praeger was uniformly helpful and pleasant. We also want to thank Emmy Friedenberg for preparing the index while under considerable time pressure.

In addition, Juddi would like to thank Carol Fathman for her professional and dedicated help in preparing the manuscript, Lene Taylor and Gay Gauder for their consistently reliable research help, the many University of Cincinnati students in her political communication classes, Communication Department colleagues, and political communication colleagues across the country who provided valuable comments about the fourth edition. And most important, she would like to thank Jimmie for his constant support throughout this and all other endeavors.

Moreover, Bob would like to acknowledge the consistently excellent support he has received from the Miami University libraries. Librarians Becky Zartner and Lynn Huff were particularly helpful in the preparation of this edition. He would also like to acknowledge the *Journal of the American Forensic Association* for permission to use portions of two articles he originally wrote for *JAFA*. He would also like to thank his many Miami University Political Communication students for their helpful comments on the third edition. Finally, he would like to acknowledge the wonderful support he received throughout the writing of every edition of this book from his mother, Florence, from his children, David and Laura, who are an unending source of delightful distraction whenever writing becomes difficult, and most of all, from his wife, Emmy, for all of her support in so many ways.

Part I

Principles of Political Campaign Communication

Chapter 1

Communication and Political Campaigns: A Prologue

It has become fashionable to criticize our electoral system. Campaigns are too long and too expensive. Candidates are dishonest, concerned only with the image they project, and speak only in sound bites. Voters are bored with the process, distrustful of government and politicians, and frequently do not vote. Although we express these and other complaints, elections, and the political campaigns that are a part of them, are vital to us in at least three different but complementary senses.

IMPORTANCE OF POLITICAL CAMPAIGNS

Elections are important because they allow us freedom to actively participate in selecting our leaders. They are the core of democracy. Nowhere in the world are more people more freely engaged in active, responsible participation in the choice of leadership than in the United States. Whether the election will determine the occupants of two seats on the city council or one chair in the oval office of the White House, the political election campaign is an essential element of a democratic system.

Elections provide us with the opportunity to determine how our own interests can best be served. We may, for example, try to decide which board of education candidate does not favor increasing our property taxes. We might also ask if the Republican candidate for governor sees the need to create jobs as the state's top priority or if the Democratic challenger running for Congress supports increasing money for education and public transportation. Once we feel enough questions have been answered, we must decide how actively to participate in the campaign.

Will we try to ignore it? Will we work for the candidate or political party we favor? Will we vote? Any decision contributes to our self-development and expression.

Elections not only give opportunities for quiet decision making or overt participation in determining who will govern; they also provide the legitimacy with which to govern. The winners of elections receive a general acceptance of their right to power. No matter how large or small the margin of victory, the candidate who receives the necessary votes has been granted a legitimacy quite distinct from power. Any election can give the winner power. Only a democratic election will provide the sense of "rightness" or even "genuineness" necessary to govern or be governed. We may no longer "like" the president for whom we voted two years ago, but we recognize that he has a legitimate claim to the office until the next election. The president, like all other candidates we elect, can only be "overthrown" as a consequence of the next election.

Thus, in pragmatic ways, our electoral system is important to us. No less significant are the symbolic aspects of election campaigns. The British historian J. H. Plumb maintained that there are two histories: the actual series of events that once occurred and the ideal series we affirm and hold in memory. In other words, the past is composed not only of historical "fact" but of what is "made" of history. It is, in the largest sense, the collective memory—the national myth—that unites us as a people. No only do elections provide leaders and grant them authority to govern, they also add to our memory or image of the electoral process and thus give proof that the system is a good one. The fact that we have elections, that leaders are not overthrown by revolution, that citizens freely discuss and participate in the selection process, or that the Constitution "worked" during the Watergate crisis of the 1970s grants support for the belief that the "American Dream" is real and that this country really is destined to be the mighty keeper of liberty. All the fanfare and excitement of the political campaign, be it bands and parades, buttons and billboards, speeches and rallies, television ads and debates, or Internet chat rooms and homepages, is important for the reinforcement provided about the rightness of what we do and the way we do it.

Now, all of this is to tell you that the subject matter of this book is worthwhile. Although aspects of our electoral system may need repair from time to time, the process and the product are worth the effort. While the value of elections has remained constant, the manner in which they are conducted has changed enormously in recent years. As a matter of fact, the political campaign has undergone such a radical transformation that those principles and practices accepted by practitioners and theorists even 15 years ago are largely irrelevant today. Thus, before we can describe and analyze any of the dimensions of campaign communication in the chapters that follow, we must examine those changes that, to the greatest extent, comprise the essence of the new politics. There are four of them that will be discussed in the following order: (1) the decline in the influence of political parties; (2) electoral financing legislation; (3) political action committees; and (4) technological advancements.

CHANGES IN THE POLITICAL CAMPAIGN

The legendary party bosses once determined who would run for political office. In national and state politics, these people were often called kingmakers, who from the sanctity of the so-called smoke-filled rooms at nominating conventions handpicked "their" candidate to be the party nominee. In local politics, especially in the large cities, party bosses, through a system that combined the disposition of jobs with political favors, support, and even protection, controlled the votes, the party, and thus the selection of all candidates.

Decline of Political Parties

Undoubtedly, the most significant change in presidential politics occurred in 1976 when the reform rules adopted by the Democratic party and, to a lesser extent the Republican party, forced changes in state laws regarding delegate selection. Under party rules adopted before the 1976 campaign, the caucus convention procedure was wide open for participation by everyone, and any candidate who could inspire a following had a chance to win delegates. By changing the process of delegate selection, political reformers aided in reshaping the presidential nominating system. In 1968, there were only 15 primaries in which less than 40 percent of the delegates were chosen. In 1976, however, 77 percent of the delegates at the Democratic Convention had come from 30 primary states, reducing the strength of delegates from caucus states to 704 of the 3,008 delegates. In 1996, there were 43 primaries that determined the choices of 77 percent of the 4,289 delegates to the Democratic Convention and 88 percent of the 1,990 delegates to the Republican Convention.

Clearly, then, the reform rules changed the nature of the presidential nominating system by transferring power from party officials to citizens who voted in state primary elections. In fact, by 1982, two years before the 1984 campaign, some Democrats were so concerned about the shift in power that the party accepted a plan proposed by its Commission on Presidential Nominations to add 548 (or 14 percent) uncommitted members of Congress, governors, mayors, and party officials to its 3,675 delegates. For the 1996 campaign, the Democratic party increased the number of uncommitted delegates to 768. Although the proposals sought to return a little of the clout from citizen activists to elected officials, they simultaneously reaffirmed the 1976 commitment to reform, since 82 percent of the delegates to the convention continued to be determined in state primaries and caucuses.

The result is that the change in rules and the proliferation of primaries have weakened political parties, the traditional vehicle for building coalitions and forging consensus. In the past, candidates had to work their way up through party ranks and appeal to party bosses, but since 1976 successful candidates at all levels have often ignored the party regulars, built their own organizations, and taken their campaigns directly to the people. As presidential chronicler and political journalist Theodore H. White reflected, "the old bosses are long gone and with them the old parties. In their place has grown a new breed of young professionals whose working skills in the new politics would make the old boys look like stumblebums."[1]

While for our purposes it is unnecessary to trace the fall of the political bosses from "kingmaker" to "stumblebum," it is important to realize that citizens feel little allegiance to political parties. Each year since the mid-1960s, the results of the election studies conducted by the Center for Political Studies at the University of Michigan have shown that fewer and fewer voters identify themselves as Republicans or Democrats, while more and more call themselves Independents. In 1964, approximately 24 percent of the population eligible to vote labeled themselves as Independents. Thirty years later, in 1994, the Center for Political Studies reported that 35 percent identified themselves as Independent Democrats, Independent Independents, and Independent Republicans. Furthermore, respect for the parties as institutions that represent the public has also decreased.

Finance Reforms

The decline in party identification and influence is not the only element that has altered the nature of the election campaign. Closely related are the reforms in financing which, although initially affecting presidential candidates, have had some effect at all levels.

The Federal Elections Campaign Act of 1974 and the amendment to it in 1976 changed much of the character of presidential campaigning, particularly in the early portion of the electoral process. The act provided for voluntary income tax check-offs, and the money was used by the U.S. Treasury to provide matching grants to presidential candidates who had raised $5,000 in amounts of $250 or less, from citizens in at least 20 states. The maximum any individual could give a candidate was $1,000. But the Supreme Court ruled in 1976 that this ceiling could not prevent individuals or committees from spending unlimited amounts of money in support of a candidate so long as the effort was separate from the candidate's campaign, without any consultation or coordination. Suddenly, "running for president" became a possibility for people who were not wealthy. In fact, in the three elections that immediately followed passage of the act, 36 people were serious enough as presidential contenders to have qualified for federal matching funds. Two of the 36 candidates who qualified, Marion G. (Pat) Robertson in 1988 and John Connally in 1980, refused to use the funds, thereby freeing their campaigns from having to impose spending limits during the primary elections. And in the 1996 presidential campaign, two Republican hopefuls Malcolm S. (Steve) Forbes, Jr., and Maurice (Mory) Manning Taylor, Jr., spent their own money on their campaigns, as did Independent candidate H. Ross Perot.

Not only has the finance law resulted in generating more participation, it has also forced presidential hopefuls to establish themselves among small donors in a number of states. Contenders can no longer rely on the traditional "fat cats" who financed "favored" candidates in the past.

In spite of the limits imposed by legislation, campaigns during the decade of the 1980s and the first six years of the 1990s became more and more expensive. For example, in the 1980 election, candidates for Congress spent $228.8 million, which was well over the 1978 amount of $192.2 million; in the 1984 election, presidential hopefuls spent over $325 million, or double what was spent by those who sought the presidency in 1980; and spending on the total 1984 campaign (local, state, national) reached $1.8 billion, a 50 percent increase over that spent for the total campaign in 1980. Advertising has become a major factor in rising campaign costs. For example, in 1996, President Bill Clinton spent $12 million of his $30 million limit on television ads during the primaries and another $44 million in the general election. Republican challenger Senator Robert Dole spent a total of $78.2 million on advertising and Independent challenger H. Ross Perot spent $22 million, or over 75 percent of his money, on television advertising. In total during the 1996 elections, according to the Television Bureau of Advertising, politicians spent a record $500 million on local and network broadcast TV, and another $30–35 million on cable, or about 30 percent of total campaign spending. In 1988 the cost of a successful United States Senate campaign was $3.1 million, 33 percent more than it had been in 1982. However, by 1996, the average cost of a winning United States Senate race had increased to $4.7 million.

Not only do candidates continue to spend vast amounts of money, they find that they can raise it themselves: In Cincinnati, conservative Republican Baptist minister Charles Winburn, who ran for a seat on City Council in 1993, raised $307,147 and in so doing, doubled the previous fund-raising for a Cincinnati City Council campaign. In fact, in that campaign, 21 candidates spent over $2 million for nine council positions that pay approximately $40,000 a year. Thus, for many who run even for City

Council, governorships, and Congress, the ability to raise money has been the most important effect of the reforms. It has widened the electoral process by bypassing the political parties. Candidates run their own campaigns and frequently hire their own professionals to raise funds— often completely independent of party support or discipline. In turn, raising money has become more challenging because individual voters who view themselves as political independents are contributing to specific candidates and causes and not to political parties.

There have been several challenges to existing campaign finance laws, but none has come as close to passage as the McCain-Feingold bill in 1997. While there was a great deal of posturing about the issue of campaign finance reform by Republicans and Democrats, in the end, nothing was accomplished.

Thus, two factors—the decline of the influence of political parties and the 1970s campaign finance legislation—have combined to change contemporary political campaigns.

Political Action Committees

There is, however, a third and related element that has altered the way in which campaigns are waged—political action committees (PACs) or single-issue groups.

Pressure groups have existed since the founding of the republic. Over the years, the efforts of some of these groups have brought about important changes, such as the abolitionists who helped eliminate slavery and the suffragettes who helped give women the right to vote. However, in recent years, pressure groups have become so powerful and so numerous that their efforts to influence legislation and elections have had a dramatic impact on electoral politics. Their campaigns for or against proposed legislation have often served to fragment the political system, and their efforts to affect the election of specific candidates have contributed to the declining influence of political parties.

Although by definition the single-issue or pressure groups are small, they have nonetheless become increasingly powerful. By the 1980 election, pollsters estimated that one in four votes was willing to vote against politicians for their position on a single issue, and the issues themselves affected 10 to 15 percent of the general electorate. While the issues around which the groups coalesce vary all the way from import quotas to environmental control, it is the so-called emotional or passionate issues (such as abortion, gun control, prayer in school, and sexual preference) that attract the most attention and motivate groups to spring into action quickly if they feel that a proposed bill, or even an individual legislator, threatens their interests. They concentrate on the grass roots, pressuring city councils and state legislators, while simultaneously bombarding members of Congress with telephone calls, telegrams, letters, personal visits, heckling during public appearances, or letting them know that without support for the issue, the PAC will work to defeat them in the next election.

In 1950, there were fewer than 2,000 lobbyists in Washington. However, by the 1978 elections, pressure groups had proliferated to such an extent that there were 15,000 lobbyists based just on Capitol Hill to work for the interests of over 500 corporate lobbies, 61 lobbies working on Japan's interests, 53 minority group lobbies, 34 social welfare lobbies, 33 women's lobbies, 31 lobbies for environmental interests, 21 lobbies for religious interests, 15 lobbies for the aging, 10 for Israel, 6 for population control, and 12 for gun related issues.[2] According to the 1990 *American Lobbyists Directory*, there were more than 65,000 individual lobbyists and 30,000 organizational lobbyists. Although some of these groups had been around for a long time, by 1991 they had formed 4,094 PACs and were much more aggressive in their attempts to influence legislation than they had been in the past. And by 1996, the number of PACs had increased to 4,600.

Through the use of computerized mailing lists that identify supporters, many PACs have been able to raise large sums of money that is spent not only to lobby for their specific issue but to defeat legislators who do not support them and to elect others who do. The ability of the PACs to do this is directly related to the election law reforms we have already discussed. When Congress limited individual campaign donations to $1,000 per candidate, per race, it simultaneously permitted corporations, unions, and other groups to become involved in making direct political contributions to candidates if they established political action committees. While companies are prohibited from contributing corporate funds, through their PACs they may solicit voluntary contributions from employees and stockholders and then give up to $5,000 to candidates in each of their primary and general election campaigns. Thus, for example, a congressional candidate who is oriented toward business can receive tens of thousands of dollars in so-called "soft money" from dozens of corporate PACs, and a union-oriented candidate can receive tens of thousands of dollars from union PACs.

During the 1996 presidential campaign, soft money raised by PACs was most frequently used for media purchases. For example, Republicans aired a commercial that advocated supporting the Republican party, although it did not discuss the support of their nominee, Senator Robert Dole. Similarly, the Democratic National Committee spent an unprecedented $42.4 million on President Bill Clinton's television ads, which appeared on airwaves a year and a half before the election. According to the *Washington Times*, the president conceded after his reelection that the television ads purchased with soft money contributions directly aided his presidential campaign.

The ability of the PACs to raise money to contribute to the campaigns of "friendly" incumbents and "promising" challengers cannot be taken lightly. It is an ability that has been proven in every election since the election law reforms. For example, EMILY's List (which stands for Early Money Is Like Yeast, because it makes the dough rise) raised $6,717,970 for candidates, including $6,319,547 in member contributions to 42 pro-choice Democratic women's campaigns. As such, EMILY's List was the largest funder of United States congressional candidates in 1992 and 1996. During the 1995–1996 election cycle, all of the PACs raised $437.4 million, an increase of 12 percent over 1994, and spent $429.9 million, an 11 percent increase over 1994. Corporate PACs gave $78.2 million to candidates; labor PACs, $48 million; and trade membership PACs, $60.2 million. Among the biggest spenders was the tobacco industry, which contributed $9,988,361, nearly double the industry's contributions in the 1992 election cycle. Philip Morris was the leading contributor, with $4,208,505.

The majority of PAC money goes to incumbents, although in recent election cycles contributions to challengers has been on the rise. In 1988 PACs contributed $66 million to congressional incumbents and only $7 million to those who challenged their seats. However, in 1992, and again in 1996, although PACs contributed far more to incumbents than to challengers, total contributions to incumbents somewhat decreased. In 1996, for example, 65 percent of the PAC contributions were channeled to incumbents, while in 1998, PACs contributed 84 percent of their total contributions to incumbents.[3] In spite of the fact that PACs have increased their contributions to challengers, PACs continue to contribute more to incumbents. The reason for this obvious disparity is that PACs understand that incumbents are far more likely to win elections than are newcomers.

Just as the PACs work toward specific candidates' success, so can they work for their defeat. For example, in 1980, the NCPAC (National Conservative Political Action Committee) targeted five prominent liberal Democratic senators for defeat and ran an extensive media campaign against each. All five, George McGovern of South Dakota, Warren Magnuson of Washington, Frank Church of Idaho, Birch Bayh of Indiana, and John Culver of Iowa were beaten, and because of its financial involvement and the publicity generated by announcing its campaigns against the senators, NCPAC received much of the credit or blame. In 1991 a group of young adults concerned about the nation's economic and social future, who called themselves the Third Millenium, rated and ranked congresspersons on their commitment to the nation's long-term prosperity. "The lawmakers were ranked by their votes on 10 issues with implications for the circumstances of citizens in the twenty-first century, ranging from the federal budget to housing policy and grazing fees, and from economic development to national service and savings and loan bailouts."[4] From those scorecards, the group categorized the politicians into lists of Third Millenium's friends and enemies and directed their money accordingly.

Thus, it would make little sense to discuss contemporary political campaigns without acknowledging the effect of political action committees. They have become an important element because they breach party lines and make uncompromising, all-or-nothing demands on legislators and candidates. They care little for party loyalties, legislative voting records, or a candidate's overall philosophy or platform. They view every legislative roll call and every election as a major test of their cause. And, perhaps because of their zealotry, they have been highly successful in raising money. At any rate, the large-scale entrance of single issue groups into the electoral process has contributed mightily to the changed nature of the electoral process for many statewide and national elections.

It is, however, important to remember that although PACs contribute a good deal of money to specific campaigns, the primary source of funds remains private citizens. It is also interesting to note that because PACs and special interests had become negatively associated with politicians, President Bush refused all external PAC donations made to his 1992 reelection campaign. According to a confidential source at Republican National Committee Headquarters, all checks sent to Bush by all special interest groups were returned promptly.[5]

Technology

Perhaps the most obvious transformation in political campaigns has been in the area of technology. Although the additions of radio in the 1920s and television in the 1950s brought with them a number of alterations to U.S. political campaigns, as technological advancements, they were only the beginning. Today, campaigns from county to national level rely on a number of devices sophisticated enough to have hardly even been envisioned in a campaign as contemporary as Jimmy Carter's in 1976. In so doing, their nature as well as the people who run them have changed. For example, in statewide as well as presidential campaigns, the old electoral map on the headquarters wall showing in what districts the voters live has been supplemented with a map of the major media markets. The new map decides how and where the candidate travels, carves new political regions around the interstate television centers, and pinpoints with the help of the computer, the exact demographic audiences who should serve as the targets of the candidate's campaign. Specialists, not county or state party leaders, now conduct campaigns for the candidates. The specialists who understand the media map can appreciate the intricacies of demographic target selection or the even newer geodemographics. Today's candidates for state legislature, governor, Congress, and president pick their media consultant almost before they do anything else. In fact, as Sidney Blumenthal writes in his book, *The Permanent Campaign*, early in the contest, candidates are often viewed as successful or not successful by the person they are able to hire to run their campaign.[6] The bigger the name of the consultant, the more serious a contender the candidate is considered to be.

Not only have the media consultants taken over the modern political campaign, they are assisted by other specialists—in media advertising, in public opinion polling, in direct mail fund-raising, in street and telephone canvassing, and even in ethnic analysis. As White has written, everything has changed including the vocabulary. Anyone who has the direct ear of the candidate is now called a "strategist," the old-fashioned hatchet man out on the hustings is now styled a "surrogate,"[7] and a sudden rise in the public opinion polls conducted by the candidate's polling specialist shows "momentum." Thus, the sophisticated use of modern technology has brought significant alterations to political campaign communication. When these changes occurred is not really important. Whether they began in 1952 when Dwight Eisenhower first brought television commercial spots to presidential campaigns, in 1960 when John Kennedy became the first presidential candidate to use his own polling specialist, in 1972 when George McGovern pioneered mass direct mail fund-raising, in 1980 when Jimmy Carter campaigned by conference phone calls to voters in Iowa and New Hampshire, in 1984 when Ronald Reagan used satellite transmissions to appear at fund-raisers and rallies, in 1988 when a number of presidential hopefuls used videotapes to deliver their message to voters in the early primary states, in 1992 when former California Governor Edmund G. (Jerry) Brown introduced his 1–800 telephone number for fund-raising and answering questions, or even during the 1996 presidential candidate when candidates rushed to establish a presence on the Internet, the result is the same. Technology has changed the manner in which candidates run for office.

TECHNOLOGY IN THE 1996 PRESIDENTIAL CAMPAIGN

Technology played a significant role in the 1992 presidential election campaign, but by 1996 the use of both old and new technology was even more intensified. Talk television and radio, which first played a prominent role in national political campaigns in 1992, became primary fixtures in the 1996 presidential campaign. Television advertising was once again a major component of candidates' campaigns. President Bill Clinton and Senator Bob Dole relied on 30-second advertisement spots, while H. Ross

Perot's campaign produced 15-second spots as well as nine one-half hour infomercials.[8]

New technological advances helped candidates and parties reach large numbers of people in short periods of time. Blast faxes, for example, sent information to 300 people in just two hours, and teleconferences linked more than 100 callers at a time. The most cost-effective medium was the Internet. For a cost of $8,000, Senator Phil Gramm's campaign set up a homepage that received 197,425 visits or hits. In contrast, the same amount of money spent on a direct mail campaign would have reached only 25,000 people.

Indeed the Internet's potential was realized as the 1996 campaign saw a dramatic increase in Internet-based online services developed by the candidates, parties, news media, and groups of all kinds. Senator Bob Dole established a presence on the web with the *Dole for President* home page, and President Bill Clinton's campaign maintained two Internet sites, the official White House home page and the Clinton-Gore site. With the help of his college-aged son, former Tennessee governor and Republican hopeful Lamar Alexander, targeted university students with his Internet site. The interactive feature of the Internet provided candidates opportunities to hold question and answer sessions with voters and journalists and also allowed political parties to invite instant feedback from voters. Linking web sites with other information sources was another practice employed to reach as many voters as possible. By August 1996, Republican and Democratic web sites formed 59.2 percent of 477 direct links to the party home pages listed on Yahoo!, a popular Internet search engine.[9]

In short, advances in technology as well as the advent of the single-issue group, the election law reforms, and the decline in the influence of political parties have combined to transform the nature and manner of our electoral system. Whether we like it or not, one significant result of these changes has been that we can scarcely avoid taking part in the campaign process. Those who choose not to participate directly become involved at some level, even if it is only to explain to friends why they are refusing to respond to a candidate's telephone survey or why they are turning off the television to avoid political programs and advertisements. "We must actively choose not to be active; hence we are participating symbolically even if not actually" because the political campaign is ubiquitous.[10] Somebody is always seeking elective office and the "somebodies" are no longer strangers but your neighbor, the clerk in the store, or the mother of your best friend. The modern campaign knows no season. It seems that as one ends, another begins. Candidates start running for office months and even years in advance of the primary election. Thus campaigns are now an unavoidable part of our environment, forcing us to become consumers of political communication.

COMMUNICATION AND POLITICAL CAMPAIGNS

The major argument of this book is that political election campaigns are campaigns of communication. Certainly, numerous forms or combinations of economic, sociological, psychological, and historical features are crucial to or reflective of the electoral process. However, the core of each campaign is communication. This is not to argue that a variety of economic and situational needs, power relationships, and a whole host of additional elements and demands do not affect the campaign process or outcome, but rather to say that all of these other factors become important in the electoral system principally through the offices of communication. It is communication that occupies the area between the goals or aspirations of the candidate and the behavior of the electorate, just as it serves as the bridge between the dreams or hopes of the voter and the actions of the candidate. It is through communication that a political campaign begins. Individuals verbally announce their intention to run, and posters/billboards announce nonverbally that election time has begun. During the campaign, candidates and their staffs debate, appear on television, answer call-in questions on radio and television talk shows, prepare and present messages for media commercials, take part in parades and rallies, wear funny hats, submit to media interviews, write letters and position papers, and speak at all forms of public gatherings. They kiss babies, shake hands at factory gates and supermarkets, prepare and distribute literature, produce campaign videotapes, wear campaign buttons, and establish phone banks to solicit money, workers, and votes. In addition, countless hours are spent during the campaign trying to raise enough money to buy radio and television time or computerized lists of voters. All of this effort is for the single purpose of communicating with the electorate, the media, and each other. And when the time comes, it is through communication that the campaign draws to a close. Candidates verbally concede defeat or extol victory, and the posters/ billboards are taken down announcing nonverbally that one campaign is over, even as another begins.

Hence, communication is the means by which the campaign begins, proceeds, and concludes. It is, as we suggested, the epistemological base. Without it, there is no political campaign. It is, therefore, not enough to approach the study of political campaign communication by analyzing the demographic characteristics or the attitudes of the electorate, although the information provided by such work is significant for our overall understanding of the phenomenon. It is also not enough to examine political campaign communication by studying only psychological construct theory or even the relationship and effect of the mass media on the campaign, in spite of the fact that each explains much about the contemporary electoral process. What is needed is a study that provides a communication perspective of a communication event or series of events—the political election campaign. Although you will find references to the works of political scientists, historians, and psychologists, as well as political journalists, we have drawn primarily on the work generated by scholars in communication.

In exploring such theoretical concerns as agenda setting, uses and gratifications, framing, gatekeeping, information diffusion, positioning and repositioning, functionalism, and legitimizing, or even in analyzing the pragmatic details of planning, organizing, and presenting speeches, television ads, debates, or fund-raising appeals, we have been guided by one question: What is it that we ought to study as political campaign communication? Our answers are contained in the subject areas we examine in the following chapters.

ORGANIZATION AND PREVIEW OF CHAPTERS

This book has two parts. Chapters 2 through 5 analyze important principles and theoretical concerns of political campaign communication, while Chapters 6 through 10 examine the crucial practices of contemporary political campaign communication. Although this distinction is designed to help you better understand the phenomenon, in the real world of political campaigns principles and practices blend. As you read the section on principles, keep in mind that in political campaigns principles often generate practices and practices often generate principles. For example, in Chapter 2 when we discuss the principles involved in an individual's surfacing as a viable candidate, principles cannot be meaningfully presented without examining the practices of many individuals who have surfaced. In turn, those practices have subsequently generated many of the principles. Similarly, in Chapter 6 when we discuss the practice of political speechwriters, we cannot readily examine it without developing some of the principles that speechwriters utilize. Thus, artificial as the distinction is, it does provide us with a pedagogically useful organizational framework from which to view political campaign communication.

Following this introductory chapter, the next four chapters focus on principles of political campaign communication. Political communication is a broad term. It has been used to describe the communication involved in winning elections, governing a nation, reporting on governmental activity, gathering and determining public opinion, lobbying, and socializing people into a nation. We have deliberately chosen to narrow the term and focus not on political communication, but rather on political campaign communication. We do not deny of the validity of studying other forms of political communication. However, in a democratic society, to govern one must first win an election. To report on governmental activity, there must first be an elected government about which to report. To lobby, there must first be elected officials to be persuaded. To gather and determine public opinion about candidates and their progress, there first must be a campaign. And to socialize people so that they accept cultural norms, elected officials must first help set the norms. In other words, we believe that political campaign communication is the root of all other forms of political communication. It is undoubtedly for this reason that political campaign communication has been the focus of far more scholarly and popular journalistic inquiry than any other form of political communication. In addition, the number of elaborately planned and professionally implemented campaigns is growing each election year. Thus, it is particularly appropriate to limit our examination of political communication to political campaigns.

Chapter 2 examines the four stages of a political campaign, discussing the many pragmatic and symbolic functions provided by communicative acts to the electorate, the candidates, and the media.

Chapter 3 analyzes the communicative strategies and styles that incumbents and challengers have used in U.S. elections from 1789 to the present. In addition, a third style, one popularized by the two campaigns of Ronald Reagan, is examined.

Chapter 4 presents an examination of the means or channels used in contemporary political campaigns. Theoretical approaches used to study the effect of mass media on political campaigns are discussed.

Chapter 5 discusses the communicative types and functions of televised political advertising. In addition, the way in which women appear to use televised attack advertising in their campaigns is examined.

At the conclusion of these four chapters, many of the principles associated with political campaign communication will have been explored. We hope that by the end of Part I, our readers will have an appreciation of the theoretical basis of campaign communication from the vantage point of a consumer, but we also hope that campaign communication principles will be understood from the vantage point of the user, one actively involved in campaigning for public office. We are aware that readers majoring in such fields as speech communication, mass communication, and public relations may anticipate being involved in political campaigns professionally. Many other readers may also participate in campaigns, if not professionally, at least as highly interested citizens concerned with their communities. We believe that Part I can provide a valuable understanding of the principles of campaign communication from any vantage point that readers choose to follow in the future. Part II focuses on the practices of political campaign communication. In this section, we will discuss five of the most common communication events in contemporary political campaigns.

Chapter 6 examines public speaking in campaigns. It explains how political candidates decide where and when to speak, how they develop speeches, and how they utilize speechwriters and surrogate speakers.

Chapter 7 also focuses on public speaking in political campaigns. But whereas Chapter 6 concentrates on the normal day-to-day public speaking that characterizes campaigns, Chapter 7 examines forms of speeches that occur in most campaigns, are unique unto themselves, and are not day-to-day occurrences. Portions of the chapter deal with announcement speeches, press conferences, speeches of apologia, and acceptance speeches. Each of these forms takes place in virtually every campaign. The purposes and strategies involved in each genre are presented.

Chapter 8 deals with political debates. Debates are often the most anticipated and most publicized communication activity engaged in by candidates. The chapter presents a history of political debating and then discusses the factors that motivate candidates to accept or reject the opportunity to debate, the strategies that are used, and the effect of political debates.

Chapter 9 examines interpersonal communication in political campaigns. Three interpersonal communication situations, typical of all campaigns, are analyzed in light of current interpersonal communication theory.

Chapter 10 concludes the section on practices by considering the advantages and disadvantages of a variety of media used for political advertising in campaigns. It also discusses the key players in political advertising, the consultants.

We find the study of political campaign communication to be fascinating and believe that some of our enthusiasm for the subject is apparent in the following pages. We hope readers come away from this book not only better informed, but also with renewed understanding and interest in a political system that, although abused and attacked in recent years, does not depend on coercion or force but derives its strength from the fact that it relies on human communication, largely as manifested in political campaigns, as a major means of decision making.

NOTES

1. Theodore H. White, "The Search for President," *Boston Globe*, February 24, 1980, p. A1.
2. Leslie Wayne, "Challengers to Incumbents Are Fighting Uphill Battle," *New York Times*, November 11, 1998, p. A26.
3. "Single-Issue Politics," *Newsweek*, November 6, 1978, p. 49.
4. "Generation X Advocacy Groups 11 Legislators 'Enemies'," *Cincinnati Enquirer*, February 20, 1994, p. A1.
5. Telephone interview with confidential source at the Republican National Committee Headquarters, May 12, 1993.

6. Sidney Blumenthal, *The Permanent Campaign: Inside the World of Elite Political Operatives* (Boston: Beacon Press, 1980).

7. White, "The Search for President," p. A1.

8. L. Patrick Devlin, "Contrasts in Presidential Campaign Commercials of 1996," *American Behavioral Scientist* 40 (1997): 1058–84.

9. Michael Margolis, David Resnick, and Chin-chang Tu, "Campaigning on the Internet: Parties and Candidates on the World Wide Web in the 1996 Primary Season," *Press/Politics* 2 (1997): 59–77.

10. Bruce E. Gronbeck, "The Functions of Presidential Campaigning," *Communication Monographs* 45 (November 1978): 271.

Chapter 2

Communicative Functions of Political Campaigns

One of the ways to examine political campaigns is to analyze their communicative functions, that is, to investigate what functions the various forms or acts of campaign communication provide to the electorate and to the candidates themselves.[1] Many of these functions are instrumental or pragmatic in that they make specific tangible contributions. Others are consummatory or symbolic in nature; they fulfill ritualistic expectations or requirements. Both are discussed in this chapter.

The modern political campaign passes through relatively discrete stages, which can be categorized as preprimary, primary, convention, and general election. This chapter is organized and divided analogous to the campaign itself; the different functions are discussed in terms of these four specific stages. It is important to remember that each stage, although discrete, has a direct relationship to and bearing on all that follow. In other words, the functions of each stage affect the entire campaign.

FIRST POLITICAL STAGE: SURFACING

Although the first or preprimary stage has been called the "winnowing period,"[2] we have labeled it "surfacing" because this term more completely conceptualizes those communication activities that occur. Surfacing was originally labeled and defined as "the series of predictable and specifically timed rhetorical transactions which serve consummatory and instrumental functions during the preprimary phase of the campaign."[3] It would be difficult to set an exact time limit on the first stage because it can vary from candidate to candidate and election to election. Political hopefuls must assess their visibility and credibility as well as determine their financial backing and organizational strength. Predictable rhetorical activities (the verbal and nonverbal communication acts) during the surfacing stage include building a political organization in each city, district, state, or region (depending on the geographic scope encompassed by the office being sought), speaking to many different kinds of public gatherings in an attempt to capture attention (media attention for state and national campaigns), conducting public opinion polls to assess visibility or to determine potential issues for which stances will later have to be devised, putting together an organizational structure and campaign blueprint, and raising money. These activities take time whether an individual is running for mayor or for president. As one woman who was elected to a seat on her city council told us, "I didn't just start campaigning. I started planning in January for the November election. And this involved an organized plan—contracting for billboards, purchasing material for signs, mapping out financing and finding volunteers for sign lettering and door-to-door canvassing."[4] A gubernatorial contender, who announced his candidacy 13 months before a Democratic primary in Ohio, justified his early start by saying that his campaign could not be tied to traditional timetables because he had to let people know who he was and what his ideas were so that voters would know that alternatives existed to the "same old names."

If surfacing takes months for city council and gubernatorial candidates, it appears to take even longer for presidential contenders. For example, Vice President George Bush was an early participant in the first stage of the 1988 presidential campaign. Thirty months before the New Hampshire primary, Bush announced the formation of a 476-member national steering committee composed of Republicans from all 50 states. Similarly, in 1989, three years before the 1992 campaign, Senator Bill Bradley began taking public speaking lessons and building a national fundraising base, two sure signs of "presidential fever." In 1990, two years and eight months before the 1992 presidential election, Georgia Senator Sam Nunn was certainly at least thinking about a run for the White House. He resigned from a golf club that does not allow women as members or even as guests and told friends that he would announce his decision about running two weeks after the 1990 Congressional election.[5] Most interesting in 1990, however, was the fact that two years before the 1992 general election some of the most likely Democratic presidential contenders called press conferences, not to announce that they would be candidates for president, but to explain that they would not be entering the race.

It was not that Democrats such as House Majority Leader Richard Gephardt, Senate Majority Leader George Mitchell, or Senators Albert Gore, Jr. and John (Jay) Rockefeller IV had no desire to retake the White

House. It was just that they believed the incumbent president could not be defeated. In January 1991, 13 months before the Iowa caucus and the New Hampshire primary, George Bush, as commander in chief, and therefore, one of the heroes of Desert Storm (the Persian Gulf War that had been played out on American television), had one of the highest approval ratings ever recorded for a sitting president. A *Washington Post/ ABC News* poll[6] found that 90 percent of Americans surveyed approved of his handling of the war and a *USA Today* survey indicated that 91 percent of those polled approved of the job he was doing as president.[7] Thus, those who might have run surfaced early but became frightened by the popularity of the incumbent and declined. And in preparation for the 1996 presidential campaign, at least six Republican hopefuls were showing up at all manner of public events in New Hampshire shortly after President Clinton was inaugurated in January 1993. By May 1993, C-Span had already resumed its campaign program *Road to the White House*.[8] By June 1994 a relatively obscure Republican governor, Carroll Campbell, Jr. of South Carolina, who said he had been planning a 1996 presidential bid by raising money and making trips to Iowa and New Hampshire, announced that he had changed his mind. Considering the two-year campaign that would have faced him, he said "financial considerations had helped him decide to abandon the quest."[9] And on June 25, 1994, according to leaders in the Iowa Republican party, a straw poll of potential Republic contenders won by Senator Robert Dole was the "unofficial kick-off for the 1996 presidential campaign."[10]

The presidential campaign of 2000 had any number of unofficial beginnings. It could have begun in May 1997 when Senator John McCain of Arizona, Senator Don Nickles of Oklahoma, and publisher Malcolm S. (Steve) Forbes, Jr. traveled to New Hampshire (which traditionally holds the first presidential primary) and delivered speeches to "test the waters." Or it could have had its start in August 1997 when more than 1,000 Republicans attended the Midwest Republican Leadership Conference to hear such Republican presidential hopefuls as House Speaker Newt Gingrich, Texas Governor George W. Bush, and Senator Fred Thompson. But one thing is clear, the campaign had certainly begun by September 1997, when Vice President Albert Gore and House Minority Leader Richard Gephardt, the two early frontrunners for the Democratic nomination, were campaigning for organized labor's support for campaign 2000.

Although it is impossible to place a definite time structure on the first stage, we have listed some of the important rhetorical activities the period demands. Thus surfacing begins with candidates' initial efforts to create an interest and image of themselves as candidates and extends through a variety of public rhetorical transactions prior to the first primary election.

But not only do we know what is typically demanded of the candidate during the first stage, we also have some idea of the characteristic functions served by the communication acts of the surfacing period. Although these can vary with the level of office sought (just as the time period does), we have observed seven functions that appear to be important in all political campaigns.

The first function is to provide an indication of a candidate's fitness for office—the "caliber" of the individual. During the campaign, especially the earliest portions when public images of potential candidates are beginning to be formed, the electorate draws inferences from campaign actions about how a particular contender would behave as mayor, or governor, or even president.

The electorate does not want elected officials who are viewed as dishonest, dull, unjust, immoral, corrupt, incompetent, or slick—or even those who are the brunt of television hosts David Letterman and Jay Leno's late-night jokes. In other words, U.S. voters have some preconceptions about people who run for public office. Generally, successful candidates will be perceived as trustworthy, intelligent or competent enough to do the job, compassionate, articulate, poised, and honorable. The higher the office, the more judgmental voters become. For example, voters expect those candidates who run for or serve as our chief executive to be of "presidential timber"—to possess special qualities not always found to the same degree in all people. And although there is not a one-to-one relationship between the two, campaign actions are taken as symbolic of actions as president. We do not want presidents who hit their heads on helicopter doors, fall down steps, mispronounce words, or who are attacked by "killer rabbits." These are behaviors that cause a candidate to be characterized as "clumsy," "dumb," or a "loser" as Gerald Ford and Jimmy Carter were labeled during the surfacing period of the 1976 and 1980 campaigns. As a matter of fact, perhaps conditioned by the negative perceptions of Ford and Carter's actions, voters' assessment of many of the 1988, 1992 and 1996 presidential hopefuls were sometimes harsh. For example, in 1988, before his confrontation with CBS News anchor Dan Rather, then Vice President George Bush was perceived as being a "wimp, a tinny-voiced preppy" who didn't possess the toughness to be president.[11] In 1992, Senator Tom Harkin came to be viewed (in spite of his championing of the poor, ethnics, and laborers) as mean to the people around him, especially those who waited on him. In 1996, former Vice President J. Danforth (Dan) Quayle was perceived to lack the intelligence to be president. Also in 1996, Republican presidential hopeful Phil Gramm was considered nasty, negative, and "charismatically challenged."[12]

Potential presidents are not supposed to be considered wimps or mean people, but neither should reference to them produce laughter. This was the problem with the general perception of Dan Quayle during his vice presidential campaigns and as an early presidential hopeful in the 2000 election. There have been few other national political figures who have been the brunt of so many "dumb" jokes—jokes that were frequently the result of his own misstatements. Among the many infamous Quayle quotes is one made during a speech to the United Negro College Fund when he said: "What a waste it is to lose one's mind or not to have a mind is very wasteful."[13] What he meant to say, of course, is that "a mind is a terrible thing to waste." Whatever the ultimate judgment, certainly one function of the preprimary period is to provide an indication of a candidate's fitness for office.

A second communication function of the surfacing stage is that it initiates the ritualistic activities important to our political system. In his book, *The Symbolic Uses of Politics*, social scientist Murray Edelman discusses the idea of U.S. political campaigns as traditional, rule-governed rituals and then discusses rituals as a kind of motor activity that involves its participants symbolically in a common enterprise.[14] While each of the stages of the campaign demands certain rituals, none is more clearly defined than the activities surrounding the preprimary announcement speech. (Although the announcement speech itself will be discussed in Chapter 7, here we will consider its ritualistic aspects.)

When candidates decide to enter the political arena formally, there are certain protocols that must be performed because they are expected. For example, a press conference is called, the candidate is surrounded by family and friends while announcing the decision to run for office, and then embarks immediately on a campaign swing through the district, state, or nation. The candidate may only be announcing a campaign for the mayor's office, but there are expectations concerning how it is done. However, to capture the full flavor of the announcement ritual, it might be best to consider the presidential campaign of 1996.

The 1996 ritual began on February 24, 1995, when Senator Phil Gramm became the first officially announced candidate for the Republican presidential nomination. Surrounded by cadets and flags, Gramm made his announcement at Texas A&M, where years earlier he had been a professor of economics.

Former Secretary of Education Lamar Alexander returned to his hometown of Maryville, Tennessee to deliver his announcement speech on February 28, 1995. Wearing his signature statement red plaid shirt and surrounded by townspeople, Alexander presented himself as a Washington outsider. His announcement concluded with his Ragtime band playing a chorus of "Rocky Top."

Senator Robert Dole went home to Russell, Kansas, and delivered his announcement address on April 10, 1995. Amidst a shower of balloons, he positioned himself as seasoned and experienced, yet someone who was able to change and keep up with the times.

On September 23, 1995 *Forbes* magazine publisher and millionaire Steve Forbes, Jr. proclaimed his candidacy at Washington's National Press Club. He declared himself to be a Washington outsider who planned to finance his campaign with his own money. He announced his campaign centerpiece, the flat tax proposal, which promised income tax cuts for almost everyone. However, none of the 1996 candidates matched the detailed pageantry of Marion G. (Pat) Robertson's formal "beg me to run" announcement in the 1988 campaign.

During the summer of 1985 Robertson let the media know that people were asking him to run for president. By October 1985 he "allowed as how" he was considering a run for the presidency and was praying about it, seeking God's counsel. Apparently his prayers were answered a few weeks later when he formed an exploratory committee and founded a think-tank called the National Perspectives Institute. On September 17, 1986, Robertson went to Constitution Hall in Washington and on closed circuit television, in a three-hour production of trumpet fanfare, and patriotic song, announced that if three million registered voters signed petitions "telling me that they will pray—that they will work— that they will give toward my election, then I will run."[15] He set a deadline of one year for a show of support that would include the signatures of three million voters on petitions and raise three million dollars by mid-1987. Clearly, one communicative function of the surfacing stage is that it initiates the ritual vital to U.S. politics.

Thus far in discussing the preprimary period, we have been focusing on what has been termed "consummatory functions of campaigning." These functions are essentially symbolic in nature—functions that seem to be rooted more deeply in the heart or soul rather than in the mind of the electorate. In other words, as communication scholar Bruce E. Gronbeck has written, "campaigning creates second-level or metapolitical images, personae, myths, associations, and social-psychological reactions which may even be detached or at least distinct from particular candidates, issues, and offices."[16]

Thus communication during the first stage plays two symbolic but important roles: it provides an indication of a candidate's fitness for office and initiates the ritual we have come to expect in political campaigns. However, there are five additional contributions provided by the communication acts and symbols during the surfacing period. These functions are related to the pragmatic aspects of the campaign and have thus been labeled "instrumental."

The first of these functions is that the electorate begins to have some knowledge about a candidate's goals, potential programs, or initial stands on issues. During the surfacing period, in an attempt to determine if and with whom their campaign has any appeal, candidates must speak at countless neighborhood coffees, potluck dinners, and service club meetings. During these appearances, they often have to answer questions about why they are running for office as well as state their positions on specific issues important to those attending the gathering. Answers may at first be sketchy, but as the frequency of the speaking occasions and the perceived receptivity of the audiences increases, so does the candidate's confidence. Statements about political goals and aspirations as well as positions on issues become refined. What was in the beginning somewhat tentative, now becomes more definite as the candidate proceeds to formulate statements of philosophy apparently acceptable to most potential constituents. For example, when Congresswoman Elizabeth Holtzman decided to enter the 1980 New York senatorial race, she began scheduling a number of appearances throughout the state months before the primary. Countless efforts were made not only to expand her visibility from one congressional district to the whole state but also to let the electorate know what her positions were on issues wider than those facing her current constituents.

During the eight years in which Holtzman had been a member of the House of Representatives, she had demonstrated an ability to work for the fairly narrow concerns of her Kings County constituents. But with the decision to move from the House to the Senate, the congresswoman had to establish her understanding of and commitment to problems and issues facing a larger and more diverse audience. The surfacing period provided Holtzman the opportunity not only to determine what the issues were but to formulate positions that could be and were used during the second or primary stage of her campaign for the United States Senate.

Closely related is the second instrumental function—voter expectation regarding a candidate's administrative and personal style begin to be established. For example, candidates who have well-organized and disciplined staffs provide some knowledge about the kind of administration they might have if they are elected. Even in a campaign for a seat on the local school board, those candidates who right from the beginning appear to be operating from a precise plan or blueprint with regard to where and when they will canvass the district, or distribute literature, or speak at neighborhood coffees provide voters with information regarding the level of organization and efficiency it might be reasonable to expect if and when they are elected to the school board.

The personal style of a candidate is also revealed during the early days of a campaign. Perhaps one of the most interesting examples occurred during the preprimary period of the 1980 presidential campaign. Before Edward Kennedy began his pursuit of the presidency, he, like his brothers before him, had been perceived as an excellent speaker, a master of the art of campaigning and campaign rhetoric. Thus the expectations of the public were high—so high that it is unlikely that any candidate could have lived up to the dimensions of the Kennedy mystique. But in the first few ventures away from Washington and Boston, the senator fell far short. He read his speeches (he always had, but no one ever seemed to have noticed before), mispronounced words, seldom looked up from manuscripts to establish eye contact with his audience, stumbled frequently using vocal pauses or qualifiers such as "uh" or "ah," appeared confused in answers to questions on material and issues he should have known, rambled, and appeared unable to speak without constant reliance on manuscripts and specially prepared charts. Deficiencies were exaggerated because of high expectations, but the point is that the surfacing period is important for its revelations of a candidate's personal and administrative style.

The third instrumental function of surfacing is that it aids in determining what the dominant theme or issues of the campaign will be. The early candidates set the rhetorical agenda for the campaign. As they crisscross the country, state, congressional district, or even the city, they begin to come to grips with the issues on people's minds, begin to address themselves to those issues, and, as we noted earlier, begin to formulate "solutions" to problems that seem to be compatible with popular perception. In national or statewide elections, the media repeat a candidate's statements and thus aid in translating the problems and positions into national or state issues. In local campaigns, candidates often determine the problems by word of mouth rather than the media. A friend of ours who ran for a seat on a city council had a fairly direct method for determining the issues on voters' minds. Instead of polling, which he could not afford, or public appearances before various groups, which he wished to avoid until the announcement of his candidacy, he simply began attending weekly meetings of the city council nine months before the election. In this way, he had some guidance in selecting issues for his campaign because he was able to learn on a firsthand basis which issues were important or controversial enough to be discussed in council meetings. Thus, the surfacing stage is important because the rhetorical agenda begins to be established. If these early concerns are widespread enough, they can become the dominant issues in succeeding stages of the campaign. And those candidates who surface early help determine what will be the agenda.

The surfacing stage in 1996 was like most others. During their campaigning in New Hampshire and other early primary/caucus states, candidates became aware of issues on voters' minds and began to formulate agendas to match popular concerns. Among the issues tested by early Republican contenders were those related to the economy and to the economic anxiety of many American families. Phil Gramm, for example, talked about the need to cut government spending and taxes and the benefits of balancing the federal budget. Lamar Alexander discussed the need to overhaul the welfare system so that people in real need could receive financial assistance. And Steve Forbes, Jr. touted his plan to implement a flat tax and the economic benefits that would derive from it. However, it was Pat Buchanan who tapped into the economic anxieties felt by many voters. He blamed economic concerns (job security, underemployment, and income stagnation) on corporate downsizing and relocating overseas, free trade pacts and agreements on tariffs, illegal immigration, and on the "New World Order" that would create a single government and overtake the United States.[17]

The Republican contenders were not alone in their focus on economic insecurity issues; the 1996 Democratic incumbent president also joined the dialogue. In fact, President Clinton's early television advertising campaign went beyond simple discussion and placed blame on Republicans for not working with his administration to solve budget and economic problems and criticized congressional Republicans for wanting to cut Medicare and Social Security Programs. Clinton's condemnation of Republicans as responsible for the nation's economic insecurities continued throughout subsequent stages of the campaign and contributed to Clinton's eventual defeat of his challenger.

The first stage is also important because it begins the process of selecting front-runners or separating the serious contenders from the not so serious. Becoming a serious candidate during the surfacing period involves obtaining visibility. Even in small races, much less in state or national contests, obtaining visibility requires persuading the media that one is a viable enough candidate to deserve attention.

Almost from the beginning, at least in state and national contests, the media strongly influence who will be considered a major candidate. Despite the fact that Lamar Alexander began organizing his campaign for the Republican nomination immediately following the November 1992 election, the media did not make him visible and he dropped out of the race without winning a primary. Texas Senator Phil Gramm organized his fund-raising long before the first primaries in 1994 and acquired enough money to frighten off potential challengers. However, he was beset by image problems and removed himself from the race after he placed fifth in the Iowa Caucus. Pennsylvania Senator Arlen Specter entered the 1996 presidential race in March 1995. When he withdrew from the campaign less than eight months later, he had not achieved any noticeable increase in national visibility.[18]

Visibility during the surfacing period is often the initial reaction of the media to a candidate's past or present self. This has been illustrated a number of times when people who have achieved national recognition in the nonpolitical arena have decided to run for public office and the media have, in a relatively short period of time, turned them into serious candidates. Consider the cases of Senator John Glenn (one of the first U.S. astronauts), Senator Bill Bradley (a former All American and All Pro basketball player, and a Rhodes scholar), California mayors Clint Eastwood and Sonny Bono (famous actor and singer), the former governor of California, Ronald Reagan (a movie actor and television host) and H. Ross Perot (the Texas billionaire). This was demonstrated, for example, during the surfacing period of the 1988 presidential campaign when Gary Hart and Jesse Jackson, because of previous roles, were selected by the media as serious presidential contenders and thus accorded early and extensive coverage. To a lesser extent, this had also been a factor affecting Governor Jerry Brown and Senator Edward Kennedy during the surfacing period in 1980. However, in 1980, neither the past nor current positions of Brown and Kennedy were as important in generating visibility as was the fact that each was challenging his party's incumbent. Intraparty challenges such as theirs in 1980, Ronald Reagan's in 1976, Eugene McCarthy's in 1968, and Pat Buchanan's in 1992 normally attract media attention.

Who candidates are and their current position also aid in determining initial visibility. For example, George Bush and Robert Dole were considered the leading contenders during the early stage of the 1988 presidential campaign because of their positions as vice president and Senate minority leader. The capability of some jobs to generate visibility was also demonstrated by two people who held powerful positions outside of the federal government during the surfacing period of 1988. In fact, Mario M. Cuomo, governor of New York, and Lee Iacocca, chairman of the board and chief executive officer of the Chrysler Corporation, received so much attention from the national media regarding their presidential prospects that each had to call a press conference to announce he was not then a candidate and would not be a presidential candidate. Conversely, Pat Robertson, Alexander Haig, Bruce Babbitt, and Pierre DuPont were not thought of as serious candidates by the media because they did not have current or powerful positions in government. A second run for the presidential nomination can foster high visibility, as exemplified by Senator Robert Dole's campaign during the 1996 presidential election. As Senate majority leader and previous presidential hopeful, he had national visibility that no other Republican contender could match. In fact, as early as December 1993, a public opinion poll proclaimed him the leading Republican candidate.[19]

Quite apart from persuading the media that one is a front-runner based on roles and present positions, a candidate may also emerge from the surfacing period as a possible leading contender by successful grassroots organizing and fund-raising. Acquiring sufficient money to generate the momentum necessary to do well in the primary stage has always been and continues to be important for local, state, and congressional candidates. But with the advent of the campaign-financing laws, motivating enough support to raise the money to qualify for federal matching funds has become crucial to presidential contenders.

Becoming a front-runner because of early grassroots organizing and successful fund-raising helps explain the initial successes of presidential contenders such as Jimmy Carter in 1976, Michael Dukakis in 1988, and Bill Clinton in 1992. Not one of them had been considered a serious candidate by the media prior to the first or second competition. Each used the surfacing period to gather the strength necessary to do well in the first contests (Iowa and New Hampshire) and thus forced the media to acknowledge them as serious presidential candidates.

On the other hand, not using the surfacing period to become a front-runner through grassroots organizing and fund-raising in the early primary/caucus states helps explain the initial losses experienced by at least three of the 1996 contenders.

Indiana Senator Richard Lugar announced his intention to run on April 19, 1995 with only a "bottoms up" operation in Iowa and New Hampshire. He had no established campaign operation in any of the early primary states. And since he began many months behind the other contenders, he did not have any big name political support, because they were already committed to other candidates. In addition, he had raised only $4 million compared to the $20 to $25 million that the "leading" contenders collected. On top of all of this, Lugar's announcement to run was "all but drowned out in the press by the Oklahoma City bombing that very day."[20] Not surprisingly, on March 7, 1996 Lugar withdrew from the race, having finished no better than fifth in any of the first eight primaries.

Similarly, on March 29, 1995, when Patrick J. Buchanan announced that he would run for the presidency, he did so without first raising the money or organizing a campaign that could effectively carry him through the 1996 primaries and caucuses. A veteran of the 1992 primaries, he had been unsuccessful in overthrowing the sitting president of his own party (although he had weakened Bush enough to aid in making him vulnerable to the Democratic attack during the general election). Throughout his candidacy, Buchanan operated with a minimal budget. The campaign did not have a pollster, and Buchanan did his own speechwriting and fund-raising, just as he had done in 1992. By the end of February, Buchanan had to abort a plan to challenge Robert Dole in North and South Dakota, because resources had to be directed to the Arizona and South Carolina primaries.

Steve Forbes, Jr. announced his candidacy for the Republican nomination on September 23, 1995. Although he planned to finance his campaign with his own fortune, he lacked organizational support and placed fourth in the February 12 caucus. He eventually had more success, but by the time of "Junior Tuesday" and the New York primary, the race came down to Dole's organizational support and Forbes' money. Clearly there were other dimensions, but the organization of the Dole campaign in each of the primary/caucus states was the dominating factor.

If surfacing has ever been difficult for candidates to negotiate, by the time of the preprimary stage of the 2000 campaign, it became almost impossible—at least for those presidential hopefuls not well known or well financed. In October 1998, California Governor Pete Wilson signed legislation to move his state's presidential primary to March 7, 2000— the same date of the primaries in New York, Connecticut, Maryland, and Massachusetts. Moving the California primary from June to early March will virtually force candidates to run simultaneous campaigns in the two largest and most expensive media markets, California and New York. Thus, early grassroots organizing and fund-raising are likely to be major factors in determining who will be successful and who will not.

The final communicative function of the surfacing stage is that the media and the candidates get to know one another. While this function is often not vital for local campaigns, it can be important in congressional and state races, and it is absolutely crucial in presidential campaigns. It is in these contests where we can most completely understand the significance of the function to the entire campaign.

At each stage of the campaign, the relationships between candidates and the media who cover them are vital not only to the candidate but to the individual media representative. The candidate needs the visibility that only the media can provide and the media need information that only access to the candidate or immediate campaign staff can provide. It is not, especially in the preprimary period, the adversarial relationship as is commonly pictured. As one analyst who studied the media-press relations of the 1976 Carter campaign summarized:

A symbiosis of the goals of journalists and those who manage campaigns provides for a good deal of mutually beneficial interaction. On the one hand, news reporting organizations certainly define the presidential race as a story which must be covered . . . and are willing to expend considerable resources in news gathering. . . . Presidential candidate organizations, on the other hand, seek to use the news reporting process as a relatively inexpensive means of communicating with voters and political activists. Campaigns, therefore, are happy to facilitate journalists in the conduct of their work.[21]

Relationships can be established during the surfacing stage because there are few media representatives assigned to cover a specific candidate and because the candidate has a skeleton traveling staff—perhaps only the campaign director and candidate. Contact is informal; candidates and staff are accessible. It is a time for finding out details and learning enough about one another to know who can be counted on when or if the candidate's campaign begins to gather momentum. Conditions change from the first stage to the second, and it is the surfacing period that allows media and candidate to get to know one another. The importance of the relationship is first that it provides the opportunity for local media/candidate interaction, which is not always available after candidates find they can get national exposure, and second it gives both candidate and national media representatives a contact to be used later. In other words, the reporter soon discovers who on the staff will have the "real" story or lead and the candidate's people know not only who they can trust but which reporter has the best chance of getting stories in print or on the air. Similarly, candidates themselves frequently try to establish relationships with a few of the major political journalists. Throughout the early stages of the 1992 campaign, Clinton, for example, sought the advice of writers his staff referred to as the "new breed of journalists," columnists such as E. J. Dionne, Jr. of the *New York Times*.[22] In other words, it is a reciprocal relationship and a significant function of surfacing.

These, then, are the necessary functions served by communicative acts during the first political stage. The period is crucial because of the functions it provides. Candidates who announce late and thus do not participate in surfacing activities or those who fail to use the period wisely have little success and frequently do not even advance to the second stage.

SECOND POLITICAL STAGE: PRIMARIES

Primary elections are, at any level, "America's most original contribution to the art of democracy."[23] Under the primary system, voters who make up the political party determine who the party's candidates will be. Although the system varies from state to state, generally, primaries provide for a full-fledged intraparty election with the purpose of choosing a single candidate from each party to run in the general election. Direct primary elections, unlike the presidential primary, normally have a degree of finality in that the winning candidate is automatically placed on the November ballot. But in instances where there are a number of candidates competing for the same office, it is often necessary to have a second or runoff primary because one candidate usually does not capture a majority of votes in the first election. In the case of the presidential primary, even after all of the state elections have been held, the party nominees still have not been chosen. The national nominating convention (the third political stage) officially selects the candidate. Thus in presidential campaigns, primary elections are only one phase of the nominating process, not the final act or choice.

There are almost as many variations of primaries as there are states. For example, Wisconsin for many years had what was known as the most "pure" of the open primaries because voters could vote in any primary (it was not necessary to be preregistered and vote as a Republican or as a Democrat and vote only in that party's primary) and have their vote remain secret. Registration took place on primary day and crossover voting was the norm. Connecticut, on the other extreme, only began holding full-fledged presidential preference primaries in the 1980s. For many years, the state allowed party leaders to choose its statewide candidates without fighting it out in primary elections.

Not only are there different forms of state primaries, some states do not even hold direct primaries but operate under the caucus system to determine nominees. To further complicate the process, the political parties within one state may vary in terms of their selection procedure. For example, in 1980 Michigan Republicans stayed with the direct primary, while Michigan Democrats switched to a caucus system after they were unsuccessful in their efforts to get the legislature to change the state's law to prevent or inhibit crossover voting. By the time of the 1988 presidential election, however, it was the Michigan Republicans who changed the process. In an attempt to play a significant role in determining the presidential nominee, Republicans established a multitiered delegate selection process that began with party precinct elections on August 5, 1986. Although Michigan Republicans were clearly hoping to replace Iowa's influence in 1988, Iowa remains one of the two best known caucuses or primaries because since 1976 it has so frequently been the first real presidential testing ground for candidates of both political parties. In 1996 the Iowa caucus began the night of February 12, in living rooms, schools, church basements, and firehouses. Democrats and Republicans gathered by precinct to elect delegates to county conventions who in turn chose delegates to state conventions and finally to the national conventions. The whole process took until June. In 1992, the Iowa caucus played little or no role in the presidential campaign because Iowa's senior Senator Tom Harkin was pretty much assured the backing of the Iowa Democratic party. However, in 1996, the Iowa caucus resumed some of its former importance in the process because the two Republicans who ultimately began to lead the pack, Senator Robert Dole and Patrick Buchanan, won first and second place in the Republican caucus, and Phil Gramm, an early favorite in terms of fund-raising, dropped out two days after the Iowa caucus results were made known.

Interestingly, Maine has essentially the same system as Iowa, but timing and precedence has given the Iowa caucuses inordinate importance. In spite of the fact that local and state nominees are not selected at the precinct level and although proportionately fewer national nominating convention delegates for either party come from Iowa, the candidates who won the precinct caucuses in 1976, 1980, 1984, 1988, and 1996 received enormous publicity boosts from the national media.

Many professional politicians and party leaders hate the primary stage of a campaign because a genuine primary is a fight within the family of the party—a fight that can turn nasty as different factions within the family compete with each other to secure a place on the November ballot for their candidate. In addition, primaries can exhaust candidates, leaving them physically, emotionally, and financially drained just before the most important battle. Charges and countercharges of candidates and their staffs often provide the opposition party with ammunition they can use during the general election campaign. Moreover, beginning with the presidential primaries of 1980, another problem developed when the unit rule forced changes in strategy and thus made the presidential primary system even more detested by party leaders than it had been. Under the new rules, there could be no winner-take-all victory anywhere. Every state and every congressional district was forced to divide its delegates in proportion to the votes the candidates had won, and then candidates would "own" the delegate chosen in their name. In practical terms, it meant that no state was worth a candidate's full attention, and yet no state could really be ignored. Each candidate had to campaign everywhere in each primary because even in losing the state, the candidate could still get a substantial share of the delegates.

Finally, primaries use a lot of money—funds not only from contributors who might have been generous for the later campaign, but money that can be a drain on state and national resources in terms of matching funds. The total amount spent by the Democratic and Republican presidential candidates in the 1992 primaries and caucuses was approximately $153 million. And in 1996, the total spent by the candidates of both parties during the primary and caucus season was more than $390 million.[24]

One reason inordinate amounts are spent on this stage of presidential campaigns is that there are so many primaries and they last so long. In 1996, for example, there were 43 primaries and 16 caucuses (not including the Alaska Republican Straw Ballot Caucus). They began on February 6 in Louisiana and did not conclude until June 14 when voters in New Mexico went to the polls. While the 1996 schedule was as drawn out as those of the previous six, it is important to note that the earliest major contests, Iowa and New Hampshire, frequently have more influence in selecting the eventual nominees than larger states simply because their caucus and primary are traditionally first. In 1996, much to the consternation of many Republican party loyalists, Louisiana grabbed the lead as the first contest. However, not all candidates participated for fear of upsetting party traditionalists. Despite their size, Iowa and New Hampshire have frequently been able to exert an inordinate amount of influence because candidates have used the win to focus national attention on their campaigns and build a momentum that has granted them front-runner status from the media. The idea is that the national surge of publicity provides a substantial "bounce" toward the nomination so that later when states with large numbers of delegates go to the polls, the race is effectively over.

At least that has been the case through the 1996 presidential election. "Campaign 2000," however, may be different because a number of states have moved their primaries closer to Iowa and New Hampshire so that they, too, will have a say in determining who will be the nominees of the two major parties. Although front-loading (the effort of states to put their primary or caucus at the front or beginning of the primary season) has been a factor in presidential politics since 1984, it will reach new heights in 2000 when two-thirds of all of the presidential state delegates are likely to be determined within two and a half weeks.

Yet, for all of the problems with this second political stage, there are five functions that the communication acts and symbols of the period provide. While we do not want to suggest that primaries (particularly the presidential primary system) need no revision, we do believe these five functions are important to the entire political campaign process. The first relates directly to the candidates and the final four to the electorate.

For candidates, the primary season is a source of feedback from the voters about their campaigns, the organization they have put together, the competence of staffs, fund-raising efforts, physical stamina—in other words, their strengths and weaknesses as campaigners. During the surfacing period, the candidates' only measures of how they are doing are the comments of the media and, in some cases, the results of polls. But the primaries provide direct feedback from the voters and thus a chance for repositioning in terms of stands on issues, themes, images, and overall campaign strategies. Obviously, for those candidates who have only one primary in which to compete (most local, state, and congressional contenders), the feedback is either of no use (except as it may account for defeat), or it is used to plan for the general election. For example, feedback from the first campaign of candidates such as John Glenn of Ohio, Lee Dreyfus of Wisconsin, and S. I. Hayakawa of California allowed them to reposition their public images from astronaut or academician to senator or governor. For presidential candidates, the early contests are direct sources of feedback that can be used immediately as preparations are made for campaigning in subsequent states. There are times, of course, when repositioning does not work, as was the case in 1984 when John Glenn attempted to reposition his image from astronaut during the Iowa caucus to experienced statesman during the New Hampshire primary. But there are other times when it has. One of the most dramatic was the repositioning of Ronald Reagan's image and campaign strategy during the 1980 primaries.

As conceived originally by then campaign manager John Sears, Ronald Reagan's 1980 quest for the presidency was to be a regal campaign, one in which Reagan would slowly but surely win the delegates necessary to assure the nomination. The front-runner campaign conceptualized by Sears would be characterized by an "above-the-battle" posture in which Reagan would campaign leisurely in each state by making only one or two appearances in any one day, not appear on forums or debates with his Republican rivals, honor his own already famous "eleventh commandment" (Thou shall not speak ill of other Republicans), and be assisted with a well-planned and well-financed media campaign.

The strategy was tested in Iowa, the birthplace of Reagan and the center of his so-called rural heartland. A week before the caucuses, Iowa newspapers talked about Reagan's failure to campaign in the state or to even appear with each of the other Republican candidates in the nationally televised forum sponsored by the *Des Moines Register*. Reagan's absence was noted throughout Iowa at countless fund-raising dinners, or as they are termed by politicians and the press, "cattle shows," where each of his Republican opponents made appearances and speeches. In fact, at some of these party functions, there were not even any signs of a Reagan campaign in the state—no campaign buttons, no posters, no candidate. By the time of the caucus, Reagan had spent only 41 hours in the state, had avoided discussing the issues, and had made only one televised speech. It had been, as one newspaper headline proclaimed, a campaign that was "Invisible to Many." In defending this strategy, Sears said that "as a front-runner, Reagan could set the pace for the campaign, decide whether to give an event like the forum the prominence of his presence, and that the job of the other candidates was to make Reagan turn around and confront them."[25]

In contrast, one Republican, George Bush, had spent a full 59 days campaigning in Iowa and had thoroughly extended his campaign organization throughout Iowa months in advance of the caucus. On January 21 it was clear that the effort had paid off when Bush upset front-runner Reagan and finished first among the Republican candidates.

Although we do not know Reagan's immediate private reaction to his Iowa upset, we do know that he must have accepted the caucus result as instructive feedback about his campaign strategy or image. By the following week, a "new" Reagan was campaigning in New Hampshire. This Reagan was talking about issues, riding a press bus, speaking at rallies throughout the state, appearing at all multicandidate Republican gatherings, participating in (in fact, pursuing vigorously) all opportunities to debate his Republican rivals, and using an expanded media campaign to present his view to New Englanders. Perhaps the clearest

indication that Reagan had used feedback from Iowa Republicans to reposition his campaign strategy and thus his image came on election day
in New Hampshire when he fired his press secretary, his operations director, and his manager, John Sears.

The 1992 primaries also saw attempts to reposition.

One of the most interesting 1992 repositioning efforts, was the attempt of Jerry
Brown to change his fairly long-standing image as a "flake" to a credible presidential contender. And although he clearly was able to tap into the anti-insider
mood of voters in a number of primaries and caucuses to eventually win the
Maine caucus five days after New Hampshire and to ultimately win 608 delegates, there was no indication that his image had undergone any significant
change. In fact, after almost six months of campaigning, Brown was still referred
to as "a nut," "a flake," "a little cuckoo," and "too much on the fringes to be
president" by Democrats during the New York primary.[26]

Massachusetts Senator Paul Tsongas was another 1992 Democratic
contender who worked to reposition himself. Tsongas, with his bright
blue Speedo bathing suit, swam daily at a nearby YMCA, before and
during the New Hampshire primary to prove that he was physically fit.
A cancer survivor, Tsongas attempted to reposition his illness (for a nation that equates cancer with dying) from a death sentence to a source
of rebirth, obligation, vigor, and personal strength. Tsongas granted media interviews poolside to show his vitality and spirit.[27]

Although the Brown and Tsongas repositioning efforts ranged from
largely unsuccessful (Brown) to marginally successful (Tsongas), Campaign '92 did not lack successful examples of candidate repositioning. In
fact, we believe that the repositioning done by the governor of Arkansas
after the April primaries in preparation for the Democratic nominating
convention and general election can be considered one of the most successful examples in recent presidential campaigning.

The effort to reposition or recast Bill Clinton's image was undertaken
to solve the governor's "character" or "trust" problem and to put him
in a better position to reach a national audience. It was called "The Manhattan Project."[28] Beginning with the Gennifer Flowers allegation of a 12-
year extramarital affair with Clinton and the Vietnam draft deferment
issue during the New Hampshire primary, through the April primaries,
the Governor continually had to defend his character. During the New
York primary, for example, Jerry Brown, his last remaining competitor,
portrayed Clinton as morally and fiscally irresponsible,[29] a hypocrite
who sought black support but played golf at a whites-only club in Arkansas,[30] and referred to him as the "prince of sleaze."[31] It was also
during the New York primary when the governor admitted that he had
smoked (but never inhaled) marijuana while a student in England.

Although Clinton won New York and the other important April primaries and was assured the nomination, public opinion polls indicated that his negative rating had shot to 41 percent, that he was generally thought of as less trustworthy and less honest than President Bush, and that people had little understanding of him and why he felt he should be president.[32]

Thus, with the May and June primaries as well as the convention and general election still to come, Clinton's campaign staff knew it was important that they begin to let Americans know more about the governor as a man: his values, what he stood for, what he had done in Arkansas, and his disadvantaged childhood.

Consequently, they revised and made more specific the ideas in his basic stump speech and extended the campaign media reach to include not only the morning and evening television talk shows but MTV, where Clinton could advance his own themes in response to 'soft' questions and directly answer viewers' questions.[33]

While doubts regarding the governor's character remained throughout the general election and into his presidency, clearly the attempt to reposition his image during the final two months of the primary period was successful. Public opinion polls indicated that Clinton's negative rating had begun to drop and he was moving ahead of both Ross Perot and President Bush.

Following his inauguration and the success of Republicans in the congressional elections of 1994 and early 1995, President Clinton again appeared to have little popular support. In fact, by summer 1994, polls showed his approval ratings to be dangerously low. In an effort to increase his credibility and viability, the president took steps to reposition or recast himself. For example, he studied Ronald Reagan videotapes with the idea of changing aspects of his rhetorical style, he merged his administration with his 1996 reelection effort, and he hired political advisor Richard Morris. Morris devised a three-prong strategy that came to be known as the Morris "triangulation" strategy. The president's position on issues moved so far to the center that Republicans (particularly the Republican presidential nominee) had little ideological space. For example, Clinton discussed the need for leadership through a "dynamic center" and proposed tax-cut initiatives he termed a "middle class bill of rights."[34] The second prong of the strategy began in July 1995, when Morris aired commercials in 20 key electoral states that attacked Republican congressional leadership (Bob Dole and Newt Gingrich) and the Republican party for cutting programs important to large segments of the American electorate, such as Medicare. By fall 1995, the ads had aired in 30 percent of the nation's media markets. Also during the surfacing period, the president began implementing the third part of the strategy, using popular, and thus safe, issues as talking points. For example, during his weekly radio addresses and on weekend trips to New Hampshire, he talked about the need for greater corporate responsibility, less violence in Hollywood, school uniforms, and drug use. The triangulation strategy was successful; the president's public approval polls went up, often 10–15 points, in primary states such as Pennsylvania, Florida, Michigan, Illinois, and Ohio.

Important also are the functions provided to the electorate. Just as the primary campaign is valuable in giving candidates the feedback necessary for repositioning, so too can it offer voters the information necessary for cognitive adjustment or readjustment.

Images are rather easily acquired by voters during primaries. As candidates crisscross the city or the state, speaking at all types of political receptions, coffees, rallies, or fund-raising events, voters have the opportunity to see and hear potential mayors, governors, or presidents. They can witness for themselves the candidate's habitual patterns of thinking and acting. They need no longer rely solely on earlier, perhaps inaccurate, accounts of a candidate's style or position on issues. A candidate for mayor does look and sound capable of coping with the city's striking sanitation and transportation workers. The Republican candidate for governor does have a plan for enticing major industry into the state. The nonincumbent candidate for city council is unable to answer a simple question about zoning ordinances. And the presidential candidate uses so many "ahs," "umhs," and "huhs" that it is impossible to understand responses to questions.

In other words, as the candidates seek all possible arenas of political talk during the primary stage of the campaign, voters can see on a first-hand basis just how candidates handle themselves verbally and nonverbally. The information they receive aids in determining or readjusting their opinions. As a matter of fact, political scientist Thomas E. Patterson has found that these early impressions gained during the primary stage tend to remain throughout the campaign.[35] From speeches and answers to audience questions, voters begin to have some information regarding the candidate's beliefs, attitudes, and value orientations. If Senator Richard Lugar was "everything a President should be," (his campaign slogan), why is it that his primary campaign never received any public or media attention? If former Tennessee Governor Lamar Alexander was really the Washington outsider he claimed to be, how could his résumé, which included stints as an aide to a senator and a president and as the secretary of education, be taken seriously? If Phil Gramm wanted to be viewed as presidential, why was his only message about the pain and hard choices Americans would have to make? Answers to these questions and countless others provide information about the candidates that allows voters to create what one communication theorist, Samuel L. Becker, has called a "mosaic model of communication," learning bits of information and then arranging those "bits" into a new or reinforced cognitive pattern.[36]

The third function of the primary period is that it involves many citizens in the democratic process. Involvement in the political process can take a number of different forms. For example, a person can engage in overt political action by participating in such activities as raising money for candidates, preparing placards, canvassing door to door for a party or for a candidate, attending a rally or a neighborhood coffee or petition drive, distributing literature, licking envelopes, or voting. While there are, of course, many other activities possible for those engaging in overt political action, involvement can also be at the social interaction level. By this we mean simply that politics gives people a variety of topics or issues for discussion at work, parties, or anyplace where people interact with one another. Involvement may be no more than talking with a friend about whether or not a particular candidate is "pro choice" or believes in "right to life," but social interaction is one form of involvement in the political process. A third form of involvement is parasocial interaction. This is interaction not with other people but interaction with the messages provided by radio, television, newspapers, brochures, and so on. In other words, it is arguing or agreeing with a negative political ad when it comes on your television set or in a candidate's speech that you read in their literature or in the evening newspaper. Finally, involvement can be a matter of self-reflection—examination of your ideas or perceptions on economic or social priorities in light of the position or platform of a given candidate.[37]

Although the other political stages of the campaign do encourage forms of overt political action, social or parasocial interaction, and self-reflection, it is increasingly becoming the primary period where involvement is most intense because the sheer number of candidates and the attention given to the primaries by the media demand it. In his book on the role of the mass media in the 1976 presidential campaign, Patterson argues that one of the changes in contemporary campaigns is that public interest now peaks more quickly. In the election of 1940, for example, interest in the campaign did not peak until the general election stage, whereas interest in the 1976 campaign rose sharply in the early primaries. Patterson also found that interest in the campaign decreased during the later primaries, and so the overall interest of voters was no greater than it had been in 1940; it just peaked earlier.[38]

In 1988 the public was once again interested in the primary stage of the presidential campaign, and once again its interest peaked early and declined. The 1988 general election turnout (only 50.16 percent of the country's eligible voters cast ballots) was the lowest in 64 years, but the early primaries set voting records. In Iowa, for example, more than 233,000 people took part in the process of selecting a president. This

figure was up from 200,000 in 1980, which was more than double the
previous high of 88,000 set in 1968 when a desire to protest the Vietnam
War drew thousands of supporters of former Senator Eugene McCarthy
to attend caucus meetings. And in New Hampshire, some 276,000 people
cast ballots, surpassing the 1980 record of 261,000.

The 1996 election was much like the 1988 one had been in that the
public was interested in the earliest of the competitions, and once again
attention peaked early and declined by the later primaries. For example,
the 1996 Iowa caucuses played their traditional role of narrowing the
field of candidates. Only the top three finishers in Iowa—Senator Bob
Dole, Patrick Buchanan, and former Tennessee Governor Lamar Alexander—were viable contenders in the New Hampshire primary. Total
Republican turnout for the Iowa caucuses was an estimated 96,451, while
on the Democratic side, which saw President Clinton unopposed for his
party's nomination, voter turnout was estimated at 50,000. For the 1996
New Hampshire primary, 301,380 people cast ballots. Although that figure was down from 1992, 44 percent of registered voters turned out for
the 1996 New Hampshire primary, whereas in later primaries, such as
New Jersey and New Mexico, voter turnout averaged about 20 percent.

Why are citizens becoming involved in the primary stage of the campaign? Although there are no certain answers, participation has undoubtedly been strengthened for three important reasons. First, with the
increased number of primaries, the public is growing more accustomed
to them and the major changes they have contributed to the process of
selecting a president over the last decade. People have discovered that
presidential primaries are exciting, almost like a carnival, as 10 or 12
presidential hopefuls, each with family, large contingents of secret service, and hundreds of national media representatives, descend on a state
for three or four weeks during the winter or spring every fourth year.
Even states such as Colorado that had never had or rarely had presidential primaries joined the swelling list by 1992. Perhaps one reason for
the excitement generated by the primaries is the direct personal contact
with a potential president. Primary campaigning allows the candidate to
meet individual voters. It is unlike the general election when the candidate is remote, isolated, and appears to be existing only for the national
media. The primaries, like the surfacing stage, are a time for interpersonal communication as candidates and citizens interact at dozens of
small group gatherings throughout an individual state.

A second reason for increased involvement may be that a larger number of presidential candidates are actively campaigning and spending
extraordinary sums of money in the primary states. For example, in Iowa
the major candidates in 1988 spent record amounts on television and
radio advertising, with most media budgets running to six figures. Each
commercial for a candidate was also an advertisement, in a sense, for

the caucuses themselves. The increased publicity given the caucuses may have led a lot of Iowans to attend them out of curiosity. In New Hampshire in 1992 the Clinton campaign spent nearly $600,000 in the last few days of the primary to buy advertising to counter negative publicity from accusations that the governor had avoided the Vietnam draft and that he had had an extramarital affair. In the 1996 presidential campaign, television advertising began in Iowa and New Hampshire in June 1995, eight months before the first primary with Lamar Alexander's 60-second commercials. A month later, President Clinton and/or the Democratic National Committee ran television ads in 12 states in 20 markets costing $2.4 million.[39] And, by the end of February 1996, with 92 percent of the primaries still in front of him, Senator Robert Dole, the leading Republican candidate, was nearing the $37 million mandated limit on spending imposed on candidates receiving federal matching funds during the primaries.[40]

Another explanation for the high levels of involvement in the second stage of the campaign is media coverage. The national media have also discovered the glamor, the excitement, the "gamelike" stakes of the presidential primary. Accordingly, each of the television network's evening news programs devotes substantial amounts of time to covering the candidates in Iowa, New Hampshire, Florida, or wherever the primary or caucus happens to be that week. In addition to regular news features, the primaries are highlighted by special programs such as the Tuesday night telecasts of primary election returns and interview programs such as *Meet the Press*. The media create "winners" and "losers" even though the "winner" may have won by only a few percentage points or maybe did not even win at all but did so much better than was expected or came so close to the "front-runner" that he is declared by the television commentators to have "won" the election. As Patterson argues, the media treat primary elections much as they do the general election—there must be a winner. Each primary is only incidentally treated as part of a larger nominating system.

There is, however, a fourth and closely related function of the primary period. As candidates campaign, regardless of what level of office is sought, they often make promises about what they will do if elected. Some promise little, others promise everything from lower taxes to increased morality, but few actually deliver once they take office. We believe that one of the important communication functions of primary campaigning is related to these promises made by candidates during the heat of the campaign. As already observed, one characteristic of primary campaigns is that they are normally more personalized than the general election stage. That is, voters have more of an opportunity for direct interaction with candidates. Campaigning is personally oriented as candidates attend countless events at which the relatively small number of people present familiarize them with the problems important primarily to their specific neighborhood, city, or state. The voters try to elicit promises of help and assistance from the candidates if they are elected. Once the promise is given, we believe that there is more likelihood of promises being kept after the election because of the physical proximity in which they were articulated and the fact that they are given to a specific individual or small groups of individuals, not an amorphous large audience or an impersonal camera.

Finally, we suggest that there is a fifth function performed by the primary stage of the campaign. The voters have a chance to determine the "real" front-runners or leading contenders for the nomination. Throughout the surfacing period, the media label candidates as "possible winner," or "dark horse," or "a favorite," or even "front-runner." With the primary, voters have the opportunity to go over and above the media and actually select the nominees or at least give true meaning to the term "front-runner." While we would not deny the influence the media have extended over the years in the self-fulfilling prophecy of their labels, there have still been a considerable number of instances when the voters, not the media, have determined the serious candidates. Consider the 1976 presidential campaign in which the media, overanxious perhaps because the surfacing period had been so long, had a whole string of candidates they labeled front-runners at one time or another. The list included senators Henry Jackson and Birch Bayh but never the former governor of Georgia, Jimmy Carter. The voters from Iowa and New Hampshire determined that Jimmy Carter was a front-runner. The 1980 campaign was pretty much the same as the media labeled candidates such as John Connally and Senator Howard Baker serious enough contenders to defeat front-runner Ronald Reagan. As it worked out, of course, the only Republican candidate who ever defeated Reagan in a primary was George Bush. The media had not even considered Bush a serious candidate until the voters from Iowa determined his front-runner status. The reverse, of course, was true in the case of Senator Edward Kennedy. Prior to the first vote, the media gave the impression that Kennedy had already defeated President Carter. The voters, however, in Iowa and New Hampshire believed that the president was the Democratic front-runner and removed Kennedy from his preprimary position. In 1988, however, after Gary Hart withdrew from the race following the Donna Rice incident, the media were unable to decide on a serious Democratic candidate (calling the seven contenders "the seven-dwarfs"). Apparently they decided to let voters determine who among the "dwarfs" was a front-runner. Voters in Iowa chose Gephardt; those in New Hampshire selected Dukakis; and the voters on Super Tuesday decided on Gore. In 1992, after the media had referred to at least three of what they had labeled the Democratic "six pack" as front-runners (Kerrey, Harkin, and Clinton), the voters in New Hampshire selected Paul Tsongas. And in 1996, despite the prominence of the person supposed to be the leader, voters in New Hampshire selected Patrick Buchanan and not Robert Dole.

These then are the communication functions of the primary stage of the campaign. They are significant because the second stage is vital to our political system. The primary campaigns allow the people to determine who the candidates will be. During the primaries, the decision making is taken from the hands of political parties and media and given to the voters. The communication functions are crucial to the process.

THIRD POLITICAL STAGE: NOMINATING CONVENTIONS

Although a majority of citizens regularly tell pollsters that they would prefer some other method for nominating presidential candidates, the national party conventions remain as they have since their inception: the bodies that make official presidential and vice presidential nominations for the Republican and Democratic parties. However, just as the first two political stages of the modern campaign have changed, so has the third. Where instrumental or pragmatic communicative functions were once the primary reason for holding party conventions, now the symbolic or ritualistic functions are, in most instances, the chief purposes. In other words, the convention stage is an important and distinct period in the four-step process because of the symbolic functions it provides. From the time that the anti-Masons held the first national nominating convention in Baltimore in 1832 until the Democratic Convention in 1972, nominating conventions could be viewed as deliberative bodies—assemblies faced with difficult and important decisions to make in a few days. In addition to participating in the "required" political rituals of the day, delegates made decisions that often determined the success or failure of their political party during the coming election. In other words, the conventions served important pragmatic or instrumental functions in that the presidential and vice presidential nominees were selected, the platforms were determined, and even the tone or "battle posture" for the general election campaigns were established. In short, the convention met to make party decisions. For many years, decisions were made and the conventions were controlled by bosses and special interests. Some of those conventions nominated candidates of top quality such as Abraham Lincoln and Woodrow Wilson, and other conventions tapped candidates of dubious quality such as Franklin Pierce and Warren Harding. Whatever the caliber of the candidates nominated or the platform written, it is important to remember that the nominating conventions actually made party decisions; in other words, they served instrumental functions.

However, beginning in 1952 and strengthened by action taken for the 1972 Democratic Convention, at least three significant changes have occurred, thus shifting the communicative functions of conventions from instrumental to symbolic. While they have been discussed earlier, their impact on the third stage of the campaign has been so enormous that they should be understood with regard to the nominating conventions.

The first change was the introduction of television to the campaign. Although television did not bring the sights and sounds of the presidential contest to millions of people until the 1952 campaign, nonprint media had been involved in the nominating conventions for many years. In 1912 movies and phonograph records captured Woodrow Wilson's acceptance speech; in 1924 the acceptance speech of presidential nominee John Davis was broadcast over a network of 15 radio stations; and by 1928 the influence of the medium was so pervasive that the time and date of Alfred Smith's acceptance speech were determined by the network of the 104 radio stations that were to broadcast the speech. However, when television was first used during the 1952 primary campaigns, it contributed to the growth of public interest. Turnout jumped from less than 5 million primary voters in 1948 to almost 13 million in 1952. The new medium brought a different dimension first to the primaries and then to the conventions by dramatizing suspense, conflict, and excitement, as well as projecting a visual image of the candidates that had never before been possible. Television gave the public a sense of involvement in the conventions, and as many delegates and reporters covering the convention soon discovered, the television viewer could see more and know more of what was going on than could the persons who were on the floor of the convention hall.[41]

During the 1952 campaign, there were 108 television stations on the air, and as one study of the election showed, the impact of the new medium was significant:

The public went out of its way to watch the campaign on television. Only about 40 percent of the homes in the U.S. have television sets, but some 53 percent of the population saw TV programs on the campaign—a reflection of "television visiting." On the other hand, the campaign news and other material in newspapers, magazines and on the radio did not reach all of their respective audiences: more than 80 percent of the population take daily newspapers and have radios and more than 60 percent regularly read magazines, but in each case the number following the campaign in these media was smaller than the total audience. . . . In the nation as a whole, television, though available to only a minority of the people, led the other media in the number of persons who rated it most informative.[42]

As important as was television's influence in 1952, it can be seen as a mere shadow of what it was to become in all stages of subsequent campaigns, including the nominating conventions. In fact, by 1976 when electorate interest in that year's presidential contest was studied, it was discovered that television coverage of the conventions boosted voter interest and attention to the campaign, especially among those who were not strong political partisans.[43] Perhaps in response to electorate interest, coverage of the 1980 conventions was increased to the point that media representatives outnumbered delegates by four and five to one at the Republican and Democratic Conventions. As a matter of fact, according to the *New York Times*, the Democratic Convention included 3,381 delegates and 11,500 reporters, editors, camera operators, and broadcasters. And although the public appeared as bored with the 1980 conventions as it had been interested in those of 1976 (network ratings showed a sharp drop in the number of people watching the 1980 conventions as compared with four years earlier), the presence of television has, nonetheless, continued to increase. For example, the number of channels has drastically increased with new electronic technologies. Compared to the earlier coverage by the three networks (ABC, CBS, and NBC), the 1992 campaign was covered by five networks (ABC, NBC, CBS, PBS, and FOX), 1,500 television stations, and two cable networks. In 1996, coverage once again increased when the number of journalists at the Republican Convention increased to over 15,000, or seven journalists for each delegate. The 1996 campaign was also the first time that one of the political parties televised its own convention. Republicans donated $1.3 million to Pat Robertson's cable Family Channel to air their sessions, and they arranged for their own commentators. In spite of this increased coverage, however, viewership of the 1996 conventions was down nearly 40 percent from those of 1992.[44]

Although fewer people appear to be viewing every televised convention activity, since 1952 the presence of television has restructured convention programming so that the party's "important" events occur during "prime time." To make certain that this happens, the convention chair often ignores the activities of the delegates on the convention floor and rushes through any official party business to make certain that those events planned to give the party the most favorable image (for example, ecumenical prayers, civic greetings, performances by show business personalities, keynote and acceptance speeches, and controlled and planned "spontaneous" demonstrations for candidates) will be seen during the hours in which most people watch television. Whether this strategy fails (as, for example, it did in 1972 when George McGovern's acceptance speech began hours after most people had gone to bed or in 1980 when Congressman Morris Udall's keynote address started as the delegates were leaving Madison Square Garden for the night) or is successful, the convention proceedings become ritual with little or no pragmatic value.

Another effect of the presence of the television has been that convention participants have become almost more aware of media presence than of convention business and thus alter their behavior and interaction. As one critic of the 1980 Democratic Convention wrote:

The omni-present camera eye contributed to the funny hat, placard, banner and button syndromes. . . . At times, the television camera introduced an almost schizophrenic atmosphere as speakers addressed themselves to an unlistening, often chaotic arena audience, while really hoping that their individual perform-ance would coincide with network coverage.[45]

The last and undoubtedly most significant effect has been that televi-sion covers only those events it decides are important, thereby altering the shape, structure, and activities of the convention. There were times during the 1980 conventions, for example, when the networks conducted interviews with relatives of the candidates while prominent convention participants were debating platform positions. In fact, there was so much "gatekeeping" by the networks covering the Democratic Convention that one scholar estimated that television viewers saw less than half of the proceedings during those times when the networks were on the air. CBS, for example, made decisions about what to show or not to show viewers based on whether Walter Cronkite judged the event to be very exciting. And during the 1984 conventions, NBC did not go to the podium for nearly an hour, preferring to present its own interviews rather than an address by Congressman Jack Kemp. An 18-minute film introducing President Reagan was carefully inserted into the convention schedule to assure airtime. However, only NBC and CNN showed the film in full. Thus, we believe communication analyst Gary Gumpert was correct when he wrote that television has helped to render the nominating con-ventions little more than "a series of arranged and controlled visual and auditory images."[46]

The second factor that has had a profound influence in changing the nature of the third political stage has been the reliance on primaries as the vehicle for selecting delegates to the national party conventions. As we discussed in the first chapter, the proliferation of primaries has con-tributed to the decline of the political parties, but now we want to em-phasize that it has also changed the role of the national nominating convention from decision maker to "legitimizer." Perhaps this statement is explained best by taking a brief glance at the history of the presidential primary.

The presidential primary is a "uniquely American institution born, after decades of agitation, in the early twentieth century."[47] In the post–Civil War era, the party organizations in many states and cities came under the control of often corrupt political machines dominated by or allied with public utilities, railroads, and others who manipulated the convention system to suit their ends. In an effort to reform the system, the Populists and later the Progressives advocated the substitution of direct primary elections for party-nominating conventions. By 1917 all but four states had adopted the direct primary method of nomination for some or all offices filled by statewide election. However, the extension of primary elections from the local, state, and congressional levels to presidential politics was much more difficult.

In 1904 Florida held the first primary election for the choice of delegates to a national party convention, and by 1916 presidential primaries were held in 22 states amid speculation that within a few years the national convention would be only an ornament for making official those decisions already arrived at by the electorate. Calculations such as these, however, were a few years premature because two decades after the first presidential primary had taken place, the movement came to a halt with the number of states stabilized at around 15. Turnout remained low, and there was little popular interest in them until the 1952 campaign when the entrance of television into the primary elections renewed voter enthusiasm and then again in 1956 when Senator Estes Kefauver became the first candidate to use the New Hampshire primary as a way to call attention to his campaign. Although the outcomes did not determine the parties' ultimate choices, they generated more interest than they had at anytime since 1912.

Twenty years later, in 1972, a major incentive for the adoption of presidential primaries was provided when the Democratic party's Commission on Party Structure and Delegate Selection to the Democratic National Committee, popularly known as the McGovern-Fraser Commission, sought to stop some of the injustices apparent to many liberals at the 1968 convention. The commission prepared 18 guidelines intended to ensure that the state Democratic parties' procedures for selecting delegates to the 1972 convention were open, fair, and timely. At least four other commissions followed McGovern-Fraser in the intervening years, and the guidelines have become so complex (to make certain that there is enough representation of minorities and women) that the state parties have found that they can best comply with them, and not disturb traditional ways of conducting other party business, by adopting a presidential primary law. Thus the number of presidential primaries has proliferated. As primaries grew, so did the number of delegates pledged to a specific candidate, and since 1972 everyone has known before the conventions begin who the candidates would be (except in 1976 at the Republican Convention when Ford and Reagan fought down to the wire). The conventions no longer determine the candidates. Voters in those states holding presidential primaries have decided who will be nominated. The convention meets to legitimize the earlier selection.

The third factor that has influenced the changing nature of the convention stage has been the emergence of the campaign specialists who, with the consent of the candidates for whom they work, determine important aspects of the convention that were once the domain of delegates and party leaders. The consultants have planned the candidate's strategies through the first two stages for the precise purpose of winning the nomination. With the nomination secured before the convention even begins, the specialists now turn to "putting on the best show" possible, or what theorists Larry David Smith and Dan Nimmo describe as the orchestration of "cordial concurrence,"[48] for the television-viewing audience. The party platform is negotiated in advance of the convention, with the staff of the candidate certain to be the nominee controlling the deliberations. If a spirited debate concerning a specific issue would enhance the "television show" or if, in the spirit of compromise, it becomes important to give the losing candidate and his supporters the chance to "air" a minority position, portions of the party's platform will be discussed during the convention itself. However, even when this has happened, as in the case of the "debate" on the MX missile at the 1980 Democratic Convention, the vast majority of the delegates paid no attention to the debaters. In fact, as one communication analyst who attended the convention noted:

Signs against the MX popped up and down in the Garden: "X-rated Missiles Aren't Sexy," "NIX the MX," "MX-Missile Madness," "No MX-Nobody Wins World War III," "MX Says Have a Nice Doomsday," "Mighty Expensive," "MX Makes US the Target." Delegates wandered around talking to friends. There were many empty seats. The clear impression was of a ceremonial occasion rather than a deliberative one. . . . The debates served the symbolic function, though, of letting off steam for those who really did care.[49]

In other words, all real decisions regarding the convention are made by the candidate, based on the advice of consultants. The candidate, not the party leaders, determines the platform, the issues to be debated, the songs to be played, the identity of those who will speak from the podium during prime time, the name of the keynote speaker or speakers, and the content and length of the "spontaneous" demonstration. As one delegate to the 1980 Democratic Convention said: "We've turned over absolute control of the nominating process to the presidential candidates, and worse, to their staffs."[50]

Thus, because of the influence generated by television coverage, presidential primaries, and campaign specialists, the overall function of the national nominating convention to the campaign has been altered. Gone is the once powerful role of decision maker. In its place is a new function. The primary significance of the modern nominating convention is symbolic—ritualistic—and as such, it serves four important communication functions.

The first function, and one of the most significant, is that convention rituals provide an opportunity for the legitimation and reaffirmation of the "rightness" of the American way or dream. The various communication acts and symbols of conventions (keynote speeches, nomination speeches, debates, demonstrations, state-by-state roll call balloting, official "greetings" from past party heroes, patriotic music, buttons, hats, placards, as well as nomination acceptance speeches) serve to renew our faith that U.S. citizens share not only a glorious tradition but a grand and proud future. In a sense, each convention can be viewed as a huge political rally where the candidate shares the spotlight with the democratic system that made success possible. When, for example, the presidential and vice presidential nominees make their triumphant entrance to the speaker's platform the last night of the convention, their appearance reinforces the belief that citizens are bound together in a noble tradition. There have been instances when nominees have acknowledged the reciprocity of the relationship during the nomination acceptance speech. For example, in 1988 Michael Dukakis said: "We are the party that believes in the American dream. A dream so powerful that no distance of ground, no expanse of ocean, no barrier of language, no distinction of race, or creed, or color can weaken its hold on the human heart. And I know, because my friends I'm a product of that dream, and I'm proud of it."[51]

He reminisced that it was the American dream that brought his family to America 76 years earlier, unable to speak English, and with only $25 in hand, but with a deep and abiding faith in the promise of America. Finally Dukakis, referring to himself, said: "Tonight, as a son of immigrants, and as a proud public servant who has cherished every minute of the last 16 months on the campaign trail, I accept your nomination for the Presidency of the United States."[52]

Certainly, conventions function to legitimize the selection of the candidates, the platform, and the unity of the party and its leaders. But in the largest sense, the communication rituals celebrate what is good about our system and thus ourselves. Convention sessions, for example, open and close with prayers (we are a spiritual and godly people). During the convention, former heroes are acknowledged (we have a sense of our roots), and countless speakers evoke selected elements of the "American Dream" (we believe that the United States is destined to become a mighty empire of liberty where everyone can share in the prosperity of society). On the final night, the selected candidates articulate their visions of a grand and more noble country (we value the traditions of reform and progress), while national songs provide periodic emotional climaxes (we have pride in and deep-seated feelings about our country).[53] The convention rituals are, in short, a kind of emotional/spiritual/patriotic catharsis in which we can, if necessary, lament current shortcomings within the party or the country while remaining proud of and faithful to our legacy.

In writing about conventions as legitimation rituals, one communication scholar found that typically the ritual has three steps: it begins with a statement and demonstration of theme (traditionally the responsibility of keynote speakers); progresses to a clustering or gathering of stereotypical character types who are given convention time for speeches or "greetings" to the delegates (the hero or heroine, the also-rans or those who fought the good fight but lost in a noble cause and are now vindicated through history, and leaders representing the right and left and all divergent interest groups within the party); and culminates in the anointing of the nominee who symbolizes and enacts the convention's theme. However, not only are there identifiable steps or phases in the convention ritual, a variety of ritualistic forms are possible. For example, the 1984 Republican Convention explored the theme of "What's Right with This Country," by stressing that Americans were better off after four years of Republican control of the White House.[54]

Not only do the communicative acts of the convention serve to reaffirm our general commitment to the electoral process, there is also a second and closely related function. The convention provides legitimation for the party's nominees. When the struggle for nomination is long and intense (as it has been for presidential nominees since 1972) or when the selection has gone to a relative newcomer (as it did when the Democrats nominated Jimmy Carter in 1976, Michael Dukakis in 1988, and Bill Clinton in 1992) or even when the convention nominates nontraditional candidates (as the Democrats did with Geraldine Ferraro on the ticket as the vice presidential candidate in 1984), the ritual of the convention confirms or legitimizes the candidate as the party's nominee as a possible governor, senator, or even president of the United States. A person may have won primary after primary, but not until the convention delegates affirm selection through their voters at the convention can the candidate become the nominee. With the act of confirmation comes added prestige and respect. The person is no longer just a candidate, but the nominee of a political party.

The third function provided by the convention stage is that the party has a chance to show its unity. Whether the cohesion is more apparent than real, the convention is the time when wounds from the primary campaigns can be addressed and healed. Perhaps the importance of a unified party to the success of the approaching campaign can be understood by examining instances when the convention ritual has failed to produce cohesiveness. In 1964 the Republican Convention that nominated Barry Goldwater appeared to repudiate Republicans whose political philosophies were more liberal than those of the conservatives who dominated the convention. The governor of New York, Nelson Rockefeller, who had been a contender for the nomination, was booed and not given the opportunity to finish a speech. When Goldwater included an endorsement of extremism in his acceptance speech, many liberals walked out of the convention. The Republican party remained divided throughout the campaign, and Goldwater lost the election by one of the largest margins in the history of presidential politics. Similarly, in 1964 and again in 1972, the Democratic National Convention failed to unify and come together to support either Hubert Humphrey or George McGovern. Humphrey was tormented throughout the 1968 general election campaign by those in the Democratic party who felt his nomination was a betrayal of party principle and a disfranchisement for liberals. McGovern, on the other hand, was never able to unify the traditional or "oldline" party leaders with his more youthful and/or liberal insurgents. In each case, the Democrats remained divided throughout the convention and general election campaign and lost in November.

Thus, even when tension below the surface is strained, the political parties strive for the appearance of unity during their conventions. At the 1976 Democratic Convention, for example, one communication analyst recalled that following Jimmy Carter's acceptance speech, party chairman Robert Strauss gathered all the party's candidates and factions on the speaker's platform as Martin Luther King, Sr. delivered the benediction to the convention:

King stunned the noisy delegates and galleries into silence, asking that they "cease walking, talking" and that "not a word be uttered unless that word is to God." In a rousing sermon that brought forth shouts of "Amen" from the audience, the father of Martin Luther King, Jr. cried: "Surely the Lord sent Jimmy Carter to come out and bring America back where she belongs. . . . As I close in prayer, let me tell you we must close ranks now. If there is any misunderstanding anywhere, if you haven't got a forgiving heart, get down on your knees. It is time for prayer." As Daddy King concluded, the delegates joined hands, linked arms, and slowly began to sing "We Shall Overcome Someday." The television cameras focused on the faces of the delegates, who wept and swayed as they achieved a cathartic moment of emotional release and affirmation.[55]

In a similar though less emotional manner, the Republicans and the Democrats in 1988 attempted to evoke images of unity in the closing moments of their conventions. Although the race for the 1988 Democratic nomination was filled with bitterness, particularly because of Jesse Jackson's feeling that neither the party nor the Dukakis staff was giving him the central role he felt he deserved, the victorious Michael Dukakis had Jackson join him at the speaker's podium after he had delivered his ac ceptance speech. Jackson was followed to the podium by those who had been opponents during the primary and caucus elections. George Bush was joined at the podium following his address by those who had been opponents during the primary and caucus elections to sing "God Bless America." In the summer of 1992, the Democratic National Convention in New York was so positive and unifying, one journalist called it the "Lovefest in Madison Square Gardens."[56]

From the beginning of the 1992 presidential campaign "season," Democratic National Chairman Ron Brown was determined that the party would be unified around a single candidate (as soon as the primaries and caucuses made clear who that person would be) and that the convention would reflect that unity:

What Brown understood from the party's twelve years out of power and from the way the 1992 primaries and caucuses had played out was that his fellow Democrats were energized by the possibility of recapturing the White House. And, given the condition of the economy, they were not in a humor to argue endlessly over how many ideological nuances could be stuffed on the head of a pin. Brown was prepared to tolerate dissent but he was not willing to allow it to spoil his convention.[57]

Accordingly, Brown and the Clinton staff oversaw every detail of the convention. And Brown instituted a basic rule: people who had not endorsed the ticket would not be allowed to speak at the convention. Thus, days before the convention opened, Jerry Brown was the only scheduled speaker who had not endorsed the Clinton ticket. And although the former California governor was entitled to speak because his name was going to be put into nomination, Ron Brown did not grant him a formal place on the program with the other defeated contenders, each of whom, had endorsed Clinton. In addition, Brown devised and implemented a Wednesday evening schedule that minimized the media exposure this one last dissenter would receive.

In contrast, the Republican convention in Houston was anything but a "lovefest." In fact, for the first time in many years, the convention exposed "significant fault lines"[58] in the Republican party. The "mean-spirited" tone of the convention had been set by the GOP platform committee which held its sessions in the days immediately preceding the opening of the convention. Although the committee had to develop a position on a variety of issues, it was the antiabortion plank, the opposition to legislation that recognized same-sex marriages, the support of home-based schools, and the charge that "elements within the media, the entertainment industry, academics and the Democratic Party are waging a guerrilla war against American values"[59] that set off the ideological sparks between the hard-line social issue conservatives who controlled the committee and the convention, and moderate Republicans.

Although the convention theme was "The American Spirit," not all of the major speakers reinforced it. For example, hard-line conservatives such as Pat Buchanan, Pat Robertson, William Bennett, and Marilyn Quayle focused on the platform planks that appeared to exclude many Americans, even those in their own party who had more liberal philosophies. Their speeches were fiery condemnations of the "evils of liberalism"[60] with direct linkages to Bill Clinton, his wife, and Senator Edward Kennedy.

Despite the fact that on the last night of the convention all factions were together at the podium to symbolize unity, the overall impression for many Americans was that the Republican party was disjointed and mean-spirited.[61]

In contrast, at the 1996 Republican National Convention the appearance of party unity was of utmost importance to Senator Dole's campaign. Before the convention, the senator proclaimed that the party would be "unified from top to bottom."[62] His campaign managers were determined to avoid the harsh rhetoric of the 1992 Republican National Convention. Every speech was reviewed by Tony Fabrizio, Dole's campaign pollster. The party brought in speakers such as retired General Colin Powell, who just nine months before had announced his status as a Republican, to illustrate the party's unity and inclusiveness.[63] Senator Alfonse D'Amato also spoke at the convention about Bob Dole's ability to unify the party "like no one else could."[64] And vice presidential nominee Jack Kemp promised a campaign that would win the support of "every single American."[65]

Another objective of the 1996 Republican National Convention was to paint an appealing image of Senator Dole and contrast his personal and policy differences with those of President Clinton. Speakers such as House Speaker Newt Gingrich and New York Republican Susan Molinari (whose selection as keynote speaker was made to appeal to women, young voters, and moderates) presented Senator Dole as a hero with character and values. Video clips were shown of Democratic promises Republicans contended were either broken or forgotten.[66]

Similarly, at the 1996 Democratic National Convention in Chicago, the Clinton campaign also focused their attention on presenting a unified party. As party chairman Senator Christopher Dodd pointed out on the opening day of the convention, "This is the first time in 60 years that a sitting Democratic President has not been challenged in his own party."[67] The convention was a week-long effort to position the Clinton-Gore ticket in the middle of mainstream America and to present the incumbents as advocates of moderation.

The opening night of the Democratic convention featured speakers such as actor Christopher Reeve and Sarah and James Brady who spoke about help for the afflicted, gun control, education, and jobs. Messages throughout the convention were intended to emphasize that President Clinton's policies had been good for Americans. In addition, Democrats depicted their ticket as more youthful and forward looking than the Republican ticket. Vice President Al Gore promised that he and President Clinton would serve as a "bridge to the future," rather than as the "bridge to the past" referenced by Senator Dole in his nomination acceptance speech two weeks earlier.[68] Both Gore and Clinton touted their administration's accomplishments and discussed specific plans for the future. Their intention was to position themselves as understanding the "problems real families face . . . and know[ing] what ought to be done about them."[69]

The fourth communication function served by nominating conventions is that they provide the public introduction of the candidate's rhetorical agenda for the general election campaign. Whether Republican or Democrat, the acceptance speeches of the nominees have frequently signaled the issues on which they plan to campaign (typically through the introduction of a specific slogan) and/or have announced an overall campaign style/plan they intend to follow (sometimes accomplished via a direct challenge to the opposition).

Franklin Roosevelt initiated the process of the nominee speaking to the delegates in person when in 1932 he flew from Albany, New York, to the Democratic Convention in Chicago. During his acceptance speech he introduced the phrase the "New Deal," which became the slogan for his campaign and subsequent administration. In 1948 Harry Truman not only announced that the central issue in his campaign would be the "do-nothing Congress," but he also explained that he was going to keep Congress in session during the summer to try and get some legislation from them. In 1960 Richard Nixon announced his intention to take the campaign to all 50 states, while John Kennedy introduced the "New Frontier" as the slogan/theme for those issues important to his campaign. In 1976 while accepting the Republican nomination, President Gerald Ford announced his intention to debate, virtually challenging his opponent to a face-to-face confrontation when he said: "This year the issues are on our side. I'm ready—I'm eager to go before the American People and debate the real issues face-to-face with Jimmy Carter."[70] In 1988 George Bush cited five major issues to draw a sharp distinction between his conservative agenda and Michael Dukakis's liberal agenda.[71] In 1992, Clinton defined the "New Covenant":

A solemn agreement between the people and their government based not simply on what each of us can take but what all of us must give to make America work again.[72]

Finally, in 1996, Robert Dole advocated a revival of the nation's "old values" of family, duty, truth, and honor.

These, then, are the communication functions served by the third political stage of the campaign. As we have pointed out throughout our discussion of this stage, though the nominating convention serves only ritualistic functions, it is no less critical to the overall campaign than are the other stages. In fact, as we suggested earlier, a campaign that fails to get the most out of the ritual demanded during the nominating convention will proceed to the fourth stage with a potentially fatal handicap.

FOURTH POLITICAL STAGE: THE GENERAL ELECTION

"Electing time"[73] means speeches, parades, debates, bumper stickers, media commercials, bandplaying, doorbell ringing, posters, billboards, polling, sound bites, town hall meetings, direct mail fund-raising, call-in talk shows, and countless television spots. As we have discussed throughout this chapter, these acts and symbols are no longer reserved exclusively for the last stage, although they remain a significant and expected part. It is almost as if all has been in readiness—a type of dress rehearsal for this final and most important scene. Certainly, candidates may have been appearing and speaking at all manner of gatherings for many months. Thirty- and 60-second television spots may have been interfering with television viewing since the primaries. Citizens may have even voted for their candidate in a primary or watched a part of one of the conventions on television. However, once the final stage begins, the campaign communication is at once more intense, less interpersonal but more direct, and certainly more important because the candidate who emerges will be the new mayor, governor, legislator, or president. It is precisely because of the importance of the general election stage that we must discuss briefly three communicative functions, which although not unique to it, are nonetheless reflective of it.

The first function is cognitive. The electorate voluntarily seeks or involuntarily learns of information about some feature of the election and/ or the candidates. News regarding the campaign is so widespread during the fourth stage that additional or restructured information may be gained from something as simple as talking with a friend, watching the evening news, or reading a newspaper or magazine. Because so much information permeates the environment during the general election, the majority of the electorate possess at least minimal knowledge about the election.

In recent years, people have been acquiring political knowledge from yet another source, the public opinion polls of the media. While syndicated polls during election years have been a regular feature of the press since the inception of modern public opinion polling in 1936, by the

1970s news organizations began to serve as their own polling agencies. News-gathering organizations were not simply printing or broadcasting the findings of others, they were creating news on their own initiative with their own polls—often extending opinion soundings down to the local level. The impact of this development is reflected in the results of a 1979 study by the National Research Council, which showed that in two parallel surveys conducted during the heat of the 1976 campaign, only 16 percent of those interviewed failed to recall hearing something "in the news or in talking with friends" about "polls showing how candidates for office are doing."[74] Twenty years later, by the time of the general election stage of the 1996 campaign, virtually every major news organization was conducting some poll each week, thus providing a constant stream of information regarding the election.

Not only do communicative acts serve as cognitions during the general election stage of the campaign, there is a second function. The general election assigns legitimacy, the idea that the campaign process itself provides further proof that the system works.

In discussing the ritualistic functions of the nominating conventions, we discovered the importance of legitimation in affirming the candidate as the party's choice and the electoral system as superior. Legitimation is also an important function of the general election. As people stand in line to greet a candidate, put up posters for "their" candidate for city council, attend a rally, watch the presidential candidates debate, discuss with a friend the merits of one of the mayoral candidates, vote, or engage in any of the participatory activities typical of the final stage of the campaign, they symbolically reinforce the values for which the activities stand.[75] Thus campaigning becomes a self-justifying activity that perpetuates two primal U.S. myths, according to Bruce Gronbeck:

Acquiescence—providing a paradigmatic, "fail-safe" rationale for choosing leaders and fostering programs with particularly "American" bents, making it difficult for anyone to object to the process (for if you do, the system's ideological web reaches out, telling you to seek the desired change by participating—running for office, pressuring the parties, voicing your opinions in public forums); and, Quiescence—reasserting the values associated with campaigning and its outcomes (free-and-open decision-making, public accountability, habitual and even mandatory modes of campaigning, the two-party system), in order to remind a citizenry that it is "happy" and "content" with its electoral system; emphasizing the mores and ceremonial rituals associated with elections which make the country "devil-proof," invincible to attacks from within or without.[76]

Finally, the fourth stage of the political campaign contributes to fulfilling our expectations regarding campaign rituals. We expect candidates to address themselves to society's problems; we expect debates, rallies, door-to-door volunteers, bumper stickers, buttons, continuous election specials and advertisements over radio and television, polls, and all manner of drama, excitement, and even pageantry. In other words, we have any number of expectations regarding political campaigns. While the previous stages also function to fulfill our "demands," the directness, intensity, and finality of the fourth stage emphasize our pleasure or displeasure with the way in which a particular election has or has not met our pragmatic or ritualistic expectations. If during the general election stage the candidates fail to address those issues of paramount importance to us, fail to debate each other, or even fail to provide for us any of the excitement or drama we normally expect, we may feel cheated. It is, in short, the climax of a political season—a time for decision and participation. It is electing time.

CONCLUSIONS

With the changes in election campaigns in recent years, there have been countless proposals to modify or alter each of the four political stages. While many of the suggestions might well prove beneficial, we hope that you can now better appreciate that our system is far from purposeless. The various verbal and nonverbal acts of communication provide a full range of instrumental and consummatory functions for the candidate and the electorate in each political stage. While some of the functions are perhaps more significant than others, taken together, they are justification enough for the routines and rituals that in this country comprise the political election campaign.

NOTES

1. Bruce E. Gronbeck, "The Functions of Presidential Campaigning," *Communication Monographs* 45 (November 1978): 268–80.

2. Donald R. Matthews, "Winnowing: The New Media and the 1976 Presidential Nominations," in *Race for the Presidency*, ed. James David Barber (Englewood Cliffs, N.J.: Prentice-Hall, 1978), pp. 55–78.

3. Judith S. Trent, "Presidential Surfacing: The Ritualistic and Crucial First Act," *Communication Monographs* 45 (November 1978): 282.

4. The commentary is taken from an unpublished 1979 survey of all women officeholders in Ohio. Partial results of the survey were presented by Judith S. Trent at the 1979 convention in St. Louis of the Central States Communication Association.

5. Roland Evans and Robert Novak, "Sam Nunn Preparing to Run," *Cincinnati Enquirer*, April 10, 1990, p. A11.

6. David Von Drehle, "Restless in Bush Country: Once Reliable Michigan Voters Demonstrate Signs of Rebellion," *Washington Post*, August 16, 1992, p. A1.

7. David Yepsen, "Another Casualty of War: Democrats' 1992 Chances," *Cincinnati Enquirer*, March 10, 1991, p. A10.

8. C. Gardner, "GOP Flocks to New Hampshire to Be Seen and Heard," *USA Today*, May 27, 1993, p. 4A.

9. "Carolina Governor Ends His Campaign for the Presidency," *New York Times*, June 5, 1994, p. A16.

10. Richard Berke, "Dole, Campaigning from Afar, Wins an Early Republican Straw Poll in Iowa," *New York Times*, June 26, 1994, p. A8.

11. Michael Oresko, *New York Times*, January 22, 1989.

12. Judith S. Trent, "The Beginning and the Early End," in *The 1996 Presidential Campaign: A Communication Perspective*, ed. Robert E. Denton, Jr. (Westport, Conn.: Praeger, 1998), p. 56.

13. Jacob Weisberg, "Making Sure Black Minds Are Never Wasted," *Los Angeles Times*, November 15, 1992, p. 3.

14. Murray Edelman, *The Symbolic Uses of Politics* (Urbana: University of Illinois Press, 1964).

15. Dudley Clendinen, "Robertson Gets Conditions for Making a Run in 1988," *New York Times*, September 18, 1986, p. D1.

16. Gronbeck, "The Functions of Presidential Campaigning," p. 271.

17. Trent, "The Beginning and the Early End," p. 63.

18. Ibid., p. 54.

19. Ibid., p. 56.

20. Ibid., p. 55.

21. F. Christopher Arterton, "The Media Politics of Presidential Campaigns: A Study of the Carter Nomination Drive," in *Race for the Presidency*, ed. James David Barber (Englewood Cliffs, N.J.: Prentice-Hall, 1978), p. 26.

22. Thomas Rosenstiel, *Strange Bedfellows* (New York: Hyperion, 1993), p. 51.

23. William R. Keech and Donald R. Matthews, *The Party's Choice* (Washington, D.C.: Brookings Institution, 1976), p. 91.

24. Trent, "The Beginning and the Early End," p. 65.

25. Adam Clymer, "Reagan's Fortunes in Iowa Caucuses Appear to Hang on His Organization," *New York Times*, January 13, 1980, p. A13.

26. Judith S. Trent, "The Early Campaign," in *The 1992 Presidential Campaign: A Communication Perspective*, ed. Robert E. Denton, Jr. (Westport, Conn.: Praeger, 1994), p. 57.

27. Although Senator Tsongas claimed in early 1992 that he had conquered the disease, he unfortunately became a victim of cancer in 1997.

28. Peter Goldman and Thomas Mathews, "Manhattan Project: 1992," *Newsweek* (Special Election Issue, November/December 1992): pp. 40–41.

29. J. Schmalz, "Brown in New York, Assails Clinton with a New Ferocity," *New York Times*, March 23, 1992, p. A1.

30. Gwen Ifill, "Bruised Clinton Tries to Regain New York Poise," *New York Times*, April 5, 1992, p. A1.

31. Ibid., p. A1.

32. Goldman and Mathews, "Manhattan Project: 1992," pp. 40–41.

33. Trent, "The Early Campaign," p. 59.

34. Trent, "The Beginning and the Early End," p. 61.

35. In studying the effects of the media on the 1976 presidential campaign,

Patterson found that even in the final stages of the campaign intense partisanship and overtly partisan media communication did not override early impressions. In fact, in 80 percent of the cases analyzed by Patterson, he found that any single impression of a candidate held during the general election was related more closely to earlier impressions of the candidate than to partisanship. Those people who thought favorably of a candidate's background, personality, leadership, or positions before the conventions also thought favorably about the candidate in these areas after the conventions, regardless of partisan leanings. See Thomas E. Patterson, *The Mass Media Election* (New York: Praeger, 1980), pp. 133–52.

36. Samuel L. Becker, "Rhetorical Studies for the Contemporary World," in *The Prospect of Rhetoric: Report of the National Developmental Project*, ed. Lloyd F. Bitzer and Edwin Black (Englewood Cliffs, N.J.: Prentice-Hall, 1971), pp. 21–43.

37. Bruce Gronbeck talks about five classes of consummatory effects in "The Functions of Presidential Campaigning," p. 272. See also Jay G. Blumer and Elihu Katz, eds., *The Uses of Mass Communication* (Beverly Hills, Calif.: Sage, 1974). For further discussion of the uses and gratifications perspective, see Jay G. Blumler, "The Role of Theory in Uses and Gratifications Studies," *Communication Research* 6 (January 1979): 9–36.

38. Patterson, *The Mass Media Election*, pp. 67–75.

39. Robert E. Denton, Jr., "Communication Variables and Dynamics of the 1996 Presidential Campaign," in *The 1996 Presidential Campaign: A Communication Perspective*, ed. Robert E. Denton, Jr. (Westport, Conn.: Praeger, 1998), p. 22.

40. Trent, "The Beginning and the Early End," p. 53.

41. David B. Valley, "Significant Characteristics of Democratic Presidential Nomination Acceptance Speeches," *Central States Speech Journal* 25 (Spring 1974): 56–62.

42. Samuel L. Becker and Elmer W. Lower, "Broadcasting in Presidential Campaigns," in *The Great Debates*, ed. Sidney Kraus (Bloomington: Indiana University Press, 1962), pp. 25–55.

43. Ibid., p. 45.

44. Denton, "Communication Variables and Dynamics of the 1996 Presidential Campaign," p. 52.

45. Gary Gumpert, "The Critic in Search of a Convention or Diogenes in Madison Square Garden," *Exetasis* 6 (October 1980): 5.

46. Ibid.

47. Keech and Matthews, *The Party's Choice*, p. 92.

48. Robert E. Denton, Jr., ed., *The 1992 Presidential Campaign: A Communication Perspective* (Westport, Conn.: Praeger, 1994), p. 87.

49. Kathleen Edgerton Kendall, "Fission and Fusion: Primaries and the Convention," paper presented at the Central State Speech Association, Chicago, 1981.

50. "Changing Times May Make Old-Style Conventions Obsolete," *Cincinnati Enquirer*, August 14, 1980, p. C3.

51. Michael Dukakis, Acceptance Address, Democratic National Convention, July 21, 1988, *New York Times*, July 22, 1988, p. A1.

52. Michael Dukakis, Speech delivered to the Democratic National Convention on July 23, 1988.

53. Kurt W. Ritter, "American Political Rhetoric and the Jeremiad Tradition:

Presidential Nomination Acceptance Addresses, 1960–1976," *Central States Speech Journal* 31 (Fall 1980): 153–71.

54. " 'What's Right with This Country' Is GOP Theme," *Cincinnati Enquirer*, August 20, 1984, p. A1.

55. Ritter, "American Political Rhetoric," p. 170.

56. Maureen Dowd, "OK on the Self-Realization; What About the Economy," *New York Times*, July 27, 1992, p. A1.

57. Jack W. Germond and Jules Witcover, *Mad as Hell: Revolt at the Ballot Box, 1992* (New York: Warner Books, 1993), p. 337.

58. Ibid., p. 416.

59. Ibid., p. 408.

60. David M. Timmerman and Larry David Smith, "The 1992 Presidential Nominating Conventions: Cordial Concurrence Revisited," in *The 1992 Presidential Campaign: A Communication Perspective*, ed. Robert E. Denton, Jr. (Westport, Conn.: Praeger, 1994), p. 70.

61. Ibid., p. 71.

62. Judy Keen, "GOP Carefully Plays to Its Audience," *USA Today*, October 15, 1996 (available at http://www.usatoday.com/elect/ec/ecr/ecr085.htm).

63. Mimi Hall, "Powell Speaks of Politics of Inclusion," *USA Today*, October 15, 1996 (available at http://www.usatoday.com/elect/ec/ecr/ecr068.htm).

64. "Dole Girds for Moment in Spotlight," *USA Today*, October 15, 1996 (available at http://www.usatoday.com/elect/ec/ecr/ecr077.htm).

65. Judi Hasson, "Kemp Vows Inclusive Campaign," *USA Today*, October 15, 1996 (available at http://www.usatoday.com/elect/ep/epr/eprjk011.htm).

66. Mimi Hall, "Molinari: Dole the Choice for All Generations," *USA Today*, October 15, 1996 (available at http://www.usatoday.com/elect/ec/ecr/ecr094.htm.)

67. "Democrats Plan to Emphasize Their Unity," *USA Today*, October 15, 1996 (available at http://www.usatoday.com/elect/ec/ecd/ecd035.htm).

68. William M. Welch, "Clinton-Gore Ticket Is 'Bridge to the Future," *USA Today*, October 15, 1996 (available at http://www.usatoday.com/elect/ec/ecd/ecd105.htm).

69. Bill Nichols and Susan Page, "Clinton's Mission: 'Focus the Race'," *USA Today*, October 15, 1996 (available at http://www.usatoday.com/elect/ec/ecd/ecd035.htm).

70. When Gerald Ford issued his challenge to Carter, he was trailing badly in the polls and needed something to give a boost to his campaign. As Bitzer and Rueter point out, Ford chose a prime moment at the convention to announce his intention to debate. In his speech accepting the nomination, Ford was aggressive and confident and when he challenged Carter to a debate, the convention audience gave sustained applause. See Lloyd Bitzer and Theodore Rueter, *Carter vs. Ford: The Counterfeit Debates of 1976* (Madison: University of Wisconsin Press, 1980).

71. George Bush, "Acceptance Address, Republican National Convention, August 18, 1988," *New York Times*, August 19, 1988, p. A-14.

72. "Clinton/Gore: 'New Covenant' for a New Generation," *Daily Report Card*, July 17, 1992 (available at http://web.lexis.nexis.com/universe/), May 3, 1999.

73. This phrase is borrowed from Edwin Black, "Electing Time," *Quarterly Journal of Speech* 58 (April 1973): 125–29.

74. Albert E. Gollin, "Exploring the Liaison Between Polling and the Press," *Public Opinion Quarterly* 44 (Winter 1980): 451.

75. Gronbeck, "Presidential Campaigning," p. 272.

76. Ibid., p. 273.

Chapter 3

Communicative Styles and Strategies of Political Campaigns

One of the central imperatives of political campaign communication is the whole notion of the manner in which incumbents seek reelection and their challengers seek to replace them—in other words, the style and strategies used by candidates as they campaign. Campaign styles have undergone significant changes over the years. There have been, for example, elections when candidates campaigned by staying home and saying nothing. There have been others when the contenders "swung around the circle" on anything from trains to jets to riverboats to buses in an effort to draw attention to themselves and to be seen and heard by as many voters as possible. And we can each recall instances of campaigns that have been waged primarily by means of the mass media. In short, there has been no one way in which local, state, or national contenders have gone about the task of getting our vote. Strategies have been as varied and sometimes outrageous as those who have used them. Perhaps because of this there has been relatively little systematic investigation or analysis of the communicative strategies and styles that have been, and continue to be, used by all manner of incumbents and challengers.

Thus the subject of this chapter is the exploration of campaign styles. While it may be that readers are more interested in contemporary examples, the present is better understood when viewed from the perspective of the past. For this reason, examples from nineteenth- and early twentieth-century campaigns have been incorporated, thereby providing a more complete catalog of the communication strategies important to all who have sought and those who will seek elective office.

Understanding of the material in this chapter will be enhanced by an examination of three preliminary considerations that are important to the way in which candidates campaign. A consideration of the term "style" is first. Second is a discussion of political image and its role in developing campaign styles. Third is an exploration of the relationship of technological advancements and styles of campaigning.

PRELIMINARY CONSIDERATIONS

Style

For many years, style has been studied by scholars who are interested in the customs and rules governing the use of language, including the choice of words (figures of speech) and the way the words are arranged (syntactical patterns) in oral and written communication. Although controversy over its meaning occurred historically because some believed style was divorced from content and only a frill or ornamentation, the conception of style as the peculiar manner in which people express themselves by means of language has been generally accepted. In other words, style traditionally has been the province of those concerned with the correctness, beauty, or even workability of language—the investigation or analysis of the words and arrangements a speaker or writer chooses in preparing a message. Thus, one of the elements to be considered in the analysis of campaign style is the language that political candidates use as they campaign.

More recently, however, communication theorists have argued that style should not be limited to language but ought to be considered a quality pervading all elements of an individual's communication. Considered in this way, style would include each of the nonverbal aspects of communication—including physical behavior, sound of the voice, body shape and movement, appearance, clothing, and choice of settings—that operate as symbols to create the meanings we infer from the transaction. In written messages, a number of symbols (in addition to language) create meaning, such as the quality, texture, size, and color of the paper and whether it is handwritten or typed for one particular person or printed and prepared for distribution to many. Thus, in election campaigns, style can be seen as a blend of what candidates say—in speeches, news conferences, talk show interviews, advertisements, brochures, and so on—and their nonverbal political acts or behavior, such as kissing babies, wearing funny hats, shaking hands at rallies, and waving at crowds from the motorcade, as well as their facial expressions and gestures while answering questions. It is what Bruce Gronbeck terms a question of "leadership style"—a combination of habitual modes of thought and action upon which individuals perceive or judge a candidate.[1]

What does any of this have to do with our analysis of campaign styles and strategies? In this chapter, style is a manner of campaigning that can be recognized by the characteristics defining it and giving it form. We have termed these characteristics "communication strategies" and the styles "incumbency," "challenger," and the combined "incumbent/challenger." Certainly, in describing each of the styles we have been concerned with the traditional dimension of language; but as you have seen in the first two chapters, we believe strongly that political campaign communication is much more than just "talk." Thus as the styles are explored, it will become obvious that many of the characteristics deal with nonverbal political behaviors as well as verbal.

Image and Campaign Style

Imagery plays an important role in the consideration of style. All candidates, whether they campaign using the strategies of incumbency or those of the challenger, must do and say whatever it is that will enhance voter perception of them. They are concerned, in other words, about their image.

Although widespread awareness regarding the significance of image creation to the political campaign did not occur until the early 1970s, it had been used for years. The first major image campaign took place in the presidential campaign of 1840 when the Whigs, after searching for a candidate they thought could defeat Martin Van Buren, found no one. So they invented a national hero, gave him a slogan, said he was champion of the ordinary citizen as well as a giant of the frontier, and elected a president.[2]

When William Henry Harrison was "discovered" by the Whigs, he was 67 years old, a long-retired army officer, and had spent four uneventful years as a senator from Ohio.

While military and legislative experience must be considered reasonable credentials for a presidential challenger, Harrison's career had been distinctly undistinguished. The Whigs, however, billed Harrison as a legendary Indian fighter and maintained that he was known widely and fondly as "Old Tippecanoe." The fact that Harrison's "glories" on the battlefield had been limited to one day, 30 years earlier, when he had repulsed a Shawnee attack at Tippecanoe on the banks of the Wabash River, did not stop his campaign managers from creating the image of a military hero. The Whig campaign ignored all issues, except those relating to the personality of their candidates, and gave image creation and "hype" a permanent place in presidential politics. When Democrats suggested that the aging Harrison might be content to spend his declining days in a log cabin "studying moral philosophy"—provided he had a barrel of hard cider at his side—the Whigs cleverly turned the attack into a reinforcement of Harrison's contrived image as a "common man."[3] From then on, every Whig rally sported cider barrels and miniature log cabins, and songs were written and sung celebrating Harrison's humble tastes (the idea being that if logs and liquor were good enough for the people, they were also good enough for the president). Lyrics from one of the campaign songs best describe the image created by the Whigs:

> No ruffled shirt, no silken hose,
> No airs does Tip display;
> But like the "pitch of worth" he goes
> In homespun "hodding gray."
> Let Van from his coolers of silver drink wine
> And lounge on his cushioned setee,
> Our man on a buckeye bench can recline
> Content with hard cider is he![4]

Image campaigns did not end with the elevation of "Old Tippecanoe" to the presidency. Instead, the place of imagery became entrenched in elective politics, especially in the area of campaign style where specific strategies must be created and utilized to keep alive the perception of an incumbent or a challenger. The Harrison campaign's visual symbol of the log cabin represents what has come to be called "image" advertising in politics. As political analyst Wilcomb E. Washburn argues, "The modern-day equivalent would be the 30-second television spot commercial."[5]

The importance of imagery is evidenced each time we see yet another television commercial of a candidate surrounded by family, talking earnestly with a senior citizen, walking through a peanut field or standing in front of a sea of flags. Television commercials that present candidates in such situations are clearly designed to build or maintain certain perceptions of the candidate. Political images, however, are more complex than simply the strategies devised to present a candidate to voters. Images should also be considered in terms of the impressions voters have— what they believe to be true or untrue, desirable or undesirable about the candidates and the campaign. As Kenneth E. Boulding wrote in his classic book, *The Image*, each of us possesses a store of subjective knowledge about the world, a collection of ideas we believe to be true. This knowledge constitutes our image.[6] While in recent years the work of a number of researchers has served to broaden the perspective by which scholars as well as practitioners view image, nonetheless, it is generally understood that the strategies candidates use to construct a public persona constitute an important area of political communication inquiry. We believe, however, that despite the importance of a candidate's role in the creation of a public perception, it is only part of the equation. In his doctoral dissertation on the construction of image in television spot commercials, Allan Louden argues that image is "more than the message projected by a candidate or even a picture created by a voter. Image is an evaluation negotiated and constructed by candidates and voters in a cooperative venture."[7] In other words, beliefs voters have about candidates are based on the interaction or interdependence of what candidates do and the evaluative responses voters have to it: a "transaction between a candidate and voter."[8]

The view of image as a transaction, however, raises questions of balance or proportion between the strategies used by a candidate to create an image and the ideas already believed by the voter. Is one more important to the creation of persona than the other? Is one more likely to influence voter behavior than the other? Generally, researchers believe that one dimension does not necessarily play a more pivotal role than the other. People have some preconceived ideas regarding what a candidate's personal characteristics and behavior should be and these ideas are continually measured against the reality of what an actual candidate says and does during the campaign. In this way, voters define the campaign for themselves—sorting through competing or contradictory messages. However, there are circumstances in which the balance between the idealized and actual can be disrupted. For example, the context in which the campaign occurs can become the dominating force—as was the Great Depression during the 1932 presidential campaign and the Vietnam War during the 1972 election. In each instance, the images of the candidates were framed by an all-consuming event that in some instances overshadowed the candidates' strategies to build an image and in others overcame voters' preconceptions of the "ideal" candidate. It is also possible that a single and dramatic campaign event can tip the scale one way or the other. During the surfacing period of the 1988 presidential campaign, Senator Gary Hart's alleged relationship with a Miami model, his challenge to the media to prove the relationship, the public accusation by reporters from the *Miami Herald*, and the subsequent intensity of national media attention completely overwhelmed anything else Hart said or did. No image strategies the senator might have utilized could have competed with public preconceptions about the way in which candidates who would be president should behave and the contrast of this with Hart's alleged behavior. And in 1984 when Geraldine Ferraro was nominated by the Democratic party for vice president, we believe that there was very little the congresswoman could have said or done to have created a public persona favorable enough to refute the preconceptions of some Americans regarding the personal characteristics or attributes vice presidents are expected to possess. She, in fact, did not look or sound like—she did not resemble—a vice presidential nominee. Thus,

for some voters the fact of Ferraro's gender created an imbalance between imaging determinants.

Even though imbalance regarding the way in which people organize
their thoughts about politics can occur, nonetheless, a consistent finding
after years of research indicates that we share a lot of beliefs about the
personal qualities candidates ought to possess—especially, presidential
candidates. Moreover, these characteristics are strongly associated with
voting preferences and, in most cases, dominate ideas (cognitions) about
the candidates and the campaign.[9] These personal qualities or attributes
tend to cluster around such leadership characteristics as competency,
experience, trustworthiness, ability to be calm, cautiousness, decisive-
ness, and boldness[10] and closely related personality characteristics such
as strength, honesty, fairness, open-mindedness, reliability, energy, and
physical attractiveness.[11] Whether or not a candidate exists who embod-
ies all of these attributes is almost immaterial in that we use the characteristics as a basis of comparison—a standard—by which to judge the
acceptability of the flesh and blood women and men actually seeking
our votes. As voters we may ask ourselves if the candidate campaigns
as an incumbent should or if the challenger fulfills expectations. Viewed
from this perspective, the reason for two common campaign activities
becomes clear. First, one of the most crucial tasks facing candidates, especially during the surfacing stage, is to determine just what attributes
voters believe are ideal for the office sought. Second, campaign activities
in later stages are designed to attempt to illustrate that the candidate
possesses these qualities.

Although we know that voter assessment of a candidate's image is a
significant factor in voting behavior (far more important, for example,
than party identification) and that voters have a mental picture of an
ideal candidate that they use as a gauge in evaluating actual candidates,
it is less clear if these characteristics vary among candidates and across
election levels. In other words, are all candidates competing in the same
race judged by the same preconceived attributes and are the dimensions
of "idealness" the same for candidates running for local offices as they
are for those campaigning for president? While scholars studying the
political campaigns of the 1970s, 1980s, and 1990s have provided few
absolutes, there has been some evidence to indicate that the relative importance of particular clusters of characteristics has remained relatively
constant from presidential election to election. For example, in a study
spanning 12 years (across three New Hampshire presidential primary
cycles), Trent, Trent, Mongeau, and Short-Thompson found that most
characteristics voters believe important for presidential candidates to
possess (competency, morality, trustworthiness, and the others discussed
above) remain constant. In 1996, as contrasted with 1992, the New
Hampshire voters who were surveyed had some change of mind about

the importance of just two characteristics: whether or not it was important that a candidate for president have experience in office and whether
or not it was important that a candidate for president be faithful to a
spouse.[12]

At this point it is uncertain if questions regarding preconceived image
characteristics are important in local races where the attributes and idi-
osyncrasies of the candidates as well as their positions on the relevant
issues are well known. However, a study in 1998 of one of the image
characteristics—physical attractiveness—in which subjects were told that
the pictures they viewed were of candidates in local and congressional
races, Trent, Trent, Mongeau, and Gauder found that physical attractiveness on initial candidate selection was an asset. In every case, across
race, gender, and age, subjects preferred the most physically attractive
candidates.[13]

Obviously, further research is needed before we can say with any degree of certainty that voter expectations either do or do not vary across
candidates and across election levels. One thing though is clear. The
creation and maintenance of image, long a part of political campaigns,
plays a dominant role because voters have a whole series of impressions
regarding the behavior of those who seek elective office that they compare with a personal vision of an ideal candidate. And although other
factors are important to the consideration of campaign style, it may well
be that the extent to which a candidate is able to achieve these idealized
expectations is the extent to which success can be achieved on election
day.

Technology and Campaign Style

During the earliest period of our electoral system, the style of political
campaigning was, at least in part, defined by the limits of our transportation system. This is one of the reasons that there were no national
political campaigns then as we think of them today. While it is true that
in 1789 and again in 1792 George Washington had no opposition, it
would have been difficult for him to have conducted a national campaign even had it been necessary for him to do so. Travel was difficult,
uncomfortable, and time consuming. Even in 1800, when the Jeffersonian
Democratic-Republicans launched the first activity that could be called
a presidential campaign, it was not a national or even a regional effort.
The rallies, parades, and leaflets were not nationally planned but the
work of individual county and state political committees. The national
road system, begun in Maryland in 1808, was the chief east-west artery,
and it did not reach even the Ohio border until 1817. Commercial water
travel started in 1807, but it took many days just to go from Pittsburgh
to New York City. Therefore, the presidential election of 1824 was the

first one in which any real mass campaigning took place. Friends of the three candidates (John Quincy Adams, Henry Clay, and Andrew Jackson) traveled within their own and neighboring states to campaign for the presidential contenders.

Although the Baltimore and Ohio Railroad began in 1829, it was 1853 before the tracks reached the Mississippi River and 1869 before the transcontinental railroad system was completed in Ogden, Utah. By 1854, although the transportation system had improved, it still took 30 hours to travel from Indianapolis to Cleveland by rail and 24 hours from Chicago to St. Louis. Thus it is small wonder that 1840 was the first time a political party conducted a national campaign by sending speakers to then all 26 states or that 1860 was the first time a presidential candidate traveled throughout the north campaigning for his own election. Moreover, it was not until 1896, after railroads serviced most of the nation and automobile production had begun, that a presidential challenger, William Jennings Bryan, was able to "whirl" through 21 states, give 600 speeches, and be seen by five million people.

Developments in the transportation network continued to affect the style of political campaigning. For example, the beginning of air travel in the 1920s allowed Franklin Roosevelt to fly to Chicago to accept the Democratic presidential nomination in 1932 just as the initiation of commercial jet service in 1959 afforded Richard Nixon and John Kennedy the opportunity to conduct "jet-stop" campaigns in 1960.

However, by the middle of the nineteenth century, a second factor had become important to the development of campaign style. With the invention of the telegraph in 1835, a communication network was able to transcend those of transportation because messages were able to move at the speed of electrical impulses rather than the speed of humans, horses, boats, or trains.[14] Moreover, the emergence of the telephone in 1876, wireless telegraph and the motion picture camera in 1895, commercial radio in 1920, and motion pictures with sound in 1927 allowed the public to "bypass the written word and extend communication senses and capabilities directly."[15] Communication scholar Frederick Williams has written that "speech and images could now span distances, be preserved in time, and be multiplied almost infinitely."[16]

Even the first advances in the communication network began to influence political campaigning. For example, one of the primary issues of the 1848 presidential campaign was the almost two-year war with Mexico. The Whigs selected one of the war's heroes, General Zachary Taylor, as their candidate. The principal reason the war could become important to the campaign was that the initiation of commercial telegraph service in 1844 and the subsequent founding of the Associated Press Wire Service had provided far more rapid news than the country had ever known. Citizens were aware of specific battles and vigorously applauded each victory over the Mexicans. In other words, the telegraph was able to inject the war into the campaign with an immediacy not known before.

By the campaign of 1884, telegraph had so unified the nation's communication system that as James G. Blain unwittingly discovered, even one election eve gaffe could be telegraphed across the country and influence election returns. The day before the election, a Republican clergyman denounced the Democratic candidate, Grover Cleveland, by saying that his party was the party of "Rum, Romanism, and Rebellion." Republican candidate James G. Blain failed to disavow the statement and therefore lost the support of Irish Catholic voters. Another thousand votes in New York, a stronghold of Irish Catholics, would have elected him.

Although each early communication development had some influence on political campaigning, certainly the most dramatic were the changes brought about by radio. Beginning in 1921, when President Warren Harding first used the new medium to talk with the public, the radio became the nation's most important means of political communication. It remained so until the widespread use of television in 1952.[17] Radio had a direct effect on campaign style because it made the personal appearances of candidates less necessary by providing an option. For the first time, candidates (even unknown ones) could become public personalities without campaigning around the country. In 1924 William McAdoo, a contender for the Democratic presidential nomination, hoped to establish a radio station powerful enough to reach all parts of the country so that he would not have to travel around the nation making speeches.[18] Although McAdoo never put his plan into action, losing the nomination to John W. Davis, subsequent candidates did. In 1928 Republican contender Herbert Hoover undertook only a few public appearances. Rather, he made seven radio speeches the focal point of his campaign. In 1936, 1940, and 1944, incumbent Franklin Roosevelt used radio extensively so that he could reach the entire nation without traveling.[19]

Thus, the early achievements in electronic media had a profound effect on the manner of political campaigning. According to Joel L. Swerdlow, "political campaigns, whether at the presidential, state or local level, rarely involve new uses of communications technologies. What becomes 'new' in politics has long since been proved in the nonpolitical marketplace. As journalist James Perry noted in *The New Politics*, 'It's not show biz that's taking over in politics; it's industrial and business technology.' "[20] Although there have been many innovations, those that have had some direct effect on campaign style include: the beginning of scheduled television broadcasts in 1941; the first electronic computer in 1942; the beginning of color television in 1951; the introduction of portable video recorders in 1968; the widespread use of microelectronic chips in 1970; the perfected development of fiber optic signal transmission in

1975; the popularity of home computers in 1980; the use of cable television in 1984; the widespread use of videocassettes and satellite transmissions in 1988;[21] the use of online computer networks and bulletin boards in 1992; and the use of candidate listservs and online home pages in 1996.

In the largest sense, television, as radio had done earlier, increased the number of campaign strategies available because candidates no longer had to be dependent on extensive national speaking tours to become well known to the public. A few nationwide television speeches, a series of well-executed and well-placed advertising spots, an appearance on one of the news/issues programs such as *Meet the Press*, campaign coverage on the evening network news broadcasts, and several appearances on the popular talk shows guaranteed public awareness. In addition, television, unlike radio, enhanced campaign swings by showing parts of them in evening news broadcasts. Although the candidate might go to one state or region of the country to campaign in person, millions of people across the country participated in the rally or parade by watching the pageantry from their own living rooms. Not only did a television campaign provide candidates with more exposure, it also allowed for more flexibility in the management of physical and financial resources. Perhaps the essence of the mass media strategy of the late 1960s and the 1970s is explained best in a memorandum written by H. R. Haldeman (and interpreted by Theodore White), in which he outlined the plan for Richard Nixon's 1968 presidential campaign:

Americans no longer gather in the streets to hear candidates; they gather at their television sets or where media assemble their attention. A candidate cannot storm the nation; at most he can see and let his voice be heard by no more than a million or two people in a Presidential year (the reach of the individual campaigner doesn't add up to diddly-squat in votes). One minute or thirty seconds on the evening news shows of Messrs. Cronkite or Huntley/Brinkley will reach more people than ten months of barnstorming. One important favorable Washington column is worth more than two dozen press releases or position papers. News magazines like *Time* or *Newsweek*, picture magazines like *Life* and *Look* are media giants worth a hundred outdoor rallies. Therefore the candidate must not waste time storming the country, personally pleading for votes—no matter what he does, he can appear in newsprint or on television only once a day. The inner strength and vitality of the candidate must not be wasted; if you do more than one thing a day, you make a mistake. If you test a man's physical strength too far, you push him beyond the realm of good judgment; both candidate and the following press must be given time to stop, rest, reflect and write. The importance of old-style-outdoor campaigning now lies less in what the candidate tells the people than in what he learns from them with the important secondary value that outdoor exertions do provide the vital raw stuff for television cameras.[22]

Although 1968 was not the first time television had been used extensively in a campaign, it was the first time that a presidential candidate had planned his entire candidacy around the medium. Richard Nixon not only used technology to help him win an election, he added an important dimension to campaign style—one that extended, in fact, to 1992 when Ross Perot became the nation's first true mass media presidential contender. Perot bypassed political parties, primaries, and traditional campaigning. Instead, he relied exclusively on television and computer technology.

In a similar fashion, the computer has made a profound impact on the manner of political campaigning in the 1980s and 1990s. Its speed in information processing and its ability to interact intellectually with us and to automate many of our methods of information analysis have provided candidates with an invaluable resource in such traditional tasks as identifying and communicating with specific publics or raising funds. It has also been enormously beneficial to the media. For example, on September 15, 1987 "The Presidential Campaign Hotline" went online. The "Hotline" is a computer network that transmits campaign information each morning to subscribers (many of them are media outlets) for a monthly fee. The purpose of the service is to keep subscribers fully appraised of developments in the race for the White House such as: late-breaking news of events in the field; forwarding news stories, editorials, and columns from influential periodicals and local newspapers in battleground states; and providing up-to-the-minute analysis from assorted campaign experts. Hotline's practice of carrying daily reports from each presidential campaign press secretary has also created a unique opportunity for each campaign to determine and circulate its own interpretation of events (spin control) before such events have had the chance to make an impact on their own.[23] Thus direct mail, instant voter prediction and analysis, and the campaign hotline are all part of the new politics facilitated by the computer.

But just as important as the past are the possibilities for the future—some of which have already been experienced in the campaigns of the 1990s. Such communication technologies as the computer, cable television service, push-button telephones, videocassettes, and videodisks have already or could completely change the nature of campaigns by allowing voters to interact with the candidate from their own living rooms. In other words, instead of a candidate simply stating a position on an issue to a mass audience during a television speech, debate, or interview, the candidate could ask a question and invite comments. Large numbers of viewers could press buttons on their television sets, phones, or computers and respond immediately to the candidate. This rapid and somewhat personal interaction might allow candidates the opportunity for repositioning their ideas and might also encourage voters to modify or change their beliefs regarding the candidate.[24]

Obviously, the effect on campaign style would be enormous. Incumbents and challengers alike could have the benefits of person-to-person campaigning without ever leaving the television studio or their office. In addition, the determination of public opinion on a given issue would no longer be subject to the intervention of third parties (such as pollsters or the press). Mass media campaigning would, in effect, become true two-way communication.

Although interactive television has not yet been a part of a candidate's communication strategy, by the 1988 presidential election it had spilled over to elective politics. During the Democratic Iowa caucus debates, participants were linked to a computer by a small box with a dial. As they watched the candidates' debate, participants were asked to continuously register their feelings about the speakers by moving the dial on a rising scale of one to seven on traits such as leadership, speaking ability, experience, and qualifications. And by the mid-term elections of 1994, congresspersons, state and local government officials, and the Democratic and Republican national committees were communicating on computerized bulletin boards. Online campaigning is inexpensive and extremely time efficient. In addition, voters have direct access and interaction with representatives and candidates in cyberspace without the filter of the media.

In 1992 and again in 1996 the major television networks (ABC, CBS, and NBC) cut their investment in covering the early campaign. Perhaps network coverage was reduced because of what appears to be a decline in public interest in network news programs. A 1998 survey from the Pew Research Center showed that the number of Americans who regularly watch the nightly news on ABC, CBS, and NBC declined from 60 percent in 1993, to 38 percent in 1998.[25]

The reduction in network coverage paved the way for a new kind of presidential campaign coverage in the 1990s, one in which nontraditional popular culture media dominated. For candidates, the popular media formats presented opportunities not experienced in the past. For example, talk show hosts or citizens who called in asked questions that were much "softer" than those typically asked by the national media. Moreover, there were rarely follow-up questions, and even when there were, no established journalist was there to push the candidate on evasions, contradictions, or half-truths.[26] There were also instances in the presidential elections of 1992 and 1996 in which the tabloids set the agenda for network news by printing a sensationalized story (e.g., the allegations of Paula Jones that, while governor of Arkansas, Bill Clinton made unwanted sexual advances toward her) that provoked candidate response and thus made coverage of the story "necessary" for the mainstream news media. It may well be that such mainstream news coverage of "interesting" versus "important" stories, as well as the increased dominance of popular culture media, has contributed to a growing public skepticism about the trustworthiness of the press. A 1998 *Newsweek* poll found that 42 percent of those surveyed believe only some of what they read and hear in the news media.[27]

One more difference regarding the use of media, which began in 1996, was that candidates came to recognize the potential of the local news stations. Beginning with New Hampshire, candidates did many of their satellite interviews with the anchors and reporters of local stations rather than with network commentators and journalists. They were able to do so because the networks were no longer able to control all of the pictures taken by their camera crews. For years, CBS, NBC, and ABC had refused to distribute pictures of national news events to their local stations until such pictures had first appeared in network newscasts. With the arrival of CNN, however, this policy began to change. To make a profit, the cable network started selling its pictures to local stations throughout the world.

Another technology that has made an impact on political campaigning is the proliferation of household videocassette recorders (VCRs). The practice of distributing campaign videos to provide primarily biographic information and to aid in fund-raising began with George Bush's 1980 presidential effort. Beginning in the 1988 campaign and continuing through the 1996 campaign, each of the presidential hopefuls produced videos that were designed to introduce themselves to voters in the early primary and caucus states and to serve as vehicles for fund-raising. For example, Bob Dole's biographical video, entitled, "Bob Dole: An American Hero," pictured his hometown, friends, and family members, as well as the struggles he endured, including his war wounds and his family's poverty. But just as videos can be used to build a candidate's public persona, so too can they undo or destroy an opponent's credibility. This power was graphically demonstrated during the 1988 surfacing period when Senator Joseph Biden of Delaware, a Democratic presidential contender, "borrowed" a stirring soliloquy from British Labor party leader Neil Kinnock without crediting him. Shortly after Biden gave the speech the *New York Times* received an "attack video" showing the Biden and the Kinnock speeches back-to-back. The *Times* ran the story on page one and the video was shown on the evening newscasts. The video set in motion a chain of events that within 11 days drove Biden from the race.

The Internet is another technological innovation beginning to influence the way in which candidates seek our votes. For example, although each of the 1996 presidential candidates had a home page (President Bill Clinton's campaign site drew 5,500 volunteers and raised between $5,000 and

$7,500[28]), it was the 2000 presidential hopefuls who pushed the technology in new directions. Vice President Al Gore conducted online chat sessions with voters and had an "open source" feature that invited users to help design and improve his site. Texas Governor George W. Bush had a site that could be read in Spanish, Representative John R. Kasich asked visitors to his site to describe their heroes, Elizabeth Dole allowed visitors to create interactive "postcards" with her picture to forward to friends, and Malcolm S. "Steve" Forbes simulcast campaign events on his web site.

The increase in the use of the Internet between the 1996 presidential campaign and the early stages of the 2000 campaign was dramatic (although it was in 1996 that the first "virtual" gubernatorial campaign occurred[29]). The number of households with access to the Internet doubled to 44 million and more than half a million households (about 18,000 every day) were coming online every month.[30]

Although it is impossible to know just what impact new technologies will ultimately have on political campaigns in the future, as we have seen before, innovations in transportation and communication have an infinite capacity to alter the strategies that candidates use to seek political office. As such, they are an important consideration in any examination of campaign style.

STYLES AND STRATEGIES OF CAMPAIGNS

Essentially, campaign styles are sets of communication strategies employed at times by all candidates, whether they run for president, mayor, governor, or legislator. Moreover, those who hold office may campaign in the manner of those who do not, just as those who challenge may adopt strategies of incumbency. In other words, those candidates who are incumbents are not restricted to a specific set of incumbency strategies any more than challengers are confined to a particular set of challenger strategies. In fact, candidates frequently combine strategies of one style with strategies of another so that there are times during the course of one contest when an individual contender may assume a rhetorical posture normally associated with incumbency campaigning and at other times may appear to be campaigning as a challenger. This combination may well be a result of the seasonless electoral process discussed in the first and second chapters. As candidates extend the length of the campaign, no one style is likely to remain appropriate for the duration. New events, as well as changes in conditions, force modification in the manner of pursuit. While in February an attack on the incumbent's economic policy might be appropriate, by August the situation may be different enough to make attack an inappropriate strategy. As such, it would be misleading to try to analyze style by only examining the practice of one candidate or one campaign. Styles (incumbency, challenger, and incumbent/challenger) are a product of whatever candidates and their staffs believe is needed at a particular time within the context of their particular campaign. Therefore, the best way to understand them is to determine the composition of each—that is, to catalog their strategies.

Incumbency Style

Incumbency campaigning in the United States is at least as old as the first presidential incumbent George Washington who ran for reelection in 1792. Its various strategies have been used by almost all who have sought election to any level of government. Given its longevity and frequent use, one might assume it would have been defined long ago and its characteristics carefully delineated. While that is not the case, incumbency has been considered a "symbolic resource"[31] and the "Rose Garden Strategy."[32] Although each idea is useful in attempting to understand what it is that candidates do and say when they appear to be "running as an incumbent," each is nonetheless incomplete. Incumbency campaigning is a blend of both symbolic and pragmatic communication strategies designed to make any candidate appear as both good enough for the office sought and possessing the office (an assumed incumbency stance). This is not an easy task. We know that image creation and maintenance take significant amounts of skill, time, and money. But developing a credible incumbency style is well worth the effort. The results of countless elections indicate that incumbents tend to win. For example, during the twentieth century, only five presidents have lost their reelection bids, and congressional incumbents, especially those in the House of Representatives, almost always defeat their challengers. In 1990 only 16 incumbent congresspersons of the over 400 who stood for reelection (about 4 percent) lost. Moreover, 74 of the House incumbents ran unopposed. In 1992, despite the anti-incumbency mood of the country, 74 percent of incumbents were reelected to Congress and in the midterm elections of 1994, only Democratic congressional incumbents were defeated; Republican incumbents were all reelected. In 1996, just one incumbent U.S. senator was unseated, while the rate of incumbency reelections in the U.S. House was 94 percent.[33]

However, 1998 stands out, by far, as the year of the incumbent. Out of 401 seats in the U.S. House of Representatives where the incumbent was running for reelection, 395—that is, all but six of the incumbents— were returned to office. The success of incumbency also benefited the U.S. Senate where all but three of the 29 incumbents were reelected. Of the three senators who lost in 1998, two of them, New York Senator Alfonse D'Amato and North Carolina Senator Lauch Faircloth, were strident critics of President Clinton. The other losing senator, Carol

Mosely-Braun from Illinois who was first elected in 1992, lost to Republican millionaire Peter Fitzgerald, in part because he was successful in highlighting several missteps by Mosely-Braun during her term of office. In other words, there were, perhaps, several factors that helped explain the loss of the only three senatorial incumbents who failed to win. Given this kind of success, it is not surprising that political scientist R. F. Fenno, has suggested that incumbency is "a resource to be employed, an opportunity to be exploited."[34]

With this understanding, we now consider the specific strategies that candidates employ when they seek the advantages of incumbency. The first four are symbolic in nature, and the remaining 11 are pragmatic or instrumental.

In exploring the symbolic characteristics of incumbency campaigning, we are, in essence, discussing presidential candidates because there is no other elective office for which the public has the same kind of feelings. In one sense the presidency can be thought of as a focus of impressions and beliefs that exist in our mind—a kind of "collage of images, hopes, habits, and intentions shared by the nation who legitimizes the office and reacts to its occupants."[35] Viewed from a related perspective, when we speak of the presidency, we are dealing with the myth of the office, the image we have possessed since childhood of the one institution that stands for truth, honor, justice, and integrity. We have a conception of an individual and an office that in ennobling each other, ennoble us. Perhaps Theodore White described it best when he wrote:

Somewhere in American life there is at least one man who stands for law, the President. That faith surmounts all daily cynicism, all evidence or suspicion of wrong-doing by lesser leaders, all corruptions, all vulgarities, all the ugly compromises of daily striving and ambition. That faith holds that all men are created equal before the law and protected by it; and that no matter how the faith may be betrayed elsewhere, at one particular point—the Presidency—justice will be done beyond prejudice, beyond rancor, beyond the possibilities of a fix.[36]

People may debate the character, quality, and personality of the men who have filled the office, and public opinion polls may indicate dissatisfaction with the performance of an incumbent, but the presidency is, for most citizens, an idealized institution, headed by a single visible individual through whom it is possible to grasp a "cognitive handle" or an understanding of "political goings on."[37]

In this context, then, the identity of a particular president is irrelevant; the concern is the office itself and the symbolic role it can play in a campaign.

Symbolic Trappings of the Office

The first strategy is the use of symbolic trappings to transmit the absolute strength and importance of the office. The presidency stands for power, and therefore incumbents take on the persona of the powerful. They are surrounded by large numbers of carefully trained and "important looking" bodyguards who appear to anticipate their every move; their song (played when they enter or leave a public ceremony) is "Hail to the Chief." Incumbents are addressed by title, never by name. When they travel, a whole contingent of secret service, media reporters, technicians, and lesser governmental officials accompany them in a caravan of planes and limousines. Their home, although the property of "the people," is heavily guarded and off limits to all who have no official business to conduct with them or their staff. Incumbents can be in instant communication with the leader of any other country of the world; they serve as commander in chief of all armed services. Incumbents can command nationwide media time, and they are always close to a small black bag, the contents of which provide them the capability to blow up the world.

Thus, it is little wonder that those who have campaigned against a president have objected to the continual and conscious use of devices that remind voters that they are seeing and hearing "the president," as opposed to "just another politician." For example, during the 1984 campaign President Reagan changed the location of his televised press conferences. He stood before an open doorway in the East Room of the White House that reveals a long, elegant corridor. The cameras recorded a majestic setting and a stately exit that dramatized the importance of the office and served to remind the audience that they were listening to the president of the United States.

Legitimacy of the Office

The second strategy involves not so much what incumbents do—that is, the use of specific tangible symbols to remind voters of their power—but an intangible tool that only they possess and about which their challengers cannot even object. The presidency stands for legitimacy, and therefore the person who holds the office is perceived as the natural and logical leader. In other words, no matter who the incumbent may be (or regardless of the incumbent's current rating in the public opinion polls), the president is accorded a kind of sociopolitical legitimacy—a public trust. As one theorist has argued, we place our faith and trust in the hands of our leaders because they project an image that seduces us into participating in the comforting illusion that through rigid adherence to the constituted ideals of the society they can guide us through whatever possible troubles the future might present.[38] Moreover, their position provides automatic legitimacy during a campaign, in that they, unlike any of their opponents, are, from the beginning, considered legitimate candidates for the job.

Competency and the Office

The third strategy is also an intangible tool that comes with the office. The presidency stands for competency, and therefore the person who holds the office can easily convey that impression. To trust in the president's competence is to accept the incumbent as a symbol "that problems can be solved without a basic restructuring of social institutions and without the threat a radical reordering poses both to the contented and to the anxious."[39] In other words, when we attribute a sense of competency to the president, it provides us with reassurance that all can be right. We want to believe that the person who is president is capable (after all, we elected the president in the first place).

As a matter of fact, our feelings about the office itself are so strong that whatever a specific president has done with regard to individual issues, a large number of people will always be supportive. For example, each year since World War II, every president has been ranked by U.S. citizens as one of the 10 most admired persons in the world.[40] Perhaps a reason for this is, as Murray Edelman suggests, that "public issues fade from attention after a period in the limelight even when they are not 'solved' because they cannot remain dramatic and exciting for long and the media then have economic and psychological reasons to softpedal them."[41]

For whatever reasons or in whatever manner goodwill is retained, our point is simply that any president possesses a sense of competency that none of his rivals can share. It is, of course, a distinct advantage of the office.

Charisma and the Office

The final symbolic strategy, like the first three, is dependent on the ability of the office to transfer its persona to the incumbent. However, this one is not an intangible resource in that it has had deliberate use since presidents began barnstorming the country for their own elections. The presidency stands for excitement, a kind of patriotic glamour, and therefore the person who holds the office takes on these characteristics. In no other way is the mystique of the presidency more visible than it is during a presidential campaign visit almost anywhere in the country. When the president comes to town (advance and security personnel have already been there for at least a week), roads are blocked, airports are closed, children are dismissed from school, bands play, television cameras and reporters are everywhere, hundreds or thousands of people converge along the streets or at the airport to greet the president; the very sight of the magnificent *Air Force One* produces a sense of awe, and for a while, we are participants in a warm and patriotic festival. It matters little whether or not we plan to vote for the incumbent; regardless of how dull and unimaginative the president may have been before living in the White House, once there, the office itself envelops the president in its aura or charisma.

Although campaign tours were not undertaken by incumbents (at least during the election period) until Herbert Hoover paved the way, their symbolic power has not been lost on any of the presidents who have succeeded him. The reasons for their trips have been as varied as have been their modes of transportation. For example, in 1948 Harry Truman whistle-stopped his way across 32,000 miles to blame what he termed the "do-nothing, good-for-nothing 80th Congress" for the nation's problems; in 1956 Dwight Eisenhower, in spite of two international crises, felt he had to undertake an extensive tour through the southern states to blunt his opponent's charges that he was too old and too sick to be president; in 1964 Lyndon Johnson barnstormed his way across the country, in part, because he felt a psychological need to be "out with the people" and experience their warmth and acceptance of him: in 1976 Jimmy Carter boarded the Delta Queen and traveled the Ohio and Mississippi rivers, campaigning at each stop, in an almost frantic effort to restore his popularity with voters; in 1984 Ronald Reagan whistle-stopped through several states, riding the same presidential caboose Harry Truman rode in 1948. In 1992 over 2,000 people turned out to shake hands with George Bush at a mall in Concord, New Hampshire and to hear him explain why he should be reelected in spite of a depressed economy. And in 1996, President Clinton's 14-bus caravan was greeted by a crowd of 25,000 in Paducah, Kentucky, during a week-long trip that Clinton stated allowed him "to see the people I've been working for for four years."[42] For the most part, other incumbents have used campaign trips for the same reasons. They have known that the glamour and excitement, the drama and pageantry of a presidential visit will, even if just for a short time, transfer the charisma of the office to them. As such, the trips are well worth the effort.

Pragmatic Strategies of Incumbency

In turning to the pragmatic strategies of incumbency, it is important to note that they are more universal than are their symbolic counterparts because they can be and have been employed by candidates who are neither presidents nor, in some cases, even incumbents. Certainly, there are those strategies which depend on the legitimate power that holding an office provides, but others have been used by candidates who only borrow the mantle or style of the incumbent.

Strategies that are examined in this section are:

1. Creating pseudoevents to attract and control media attention
2. Making appointments to state and federal jobs as well as appointments to state and national party committees
3. Creating special city, state, or national task forces to investigate areas of public concern
4. Appropriating federal funds/grants
5. Consulting or negotiating with world leaders
6. Manipulating the economy or other important domestic issues
7. Endorsements by party and other important leaders
8. Emphasizing accomplishments
9. Creating and maintaining an "above the political trenches" posture
10. Depending on surrogates for the campaign trail
11. Interpreting and intensifying a foreign policy problem so that it becomes an international crisis

Creating pseudoevents. As the use of public relations experts and publicists has increased in political campaigns, so too has the frequency of hyped or manufactured news. Essentially, pseudoevents are defined as occurrences that differ from "real" events in that they are planned, planted, or incited for the primary purpose of being reported or reproduced.[43]

While all candidates use pseudoevents to try to capture media attention, incumbents have more success because they are in a better position to create them. For example, a governor or state senator may be featured on the evening television and radio news throughout the state because of an announced "major" initiative in attracting a specific corporation to the state and thus creating new jobs. A member of Congress may receive headlines from appointment to a special committee or commission created by the president. Moreover, incumbents have many opportunities for participation in ceremonious occasions—events that are sure to bring the local media. The ceremonies can be as different as the groundbreaking for a new government building to the announcement that a special day has been set aside to honor the city's firefighters. But each can be hyped up enough to guarantee publicity for the candidate. However, not only do incumbents have more opportunities to attract the attention of the media, they are better equipped to control the kind of coverage they receive. Perhaps a politician whose experience provides one of the best examples of what we mean is the ex-mayor of New York. During his years as mayor, Edward I. Koch learned how to control the New York media. He was seen on television virtually every evening; most of the time it was as the leading participant in a special occasion or ceremony. (New York is a big city, and therefore many events can be important enough to make the mayor's attendance seem appropriate.) Equally important, was the way in which Koch controlled the kind of coverage he received. During the 1985 Democratic mayoral primaries, the mayor's opponents issued frequent press statements attacking various administration programs. In response, Koch called press conferences on those days to announce new initiatives the city government was taking in such areas as housing starts and education reforms, or even to announce park dedications. According to Koch, "my own comments were getting covered in long news stories, while the charges of my opponents were reduced to little metro briefs deep inside the paper. This is the power of incumbency."[44]

In 1996 the Clinton administration was successful in drawing favorable and widely publicized coverage of presidential initiatives—initiatives that had been frequently discussed by Republican candidates. Shortly after the 1994 election when the Democrats lost control of Congress, the president and his staff identified issues congressional Republicans had championed and began writing their own legislative proposals. Some of the proposals received daily media coverage. For example, within a two-day period, Clinton's announcements of initiatives to help schools and track the illegal sale of guns made the front pages of *USA Today* and the *New York Times*, respectively. A month earlier, ABC reported on the president's announcement of a program to combat infectious diseases and his intention to "restate his belief" that cigarettes are addictive. The wide publicity received criticism from Senator Dole, whose campaign released a statement that Clinton and his aides were "getting away with refried beans and in some cases very thin gruel, and getting coverage that makes it seem like a full platter of policy."[45] Clinton, in other words, used the media exposure his incumbency guaranteed to seize the rhetorical agenda for the 1996 presidential campaign.

In short, incumbents have at their disposal the ability to create pseudoevents that not only generate media exposure but allow some measure of control over the coverage.

Making appointments to jobs and committees. One of the most common yet powerful incumbency strategies revolves around the ability to appoint personal or political friends—or potential friends—to local, state, and federal jobs or to give them key positions on party committees. Although patronage has been condemned by reformers in both political parties, it continues largely because it is so advantageous to everyone concerned. First, it allows candidates (and is not limited to incumbents in that all contenders can hold out the "promise" of appointment) to reward those who have helped them in the past. Second, it creates potential friends or at least puts people in a position of gratitude. Third, and undoubtedly most significant, it places supporters in key positions that may well be important in later stages of the campaign or even in subsequent elections. As such, few candidates, from county commissioner to governor to president, have failed to use this strategy.

Creating special task forces. Modern candidates understand the need not only to determine which issues are of concern to the voters in their city, district, or state but to speak to those concerns. One way to do this is to announce the formation of a special task force whose purpose is to investigate the issue/problem and make recommendations to the candidate regarding steps or actions to be taken in the future. The strategy is employed by incumbents as well as those who are not incumbents because the act of forming the task force is all that is really required to create the illusion that the candidate is concerned about the problem.

The primary advantage of the strategy is that the candidate is perceived as a person who understands and cares about those issues important to a particular constituency. However, a second benefit is that the candidate is in the position to postpone taking a stand on a controversial issue—one that might create as many enemies as supporters. Thus every election year seems to bring a plethora of specially created task forces composed of concerned community/state/national citizens who investigate topics as varied as mental health facilities and taxes for a new sewer system.

Appropriating funds/grants. Absolutely no incumbency strategy is less subtle or more powerful than appropriating special grants to "cooperative" (politically supportive) public officials for their cities and states. It is reserved only for incumbents (in that the strategy does not include promises for the future) and is viewed best at the presidential level, although it is certainly done at state and local levels as well.

Although every modern president since Franklin Roosevelt has had a prodigious amount of discretionary money to distribute in the form of federal grants, by the election of 1980 the amount totaled $80 billion. Like his predecessors, Jimmy Carter was determined to use it to aid him in the primaries—especially the early contests when the campaign of Edward Kennedy was still viewed as a threat. The money was employed to reward those public officials who announced their preference for the president, to gain a public endorsement where there had not been one, or to punish those who denied or withdrew support. For example, prior to the Illinois primary, Jane Byrne, mayor of Chicago, was told by the White House that U.S. Air Force facilities at O'Hare Field would be relocated to allow Chicago to expand its major airport. However, after the mayor announced her support of Senator Kennedy over the president, the secretary of transportation said that the cabinet had "lost confidence in Mayor Byrne, and would look for opportunities to deny transportation funds to Chicago and its mayor."[46]

Thus, the Carter White House went into the 1980 campaign determined to "grease" its way through the primaries. Florida (in advance of the Democratic straw primary) received a $1.1 billion loan guarantee to an electric cooperative, $29.9 billion in grants for public housing in various counties, and $31 million for housing projects for the elderly throughout the state. Prior to its primary, New Hampshire received funds for such projects as a four-lane highway from Manchester to Portsmouth and a special commuter train from Concord to Boston.[47] In 1996 President Clinton made extensive use of his power to allocate funds. For example, federal funds were provided to enlarge local police forces throughout the country. And, after Massachusetts suffered severe flooding from the "Great Rain of '96," it was immediately announced that funds would be made available by the government to those counties hit the hardest.

Is the appropriation of funds a successful incumbency strategy? While it is impossible to claim the effect of any one element in a phenomenon as complex as a primary election, President Carter soundly defeated Kennedy in New Hampshire and virtually annihilated him in the Florida and Illinois primaries. On the other hand, the emergency federal funds President Bush promised to Florida ultimately worked against him because Florida citizens said it was too little and arrived too late.

Consulting with world leaders. While at first glance consultation with world leaders may appear to be a strategy possible for only presidential incumbents, the fact is that this strategy is employed by any number of governors and members of Congress as they attempt to build their credentials for reelection. Governors extend invitations to athletic teams or artists and may even negotiate with foreign business corporations and governments about the prospect of building a major factory in the state. Members of Congress take frequent junkets overseas in the effort to illustrate their power and importance to voters in their districts or states.

In addition to its use by incumbents, the strategy is employed by challengers who must also build credentials and convey a sense of their individual importance. Moreover, its use may be even more crucial for them because they do not possess the real authority or power of the incumbent. Thus a meeting with foreign governmental leaders grants at least a sense of legitimacy because it illustrates acknowledgment and a kind of acceptance into an important and official group of leaders. For example, in 1992 challenger Bill Clinton met Russian President Boris Yeltsin to assure him of his support for the multibillion-dollar aid package for Russia that was then pending in Congress. Following the meeting, the governor allowed as how the half-hour chat with the Russian leader was a meeting of the minds.[48] And in 1998, in anticipation of the Iowa caucus for presidential campaign 2000, Republican hopeful Malcolm (Steve) Forbes, Jr. brought former British Prime Minister Margaret Thatcher to Iowa to campaign by his side.

While significant to congressional and gubernatorial candidates, a trip abroad—especially to Russia, China, or the Middle East—is virtually a prerequisite for potential presidential contenders, particularly those whose previous experiences have not included "official" foreign travel and consultation with government officials. At the very least, it allows them to work their trips into their discourse with such phrases as, "in my meeting with the prime minister, I was told that . . ." But even more important, the strategy provides those candidates who have absolutely no foreign policy experience the appearance of seeming to be a part of or involved in international affairs. As such, it is a useful strategy of the incumbency style.

Manipulating important domestic issues. As a number of these strategies illustrate, incumbents have considerable power, which is, of course, one of the reasons they are difficult to defeat and challengers are so eager to assume their campaign style. However, the manipulation or management of important issues is one strategy that can be assumed only by the incumbent.

For example, throughout the years, the economy has been a primary area of presidential management. One way this has been done is timing economic benefits to specific groups within the electorate to ensure their vote in the election. Political scientist Frank Kessler has pointed to the following Social Security incident during the 1972 presidential campaign as a case in point:

Checks went out in October 1972, one month before the elections, with the following memo enclosed and personally approved by President Nixon to each of the 24.7 million Social Security recipients: "Your social security payment has been increased by 20% starting with this month's check by a new statute enacted by Congress and signed into law by President Richard Nixon on July 1, 1972. The President also signed into law a provision which will allow your social security benefits to increase automatically as the cost of living goes up."[49]

In using this strategy, presidents have not limited themselves to economic manipulation; other issues have been managed. For example, President Bush took a number of actions designed to win voter approval in 1992, including: supporting the sale of F-15 fighters to Saudi Arabia in time to announce it to defense workers in Missouri, signing a bill making carjacking a federal crime, announcing to farmers a complicated plan for using corn-based ethanol fuel as an antidote for urban smog, vetoing a bill that would regulate cable prices (saying that it benefited special interests rather than the public), and retooled training programs that he said could be paid for without new taxes. And in 1996, in an effort to boost his campaign, President Clinton vetoed a bill that would have outlawed some late-term abortions, signed legislation aimed at preventing gay marriages, transferred U.S. Border Patrol agents from Texas to California (where illegal immigration is a major issue), vetoed bills that would place new limits on the ability of Americans to pursue civil court claims, and signed a bill that increased the minimum wage.

Thus the manipulation or management of important domestic issues is yet another strategy of incumbency.

Receiving endorsements from other leaders. Although the growth of primaries has reduced their importance, endorsements are an attempt to identify and link the candidate with already established, highly respected, and generally acknowledged leaders. The idea is that endorsement by respected leaders signifies that the candidate is already part of their group and should therefore also be thought of as a leader; in other words, credibility by association. Obviously, this perception can be crucial for a nonincumbent who wishes to adopt the incumbency style. It is, of course, equally significant for the incumbent because continued acceptance by other governmental or political leaders is one way of advancing the perception of a successful term of office. Similarly, candidates hope they receive no endorsements from individuals or groups who are not perceived positively by large segments of society because negative association is also possible. For example, during the 1960 presidential campaign, Richard Nixon was endorsed by the president of the Teamsters Union, Jimmy Hoffa. Because Hoffa was already thought of as a "racketeer," or worse, by many citizens, it was an endorsement that Nixon tried to ignore. When reporters questioned John Kennedy about his reaction to Hoffa's endorsement of Nixon rather than himself, Kennedy responded humorously that he guessed he was just lucky, which of course reinforces our point.

Emphasizing accomplishments. One of those strategies forming the core of the incumbency style is emphasizing accomplishments. Candidates must be able to demonstrate tangible accomplishments during their term of office if they are incumbents or in some related aspect of public service if they only assume the style. This is, of course, the reason that incumbents go to great lengths to list for voters all that they have done while in office. For example, during the 1992 presidential campaign President Bush took credit for many of the events that happened in the world during his term of office, including the end of the Cold War.[50] In discussing United States foreign policy accomplishments he said:

Germany was unified. Central America was transformed through a policy based on free elections and reconciliation. The Soviet Union was dissolved peacefully and groundbreaking arms control agreements were reached. Iraq was defeated after the U.S. assembled an unprecedented international coalition to prosecute the war, opening the way for peace among the Arabs, Palestinians and Israelis.[51]

The strategy is simple as long as the deeds exist. The difficulty occurs when there have been few accomplishments or when major problems have arisen that overshadow positive contributions (taxes are higher than they were before the incumbent took office, inflation is worse, unemployment has not been reduced). When this happens, the strategy becomes more complex in that the incumbent must either deny that the current problems are important ones (normally an impossible task for even the most persuasive) or blame them on someone else—even on uncontrollable forces. Blaming someone—scapegoating—is the path normally chosen. Examples are as numerous as candidates. State legislators blame the governor, governors blame the federal government (especially Congress), presidents blame Congress, and surprisingly enough, members of Congress often blame other congressional members. A case that aptly illustrates the practice of blaming others is the 1996 budget impasse that led to partial shutdowns of the federal government. President Clinton blamed the Republican majority of Congress for not compromising, and the Republicans blamed the president for their inability to reach agreement. A budget was finally agreed upon in April 1997, but by then the government had lost some $2 billion in uncollected taxes.[52]

The practice of casting blame elsewhere is certainly not a new variation of the accomplishment strategy. However, its most interesting use is by members of Congress, especially the House. Popular perceptions of Congress are not high. For example, in 1998, a Gallup Poll found that less than 45 percent of the public expressed confidence in the United States Congress and approved of the way they were doing their job.[53] In fact, surveys on congressional job approval and disapproval ratings have shown a trend of disapproval for decades. However, despite these feelings, congressional incumbents win the overwhelming majority of their elections. One of the reasons for this paradox is that when individual representatives seek reelection, they disassociate themselves or even "run against" the institution of which they are a member. They talk about their accomplishments rather than those of Congress, and as two political communication scholars have noted, they play up the negative "myths" (Congress is a kind of shadowy process in which sinister figures operate) while projecting themselves as hardworking and honest people who work against evil.[54] In this way, then, even when genuine accomplishments may be few, scapegoating makes the strategy possible.

Above the political trenches image. Another strategy that is at the center of incumbency style is the technique in which candidates try to create the image that they are somehow removed from politics. Essentially, the strategy is composed of any combination of the following three tactics (each designed to create the impression that the contender is a statesman rather than a politician):

1. Appear to be aloof from the hurly-burly of political battle—that the office has sought them and thus they run because of a sense of love of country and duty

2. Fail to publicly acknowledge the existence of any opponent—candidates may have opponents, but statesmen do not

3. Sustain political silence (absolutely refrain from any personal campaign trips or confrontations with opponents, including not answering any charges or attacks or discussing partisan issues)[55]

While portions of the strategy are used by contemporary candidates, it has been around for a long time. As a matter of fact, its progenitor was George Washington. He did not have to create a nonpolitical or statesman image because he was not a politician. He had been reluctant to become president and, once there, never campaigned for reelection. In spite of this, for candidates who were to follow (at least presidential candidates), he bequeathed a legacy of "being above politics," in a sense, conveying the attitude that being political would somehow "dirty" the office. Thus, for many years, the public picked presidents without ever seeing or hearing what their ideas or policies were—at least during the time in which they were candidates. With only two exceptions,[56] no major party candidates, even after formal nomination, personally solicited votes. They were not expected to (even after transportation networks improved) because the prevailing attitude was that the office must seek the person; that is, the appearance of modest reluctance—of being above politics—had to be maintained. Stephen Douglas was the first to break the taboo in 1860 when he shocked people with speaking tours on behalf of his own candidacy. Although other Democratic candidates followed his example, none were successful until Woodrow Wilson was elected in 1912. Republicans remembered Washington's example longer and eschewed mass campaigning until the 1932 campaign when an incumbent was faced with a problem of such magnitude that he felt he had to travel the country explaining why he should not be blamed for the Great Depression.

Thus this strategy has a long history, and its use, in combination with the next two strategies, continues to play a central role in the development and maintenance of incumbency style.

Use of surrogates on the campaign trail. This strategy is closely related to the last one in that it is possible for candidates to assume an above-politics posture because others are overtly campaigning for them while they stay home being nonpolitical. While the strategy is employed by a wide spectrum of candidates, it is the sophisticated use by presidential incumbents throughout the 1970s, 1980s, and 1990s that allows us to see most clearly the technique at work. For example, in 1972 Richard Nixon depended on the campaign tours of over 49 surrogates (including members of his family, cabinet officers, and other high-level government officials) while he stayed in the White House during most of the fall campaign against George McGovern. As a matter of fact, Nixon was so intent on creating the illusion of a hardworking, nonpolitical statesman that not only did he rarely take a political trip or make a speech on his own behalf, but when asked once by a reporter about his campaign, he cut off questioning with the remark, "Let the political people talk on that."[57]

The use of surrogates did not end with Richard Nixon's election. As a matter of fact, it became more pronounced, especially when the media dubbed it the "Rose Garden" strategy during the stay-at-home period of Gerald Ford's campaign in 1976. What they meant was that for weeks on end, as part of a specifically designed plan, Ford did not leave the White House to campaign for his reelection. Members of his family, his cabinet, and hundreds of Republican party faithful were out on the hustings for him as he stayed close to the White House and acted "presidential." In addition, as part of the plan, the media were alerted several times each day to witness pseudoevents (the president's welcome to visiting dignitaries or his signature on legislation), most of which occurred in the area adjacent to the Oval Office, the Rose Garden (thus the name). During the midterm elections of 1982, the Republican National Committee developed a program called "Surrogate 82" in which all cabinet members were required to devote 15 days to campaign activities.[58] But what is most interesting about surrogates and rose gardens is that the strategy is a direct descendant of the "Front Porch" campaigns used by Republicans many years earlier.

In 1888 the grandson of "Old Tippecanoe," Benjamin Harrison, was the Republican candidate for president. The party believed it had lost the 1884 election because of the mistakes their candidate made. Therefore, it was decided that Harrison would campaign from his home in Indianapolis against the Democratic incumbent, giving rehearsed and dignified speeches to delegations of visitors who were invited to hear him speak while other party leaders toured the country on his behalf. In other words, the challenger would not only appear presidential, he would have little opportunity to err. Thus, when Harrison won, the Front Porch or Rose Garden strategy was born.

As is the case with most campaign strategies, success means repetition. So in 1896 Republicans went back to the porch with a new candidate and increased zest for a campaign style that was in stark contrast to the "swing around the circle" effort of the Democrats.

Although William McKinley never left his porch in Canton, Ohio, he nonetheless was part of a more vigorous campaign to return the White House to the Republicans than had been conducted for Harrison. Hundreds of visiting delegations were invited to visit his home to hear him speak. He gave as many as 12 carefully prepared speeches a day (each on a single issue specifically directed to the interests of the delegation), and copies were supplied to all major papers. Thus, while remaining at home, McKinley received daily nationwide press coverage—more in fact than did his opponent. In addition, 1,400 surrogates were sent out from party campaign headquarters to speak for him all across the country. With all this effort, McKinley defeated William Jennings Bryan.

In part because of their victories the first two times, Republicans returned to the porch for the 1920 election. While the Democratic candidate toured the country, the Republican managers sat Warren G. Harding on the front porch in Marion, Ohio (where day after day he delivered quiet and dignified platitudes about common sense and clean living) and then supplemented the porch performances with touring surrogates. Once again, the strategy worked as Democratic contender James Cox lost in the worst defeat a presidential candidate had known.

With this kind of success, it should now be easy to understand why front porches (currently called rose gardens) and surrogates have remained popular with modern presidential candidates.

Interpreting or intensifying foreign policy problems into international crises. Although variations of the strategy of interpreting or intensifying foreign policy problems into international crises are employed by incumbents at all levels, it is most completely studied as it has been used by presidents. Its purpose is simple: to create enough of a crisis situation so that voters (either because of patriotism or not wanting to change leaders at the time of an emergency) will be motivated to rally around the president. There have been many instances when the technique has been successful. In 1916 and again in 1940, presidents Woodrow Wilson and Franklin Roosevelt campaigned with the specter of war in Europe in the minds of the electorate. In 1964 when U.S. ships in the Gulf of Tonkin were fired upon, President Lyndon Johnson interrupted his "campaigning" to go on television where he pledged that the United States would take rigorous defensive measures. In 1975 when a U.S. merchant ship, the Mayaguez, was captured by Cambodian forces, President Gerald Ford (who was about to make official his bid for reelection) used the situation to build his leadership or command credentials by ordering marines to bomb Cambodia until the Mayaguez crew was released. However, one of the most adept uses of the strategy occurred in the surfacing and primary stages of the 1980 campaign when President Jimmy Carter (who had two genuine foreign policy problems with the seizure of the U.S. embassy in Iran and the Soviet advances into Afghanistan) combined the use of surrogates, a nonpolitical image, and international crises to promote his renomination campaign.

Prior to the Iowa caucus and continuing through the Maine and New Hampshire primaries, Carter pledged that he would not personally campaign until the hostages in Tehran were released. Later, when the Soviets marched into Afghanistan, the president reinforced his earlier vow when he announced that because "this is the most serious crisis since the last World War," he would be unable to leave the White House to campaign in person for reelection. In addition, when other candidates (notably Senator Edward Kennedy and Governor Jerry Brown) questioned the administration's handling of the "crisis," the president completed the strategy by suggesting that attacks on his policy were "damaging to our country and to the establishment of our principles and the maintenance of them, and the achievements of our goals to keep the peace and to get our hostages released."[59]

Until the very last round of the primaries, the president stuck to his pledge. He emerged only rarely from the White House or Camp David and left most comments on politics to his surrogates. Carter's use of incumbency strategies was eminently successful. While giving the appearance that he was too busy trying to solve the international crises to campaign for reelection, he was defeating his opponents in the Democratic primary elections.

These then are the strategies that comprise the incumbency style. There are, as we have seen, a large number of them—each somewhat different from, although often dependent on, the others and each potentially effective in the hands of candidates who understand and appreciate their power. Perhaps what is most startling about them is the extent to which they work. Normally, it takes enormous amounts of money, organization, and skill to defeat even somewhat inept incumbents. They have at their command not only the strategies we have examined but whatever privileges the office itself provides—including public awareness (visibility) and the opportunity to perform various popular and noncontroversial services for constituents. These strategies have repeatedly enabled incumbents to overwhelmingly win reelections and win by larger margins than victorious nonincumbents. As we have said before, given all of the benefits, it is no wonder that candidates who are not incumbents often assume elements of the style.

But under what conditions can incumbents lose? In other words, are there burdens of the style as well as benefits? It seems to us that there are at least four major disadvantages of incumbency campaigning. First, and maybe most important, incumbents must run (at least in part) on their record. While they may cast blame elsewhere or minimize the scope or significance of problem areas within their administration, an effective challenger can make certain that the record of the incumbent (and shortcomings can be found in virtually all records) forms the core of the campaign rhetoric. The incumbent can be kept in a position of having to defend, justify, explain—answering rather than charging, defending rather than attacking. Being forced to run on one's record can be a severe handicap particularly in the hands of a skilled challenger.

The second and related burden faced by many incumbents is simply that the public may blame them for all problems—whether or not they were at fault. Incumbents are in the public eye and if the city sanitation workers refuse to pick up the garbage for a week or if the public transportation system is shut down because of weather, an accident, or striking employees, they are held accountable. At the very least, the question of competency or job effectiveness is raised in the public mind, waiting perhaps for the skilled challenger to capitalize on it.

The third disadvantage, although quite different from the first two, can be equally troublesome. The challenger is free to campaign, but incumbents must at least give the appearance of doing the job for which they have been elected. As campaign seasons become longer, this becomes more difficult. Incumbents often find it unnerving to go about the day-to-day task of administering a city, state, or nation while their opponents spend countless hours out on the hustings, garnering media attention with attacks against them and their policies. If they respond by indulging in overt campaigning, they are criticized for not doing their job. If they ignore it, they may well be accused of having no defense and being afraid to go out and face voters. In other words, it is a real damned if you do and damned if you don't situation.

Finally, because incumbents are at the center of media/public attention far more than their opponents, expectations are great regarding their "front-runner" status. If those expectations are not met, the incumbent is in trouble. Nowhere has this been more thoroughly illustrated than in presidential primary campaigns. Even when incumbents win, if they fail to meet some preconceived percentage set by the media or even by their own staffs, they have, at least in terms of media publicity, lost.

Thus there are some burdens. Even the incumbency style does not guarantee election. With this in mind, we will now contrast the strategies of the incumbent style with those of the challenger, knowing that in each there are burdens as well as benefits.

Challenger Style

Challenger campaigning is not easy because the style demands a two-step process, the implementation of which requires not only a good deal of deliberate planning but equal portions of skill and even luck. The style can be defined as a series of communication strategies designed to persuade voters that change is needed and that the challenger is the best person to bring about the change. While the kind of change can vary all the way from shifts in a whole economic system to personality characteristics desired in the officeholder, challengers must convince the electorate that some kind of alteration is necessary if they stand any chance for success. However, the second part of the process is equally important; the voters must also be persuaded that the challenger is the candidate most likely to produce more desirable conditions or policies. Therefore, the complexity of the style is increased because not only must those who challenge call for change, they must simultaneously demonstrate their own capability in bringing about that change. As if all of this was not difficult enough, it is entirely possible that the success of the challenger may ultimately depend on the skill of the incumbent—whether or not the incumbent makes a major mistake in campaign strategy or becomes a victim of prevailing conditions. Thus, it is no understatement to maintain that the task facing most challengers is formidable.

In spite of the potential hazards or burdens, advocating change—the challenger campaign style—is not new. As a matter of fact, it probably got its start in the presidential campaign of 1800 when Jeffersonians distributed leaflets that asked: "Is it not time for a change?" Whenever it began, it has been used by many candidates who have sought elective office. Moreover, elements of the style have even been employed by incumbents such as Harry Truman and Gerald Ford who felt it would be more beneficial to their candidacies to call for a change in Congress rather than only try to explain the present problems.

The strategies examined in this section include:

1. Attacking the record of opponents
2. Taking the offensive position on issues
3. Calling for a change
4. Emphasizing optimism for the future
5. Speaking to traditional values rather than calling for value changes
6. Appearing to represent the philosophical center of the political party
7. Delegating personal or harsh attacks in an effort to control demagogic rhetoric

Attacking the record. Just as running on the record of their accomplishments is a central strategy of incumbency, so too is attacking that same record a prime characteristic of the challenger style. As a matter of fact, the ability to criticize freely (and often in exaggerated terms) may well be one of the most important benefits the challenger possesses.[60]

When there is no incumbent, candidates attack the record of the current administration (if they do not represent the same political party) or even an opponent's record in a previous position. Whatever becomes the focus of criticism, the object is to attack—to create doubt in voters' minds regarding the incumbent's/opponent's ability, to stimulate public aware-ness of any problems that exist, or to foster a sense of dissatisfaction and even unhappiness with the state of affairs generally.

In addition, a few challengers extend the attack strategy to demand publicly an investigation of some aspect of the incumbent's record or administration. This was the case, for example, during the 1989 Demo-cratic mayoral primaries in New York. Ed Koch's challengers demanded that his record be investigated because of charges of widespread corrup-tion during his tenure—charges and evidence of bribery and extortion that engulfed the mayor's most powerful allies and a few of his closest friends. Whether or not investigations such as these ever take place is almost unimportant. The tactic is to call attention to some alleged prob-lem or instance of wrongdoing within the incumbent's administration and thus imply, at least indirectly, that the incumbent has some serious difficulties and therefore does not deserve another term. In 1992, a woman who had never before run for elective office challenged a pow-erful United States senator from Pennsylvania, Republican Arlen Spector. Democratic senatorial candidate Lynn Yeakel said that her run for office was motivated by the Anita Hill/Clarence Thomas televised Senate hear-ings and her feeling that the men on the Senate Judiciary Committee, including Senator Spector, "just didn't get it." During her campaign, Yeakel worked to paint Spector as the personal embodiment of a gov-ernment on the wrong track.[61] In 1996, Senator Dole attacked President Clinton on a number of issues and tried to convince voters that problems existed that demanded attention. For example, Dole attacked Clinton's campaign for accepting large financial contributions from foreign busi-ness interests.[62] He also demanded that President Clinton forgo future pardons connected with Whitewater, the failed land deal in which Clin-ton had been accused of wrongdoing.[63] The problem for Dole was two-fold. First, the president's campaign responded immediately by counterattacking, and second, voters appeared to have little interest in his attacks on the president.

Interestingly, attack is so much a part of challenger style, that it fre-quently occurs even when the predominant public perception of the in-cumbent is that a credible job has been done. In this instance, the challenger may minimize the importance of the accomplishments, credit them to someone or something else (often another branch or level of government that happens to be controlled by their own party), never mention the accomplishments, or point out that in the years ahead ac-complishments will be viewed as problems. Few challengers, however, have been as mean-spirited in their attacks on the incumbent as was Geoffrey Feiger during the 1998 Michigan primary when, in his nonstop attack on Republican incumbent John Engler, he called him "a cheater, a liar, and a coward . . . a man of mediocre intelligence who's never done anything in life but suck off the public trough."[64]

Whatever means various challengers go about it, their ability to attack existing records or policies is a crucial tool and integral to the overall style.

Taking the offensive position on issues. Essentially, the strategy involves nothing more than taking the offensive position on issues important to the campaign—probing, questioning, challenging, attacking but never presenting concrete solutions for problems. It is the incumbent who has to defend unworkable solutions to insolvable problems; the challenger can limit rhetoric to developing problems, keeping the incumbent in a position where all actions have to be defended.[65] In a sense, it is part of a challenger's expected role—to criticize, attack, point out needs—generally guiding voters to begin thinking that the incumbent has been ineffective. Challengers are not expected to solve problems (they have had no chance as officeholders to do so). This is, of course, a major advantage (one of the relatively few), and those who abandon it often lose the election. As a matter of fact, the more detailed challengers become in offering solutions, the more material they provide to be attacked themselves. In other words, when they drop the offensive, they have essentially traded places with incumbents, thus compounding their difficulties because unlike incumbents they lack the tools to solve problems. Thus, the strategy is simply to talk about what is wrong without suggesting any precise ways in which conditions can be righted.

History is replete with examples of successful challengers who used this strategy and won. In 1932 Franklin Roosevelt never divulged the contents of his "New Deal"; in 1952 Dwight Eisenhower never suggested how he would deal with the Korean conflict except to promise that he would personally go there and look it over; in 1960 John Kennedy never shared the details of the "New Frontier"; in 1968 Richard Nixon only said he had a plan regarding the war in Vietnam but never provided any clues regarding it; in 1976 Jimmy Carter seldom offered solutions more substantive than his love and admiration for the people; in 1980 Ronald Reagan never explained just how his supply-side economics would do all he claimed for it; and in 1992 Bill Clinton presented the necessity for economic reform, health care reform, and welfare reform without providing clear details of the solutions he advocated. Clinton charged Bush with a failed economic policy and said the president had offered no plan to improve conditions. "Unlike our competitors, America has no natural economic strategy," he told employees in a manufacturing plant in Oregon. "Instead we have a series of unconnected, piecemeal efforts, and trickle-down economics. Under trickle-down economics, our manufacturing strength has trickled away."[66] At another time he said "if you look at the last 12 years, we now have a chance to assess whether the theory has worked. In 1980, we had the highest wages in the world. Now we are 13th and dropping."[67] In retrospect, it is unlikely that most of these challengers even knew how they might solve all of the problems they discussed once they were elected. Whether they did or not, solutions were not offered, and the candidates managed to keep their offensive position on the issues while forcing their opponents to defend, justify, and offer plans.

Conversely, in 1964 and again in 1972, two challengers never seemed to understand the essential nature of the strategy. Barry Goldwater and George McGovern thought they had to present specific proposals on topics as varied as welfare and the way to fight wars. As the details of their plans became known, they were subjected to intensive analysis, debated, refuted by opponents and media, and finally rejected as absurd. Goldwater and McGovern not only lost their credibility as serious presidential candidates, they lost an important advantage. Taking and keeping the right to attack without proposing solutions is a major challenger strategy that only the foolish abandon.

Calling for a change. From the beginning of each campaign season, it becomes clear that many candidates announce that they are "willing" to run for office because they believe that a change is necessary. Whether it involves specific programs and policies, philosophical assumptions regarding the nature of government, or even modification in administrative style, calling for a change has become the dominant characteristic of those who challenge.

There are various ways in which the strategy has been employed. For example, John Kennedy talked about the need to "get the country moving again"—a stylistic and substantive change from a passive attitude to aggressive, take-charge action. Jimmy Carter used a moralistic change—a return to honest, decent, and compassionate government. Ronald Reagan argued for economic as well as philosophical change, while Edward Kennedy gave the need for a change in the manner and style of presidential leadership as his only reason for an intraparty challenge. Perhaps one of the most specific uses of the strategy was exemplified by Senator John Glenn who, in the early months of the surfacing stage of the 1984 presidential campaign, called for a change of direction in budgeting for basic research and technological development as well as a dramatic overhaul of the Social Security system. Conversely, the failure of Michael Dukakis to call for a change in 1988 was one of the reasons for his defeat. According to John Sasso, the chief strategist for Dukakis's presidential campaign, "the failure to establish a clear campaign theme and a compelling case for political change" was a mistake on their part.[68] In 1992, Clinton integrated talk of reform into his overall call for change. In June 1992, Clinton told an audience, "When I got into this race, the President was at an historic high point in popularity. But I was convinced then and I am convinced now that this country needs profound change."[69] And in 1996, Bob Dole asserted that the nation needed material, or economic, as well as moral change.

Thus regardless of how it is employed, the essence of challenger style must revolve around seeking change. If a change from existing conditions, incumbents, or administrations is unnecessary, then so too are challengers.

Emphasizing optimism for the future. While most candidates, regardless of the level of office sought, traditionally spend some time during the campaign talking about their vision or their optimism for the future, the strategy is particularly important for those who would challenge the status quo. After all, if existing conditions are so bad, can they ever be better? Thus the task of the challenger is not only to attack but to hold out the promise of a better tomorrow—a day when wrongs will be righted, when justice will prevail, and when health, wealth, and happiness will be more than just vague illusions. In other words, challengers must assume a "rhetoric of optimism" as opposed to a "rhetoric of despair."[70]

This is not to suggest that candidates who employ the strategy dismiss the nation's needs from their discourse; rather, it is a question of emphasis. For example, in 1932 Franklin Roosevelt obviously acknowledged the problems caused by the economic depression, but the central focus of his campaign was hope for the future. John Kennedy talked about problems, but his emphasis was on the country's potential to get moving again. Ronald Reagan pledged that he would lead a crusade to make the United States great again, the commitment of George Bush to the spirit of volunteerism as a substitute for federal government programs was embodied in the phrases first used in his nomination acceptance speech "kinder-gentler nation" and "a thousand points of light," and the focus of Bill Clinton's rhetoric was the creation of a government that efficiently works for people, for a change. In short, a part of the challenger style is reliance on the positive—emphasizing hope and faith in the future, an optimism that the nation's tomorrow will, in fact, be better than today.

Speaking to traditional values. Even though the overall challenger style is dominated by a call for redirection or change, it does not mean a redefinition of values. In fact, it is just the opposite. Successful challengers must reinforce majority values instead of attempting to forge new ones. In other words, they must have some understanding of the way in which people view themselves and their society—some understanding of the current tenets of the American Dream. In 1992, Bill Clinton

used the challenger strategy of speaking to traditional values as both a defensive and as an offensive weapon. For example, he defended against direct attacks from Bush by saying, "I think the implication he has made that somehow Democrats are godless is deeply offensive to me ... and to a lot of us who cherish our religious convictions and also respect America's tradition of religious diversity."[71]

While this strategy has been understood by challengers such as Richard Nixon, Jimmy Carter, Ronald Reagan, and George Bush, it may be more interesting to explain it by the example of one who did not. In 1972 before suffering the worst defeat in the history of presidential politics, Democratic challenger George McGovern seemed to have little comprehension of what most citizens wanted. He talked about massive or radical changes in welfare and tax reform, military spending and inflation, school busing, amnesty for those who had left the country rather than participate in the Vietnam War, and the need for more civil rights legislation. What McGovern failed to understand was that most citizens "were tired of social reforms, tired of the 'good-cause' people; that the majority preferred to live their own lives privately, unplagued by moralities, or war, or riots, or violence."[72] Middle-class citizens viewed McGovern as a candidate of an elitist upper class whose values they did not understand except to know that they angered and frightened them. Through his failure to speak to the dreams or visions of the electorate, McGovern abandoned an important strategy of the challenger style.

Appearing to represent the philosophical center. Throughout our political history, successful challengers have been ideological representatives from the mainstream of the major parties, or they have tried to appear as though they were. While some may have been on one or two issues a bit to the right or left of the majority of the party, they have not been representatives of the outer or fringe groups. In most campaigns, the fringe groups eventually have compromised and supported their party's candidate, even though that candidate may have been more conservative or liberal than they would have preferred. In the presidential campaign of 1980 and even in 1984, Ronald Reagan, who had long been the champion of the ultraconservatives within the GOP, attempted to position himself closer to the ideological Republican middle once he had secured the nomination. In 1988, George Bush used the same strategy by repositioning himself on such issues as abortion. And in 1996, Bill Clinton modified his stand on so many domestic issues, it was difficult, and frequently impossible, for his opponent to claim even traditional Republican positions.

The only two major exceptions in contemporary presidential politics have been Barry Goldwater and George McGovern, each of whom, as the candidate of fringe groups, did not try to reposition himself in the center of his respective party. Instead, each attempted to reform the ideological majority around the ideological minority. In so doing, they failed to employ a traditional challenger strategy.

While Goldwater and McGovern did not attempt to occupy a more central ideological ground, two nominees during the 1980s were blocked from using the strategy by their opponents. In 1984 Ronald Reagan was able to position Walter Mondale as a candidate of the Democratic fringe because of the former vice president's stand on increased taxes, social welfare issues, defense spending and because of the endorsement of him by groups such as the National Organization of Women and the Gay Liberation Movement. Similarly, in 1988 George Bush, who for much of his political career had been perceived by conservative Republicans as too liberal, repositioned himself in the center and branded Michael Dukakis as a liberal even among Democrats. A liberal, according to the Bush definition, was someone who, like Governor Dukakis, was opposed to children saying the pledge of allegiance in school, was so soft on crime he let convicted murderers out of prison on weekend furloughs, and someone who did not support defense initiatives such as the MX missile. In other words, someone who was outside the mainstream of traditional American values. The label proved disastrous for Dukakis because the governor failed to reposition himself or to redefine the vice president's interpretation of a liberal.

In 1992, Bill Clinton did not allow himself to be defined by his opponents. From the surfacing period onward, he positioned himself as a "new kind of Democrat." As a matter of fact, he was one of the founding members of the Democratic Leadership Council—a group of Democrats recognized for its conservative to moderate position on many issues. However, in 1996, Republican challenger Bob Dole had a singular inability to define himself. In fact, it was his very lack of definition that allowed the incumbent and his fellow Democrats to maintain the hold on the ideological center and force Dole to the conservative right, a position that he did not always fit.

Delegating personal or harsh attacks. Although attack remains a central imperative of the challenger style, successful candidates (particularly in statewide or national races) do not themselves indulge in demagogic rhetoric. While smear tactics and political hatchet work have been a part of elective politics for years, wise challengers have left harsh or vitriolic language to running mates, surrogate speakers, or to their television advertising and printed materials. The reason for delegating this kind of attack is, at least in part, related to the symbolic nature of the campaign itself. As we have mentioned earlier, campaigns are a symbolic representation of what or how candidates might behave if elected—a kind of vignette from which voters are able to transfer campaign performance into performance as officeholders. Thus the challenger who likens the incumbent to Adolf Hitler, asserts that the president behaves like a reformed drunk, or argues that the incumbent is ignorant of foreign policy, as did George McGovern in 1972, Edward Kennedy in 1980, and Walter Mondale in 1984, is unwise.

Demagogy is never viewed as an asset and normally backfires for the challenger who employs it. In 1988 Michael Dukakis was attacked as being soft on defense, soft on crime, and soft on patriotism. However, George Bush was smart enough to leave direct attacks on his opponent to others and to his television advertising campaign. In 1992 Clinton attacked the policies of the president and his administration but was careful to show no disrespect to President Bush, even after the president referred to Clinton as a "bozo." However, in 1996, Bob Dole attacked President Clinton's personal character. Dole's attacks not only proved ineffective, as the president retained his double-digit lead in the polls, but the strategy actually persuaded some voters to oppose Dole and support Clinton because they thought personal attacks were "in bad taste and removed from the issues of being the president."[73]

These then are the strategies that comprise the challenger style. While there are fewer of them than there are incumbency strategies, they can also be powerful when used correctly. However, those who employ them, just as those who employ their counterparts, must understand the importance of image creation and maintenance. For example, it does little good if a candidate attacks the record of the incumbent but does so using demagogic language or leaves no outlet for the promise of a better to-morrow. In a similar manner, those who fail to understand the necessity of appearing to represent the values of the majority of the electorate as they call for a change in the course or direction of present policies will have little success. In short, challenger campaigning is difficult primarily because being a challenger is not nearly as advantageous as being an incumbent. Challengers win but not as often. Challengers have some advantages over incumbents but not very many. In the final analysis, challengers may be only as successful as incumbents are incompetent to employ the symbolic and pragmatic strategies their office provides.

Incumbent/Challenger: A Merger of Styles

As discussed earlier, the incumbent and challenger strategies are not absolute categories. Those candidates who are incumbents are not re-stricted to a specific set of incumbency strategies any more than chal-lengers are confined to a particular set of challenger strategies. While the rhetoric of most candidates typically reflects their actual position in the race, there are instances wherein aspects of incumbency and challenger styles have been combined. It is not uncommon, for example, for chal-lengers to assume the mantle of incumbency whenever and wherever possible; its advantages are well documented. Those who challenge must try to emphasize whatever accomplishments they have had in public life;

they must appear to be acquainted with other leaders, and they have a clear need to use whatever means available to them to gain the attention of the media. Similarly, events may, from time to time, compel incumbents to borrow strategies more frequently associated with the challenger. While we consider it unlikely that any incumbent would ever find it advantageous to drop the symbolic strategies or to call for a change, an incumbent may well emphasize ideological centrality or rely on surrogate speakers for overt/direct personal attacks on opponents. Such rhetorical borrowing between categories, perhaps in response to changing conditions, is only part of what we mean by the incumbent/challenger style.

The most prominent characteristics of the combined style are abandonment of the essential purpose or thrust of incumbent or challenger rhetoric and abandonment of the responsibilities each has. If the challenger does not attack or at least question the policies and actions of the incumbent, no real campaign dialogue occurs. In a similar vein, if the incumbent will not acknowledge problems, defend current policies or programs, or even suggest/offer a future course of action, no real dialogue can occur. Although there is little question that at many points during the 1996 campaign the incumbent president used strategies of an incumbent as well as those of a challenger, perhaps the best way to understand the incumbent/challenger style is through an extended example from the 1984 presidential campaign.

In 1984 we had two challengers; one of whom was the president of the United States. Beginning with his nomination acceptance speech, Ronald Reagan's rhetoric was heavily centered around two staples of the challenger style: (1) attacking the policies of the opposition (in this case going back to the Carter–Mondale administration) while taking the offensive position on issues; and (2) emphasizing optimism for the future. Incumbency strategies were only to enhance his campaign as a challenger. While Reagan was not the first sitting president to try to campaign for reelection in this manner, he was the first one since Harry Truman to do so successfully.

Part of Reagan's success as an "incumbent challenger" was his ability to figuratively step out of office at crucial moments and reflect on problems—"posing as a commentator who happened to live on Pennsylvania Avenue"—never admitting that he, as the result of election, was currently more responsible than any other single individual for the federal government.[74] But there was another part to the strategy—painting the portrait of a future at once so uplifting and patriotic that all problems of the moment were dwarfed by it.

Americans are by nature optimists. We believe in people—especially heroes—and in happy endings. Successful candidates have long known that optimism is the way to the hearts of the American electorate. "At the worst of times, Franklin Roosevelt uplifted with a smile, while years later, Jimmy Carter guaranteed his fate by telling us that we were suffering from malaise."[75] What was so effective about Reagan's use of cheer was his own appearance of amiability and an understanding of the political fact that Americans want to hear good news, as well as the way he managed to distance himself from responsibility when things went wrong. "It was as if he was a king who reigned but did not rule—a constitutional monarch whose performance was a symbol to his people while politicians did the dirty work of governing."[76] In 1984 he campaigned for reelection as a critic of federal budget deficits even while he had created the largest deficit in history.

In short, he offered voters, just as he had in 1980 when he had actually been a challenger, a picture of a future that did not include hard choices or sacrifices he might ask them to make after the election. However, a strategy of optimism is possible only if a candidate has managed to avoid the defensive position on issues. This was the second overt use of the challenger style employed by the incumbent president.

Throughout the campaign, it was as if there were two challengers—both attacking, probing, questioning, but the incumbent/challenger never defending his policies. In fact, by seizing the offensive on issues the president reduced his opponent to the most disadvantageous challenger posture, suggesting solutions for problems. Reagan did not have to make allowances for solving problems because he did not acknowledge the existence of problems. Unwilling to accept the issues presented by Mondale as problems, let alone acknowledging any responsibility for them, the president simply smiled and said that the trend is the thing and every day in every way, things are getting better. When Mondale charged that the nuclear arms race had heated up between Washington and Moscow and that U.S.–Soviet relations were strained, the president responded by ignoring the issue and talked about America standing tall and looking to the 1980s with courage, confidence, and hope. Finally, in a measure of absolute desperation, Mondale outlined solutions—such as the inevitable raising of taxes to deal with the national deficit. When time after time Mondale tried to push Reagan on exactly what he was going to do about the deficit, the president only responded that it was a little scary to have a deficit of a hundred and eighty billion dollars a year and that even if he had "inherited the wreckage from the Democrats," he was willing to work with them to repair the problem.

From the beginning, it appeared that the challenger and the incumbent had reversed roles. The incumbent ran against "big spending demons in Washington," "puzzle-palaces on the Potomac" and whenever he left the White House, talked about what a pleasure it was to be out of Washington. The challenger sought to tie the incumbent to problems the country faced and when there was no response, created his own solutions.

The Reagan staff had reasoned that it was unnecessary to speak to the specific issues raised by Mondale. They had determined before the campaign even began that the reelection effort would be concentrated on the president's leadership and the problems resulting from the Carter–Mondale past, without defending current programs or without proposing any new or specific programs for the future.[77] They believed their strategy would be successful because Reagan had been on the political stage for 30 years. His views were well-known by the American people. As the press secretary for his reelection campaign, James Lake, said, "It would be foolish of us to let Ronald Reagan respond to Mr. Mondale . . . people don't care. They get his message. They see him on television and read the newspaper."[78] Thus the incumbent outlined scenes and evoked symbols, leaving details—particularly unpleasant details—for later. Patriotic slogans, such as "America is back," "America stands tall," "America is too great for small dreams," or "the opportunity society" combined with the persona of the incumbent himself and his stage-managed appearances drove the 1984 presidential campaign into what one political commentator called a "collage of manufactured happiness as in an infinitely extended television commercial."[79]

CONCLUSIONS

In this chapter, we have examined an important yet frequently overlooked element of elective politics—campaign style. In so doing, we considered style as sets of communication strategies that are employed by all candidates and noted the relationship of image and advancements in transportation and communication to their creation and maintenance.

The incumbency style was defined as a blend of symbolic and pragmatic communication strategies designed to make candidates be perceived by voters as not only good enough for the office sought but appear as if they already possessed the office. Fifteen different yet complementary strategies were examined. In a similar manner, we analyzed the challenger style, defining it as a series of communication strategies designed to persuade voters that change is needed and that the candidate is the best person to bring about change. Seven different yet complementary strategies were discussed.

Finally, we considered the incumbent/challenger style and noted that the combination of strategies which compose it, at least as illustrated during the 1984 presidential campaign, can play a major role in the creation of empty political rhetoric.

NOTES

1. Bruce E. Gronbeck, "The Functions of Presidential Campaigning," *Communication Monographs* 45 (November 1978): 268–80.

2. James Tobin, *The People's Choice* (Detroit: Detroit News, 1978), p. 3.

3. Ibid.

4. See Irwin Silber, *Songs America Voted By* (New York: Stackpole Books, 1971).

5. Kathleen Hall Jamieson, *Packaging the President: History and Criticism of Presidential Campaign Advertising* (New York: Oxford University Press, 1984), p. 12.

6. Kenneth E. Boulding, *The Image* (Ann Arbor: University of Michigan Press, 1961), p. 6.

7. Allan Dean Louden, "Image Construction in Political Spot Advertising: The Hunt/Helms Senate Campaign, 1984" (unpublished Ph.D. dissertation, University of Southern California, 1990), p. 1.

8. G. R. Pike, "Toward a Transactional Model of Political Images: Collective Images of the Candidates in the 1984 Elections," paper presented at the International Communication Association Convention, Honolulu, 1985. Quoted from Susan A. Hellweg et al., "Political Candidate Image: A State-of-the-Art Review," in *Progress in Communication Sciences* 9, ed. B. Dewin and M. J. Voigt (Norwood, N.J.: Ablex, 1989), pp. 43–78.

9. Arthur H. Miller, Martin P. Wattenberg, and Oksana Malanchuk, "Schematic Assessments of Presidential Candidates," *American Political Science Review* 80 (June 1986), pp. 521–40.

10. Dan Nimmo and Michael W. Mansfield, "Change and Persistence in Candidate Images: Presidential Debates Across 1976, 1980, and 1984," paper presented at the Speech Communication Association Convention, Chicago, 1986.

11. Hellweg et al., "A State-of-the-Art Review," esp. pp. 44–53.

12. Judith S. Trent, Jimmie D. Trent, Paul A. Mongeau, and Cady Short-Thompson, "The Ideal Candidate Revisited," *American Behavioral Scientist* 40(8) (August 1997): 1001–19.

13. Jimmie D. Trent, Judith S. Trent, Paul A. Mongeau, and Gay E. Gauder, "Facial Attractiveness and Initial Choice among Political Candidates: The Effect of Sex, Race, Political Preference, and Position," paper presented at the International Communication Association, Rome, Italy, 1998.

14. Frederick Williams, *The Communications Revolution* (Beverly Hills, Calif.: Sage, 1982), p. 37.

15. Frederick Williams, The *New Communications*, 2d ed. (Belmont, Calif.: Wadsworth Publishing Company, 1989).

16. Ibid.

17. Edgar E. Willis, "Radio and Presidential Campaigning," *Central States Speech Journal* 20 (Fall 1969): 187.

18. Ibid., p. 191.

19. Ibid.

20. Joel L. Swerdlow, *Media Technology and the Vote: A Source Book* (Boulder, Colo.: Westview Press, 1988). See also James Perry, *The New Politics: The Expanding Technology of Political Manipulation* (New York: Potter, 1968).

21. Michael McCurry, "The New Electronic Politics," *Campaigns and Elections* (March/April 1989): 23–32. See also Williams, *The Communications Revolution*, 1982, esp. pp. 17–39.

22. Theodore H. White, *The Making of the President 1968* (New York: Atheneum, 1969), p. 154.

23. Swerdlow, *Media Technology and the Vote*, pp. 6–7.

24. For a discussion of the potential of what he terms "push-button government," see Williams, *Communications Revolution*, pp. 183–99.

25. Robert J. Samuelson, "No More Media Elite," *The Washington Post National Weekly Edition*, July 13, 1998, p. 26.

26. Thomas Rosenstiel, *Strange Bedfellows* (New York: Hyperion, 1993) p. 170.

27. Evan Thomas and Gregory L. Vistica, "Fallout from a Media Fiasco," *Newsweek*, July 20, 1998, pp. 24–26.

28. Becky Beaupre, "Net Wins Over Millions During Election," *Detroit News*, November 8, 1996, p. C1.

29. Carolyn Barta, "A Bridge to Where?" *Dallas Morning News*, December 15, 1996, p. 1J.

30. Terry M. Neal, "www.voteforme.com," *The Washington Post National Weekly Edition*, May 3, 1999, p. 12.

31. W. Lance Bennett, "The Ritualistic and Pragmatic Bases of Political Campaign Discourse," *Quarterly Journal of Speech* 64 (October 1977): 228.

32. Keith V. Erickson and Wallace V. Schmidt, "Presidential Political Silence: Rhetoric and the Rose Garden Strategy," *Southern Speech Communication Journal* 47 (Summer 1982): 402–21.

33. Bruce Barron, "Give Challengers a Chance," *Pittsburgh Post-Gazette*, December 15, 1996, p. B-1.

34. R. F. Fenno, Jr., *Home Style: House Members in Their Districts* (Boston: Little, Brown, 1978), p. 211.

35. Robert E. Denton, Jr., *The Symbolic Dimensions of the American Presidency* (Prospect Heights, Ill.: Waveland Press, 1982), p. 58.

36. Theodore H. White, *Breach of Faith* (New York: Atheneum, 1975), p. 322.

37. Dan D. Nimmo, *Popular Images of Politics* (Englewood Cliffs, N.J.: Prentice-Hall, 1974), p. 92.

38. John Louis Lucaites, "Rhetoric and the Problem of Legitimacy," in *Dimensions of Argument: Proceedings of the Second Summer Conference on Argumentation*, ed. George Ziegelmueller and Jack Rhodes (Annandale, Va.: Speech Communication Association, 1982), pp. 799–807.

39. Murray Edelman, "The Politics of Persuasion," in *Choosing the President*, ed. James David Barber (Englewood Cliffs, N.J.: Prentice-Hall, 1974), p. 171.

40. Denton, *Symbolic Dimensions*, p. 61.

41. Edelman, "The Politics of Persuasion," p. 171.

42. Al Cross and James Malone, "Clinton Reaches Out to Heartland," *Courier-Journal*, August 31, 1996, p. 1A.

43. William R. Brown, "Television and the Democratic National Convention of 1968," *Quarterly Journal of Speech* 55 (October 1969): 241. For a more extensive treatment of pseudoevents, see Daniel J. Boorstin's classic, *The Image* (New York: Atheneum, 1980). Originally, the book was published under the title *The Image or What Happened to the American Dream* in 1961.

44. Edward I. Koch with William Rauch, *Politics* (New York: Simon and Shuster, 1985), p. 236.

45. Howard Kurtz, "White House News Leaks of Questionable Significance Unleash Publicity Deluge," *Washington Post*, July 14, 1996, p. A16.

46. Theodore H. White, *America in Search of Itself* (New York: Harper & Row, 1982), p. 296.

47. Ibid., p. 295.

48. "Clinton Becomes Yeltsin Fan after Early Morning Chat," *New York Times*, January 24, 1992, p. A24.

49. Frank Kessler, *The Dilemmas of Presidential Leadership: Of Caretakers and Kings* (Englewood Cliffs, N.J.: Prentice-Hall, 1982), p. 313–14.

50. Andrew Rosenthal, "Bush Sounding Like His Rivals, Tones Down His Attacks, Briefly," *New York Times*, October 27, 1992, pp. A1, A11.

51. Devroy, "The Bush Campaign, Shake and Bakered," p. 11.

52. Indigo, "Shortfall in Responsibility," *Orlando Sentinel*, May 29, 1996, p. A12.

53. *The Gallup Organization—Congress Job Approval* (available at http://www.gallup.com/Gallup _ Poll _ Data/ratecong/jobapp.htm).

54. Dan D. Nimmo and James E. Combs, *Subliminal Politics: Myths & Mythmakers in America* (England Cliffs, N.J.: Prentice-Hall, 1980), p. 78.

55. Barry Brummett, "Towards a Theory of Silence as a Political Strategy," *Quarterly Journal of Speech* 66 (October 1980): 289–303.

56. William Henry Harrison in 1840 and General Winfield Scott in 1852 made, at the insistence of their managers, some speeches on their own behalf.

57. "The President," *Newsweek*, August 28, 1972, p. 15. See also Judith S. Trent, "Image Building Strategies in the 1972 Presidential Campaign," *Speaker and Gavel* 10 (January 1973): 39–45; and for a discussion of the use of surrogate speakers, see Chapter 6.

58. Robert E. Denton, Jr., and Gary C. Woodward, *Political Communication in America* (New York: Praeger, 1985), p. 87.

59. Ellen Reid Gold and Judith S. Trent, "Campaigning for President in New Hampshire: 1980," *Exetasis* 6 (April 1980): 7.

60. Nelson W. Polsby and Aaron Wildavsky, *Presidential Elections* (New York: Charles Scribner's Sons, 1976), p. 165.

61. D. Russakoff, "Putting Washington on Trial," *Washington Post*, September 7–13, 1992, p. 9.

62. David Jackson, "Campaign Financing under Attack," *Dallas Morning News*, October 24, 1996, p. 1A.

63. Jere Hester, "Irancon Figure Hits Dole," *Daily News* (New York), October 16, 1996, p. 18.

64. Ron Stodghill II, "The Motown Motormouth," *Time*, August 17, 1998, p. 30.

65. Judith S. Trent and Jimmie D. Trent, "The Rhetoric of the Challenger: George Stanley McGovern," *Central States Speech Journal* 25 (Spring 1974): 16.

66. "Clinton Hits Hard on Jobs, Economy," *Cincinnati Enquirer*, September 9, 1992, p. A8.

67. "Excerpts from Clinton Speech to National Guard," *New York Times*, September 16, 1992, p. A15.

68. David S. Broder, "The Lessons of Defeat," *Washington Post National Weekly Edition*, February 6–12, 1989.

69. Robin Toner, "Clinton Wins a Majority for Nomination but Perot's Appeal Is Strong in 2 Parties," *New York Times*, June 3, 1992, p. A1.

70. Judith and Jimmie Trent, "The Rhetoric of the Challenger," p. 17.

71. Bill Nichols, "Clinton Antagonized, the Challenger Counterattacks," *USA Today*, August 24, 1992, p. A5.

72. Ibid.

73. "Dole's New Attack Style Leaves Bad Taste with Some Voters," *Arizona Republic*, October 20, 1996, p. A25.

74. Francis X. Clines, "Friend and Foe Cite Reagan's 'Masterful' Use of Incumbency," *New York Times*, September 18, 1983, p. E5.

75. Anthony Lewis, "Dr. Pangloss Speaks," *New York Times*, October 14, 1984, p. E19.

76. Ibid.

77. Jane Mayer and Doyle McManus, *Landslide: The Unmaking of the President, 1984–1988* (Boston: Houghton Mifflin, 1988).

78. Howell Raines, "Reagan Appears to Succeed by Avoiding Specific Issues," *New York Times*, September 22, 1984, p. 14.

79. David Hoffman, "Accentuate the Positive, Put Off the Negative," *Washington Post National Weekly Edition*, March 26, 1984, p. 13.

Chapter 4

Communicative Mass Channels of Political Campaigning

× ejemplos ,USA   (   )

No other nation in the world consumes so much mass communication. By the mid-1990s, there were over 1,600 daily newspapers and about 7,000 weekly newspapers with a combined circulation of over 100 million. By 1998 there were approximately 10,000 commercial radio stations and more than 11,000 magazine titles available to us that sold about 400 million copies to subscribers and through newsstands.[1] However, the medium that continues to be devoured to a greater extent than all others is television. More than 98 percent of all households (93.1 million homes) have one television set, and approximately 64 percent have two or more, making television more plentiful than home telephones or automobiles.[2] Over 70 percent of American homes now subscribe to a cable television service and satellite television programming is growing.[3] However, more striking than the number of television sets owned is the frequency of their use. Television is the major source of entertainment and information, our primary leisure time activity. Americans have their television sets turned on more than seven and a half hours every day, and we spend 40 percent of our time watching it.[4] In other words, it is a dominant force in the lives and environments of most of the public, a fact that was called to our attention by political communication scholars Dan D. Nimmo and James E. Combs in 1990. In their book *Mediated Political Realities*, Nimmo and Combs claim that consistently since 1963 Americans have named television as their primary and most believable news medium.[5]

As we discussed in an earlier chapter, the widespread growth of the Internet and the increase in the number of Americans who have access to and use the Internet on a daily basis is another significant element in

the utilization of mass communication. Over 62 million people are regular users of the Internet for "shopping," for linking to web sites to find
out where to purchase specific products, and for access to political information.[6]

Not only is U.S. mass media consumption unequaled, in no other nation is it so inextricably linked to the electoral process. Mass communication has become the center stage for all major political events. For
example, daily newspapers and weekly magazines keep political people
and issues in our minds as they frequently report the result of the latest
poll taken to measure how individuals feel about the president, governors, members of Congress, candidates, and specific issues and controversies. Radio programming is punctuated with five- and ten-minute
news reports regarding some aspects of politics or with 10-, 30- and 60-
second spot advertisements for candidates and local "vital" issues. Moreover, by the 1992 presidential campaign, radio political talk and call-in
shows had reached a zenith in popularity all over the nation. And by
the time of the midterm elections in 1994, the more than 900 shows and
their hosts had become a political reality in local, state, and national
races. But it is television that has most dramatically linked us to large-
scale political campaign events such as presidential debates, national
nominating conventions, primary victories and losses, candidates' gaffes,
campaign trips, news conferences, election eve rituals, campaign
speeches, biographies, negative commercials and, in the late 1990s, even
hearings and investigations. It was television that brought Ronald Reagan to national political attention in 1964 as he delivered one of history's
most financially successful speeches; just as 28 years later, Texas billionaire H. Ross Perot announced on CNN's "Larry King Live" that he
would run for president if citizens would be willing to gather enough
petition signatures to place his name on the ballot in all 50 states. And
in 1998, the public watched as the results of the Minnesota gubernatorial
election made clear that Jesse "The Body" Ventura, a former professional
wrestler (well known to many because of televised wrestling matches),
had defeated Republican and Democratic opponents to become that
state's new highest elected official. In short, the mass media and particularly television have had a profound impact on the electoral process by
connecting citizens and political campaigns.

In spite of this, the influence of mass communication on political behavior remains uncertain. Although media effects is one of the most
studied areas in the social sciences, after almost 80 years of intense research there are relatively few absolutes, largely because the findings of
one generation of scholars are frequently challenged by the next.

Thus, the purpose of this chapter is to sort through the major theories,
perspectives, hypotheses, and models that have been advanced regarding the media's relationship to political behavior and attempt to draw at

least some general conclusions. In so doing, it may be helpful to understand that for some scholars the "theories" are not theories at all because they are not all unambiguous, deductive, and interrelated structures from which empirically ascertained and consistent laws or general principles have been derived. For our purposes in this chapter, however, theories come in various packages. Although most have been empirically derived, not all are unambiguously and deductively determined. Moreover, if we insisted that the theories presented here must account for or predict general principles, there would be relatively little to discuss. Few of the perspectives or hypotheses have provided the consistency needed for determining general laws or principles. In other words, when it comes to the question of the role of media in determining political behavior, there is no one grand theory. There are a number of partial theories or what (in another context) communication scholar Frank E. X. Dance refers to as particularistic theoretical bits and pieces,[7] but no single theoretical development that can account for or predict related phenomena. It is for this reason that we discuss a number of the major perspectives and approaches that have generated research. Whether or not multitheoretical conceptualizations are desirable or undesirable, the fact is that almost eight decades of research have frequently led to conclusions that contrast with one another. This is one element to which we pay special attention as we proceed through the various theoretic approaches.

We define "mass" in a standard way as consisting of people representing all social, religious, and ethnic groups, from all regions of the country. Moreover, they are anonymous (do not necessarily know one another) and therefore act not in concert but spontaneously as individuals. We use the terms "mass channels" and "mass media" interchangeably to refer to the primary means of mass communication (radio, television, newspapers, and magazines). While we would not deny the existence of other modes of mass communication such as books, music and motion pictures in the political campaign any more than we would refuse to recognize forms of "mini" communication such as posters, billboards, and campaign literature, they are simply not as important. The major perspectives have been generated from studies of radio, television, newspapers, and magazines although we believe that the Internet will be added to this list as more studies are undertaken regarding its use.

Finally, it is important to understand that the focus of this chapter is not candidates and the campaign process but voters and the campaign process. The principles that are analyzed center around the effect of mass communication on the political behavior of citizens. As such, we will be concerned with the way researchers have answered such questions as: (1) to what extent do the media influence cognitions and behavior? (2) what are the primary mass communication models that have guided research? (3) what have been the effects of the media on the electoral process itself? (4) how do people use the media in the political process?

The chapter is organized chronologically in that the general conceptualizations from early and contemporary research compose separate sections. Within each, major studies are examined and any specific hypotheses or models that have been derived from them will be discussed. The conclusion focuses on a summary of principles regarding the influence of the media that are most important in understanding the nature of political campaign communication.

EARLY STUDIES

The media's influence on political behavior has been a subject of scholarly investigation since the 1920s. Although readers might question the need to be aware of anything other than the most recent research findings, many of the early studies have been of tremendous importance. In fact, their impact has been so profound, they are considered "classics," and the conclusions they articulated as well as the methods they employed influenced all who followed. Thus we will discuss each of the major perspectives as well as the general models or hypotheses that were derived from them during the 30-plus-year period in which they dominated mass communication research.

Hypodermic Effect

The assumption that the press is a powerful force in shaping public opinion had been around for centuries. In 1529, 50 years after the printing press had been introduced to England, King Henry VIII seized control of the printing industry. Licensed printers held their patents only if what they printed pleased him.[8] In the mid-1600s the Puritan establishment in Massachusetts Bay Colony maintained strict control over printing because they feared that a free press might threaten the government and promote religious heresies.[9] In 1722 the founder and editor of a Boston newspaper, the *New England Courant*, was jailed for three weeks because of his attacks on the government.[10] Years later, the press was thought to have been a powerful force in creating revolutionary fervor in the United States, in providing passion and visibility to the abolitionist movement, and in provoking Congress to go to war with Spain.

However, it was not until the 1920s and 1930s that researchers actually tried to determine the power of mass communication in shaping values and behaviors of citizens. The motivation to learn more about the ways in which media could influence the public was provided, in large measure, by Adolf Hitler's propaganda machine, which seemed to have captured the minds of the German people through movies and staged rallies, and the use of the radio by Benito Mussolini in Italy and Father Charles Coughlin in the United States to stir public support and sentiment for the fascists. The Information and Education Branch of the United States Army began recruiting social scientists to study the influence of media persuasion. As researchers analyzed the effects of propaganda films such as *The Battle of Britain* or the pro-German magazine, *The Galilean*, they confirmed what had been assumed for centuries. The media really were powerful; they had the strength not only to change people's attitudes but to alter their behavior. And because citizens were often helpless to resist the persuasion of propaganda, they were easily "bamboozled." Moreover, according to the researchers, these effects occurred in all people because, despite individual attributes and characteristics, individuals responded in the same way when they received similar messages. Audiences were like mobs; there were no individual minds but only a group consciousness. Messages went directly from the media to the individual where they were immediately assimilated. "Messages were literally conceived of as being 'injected' into the mind where they were 'stored' in the form of changes in feelings and attitudes. Eventually such feelings or attitudes produced the behavior desired by the message source."[11] This is, essentially, what researchers called the hypodermic effect or the hypodermic needle model.

Although it may be difficult for us to subscribe to specific aspects of the hypodermic model, it must be viewed in terms of the context in which it was developed. The 1920s through the early 1940s was a time of worldwide social, political, and economic unrest, passion, and violence. Economic depression, the rise of fascism and Hitler, and the domination of the Nazis throughout much of Europe suggested irrational yet somehow controlled mass group behavior. It seemed entirely likely that people's minds were being manipulated by powerful propaganda devices. In the view of many who were studying it, the "mass media loomed as agents of evil aiming at the total destruction of democratic society. First the newspaper and later the radio, were feared as powerful weapons able to rubber-stamp ideas upon the minds of defenseless readers and listeners."[12]

By the late 1930s, the hypodermic effect was widely enough accepted (even by those social scientists not involved in the government propaganda research program) to be applied specifically to the electoral process. One of the first systematic attempts to determine the political impact of the press was undertaken in 1937. Harold F. Gosnell studied the relationship of social and economic characteristics and newspaper-reading habits to election returns in several Chicago neighborhoods and found that the endorsements of newspapers could influence the way readers voted.[13] Thus social scientists were provided with additional proof of the seemingly unlimited power of the media to persuade.

Limited Effects or the Social Influence Model

Although the work of many of the army's psychologists and sociologists who were studying the effects of propaganda continued to reflect the hypodermic thesis, by the early 1940s, the findings of some researchers began to challenge the idea that the media were so potent that the public was mesmerized by them. One of the most important challenges occurred when three social scientists from Columbia University's Bureau of Applied Social Research, Paul F. Lazarsfeld, Bernard Berelson, and Hazel Gaudet, studied the 1940 presidential campaign and discovered (much to their surprise) that campaign propaganda had little impact on the way the electorate had voted. This study and others that followed began to build a competing explanation for media influence, one that was in stark contrast to the presumption that people were unable to control their own destinies or the destiny of the nation. It was, of course, a much more comforting thought than the hypodermic thesis because it provided reassurance that in the United States individual rationality and society's sense of order could not be overthrown because of the seizure or control of the media by a demagogue or someone who had gone insane.

The 1940 study began to form what became known as the social influence model. Twenty years later, mass communication scholar Joseph Klapper, in summarizing the conclusions of the work done on the impact of the media during the 1940s and 1950s, concluded that media effects are limited and, even in cases where they do occur, are mediated by other factors.[14] Thus he coined the term "limited effects model," a label that obviously stands in direct contrast with the earlier hypodermic perspective.

To understand this shift, it may be best to take a closer look at those studies that are regarded as the classics and that collectively influenced generations of mass communication scholars and their view of media and politics.

The first study by Lazarsfeld, Berelson, and Gaudet was conducted in Erie County, Ohio, a section of northern Ohio fairly equally divided between a city and farmland. Lazarsfeld and his colleagues wanted to measure the repercussions of campaign press coverage during a presidential election. At the outset they divided potential political effects into three categories: first, they believed the media could arouse public interest in the campaign and encourage voters to seek out more information about the candidates and issues; second, they reasoned that the press could reinforce existing political beliefs to make them stronger and more resistant to change; and third, they hypothesized that the media were powerful enough to convert attitudes, changing voters from supporting one candidate or party to supporting the opposition.

From May to November, a member of the research team interviewed someone each month in every twentieth house or apartment in the county. In total, 600 people were questioned about political parties, candidates, issues, and the news. Interviewers kept carefully structured records of each talk, and from these records Lazarsfeld and his colleagues were able to reconstruct how Erie County citizens made their decision between Franklin Roosevelt and Wendell Wilkie. The results were published four years later in a book called *The People's Choice*.[15]

Although Lazarsfeld and his colleagues believed that their research would confirm the prevailing thesis that the media were capable of controlling individual thought processes, they instead found that very few people changed their vote in response to the campaign propaganda and that those who changed did not attribute their conversion to media information. Specifically, they learned that:

1. People who read or listened to a substantial amount of campaign media coverage were more likely to become more interested in the election.
2. Their interest and activation were selective in that they tended to seek out stories that were consistent with prior political attitudes.
3. Those relative few who did change their minds did so not because of attending to the media directly but by the filtering of information to them from people in the community whom they respected. Such people were perceived to be highly active, highly informed, interested in politics, and therefore more likely than others to read or listen to media coverage of the campaign. These individuals were labeled "opinion leaders."

In the largest sense, the results of the Erie County study were not as important as the two explanations that Lazarsfeld and his colleagues offered for their findings. The explanations formed the cornerstone of the social influence theory. The researchers maintained that if a message presented by the media is in conflict with group norms it will be rejected. "Since groups have opinion leaders who transmit mass media information to individuals who do not attend to the media, these leaders influence whatever opinion change takes place in the followers; media messages do not have direct impact."[16] The second explanation given for their findings was that people are selective in those campaign messages to which they attend. They only listen to or read messages that are most consistent with their own beliefs, attitudes, and values. In other words, voters use the content of the media to support or reinforce the voting conclusions they would have reached because of their social predispositions. Interestingly, the concept of selective exposure was based on an analysis of only 122 persons who by August had not yet decided for which candidate they would vote. While 54 percent of those people with a Republican predisposition exposed themselves to Republican material and 61 percent with a Democratic predisposition exposed themselves to Democratic material, 35 percent of the Republicans and 22 percent of the Democrats did expose themselves to material from the other party— material that presumably was inconsistent with prior beliefs or social predispositions.

These percentages were never explained and the concept of selective exposure became a widely accepted phenomenon not only for the sociologically oriented voter studies but also by psychologists, who eventually incorporated it into a series of studies regarding involuntary and voluntary exposure to information to reduce psychological dissonance.[17]

The second of the classic studies conducted by the Columbia group was also staged in a single location. In 1948 Paul Lazarsfeld, Bernard Berelson, and William McPhee went to Elmira, New York, to determine voter behavior during the presidential campaign. The Elmira results, published in 1954 in *Voting*, supported the Erie County findings that campaign press coverage converted few voters and that information was disseminated from opinion leaders.

The third single-location study was mounted in Decatur, Illinois, and was reported by Elihu Katz and Lazarsfeld in the book *Personal Influence*. The researchers interviewed 800 women regarding "four arenas of everyday decisions: marketing, fashions, public affairs, and movie-going." For each arena respondents were asked "not only about themselves and their own behavior but about other people as well—people who influence them, and people for whom they are influential."[18]

Essentially, the results of the Decatur study confirmed the social influence model, although they also produced a more precise conceptualization of "the two-step flow of communication." The idea that had been hypothesized from the Erie County data suggested that "ideas often flow from radio and print to the opinion leaders and from them to active sections of the population."[19] However, in Decatur, the Columbia group wanted to compare the media behavior of opinion leaders and nonleaders "to see whether the leaders tend to be the more exposed, and the more responsive group when it comes to influence stemming from the mass media."[20] They discovered that the women they studied were willing to admit that they were influenced by other women, that leadership varied by topic, that leaders for each topic had different social and psychological characteristics, and that no single leader exercised control over the political beliefs of others. However, their most important finding, in terms of media impact on the electoral process, was that "opinion leaders were not more likely than followers to attribute influence upon their beliefs or opinions to the mass media."[21] Thus as a result of the third Columbia study, the role of the media was reduced even further in the minds of most social scientists. It appeared as if no group sizable enough to be measured was persuaded by media messages during a political campaign.

In 1952 another group of researchers began examining voters' behavior. Using the 1952 presidential election as their base, the University of Michigan Survey Research Center, or SRC, (now called the Center for Political Studies, Institute for Social Research at the University of Michigan) soon replaced the Columbia group as the dominant research force in large-scale voting studies. Methodologically as well as conceptually, the work of the Michigan group represented a major shift in the effort to examine voters and their behavior.[22] For example, the SRC relied on panels of potential voters based on national probability samples rather than a single community. In focusing on national behaviors, they moved away from sociological explanations (the emphasis on traditions, structure, composition, and the sociological nature of major institutions within single communities), which the Lazarsfeld group had presumed were the reasons for voters' predispositions. Instead, the Michigan researchers sought cognitive and attitudinal reasons for voting decisions. They asked citizens to indicate their party affiliation (Columbia had studied parties only in terms of social predispositions that led voters to choose one candidate over another). Thus with party identification as a key factor in explaining voters' attitudes and evaluation of candidates, the idea of interpersonal communication and the two-step flow conceptualization as the primary means of information diffusion was relegated to a "relatively unimportant position in the SRC model."[23]

However, in one important respect, the early SRC studies did not differ from their Columbia counterparts. Despite the fact that in 1952 television played a role in the presidential primaries, in the nominating conventions, and in the general advertising campaigns of at least one of the candidates, the Michigan researchers concluded that the impact of the mass media on the electoral process was minimal.[24] In fact, in *The American Voter* (a book based on the data collected in 1952 and 1956), the researchers indicated that it was party identification and not television that was the important factor in the development of political cognitions, attitudes, and behavior.[25]

Finally, in 1963, undoubtedly in an attempt to revitalize a theory that was being challenged by many, Lazarsfeld and his colleagues described a modification of the two-step flow. In the new conceptualization, information from the media was relayed from one opinion leader to another before it was passed on to followers. The revision became known as the "multistep flow" and because more people were added to the transmission process, the persuasive power of the media was viewed as even less significant than it had been before. Moreover, information not only traveled from opinion leader to opinion leader, but any one of these people could act as a "gatekeeper" and thereby prevent a follower from even being exposed to part of the information. In other words, opinion leaders functioned not only as conveyers of information among each other and finally to their respective "audiences," they also determined just what information would be transmitted. Although gatekeeping was discussed by Lazarsfeld in relationship to the multistep flow in 1963, the idea was not new. As early as 1950, one study had examined the selection and rejection of messages by gatekeepers. One of the key findings confirmed in many studies that followed was that when media gatekeepers made decisions, they did not have the audience in mind.[26]

Essentially, a gatekeeper is any person in the news gathering process with authority to make decisions affecting the flow of information to the public. "The image is precisely that of a turnstile gatekeeper at a sporting event—he examines the qualifications of each person in line, and decides whether or not to let him in. The difference is that what gets let in or left out is not a person, but a piece of news."[27] One of the reasons the gatekeeping function has received so much attention is that there are a variety of people in the media who must make decisions regarding the presentation of information and news. Examples include telegraph and wire service editors, reporters, film editors, headline writers, radio and television producers, news program anchors and commentators, and even other media (small newspapers and radio and television stations frequently take their news from the larger and more established media). Thus given the wide spectrum of people who daily determine which of the many possible news items will be presented to the public, it is little wonder that gatekeeping has been the subject of scholarly investigation as well as public consternation. Undoubtedly one of the most famous attacks against media gatekeepers was leveled in 1969 by Vice President Spiro Agnew. One of the broad areas of his criticism concerned the similarities of the various media decision makers. In an address before the Midwest Regional Republican Committee in Des Moines, Iowa, Agnew charged that

a small group of men, numbering perhaps no more than a dozen "anchormen," commentators and executive producers, settle upon the 20 minutes or so of film and commentary that is to reach the public. . . . We do know that, to a man, these commentators and producers live and work in the geographical and intellectual confines of Washington, D.C. or New York City—the latter of which James Reston terms the "most unrepresentative community in the entire United States." . . . We can deduce that these men thus read the same newspapers, and draw their political and social views from the same sources. . . . The upshot of all this controversy is that a narrow and distorted picture of America often emerges from the televised news.[28]

Whether or not Agnew's charges were true, they did provoke public discussion as well as a good deal of media response. In addition, gatekeeping continued to be a subject of scholarly investigation throughout the 1960s and 1970s.[29]

In summarizing the major ideas advanced by the early studies of media influence, it is tempting to conclude that in spite of the label of some of them as classics, almost four decades of investigation has had little relationship to contemporary theory. Researchers went from one extreme to the other; first media propaganda was the harbinger of all that was evil, and then it had little impact at all. Effects were seen primarily on a one-dimensional level—persuasion. The informational or cognitive function was largely ignored because of the dominance of selective exposure, a concept with little empirical validation then and clearly inadequate now.[30] Moreover, investigators were so intent on confirming the basic tenets of the social influence model that they ignored media effect in such important areas as voter turnout, political activation, and information seeking. The studies were conducted at a time in which home television sets were far less plentiful than they are today, and so the medium was viewed as having little direct influence on political behavior. Radio and newspapers were important only in their role as reinforcers rather than opinion formers, thus suggesting that voters were limited perceptually by their past.

However, in spite of all this, the early studies remain an important part of our media research heritage for at least four reasons. First, they pointed the way toward research methodologies that were more sophisticated than those that had been used. Moreover, the Columbia studies were the last massive single-community analysis for many years. And the Michigan studies of the national electorate continue to provide the most authoritative source of election data available. Second, the social influence model did rescue social scientists from the mass media hysteria symbolized by the hypodermic thesis. Third, although the Columbia studies may have carried the sociological explanation of voters' behavior to the extreme, they did begin the path toward the study of mass media and interpersonal relationships, obviously an important area of political campaign communication. Finally, the limited effects theory served as a catalyst for later scholars who would challenge the idea that the mass media had little impact on voters' behavior or the electoral process. Indeed, the sheer attempt to disprove the theory may well have led to the multiperspectivism that characterizes contemporary mass communication research.

CONTEMPORARY STUDIES

Just as the hypodermic thesis reflected society's turmoil and the social influence model depicted a quiet, reflective people not swayed by campaign propaganda, the mass media research of the 1960s and 1970s was a product of or at least representative of its time. If the decade of the 1950s is described by such words as quiet, inactive, or dull, the following years can be characterized as disquieting, tumultuous, and wild. While the federal bureaucracy grew in size and influence, so did citizen involvement in public affairs. Beginning with the civil rights struggle, which brought local groups together to form national organizations, a number of large-scale political and social movements appeared on the national scene. Each of them demanded new social and economic legislation to ensure equality and to guarantee their rights as citizens to help formulate national and international policy. However, each of them also needed various forms of mass communication not only to recruit, organize, and maintain their movements but to publicize their demands by drastic and frequently passionate actions.

The changes in society and the escalation of the social movements corresponded to alterations in the mass media system. It too was growing, largely because of the widespread use of television. More people owned television sets, and it was beginning to replace interpersonal conversations and meetings as a leisure time activity.[31] Television was becoming the most revolutionary branch of journalism. While in the 1950s, television news was typically read by one person seated in front of a wall map, during the next 20 years it became a drama featuring live coverage of national and international events. The sit-ins and marches of the social movements, the urban riots and burning of U.S. cities, the funeral of a young president and the assassination of his alleged killer, and the bloody battles of the war in Vietnam all contributed to the transformation of U.S. news-gathering and of those social scientists who studied it.[32]

It was in this atmosphere that many mass communication scholars began to question the basic tenets of the social influence model. Although they had no one holistic theory with which to replace it, maintaining that the media had little influence on or played no major role in the electoral process appeared a direct denial of what was happening all around them. A few researchers looked to the reigning paradigm for new explanations. For example, one study in 1962 indicated that uninvolved voters are susceptible to attitude change if any new information reaches them,[33] and another showed that, under certain conditions, it is possible for large audiences to get information directly from the media without the intervention of an opinion leader, suggesting that mass communication does not always work in a two-step flow.[34] However, the most important break with the social influence model occurred when social scientists, Jay G. Blumler and Denis McQuail, discovered in a study of the 1964 British parliamentary election that "regular viewers of television news developed significantly different perceptions of the Liberal and

Conservative parties."[35] Clearly, it was possible for media to do more than simply reinforce the status quo.

Beginning roughly about the time that the work of Blumler and McQuail appeared to suggest a new perspective for viewing media influence in politics, other theories or quasi theories were being articulated. In the remainder of this section, we discuss the basic assumptions or tenets of four of the most important approaches undertaken during the 1960s and 1970s and reexamined, reformulated or extended during the 1980s and 1990s.

Diffusion of Information

One of the approaches that bridges the gap between the limited effects model and the contemporary conceptualizations is the diffusion of knowledge perspective. It is related to the research that characterizes social influence theory largely because it was initiated in that era and because it acknowledges the importance of interpersonal communication to the dissemination of information. However, it differs from that theory in at least two important respects. First, diffusion research maintains that, under certain conditions, media transmission of information will have a direct impact on individuals and can produce changes in their knowledge or even their behavior. Interpersonal communication occurs after the mass media transmit information about news events and is therefore only a response to media reports.[36] The second way in which diffusion research is distinct from social influence is that it does not study attitude changes in voting behavior during political campaigns but focuses instead on the influence of the mass media on the acquisition of political cognitions. In other words, diffusion research is concerned with such topics as knowledge of campaign issues, candidates, and general public affairs. It is also used to investigate possible stages of information dissemination, how specific groups within society become aware of particular political matters, what factors contribute to the acceptance or rejection of political ideas, and what conditions mediate the flow of information about events.

Although diffusion has been defined in a variety of ways, generally conceptualizations of it in communication research capitalize on the idea of movement—the spread of adoption of new ideas (innovations) through time and space from one individual or group of people to another. In spite of the fact that diffusion research and the resulting diffusion model have roots in the physical sciences, it is employed by a number of disciplines within the social sciences. In the area of our interest, much of the early important work was done by Everett Rogers. In his 1961 book, *Diffusion of Innovations,* and in his later work with Floyd Shoemaker, Rogers discovered a multistage process of innovation diffusion. The four stages are: (1) information or knowledge; (2) persuasion; (3) decision or adoption; and (4) confirmation or reevaluation. In other words, new information is transmitted through society (or from person to person) in a particular sequential pattern. While it can be argued that these stages will not always be either separate or sequential under some conditions for some people, according to Rogers and Shoemaker, the media are important primarily in the first or information stage, where an interest in, awareness of, and understanding of the innovation can be created. Interpersonal communication is important during the last three stages as people seek confirmation or interpretation of the information they have received from the mass media.[37]

To support the view that the media were the predominant sources of information about political news events, early diffusion research in political communication was designed to measure the extent to which messages were transmitted. For example, it was discovered that the media informed most people about the death of Senator Robert Taft, President Eisenhower's decision to seek reelection, the dropping of Senator Thomas Eagleton as the Democratic vice presidential candidate, and the assassination of John F. Kennedy.[38] To a large extent, much of the diffusion research even during the 1970s continued to be concentrated on the extent and veridicality of information flow. Thus researchers appeared to be more interested in the attention arousal and information-seeking characteristics of the first stage of the process rather than the later adoption or persuasion stages.[39] In fact, after reviewing the diffusion approach to political communication studies published during the 1970s, Robert L. Savage reported that with the exception of news dissemination studies very little use had been made of it. He urged scholars to investigate such questions as: Are diffusing messages causes or effects of human actions? What latent and/or dysfunctional consequences follow from existing diffusion patterns? He appeared to doubt that political communication scholars had used the approach for all relevant forms of political information.[40] In a similar vein, mass communication scholar, Steven H. Chaffee, acknowledged that the diffusion approach had not yet lived up to its potential when he called for research that would lead to the development of a universal scheme for categorizing different types of diffusion items according to the type of communication that transmits them and the type of person most receptive to them, and determining the way in which items are relevant from the perspective of the political system.[41] And authors Sidney Kraus and Dennis Davis suggested that the diffusion model be supplemented by stipulating specific patterns of media use and perception to understand better the conditions that mediate the flow of information.[42]

Unfortunately, those researchers who continued to use the diffusion perspective during the 1980s rarely broadened or extended the scope of the topics investigated or the ways in which human behavior was affected—especially political behavior. Studies continued to focus on crisis news events (such as the shootings of President Reagan and Pope John Paul II in 1981), the relative roles of interpersonal and mass communication in the dissemination process (which one is the primary source of information and under what conditions for what people), and the rate at which information is diffused through the population.[43] In short, the model was never really expanded as some political and mass communication scholars hoped that it would be.

Thus, while the diffusion of information perspective helped redirect the focus of media/political research away from the unidimensional thrust of the social influence model, its potential has yet to be realized.

Uses and Gratifications

A crucial assumption of the uses and gratifications perspective is that a wide range of motives exists for using the mass media and that an individual's media requirements are dictated by such factors as their social roles, situations, or personalities. In other words, media audiences should not be thought of as huge collectivities who watch television shows, attend movies, and read newspapers and magazines for the same reasons.[44]

In one sense, the uses and gratifications perspective is similar to some of the other research approaches discussed in this chapter in that there is really no single theory. We do not mean to imply that the perspective is atheoretical but simply that there are numerous theoretical bits and pieces that compose the perspective. However, as one of its principle advocates, Jay G. Blumler, has argued, the various theories about the phenomena "share a common field of concern, an elementary set of concepts indispensable for intelligibly carving up that terrain, and an identification of certain wider features of the mass communication process with which such core phenomena are presumed to be connected."[45]

Although a diverse range of research has been conducted under the uses and gratifications paradigm, essentially it has been concerned with determining those uses people make of the mass media in the circumstances of their own lives as well as the gratifications they seek and receive from such consumption.

To an extent, part of the popularity of the approach is that it has served as a means of integrating ideas of massive effects (the hypodermic thesis) with limited effects (the social influence model) to form a middle-ground position where the audience is viewed as active, thinking receivers who are neither susceptible to all persuasive media messages nor impervious to them. In fact, it has been argued that it is in this role as an integrative component in an effects model "that the uses and gratifications perspective offers its greatest promise to the study of political communication."[46]

Not only, however, is the approach used for its bridge between the effects models, it has the additional benefit of allowing researchers to study more than just effects—to get at the functions mass media may provide during a political campaign. While some of these functions may be obvious (we read a newspaper account of a candidate's speech to gain more information about the candidate and the campaign), others may be latent (we watch a television commercial about a candidate so that we have enough information about the campaign to maintain our social status as an informed citizen). In other words, the functions served by the media during a campaign are not necessarily what they appear to be. Information or cognitive gain may serve many important purposes for the individual and the uses/gratifications perspective provides a way to examine them.

Although the uses and gratifications paradigm began to be especially popular during the 1970s, research conducted under its label goes back as far as the beginning of World War II when studies were published that dealt with the use of radio for entertainment purposes. Similarly, during the following two decades, when commercial television became important, the approach was used to generate data regarding entertainment programming. It was not until the landmark Blumler and McQuail study, published in 1969, that the perspective came into major use in examining political campaigns. In fact, it was this investigation of the 1964 British election that really spelled out the basic assumptions for researchers in political communication. Other studies followed, and in 1974 Blumler and Katz summarized much of the research the perspective had stimulated in *The Uses of Mass Communication*.

In spite of the fact that multiple studies have been conducted under the uses and gratifications paradigm, there remains not only the lack of one unified theory, there is still some disagreement about such basic tenets of the perspective as the meaning of an "active audience" and if media gratifications differ in any important way from one set of ideological beliefs to another or from one culture to another—in other words, the relationship of social structure to the understanding individual citizens bring to political messages/events. The question of the sociocultural bases upon which or through which the meanings of political messages are constructed and responded to was not clear in the original categorical scheme used by Blumer and McQuail. The five types of gratification orientations to political television programming employed in their study of the British national election were: using the political content of the media for vote guidance, reinforcement of decisions already made, general surveillance of the political environment, excitement, and anticipation of using the information in future interpersonal communication

situations. The three types of avoidance were: feelings of political alienation, partisanship, and relaxation.[47] However, in more recent years,
some researchers—including Blumer—have emphasized the importance
of the social structure, or the culture, in arriving at any understanding
of the meaning people give to messages (or their motivation to use or
avoid media). For example, in 1985 Blumer and his colleagues reported
that they "never meant to talk about abstracted individuals, but about
people in social situations that give rise to their needs. The individual is
part of a social structure and his or her choices are less free and less
random than a vulgar gratificationism would presume."[48] Whether or
not Blumer and McQuail simply assumed the role of sociocultural influence in their gratification and avoidance categories without specifically
discussing it is not as important as the fact that in recent years researchers have begun more clearly to acknowledge the role played by social
structure.

The second area of disagreement within the uses and gratification research is closely related to the first. Not only must the social determinants of the audience's media needs and expectations be considered, so
too must the idea or definition of an active audience be considered. As
at least one theorist has argued:

If the uses and gratifications paradigm is truly to come to grips with the nature
of the audience's media experience, it will have to give up the optimistic and
simplistic notion that an active audience implies a powerful audience. It must be
recognized that the concept of an active audience, as traditionally explicated in
the literature, may in fact obscure the powerlessness of the audience. Certain
audience media expectations are never voiced because they are perceived as inappropriate or as so unlikely as to make their articulation sound foolish or naive.
. . . Other expectations, for some individuals, when expressed, may be significantly modified or tempered due to the sense of powerlessness they feel with
respect to the political and social system. . . . In-depth probing of individual's
media expectations may reveal more about the assumptions these individuals
hold regarding their locations in the social and political system than about any
true media needs. In-depth analysis of the meaning of a commonly expressed
media expectation such as diversion may reveal the use of standard media fare
not so much for polite relaxation but for opportunities to ridicule a presentation
of reality which does not correspond to one's experience as opposed to mediated
life.[49]

Thus, while the uses and gratifications perspective has been the focal
point of a good deal of research and although the paradigm itself has
served a useful function by illustrating that people pay attention to the
political content of the media, it is interesting to note that in 1997 Dennis
McQuail argued that the research emanating from the uses and gratifications theories has produced little in regard to predicting or explaining

media choice. He wrote that connections between attitudes toward the media and media behavior are difficult to document because the "typologies of 'motives' often fail to match patterns of actual selection or use and it is hard to find a logical and consistent relation among the three sequentially ordered factors of liking/preference; actual choosing; and subsequent evaluation."[50] In general, he described uses and gratifications as an approach that "overestimates the rationality and activity of audience use behavior. Most actual audiences also turn out to be composed of people with varied, overlapping and not always consistent expectations and subjective motives."[51] Although the perspective continues to spark research (particularly in terms of its utility in studying the uses and gratifications of the World Wide Web),[52] we believe it may only reach its potential when researchers who employ it give full attention to the social bases of message construction and response.

Agenda-Setting Hypothesis

Undoubtedly, the most popular contemporary approach for studying the relationship of media and politics is the agenda-setting hypothesis. It has generated more research than any of the others. It clearly separates the persuasive and informational communicative functions of the media. It comes closer than any of the other approaches to reaffirming the early basic assumption that the media do have a great deal of influence on politics; the media may not always dominate, but they do have a significant impact on what we think about (our focus of attention). Finally, the perspective is important for another reason. The most frequent site for agenda-setting research has been election campaigns, and this has clearly not been the case with either the diffusion of information or uses and gratifications perspectives.

The underlying assumption of agenda-setting was first articulated by a political scientist, Bernard C. Cohen, in 1963. Cohen argued that the press may not be successful in telling its readers what to think, but "it is stunningly successful in telling its readers what to think about. . . . The editor may believe he is only printing the things that people want to read, but he is thereby putting a claim on their attention, powerfully determining what they will be thinking about, and talking about, until the next wave laps their shore."[53]

Just two years later, empirical verification of Cohen's ideas began to appear. In a study of the 1964 presidential campaign, researcher Jack McLeod found that the stories from two newspapers revealed clear differences in their reports of two issues in the campaign—federal spending policies and control of nuclear weapons. Specifically, the study revealed that respondents who read the paper that provided a good deal of coverage to nuclear control (the Democratic issue) ranked it higher than they did the economic issue. Correspondingly, those who read the paper that focused on spending policies (the Republican issue) ranked it higher than they did nuclear control.[54] In 1972 Maxwell E. McCombs and Donald L. Shaw explored the power of the press to set the agenda by studying the 1968 presidential campaign. Specifically, they hypothesized that "the mass media set the agenda for each political campaign, influencing the salience of attitudes toward the political issues."[55] Before the election, the researchers interviewed 100 people in five precincts in Chapel Hill, North Carolina, who had not yet decided whether they were going to vote for Hubert Humphrey, Richard Nixon, or George Wallace. The undecided voters were the only people interviewed on the presumption that they would be the most receptive to campaign information. McCombs and Shaw compared what voters said were the key issues in the campaign with the amount of space devoted to those issues in the particular medium used by the voters. They found a strong relationship between the emphasis given by the medium to specific campaign issues and the judgment of voters relating to the salience and importance of those issues. A third study, this time a national one conducted from 1964 to 1970, compared what people identified as the most important problems facing the United States (according to data from Gallup Polls) with listings of the content of news magazines. The researcher, G. Ray Funkhouser, concluded that "the average person takes the media's word for what the 'issues' are, whether or not he personally has any involvement or interest in them."[56]

In these three studies and many others that followed them during the 1970s, the agenda-setting functions of the mass media gained wide acceptance from social scientists. In part the perspective was well-received because it did not suggest that media have the all-powerful attributes envisioned by the hypodermic thesis. Instead the theme from the corpus of work undertaken was that the media set public priorities just by paying attention to some issues while ignoring others. They determine which issues are important and in this way play an important role in structuring our social reality. In other words, people not only learn about issues through the media, they learn how much importance to give them because of the emphasis placed on them by the mass media.

Throughout the 1970s and 1980s, the perspective remained important because it illustrated "how significant communication variables" could be "operationalized and linked to concrete political processes such as election campaigns."[57] It stimulated a good deal of research (although few consistent conclusions) on such important areas as the distinct agenda-setting roles of newspapers and television, the differences between the intrapersonal agenda (operationalized in most studies in terms of what each individual considers personally most important) and the interpersonal agenda (what each individual talks about most often with others), and the length of time required for agenda-setting effects to manifest themselves in the public agenda.[58] Moreover, the approach continued to be employed in the 1990s to study, for example, public opinion during the Gulf War[59] and the relationship between public opinion in the United States about foreign countries and their visibility in our television news programs.[60] In 1982, however, perhaps in part because the campaign of 1980 and the subsequent election of Ronald Reagan reemphasized that television had become "the single greatest mediator of political outcomes in both everyday and campaign arenas,"[61] agenda-setting research was extended by some researchers to include evaluation. In other words, not only did the media tell us what to think about, it told us what to think about it. Evaluation was a major extension of the original formulation and, for those who subscribed to it, helped place in perspective the apparent power of such campaign tools as televised political advertising (the subject of the next chapter) during the political campaigns of the decade. Among other things, these researchers argued that news stories not only suggest the importance of the subject matter but the contextual cues or frames by which to evaluate the subject matter.[62] In one study, it was found that when the media concentrate on a particular news story, not only do program viewers become convinced that the subject is important, through this process they become " 'primed' to evaluate the president, in part, by his apparent success in dealing with this issue."[63] The researchers Shanto Iyengar and Donald Kinder also sought to assess the influence of priming in elections. They found that the issues over which voters appear most concerned as they prepare to cast their ballots for president or for the U.S. House of Representatives are shaped by whatever issues have most recently been the subject of television news.[64] And in a related study, published in 1983, scholars Gladys Engel Lang and Kurt Lang argued that Watergate never really became an issue in the 1972 presidential campaign (in spite of the extensive coverage of it) because it was cast as a partisan issue, just another example of election year politics.[65] The assertions of candidate George McGovern were "balanced" by denials from the Nixon White House. The Langs found that most people did not pay much attention to Watergate until Judge Sirica was "presented by the media as a credible and presumably objective spokesperson for the cover-up scenario. Subsequently, the press abandoned its practice of balancing Watergate stories and printed news that was more or less exclusively supportive of the cover-up narrative."[66] They termed the "framing" and "balancing" media activities as agenda-building.

The framing or balancing studied by the Langs in regard to Watergate and the 1972 presidential election was also the subject of a 1991 book by Shanto Iyengar titled *Is Anyone Responsible? How Television Frames Political Issues*. In this book, Iyengar developed the idea that television news frames issues in two different ways, both of which affect public opinion. Episodic framing, or event-based news reports, is more frequently used but thematic framing can be powerful because it provides a broader perspective by placing an issue or event in a context or as part of a trend or public debate.[67]

Without much question, the agenda-setting perspective has generated more research than the other approaches we have discussed. Its growing volume is documented by a steady rate of publication and by its application in a variety of social science disciplines,[68] especially in political campaigns and advertising. With the addition of the concepts of priming and framing, agenda-setting seems destined to remain an important perspective by which to explain the influence of the media in, at least, American politics and election campaigns.

Reconceptualization of the Classics

Although not a complete perspective like information diffusion, uses and gratifications, or agenda-setting, we nonetheless include in this section a brief summary of the major tenets of a 1976 study that, while modeled after those of the Columbia Bureau of Applied Social Research, came to opposite conclusions. We believe that one of the reasons this study is important is because it laid a foundation for research during the 1980s and 1990s that explored the relationship between the media and political campaigns.

In an effort to provide a body of knowledge that would "contribute to an understanding of election coverage and the American voter,"[69] Thomas E. Patterson implemented the "most comprehensive panel survey ever conducted for the study of change during a presidential campaign."[70] The study and its results were described in the book, *The Mass Media Election*.

Although the Patterson investigation resembled the earlier work of Lazarsfeld and Berelson, there were major differences that are important to our consideration of political campaign communication in two respects. The first concerns the overall design of the study, and the second relates to the conclusions. We will begin by comparing designs.

In each of the Columbia studies, respondents were interviewed a number of times to determine if their attitudes were changing as the presidential campaigns were proceeding. Panel surveys were the single source of data for findings. Moreover, each of the Columbia studies interviewed 600 to 800 potential voters, and each was conducted in a single community. By contrast, the design of the 1976 study was more comprehensive. First, more people were interviewed (1,236). Second, they were interviewed in seven waves (five face-to-face interviews and two over the telephone) that were timed to correspond with each of the important intervals and stages in the campaign (just before the New Hampshire primary, after the early primaries, after the final primaries, after the conventions, before the general election, after the first and second presidential debates, and after the election). Third, respondents represented two communities that had substantially different populations and media (Erie, Pennsylvania, and Los Angeles, California). Finally, data collected from repeated interviews represented only one of the sources of evidence. The other was a content analysis of election year political news stories that appeared on evening newscasts of the three major television networks, two news magazines, two national newspapers, and two local newspapers (one in each of the selected cities). The content analysis was conducted from January until after the general election in November, and the interviews began in February and also concluded when the election was over. In short, the Patterson study was not only a more ambitious undertaking than any of the Columbia efforts had been, it was the largest project attempted in the intervening years—years in which research regarding the influence of mass communication was beginning to illustrate that the media were not passive entities in the political process.

As we discussed earlier, the primary conclusion derived from the Lazarsfeld/Berelson work was that the media did not play a major role in determining voters' attitudes during a presidential campaign. In fact, media messages were far less important than the messages relayed through interpersonal communication channels. Political opinions were determined by party and social affiliations, and therefore if the media were not absolutely powerless they were of minor importance in influencing how people voted.

However, in reporting the results of his 1976 investigation, Patterson argued that the presidential campaign is essentially a mass media campaign. He felt that for the "large majority of voters, the campaign has little reality apart from its media version."[71] In other words, far from being an unimportant factor, media are a significant part of the campaign process itself. As a matter of fact, virtually all of the conclusions from the 1976 study contradicted those articulated by the Columbia researchers. Among the conclusions Patterson discussed, the following three are particularly important for us:

1. Although the media do not change attitudes, they do influence because people rely on them for information, thereby placing media in a position to influence perceptions.

2. The stories that voters see in newspapers and watch on television "affect what they perceive to be the important events, critical issues, and serious contenders: [media] will affect what they learn about the candidates' personalities and issue positions."[72]

3. Thus, the power of the press "rests largely on its ability to select what will be covered and to decide the context in which these events will be placed."[73]

Therefore, the Patterson investigation of the ways in which voters were influenced by the media in 1976 is important. First, it firmly dispelled the long-term myths created by the Columbia studies and, second, it provided the comprehensive data necessary to begin updating and solidifying our knowledge of the ways in which voters, candidates, and the mass media interact with each other in contemporary political campaigns. In fact, thirteen years after the publication of *The Mass Media Election*, Patterson was even more convinced of the media's power in election campaigns. In *Out of Order*, published in 1993, Patterson's thesis is that the news media has become the "chief intermediary between voter and candidate."[74]

CONCLUSIONS

As we have seen, beliefs regarding the political influence and power of the mass media have come almost full circle during the almost 70 years researchers have been studying them. First, it was believed that the media were all-powerful. Then their power was seen as limited and of secondary or minor importance. In each instance, conclusions were frequently based on substantial evidence but gained prominence because they reinforced the dominant attitudes and context of the time in which they were articulated. The effective use of propaganda in the 1930s and the early 1940s convinced researchers that the power of the media was massive. Indeed, the media were virtually unlimited in the ways they could change attitudes and produce behavior modification or conformity. Whereas in the 1950s, the opposite viewpoint was held because in the context of those years it seemed difficult to subscribe to the belief that U.S. citizens could be reduced to puppets who would follow the ravings of any demagogue. Moreover, it must be remembered that when the classic Columbia studies were undertaken (during the 1940 and 1948 presidential elections), television was not yet a real factor in politics or in the environment of voters. However, by the 1960 presidential campaign, television was on its way to becoming a political force. Both candidates were using the medium for spot commercials, and their precedent-setting debates broke all previously established viewing records. When over 100 million people watched the debates and subsequently talked about their perceptions and reactions to the candidates, it became increasingly difficult for social scientists to deny that media, particularly television, had any impact.

Thus as the context/environment changed, some researchers began to question the limited effects model just as 20 years earlier they had challenged the validity of the hypodermic thesis. Eventually, most conceded that the media possessed some influence—even if it did not create massive changes in voting behavior. Some acknowledged the media's ability in the transmission and diffusion of information regarding candidates, issues, or the campaign itself. Other researchers suggested that people use the media for a variety of political reasons: for information, entertainment, increasing the range of topics for social exchange and acceptability, meeting expectations of peer groups, or for intrapersonal communication. And there were those who argued that the media are important because of their power to determine what information or news would be presented. Thus by the middle of the 1970s, many social scientists had begun to believe that media influence in the electoral process could not be ignored. Finally, in 1976 a study was undertaken that provided enough data to confirm many of the trends evident since 1960.

But the pendulum continued to swing. During the 1980s and 1990s when every election year appeared to bring with it an ever increasing reliance on television to frame candidates' rhetorical and visual messages, some worried about the omnipotence of the media. Thus when we asserted at other points in this chapter that beliefs regarding the influence of the media had come full circle, we were not exaggerating. But do these perspectives from mass media research contribute to the understanding of campaign communication? We think they can and suggest seven principles of campaign communication that can be drawn from them.

The first of these principles is that the most important effect of media influence is seldom direct persuasion but providing information that affects perception and may ultimately persuade. Persuasion theorists have consistently determined that a "one-shot" persuasive effort or message does not change attitudes—at least does not change attitudes from one extreme to the other. There may be behavior modification or conformity when conditions include threat, punishment, or even reward, but not internalized attitude change. And it is naive to assume that it is any different in the context of a political campaign. Instead, persuasive information about a candidate, about the issues for which the candidate stands, even negative information regarding the candidate's opponent will affect perception and thus help to draw attention to the candidate and campaign and may even influence later perception. Therefore, we conclude that the media are important to and powerful in a political campaign not in necessarily changing votes because of a single message but in drawing attention to candidates and thereby providing information for a full range of attitude formulations (including reinforcement, reformulation, and repositioning).

The second principle is simply that the contemporary candidate needs the mass media, in part because voters have expectations regarding the media's role in providing information about the candidate and the campaign. Citizens rely on newspapers, newscasts, and televised political advertising to tell them about candidates, issues, and the campaign itself.

Moreover, candidates have found that they can efficiently reach potential voters only through the mass media. And with the proliferation of cable channels and hundreds of additional channels, narrowcasting provides candidates with special challenges and opportunities in regard to communicating their messages to voters via the mass media.

The third principle is that the media have tremendous power in determining which news events, which candidates, and which issues are to be covered in any given day. Thus a candidate's campaign must be focused, in large measure, around those sorts of issues, photographic opportunities, and events that will draw media attention and provide "sound bites" for the evening television newscasts. Whether these are pseudoevents or real, pseudoissues or real, modern candidates do those things that will "play" to the media—that will call attention to themselves and their campaigns. Perhaps more important, because of the media, candidates do not do some things and do not discuss some issues. Often what they fail to do is just as important as what they do.

The fourth principle may be less obvious. Although candidates attempt to use the media for their own purposes, they are not always able to control it. While a candidate can send a press release, its use is not guaranteed. Although an appearance at the state fair is planned, there is no assurance the event will be used in the evening newscasts. It may well be that election coverage will focus on an opponent or on yesterday's gaffe. Moreover, media have the power to penetrate even the most expertly contrived image—the newspaper reporter catches the wording of the answer to a question, or the television camera records unplanned nonverbal behavior. The point we make is simply that candidates may spend most of their campaign resources on the many avenues of the mass media, they may depend on them to present persuasive information regarding their candidacies, but with the exception of their own advertisements, they cannot control the media.

The fifth principle is that mass media influence is important to our knowledge or appreciation of the electoral process itself. The media allow us to witness political events, they teach and instruct, thereby adding to our expectations about the democratic process. Most of the crucial events of at least recent presidential elections have occurred on television. Indeed the 1996 election was a television campaign—it was the medium through which the candidates became known to the public through such formats as ads and appearances on talk shows and on news programs. While this may increase or decrease our liking for particular candidates, issues, or campaigns, it does provide a sense of involvement as we affirm (or deny) our role as citizens.

The sixth principle regards how the mass media, primarily television, has changed the way in which candidates campaign for office. As we noted in an earlier chapter, we greet candidates in the living rooms of our homes via the television screen rather than at a political rally. More-over, the candidates' television advertising and appearances on televi-sion talk shows and town meetings are the electronic age equivalent of the whistle-stop tours.

Finally, we believe that the influence or power of the media has con-tributed mightily to the many changes in the electoral process. For ex-ample, the surfacing and primary stages of the campaign have become more important to the final outcome, receive more precise and planned attention by candidates, and generate more excitement and enthusiasm from the general public than before television entered the political arena. This has happened because the media treat these preliminary events in much the same manner as they treat the later stages. In fact, because of high media involvement, the first two stages have replaced not only the attention-getting power of the nominating conventions and the general election, they have also seized much of their legitimate power.

In the largest sense, we conclude this chapter as we began it—con-vinced that the mass media (especially television) have a tremendous impact on political campaign communication.

NOTES

1. David L. Paletz, *The Media in American Politics: Contents and Consequences* (New York: Longman, 1999), pp. 28–34.

2. "Nielsen Tunes in to Politics: Tracking the Presidential Election Years (1960–1992)," Nielsen Media Research, 1993.

3. Paletz, *Media in American Politics*, p. 34.

4. "Nielsen Tunes in to Politics," p. 213.

5. Dan D. Nimmo and James E. Combs, *Mediated Political Realities*, 2d ed. (New York: Longman, 1990), p. 25.

6. www.greenfield.com/dlrci/content/html.

7. Frank E. X. Dance, "Human Communication Theory: A Highly Selective Review and Two Commentaries," in *Communication Yearbook II*, ed. Brent D. Ruben (New Brunswick, N.J.: Transaction Books, 1978), pp. 7–22.

8. Peter M. Sandman, David M. Rubin, and David B. Sachsman, *Media* (En-glewood Cliffs, N.J.: Prentice-Hall, 1972), p. 20.

9. Ibid., p. 23.

10. Ibid., p. 25.

11. Sidney Kraus and Dennis Davis, *The Effects of Mass Communication on Po-litical Behavior* (University Park: Pennsylvania State University Press, 1976), p. 117.

12. Elihu Katz and Paul F. Lazarsfeld, *Personal Influence* (New York: Free Press, 1955), p. 16.

13. Harold F. Gosnell, *Machine Politics Chicago Model* (Chicago: University of Chicago Press, 1937).

14. Garrett J. O'Keefe, "Political Campaigns and Mass Communication Re-

search," in *Political Communication: Issues and Strategies for Research*, ed. Steven H. Chaffee (Beverly Hills, Calif.: Sage, 1975), p. 133.

15. David Blomquist, *Elections and the Mass Media* (Washington, D.C.: American Political Science Association, 1981), pp. 4–6.

16. Kraus and Davis, *Effects of Mass Communication*, p. 117.

17. For a discussion of the methodological difficulties of the selective exposure concept, see, for example, Lee B. Becker, Maxwell E. McCombs, and Jack M. McLeod, "The Development of Political Cognitions," in *Political Communication: Issues and Strategies for Research*, ed. Steven H. Chaffee (Beverly Hills, Calif.: Sage, 1975), pp. 28–31; Kraus and Davis, *Effects of Mass Communication*, pp. 51–54; and David Sears and Johnathan Freedman, "Selective Exposure to Information: A Critical Review," *Public Opinion Quarterly* 31 (Summer 1967): 194–213.

18. Katz and Lazarsfeld, *Personal Influence*, p. 138.

19. Ibid., p. 309.

20. Ibid.

21. Kraus and Davis, *Effects of Mass Communication*, p. 120.

22. Becker, McCombs, and McLeod, "The Development of Political Cognitions," p. 32.

23. Ibid., p. 33.

24. Kraus and Davis, *Effects of Mass Communication*, p. 53.

25. Angus Campbell et al., *The American Voter* (New York: John Wiley and Sons, 1964).

26. David M. White, "The 'Gate Keeper': A Case Study in the Selection of News," *Journalism Quarterly* 27 (Fall 1950): 383–90.

27. Sandman, Rubin, and Sachsman, *Media*, p. 103.

28. Ibid., p. 109.

29. See, for example, Lewis Donohew, "Newspaper Gatekeepers and Forces in the News Channel," *Public Opinion Quarterly* 31 (Spring 1967): 62–66; Jean S. Kerrick "Balance and the Writer's Attitude in News Stories and Editorials," *Journalism Quarterly* 41 (Spring 1964): 207–15; and G. A. Donohue, P. J. Tichenor, and C. N. Olien, "Gatekeeping: Mass Media Systems and Information Control," in *Current Perspectives in Mass Communication Research*, ed. F. G. Kline and P. J. Tichenor (Beverly Hills, Calif.: Sage, 1972).

30. Studies in the late 1960s and in the 1970s have consistently indicated that voters use the media for purposes other than reinforcement of their views. Moreover, other studies have shown that there are cases wherein voters prefer messages that contradict their views. Finally, with the decline of party affiliation, there is reason to believe that voters are not holding onto preconceived political beliefs but enter a campaign season with a willingness to be persuaded on issues. Steven H. Chaffee and Michael Petrick call the concept of selective exposure "too simplistic." See their book *Using the Mass Media* (New York: McGraw-Hill, 1975), p. 141.

31. Kraus and Davis, *Effects of Mass Communication*, p. 123.

32. Blomquist, *Elections and the Mass Media*, p. 7.

33. Ibid.

34. Ibid.

35. Ibid., p. 8. See also Jay G. Blumler and Denis McQuail, *Television in Politics* (Chicago: University of Chicago Press, 1969).

36. Kraus and Davis, *Effects of Mass Communication*, p. 126.

37. Ibid., p. 128.

38. Ibid., p. 127.

39. Robert L. Savage, "The Diffusion of Information Approach," in *Handbook of Political Communication*, ed. Dan D. Nimmo and Keith R. Sanders (Beverly Hills, Calif.: Sage, 1981), pp. 104–7.

40. Ibid., p. 115.

41. Steven H. Chaffee, "The Diffusion of Political Information," in *Political Communication: Issues and Strategies for Research*, ed. Steven H. Chaffee (Beverly Hills, Calif.: Sage, 1975), p. 125.

42. Kraus and Davis, *Effects of Mass Communication*, p. 130.

43. See, for example: Walter Gantz, "The Diffusion of News about the Attempted Reagan Assassination," *Journal of Communication* 33 (Winter 1983): 56–66; Charles R. Bantz, Sandra G. Petronio, and David L. Rarick, "News Diffusion after the Reagan Shooting," *Quarterly Journal of Speech* 69 (August 1983): 317–27; and Ruth Ann Weaver-Tarisey, Barbara Sweeney, and Thomas Steinfatt, "Communication during Assassination Attempts: Diffusion of Information in Attacks on President Reagan and the Pope," *Southern Speech Communication Journal* 49 (Spring 1989): 258–76.

44. Jay G. Blumler, "The Role of Theory in Uses and Gratifications Studies," *Communication Research* 6 (January 1979): 21.

45. Ibid., pp. 11–12.

46. Jack M. McLeod and Lee B. Becker, "The Uses and Gratifications Approach," in *Handbook of Political Communication*, ed. Dan D. Nimmo and Keith R. Sanders (Beverly Hills, Calif.: Sage, 1975), p. 71.

47. Ibid., p. 87.

48. David L. Swanson and Dan D. Nimmo, eds., *New Directions in Political Communication: Resource Book* (Newbury Park, Calif.: Sage, 1990), p. 18.

49. Carl R. Bybee, "Uses and Gratifications Research and the Study of Social Change," in *Political Communication Research: Approaches, Studies, Assessments*, ed. David L. Paletz (Norwood, N.J.: Ablex Publishing Corporation, 1987), pp. 209–10.

50. Denis McQuail, *Audience Analysis*. (Thousand Oaks, Calif.: Sage, 1997), p. 73.

51. Ibid.

52. Diane F. Witmer and Chutatip Taweesuk. "Flow or Function? Examining Uses and Gratifications of the World Wide Web by Mexican and U.S. Communicators," paper presented at the NCA and ICA Conference, Rome, Italy, July 15–18, 1998.

53. Bernard C. Cohen, *The Press and Foreign Policy* (Princeton, N.J.: Princeton University Press, 1963), p. 13.

54. Kraus and Davis, *Effects of Mass Communication*, p. 216.

55. Maxwell E. McCombs and Donald L. Shaw, "The Agenda-Setting Function of Mass Media," *Public Opinion Quarterly* 36 (Summer 1972): 177.

56. G. Ray Funkhouser, "Trends in Media Coverage of the Issues of the '60s," *Journalism Quarterly* 50 (Autumn 1973): 538.

57. Kraus and Davis, *Effects of Mass Communication*, p. 214.

58. Maxwell E. McCombs, "The Agenda-Setting Approach," in *Handbook of*

Political Communication, ed. Dan D. Nimmo and Keith R. Sanders (Beverly Hills, Calif.: Sage, 1975), pp. 127–30.

59. John Mueller, *Policy and Opinion in the Gulf War* (Chicago: University of Chicago Press, 1994), p. 130.

60. Holli A. Semetko, "TV News and U.S. Public Opinion about Foreign Countries," *International Journal of Public Opinion Research* 4(2) (Summer 1992): 126–47.

61. Bruce E. Gronbeck, "Popular Culture, Media, and Political Communication," in *New Directions in Political Communication: A Resource Book*, ed. David L. Swanson and Dan D. Nimmo (Newbury Park, Calif.: Sage Publications, 1990), p. 85.

62. Anne Johnston, "Trends in Political Communication: A Selective Review of Research in the 1980s," in *New Directions in Political Communication: A Resource Book*, ed. David L. Swanson and Dan D. Nimmo (Newbury Park, Calif.: Sage Publications, 1990), pp. 336–38.

63. Ibid., p. 337.

64. Shanto Iyengar and Donald R. Kinder, *News That Matters* (Chicago: University of Chicago Press, 1987), p. 110.

65. Gladys Engel Lang and Kurt Lang, "The Media and Watergate," in *Media Power in Politics*, 2d ed., ed. Doris A. Graber (Washington, D.C.: Congressional Quarterly Books, 1990), pp. 255–62.

66. Dennis K. Davis, "Development of Research on News and Politics," in *New Directions in Political Communication: A Resource Book*, ed. David L. Swanson and Dan D. Nimmo (Newbury Park, Calif.: Sage Publications, 1990), p. 171.

67. Shanto Iyengar, *Is Anyone Responsible? How Television Frames Political Issues* (Chicago: University of Chicago Press, 1991), p. 18.

68. Maxwell E. McCombs and Donald L. Shaw, "The Evolution of Agenda-Setting Research: Twenty-Five Years in the Marketplace of Ideas," *Journal of Communication* 43(2) (1993): p. 59.

69. Thomas E. Patterson, *The Mass Media Election: How Americans Choose Their President* (New York: Praeger, 1980), p. 8.

70. Ibid., p. viii.

71. Ibid., p. 3.

72. Ibid., p. 95.

73. Ibid., p. 53.

74. Thomas E. Patterson, *Out of Order* (New York: Knopf, 1993).

Chapter 5

Communicative Types and Functions of Televised Political Advertising

During the electoral campaigns of the 1980s and continuing through the 1990s, it became increasingly apparent that political advertising on television is a central communication strategy for the growing numbers of those who seek our vote. While during the previous two decades those who fancied themselves president had demonstrated a willingness to explore all manner of television commercials to champion the rightness of their cause, it was the 1980s that brought the television advertising attempts of all manner of candidates to our attention. Whether running for a seat in the United States Senate or for a chair on the Cincinnati city council, it seemed that every candidate was using television spot advertising. Political ads came to dominate whatever portion of public attention is reserved for things political. In fact, by 1990, during the first election of the new decade, there was at least as much discussion about the number and nature of the ads being used as there was about the candidates themselves. Voter or journalist, consultant or scholar, the central focus was television advertising. Criticism of the ads and their prominent role in the campaigns of 1988, 1990, 1992, 1994, and 1996 was broad based. However, attention centered around what appeared to be a growing reliance on negative as opposed to positive ads, replacement of campaign dialogue with television commercials, the extraordinary cost of the spots, fear that the ads, especially those that were negative, determined electoral results, and the idea that television advertising had "turned off" the public.

Televised political advertising occupies a pivotal position within a candidate's campaign. Thus, in this chapter, we will take a brief look at the development of television advertising in presidential politics, explore the principles underlying different types of political commercials, and then discuss some of the most important communicative functions they perform during the campaign. In so doing, we will examine the use of one kind of commercial, the attack or condemnation spot, by candidates who are women. We will conclude our discussion by reviewing the major question that has developed around the use of attack advertising. Because in Chapter 10 we examine all forms of media advertising, for now our consideration is limited to the ads candidates use on television.

HISTORICAL DEVELOPMENT

Televised political spots entered presidential politics in 1952 when the Republican nominee, General Dwight D. Eisenhower, filmed 40 commercials that were titled "Eisenhower Answers America." Although the 28 ads that were aired in 40 states revolutionized the way in which presidential candidates went about the job of getting elected, in terms of narrative and cinematography, the Eisenhower spots were but a primitive form of those we have seen more than 40 years later when Bob Dole was the Republican nominee. The format for all of the spots was exactly the same: a male voice announced "Eisenhower Answers America." A regular citizen or "person-on-the-street" (actually a line of people waiting to get into Radio City Music Hall in New York City) would ask Eisenhower a question and the General would respond with a one-or-two sentence answer which implied that it was time for a change. For example, "a man on the street" would say: "General, the Democrats are telling me I've never had it so good." Eisenhower would respond, "Can that be true when America is billions in debt, when prices have doubled, when taxes break our backs, and we are still fighting in Korea? It's tragic and it's time for a change."

The 1952 and 1996 spots did, however, have at least one common characteristic—each brought the techniques used in persuading Americans to buy commercial products to the front door of the White House. One of the most interesting aspects of the application of "Madison Avenue" strategy to the 1952 campaign was that it was totally unnecessary. Eisenhower, a genuine American hero, was, according to a 1952 Roper poll, the most admired living American. Although Eisenhower used the ads, his opponent, Illinois Governor Adlai Stevenson, rejected the idea of appearing in spot commercials—at least during the 1952 campaign. By 1956, when Governor Stevenson was again the Democratic nominee for president, he changed his mind about participating in spots—largely because the experts in both political parties believed television advertising had become a necessary part of the campaign effort. In fact, as political communication scholar Kathleen Hall Jamieson has written, "The major innovation of the '56 campaign was its increasing reliance on the five minute spot."[1] The ads in 1956 and the ones that followed in 1960 frequently consisted of the candidate talking directly to the television audience (the "talking head" ads) or those that made it seem as if "the viewing audience was eavesdropping on the candidate as he addressed a rally."[2] In spite of relatively minimal production techniques, by the time of the 1960 campaign it was clear that with the technology of television editing, ads could provide additional arguments for or against a candidate simply by juxtaposing a still photograph of the candidate, a name, or even part of a speech with specific visuals to create a whole range of image messages. Some of the images were positive (American flags, the Liberty Bell, waving fields of grain), others were negative (deserted factories, foreign demonstrators throwing rocks at cars, farmers standing in front of empty grain bins), but all were examples of arguments by visual association. As Jamieson noted in her chronology of the evolution of American political advertising, arguments by visual association (positive and negative) were used in the presidential campaigns of 1964 and again in 1968. Moreover, argument by positive association characterized the Ford and Carter campaigns of 1976, and remained a staple of political advertising through the early campaigns of the 1980s.[3] Although ads that utilized negative visual images (concepts) were used from at least the 1964 campaign forward, frequently those spots that directly attacked the opponent did not picture the candidate or the opponent. Attacks were left to running mates, other surrogates, or to unnamed, unknown voiceovers.

Without question, the best known of the negative concept ads aired only once (because of the legal and ethical questions it raised) and it never even mentioned the opponent's name. Nonetheless, the "Daisy Girl" ad so effectively cemented perception of the Republican nominee, Senator Barry Goldwater, as a warmonger—a man who could not be entrusted with our nation's national security—that he was never able to rid himself of the negative image. The force of the following ad was its ability to engage viewer's emotions and associate their negative response with Goldwater:

Video	Audio
Camera up on little girl in field, picking petals off a daisy.	Little girl: "One, two, three, four, five, seven, six, six, eight, nine, nine—"
Girl looks up, startled; freeze frame on girl; move into her eye, until screen is black.	Man's voice, very loud as if heard over a loudspeaker at a test site: "Ten, nine, eight, seven, six, five, four, three, two, one—"

Cut to atom bomb exploding. Move into explosion.	Sound of explosion.
	Johnson: "These are the stakes—to make a world in which all of God's children can live, or to go into the dark. We must either love each other, or we must die."
Cut to white letters on black background: "Vote for President Johnson on November 3."	Announcer: "Vote for President Johnson on November 3. The stakes are too high for you to stay home."[4]

In many instances, ads were targeted to appeal to voters in the opposition political party. For example, in 1964 several of Lyndon Johnson's spots openly called to Republicans "worried" about voting for Goldwater to join him. And in 1972 Richard Nixon used negative association or concept ads whose air time was paid for by an organization called Democrats for Nixon.

Typical of these ads was one titled the "McGovern Defense Plan:"

Video	Audio
Camera up on toy soldiers.	Military drumbeat underneath. Announcer: "The McGovern defense plan.
Hand sweeps several away.	He would cut the Marines by one-third.
Cut to another group of toy soldiers; again, hand sweeps several away.	The Air Force by one-third.
Cut to another group of toy soldiers; again, hand sweeps several away.	He would cut the Navy personnel by one-fourth.
Cut to toy planes; hand removes several.	He would cut interceptor planes by one-half,
Cut to toy ships; hand removes several.	the Navy fleet by one-half,
Cut to toy carriers. Hand removes several.	and carriers from sixteen to six.
Cut to toys in jumble. Camera pans across.	"Senator Hubert Humphrey has this to say about the McGovern proposal: 'It isn't just cutting into manpower. It's cutting into the very security of this country.'"
	[Music comes in: "Hail to the Chief."]
Cut to Nixon aboard naval ship.	"President Nixon doesn't believe we should play games with our national security. He believes in a strong America to negotiate for peace from strength."

Fade to slide, white letters on black
background: "Democrats for Nixon."[5]

Jamieson argued that in 1976 two new types of attack ads replaced the
association or concept type—personal witness and neutral reporter.
These ads featured ordinary Americans (not actors) expressing their beliefs about the opposing candidate (personal witness) or they presented
a list of factual statements and invited people to make a judgment call
(neutral reporter). As such, they appeared less harsh than the concept
ads and somewhat removed or apart from the candidate. Typical of these
ads was the following example used by the Ford campaign:

Video

Camera up on slide: white letters
against black background. "Those who
know Jimmy Carter best are from
Georgia. That's why we thought you
ought to know": Photo of Gerald Ford
appears and holds underneath crawl:
tough, unsmiling. Script already on
screen crawls upward, being replaced
by new material:

"The Savannah, Georgia, *News* endorses Gerald Ford for President.

"The Augusta, Georgia, *Herald* endorses President Ford.

"The Atlanta, Georgia, *Daily World* endorses President Ford.

"The Marietta, Georgia, *Journal* endorses President Ford.

"The Albany, Georgia, *Herald* endorses
President Ford.

"The Augusta, Georgia, *Chronicle* endorses President Ford.

"The Savannah, Georgia, *Press* endorses—"

The spot fades out midsentence, suggesting more papers to be named.[6]

Audio

Sound of teletype underneath. An-
nouncer reads script from slide and
crawl.

In 1980, the personal witness or "man-in-the-street" ads were used
once again. In addition, a longer ad, the documentary (spots designed
to present a candidate's accomplishments) were utilized—especially by
Ronald Reagan. But in the 1984 election, and again in 1988, the negative

visual association or concept ad returned in such force that each was, at some point, termed the "year of the negative campaign."

Another element that has undergone change from campaign year to campaign year is the preferred length of commercials. There have been half-hour speeches or biographies; 4- or 5-minute documentaries or other special appeals squeezed between evening entertainment programs or right before or after the late night news; and there have been 20-, 30-, and 60-second segments. In other words, over the years, sandwiched in between programs and product commercials, political ads have taken a variety of time frames. However, during the decade of the 1980s, 30-second spots became dominant—largely because research had documented that they were just as effective as longer spots in getting the message across. For the most part, campaigns have come to reserve longer ads, such as the 5-minute documentaries or biographies, for specific functions such as introducing a new candidate, raising money, or an election eve message.

Thus, since their entrance into the presidential campaign arena, the form and style of televised political spots have, from election to election, undergone change. In some instances, stylistic changes were temporary and reappeared just four years later. In other cases, revisions or reformulations were more permanent. Over the years, however, political ads have reflected two patterns with some regularity. While neither is surprising, each is important enough to our understanding of televised ads as a critical tool of the campaign to spend some time discussing them. First, the style or form political ads take is frequently a reflection of the larger society of which they are a part. For example, in the two campaigns of the 1950s and even in 1960, the spots were neither hard-hitting nor very specific (particularly those in which the candidates themselves appeared), largely because Americans did not yet equate the techniques and manipulations of Madison Avenue advertising and public relations with their presidential candidates, and the candidates themselves were concerned that they not appear too "political" as opposed to "presidential." Between 1964 and 1972 we believe that the harshness of the negative associations used in commercials has to be seen within the context of the national anguish created by the escalating war in Vietnam and the civil rights movement. In the campaigns of 1976 and 1980, the number of positive ads and the "feel good" mood that was their theme, as well as the indirect and less attack-oriented negative spots, must be viewed as a reflection of public distrust and disillusionment with politics and politicians in the aftermath of Vietnam and Watergate. And the reemergence of strident and graphically explicit negative association or concept spots in 1984 and 1988 (whose meaning is perhaps less clear-cut because of their relative proximity to us in time) may well have occurred because the campaigns did not generate any major issues or themes.

From the surfacing through the general election stage, the focus was the character and image of the candidates rather than the identification and discussion of "burning issues" facing the electorate.

Not only, however, have political spots reflected broad societal problems/attitudes/preoccupations, they have also reflected the prevailing philosophical and stylistic "schools of thought" operant in commercial or product-oriented advertising. While we would hesitate to contend that the process never works the other way—that is, particular strategies are used first in the political world and then by Madison Avenue—in general, those political consultants who work in most of the statewide to national races apply techniques that have been found successful in commercial advertising. In fact, after studying 669 political ads made in 1984 and 1986 for candidates on all levels, and after interviews with more than 800 campaign and media consultants, author Montague Kern wrote that during the 1980s the "world of political advertising absorbed its commercial counterpart and became as one."[7] Kern argues that political spots in the campaigns of the 1980s were like their commercial counterparts in that they evoked feelings or experience, relied heavily on visual and aural effects, developed messages in which the candidate and a single issue were blended, and frequently attempted to associate a candidate with an affect-laden symbol that already had meaning for us.[8] And as the campaigns of the 1980s became the campaigns of the 1990s, there were no discernible differences in the ads. The attempt to develop spots that provoke strong feelings continued through the 1996 presidential campaign.

In a study of presidential advertising in the 1992 campaign, researcher Lynda Lee Kaid found that emotional appeals were used in 52.6 percent of the ads produced for the Perot campaign and 46.2 percent of the ads produced for the Clinton campaign, and that 56.3 percent of the spots produced for the Bush reelection campaign contained fear appeals.[9] Similarly, Kaid's study of presidential advertising in the 1996 campaign found that 63 percent of Dole's general election ads contained emotional appeals, while 84 percent of Clinton's ads used emotional appeals.[10] While we do not intend to trace the historical development of commercial advertising, the ways in which its methods and techniques have been used by a variety of candidates will become obvious in the next sections as we explore the types and functions of televised political ads and the questions and controversies they have generated.

TYPES AND FUNCTIONS OF POLITICAL ADS

As the number of televised spots used during election campaigns have increased, so too have the number of people writing or talking about them. Whether the report of a practitioner or the analysis of a scholar, all seem to have contributed a name to describe the ads they have studied or those they have used. For example, in their book, *The Spot*, authors Edwin Diamond and Stephen Bates argue that political advertising goes through four phases and thus produces four types of ads. Phase One brings ID Spots (ads that are biographical and are intended to introduce or identify the candidate—provide a sense of the candidate in the surfacing or primary stages of the campaign). Phase Two produces Argument Spots (ads that identify the candidate's causes, ideas, concerns— what the candidate stands for). Phase Three is the time for Attack Spots (ads that are direct and personal attacks meant to reduce the credibility of the opposing candidate—create doubt, stir fear, exploit anxiety, or motivate ridicule). Phase Four produces Visionary Spots (ads that are used as the campaign draws to a close to provide a reflective/thoughtful/dignified view of the candidate—create the impression that the candidate has the leadership ability and the vision to move the country/state/city forward).[11]

In his analysis of presidential television commercials used from 1952 through 1984, L. Patrick Devlin describes spots in terms of categories such as: talking head ads; negative ads (those spots that tear down the opponent); cinema verité ads (those in which the candidate is filmed in a real life setting interacting with people); documentary ads (spots that present the accomplishments of the candidate); man-in-the-street ads (those in which real people talk positively about the candidate or negatively about the opponent); testimonial ads (spots in which prominent people speak on behalf of the candidate); and independent ads (those that are sponsored by organizations separate from the candidate).[12] Montague Kern contributes two additional types of spots from her book, *30-Second Politics: Political Advertising in the 1980s*. She defines platform ads as those that present a candidate's commitment to a position or to opposing the opponent's position and slogan ads as those that contain no policy statement, why statement, nor any answer.[13]

In a study of political advertising and its meaning in American elections, Richard Joslyn identifies four different perspectives or approaches by which the contemporary election can be understood and argues that within each perspective specific kinds of appeals are used in the television commercials. After examining 506 of these commercials, he found that the most prevalent type of appeal is one he labeled "benevolent leader." Benevolent leader ads, according to Joslyn, focus on a candidate's personality traits rather than programmatic actions, policy positions, or political values and "attempt to accomplish a correspondence between the role expectations for a public office and the persona of the candidate."[14] For example, the benevolent leader ads might focus on such traits as the candidate's courage, honesty, strength of character, sense of fairness and justice, or compassion. The ads can be in the form of biographies or documentaries in which the candidate is shown in situations wherein the traits discussed are evident, in testimonials in which a prominent person discusses a specific characteristic of the candidate, or even in a man-on-the-street format in which a number of people are featured as they remark on the candidate's virtues. Whatever form the benevolent leader ad might take, its focus is the candidate's personality or character strengths.

Not only have scholars offered a classification scheme for the variety of televised commercials, some have suggested that negative ads can be divided by specific types. As mentioned earlier in this chapter, Kathleen Hall Jamieson suggests three kinds of negative spots that she terms concept ads (those that juxtapose unrelated visual images to suggest false inferences), personal witness ads (which feature regular citizens giving unscripted negative opinions about the opponent), and neutral reporter ads (those in which a series of informational statements are made and then the voter is invited to make a judgment or draw a conclusion about the opponent).[15] In 1985, and again in 1994, Bruce E. Gronbeck identified negative ads as implicative (those that operate by innuendo without attacking directly), comparative (ads that juxtapose the opponent's record or positions on issues with those of the candidate), and assault (those directly assaulting the character, motivations, associates, or actions of an opponent).[16]

Although this summary is certainly not exhaustive, it may help you appreciate the complexity of trying to understand and distinguish among the types of televised commercials that have been used since 1952. However, we have no real desire to contribute either to the proliferation of ad types or to the difficulty of describing contemporary political advertising. Rather, our goal is to reduce ambiguity by classifying spots according to their primary rhetorical purpose. Within each category, we subdivide only in terms of videostyle factors (verbal content, nonverbal content, film/video production techniques)[17] that appear to have characteristics significant enough to distinguish them one from another. In some cases, you will see that at least one component of videostyle (usually film/video production techniques) overlaps from category to category, although the overall purpose of the ad is unchanged. You will also note that what we term videostyle factors, other theorists have classified as types of ads.

We suggest that the only important reason to categorize types of political commercials is to gain some understanding of their rhetorical purpose. While ads are used by candidates to fulfill a variety of functions (which we will discuss shortly), they have three primary rhetorical purposes: to praise the candidate, to condemn the opponent, or to respond to charges. Although from time to time these purposes may overlap, essentially, ads can be understood in terms of their primary rhetorical purpose. Thus, we characterize televised political commercials and the communicative functions they perform in the following manner.

Ads Extolling the Candidate's Virtues

The videostyle factors available to be used in ads whose overall purpose is to praise the candidate are virtually unlimited. Over the years techniques such as testimony, documentary, talking head, cinema verité, man-on-the-street, slogan, platform, or benevolent leader have all been used. And although some election years and the campaigns of some candidates have made extensive use of a particular videostyle (for example, in 1980, 41 percent of the Reagan campaign's television commercials were documentaries)[18] most campaigns that have the financial resources to do so use a variety of the videostyles to promote the virtues/strengths of their candidate. It is important, however, that the videostyle not detract from the ad's primary objective—extolling the candidate and ignoring the opponent.

The communicative functions performed by ads of this nature are as varied as the videostyles. Moreover, they are critical for both incumbents and challengers, although the extent to which they are used may vary in relationship to other conditions. For example, if the candidate is a relatively unknown challenger running against an entrenched incumbent, it is critically important that the campaign tell the candidate's "story." In other words, provide information on her background, accomplishments, positions on issues, strengths of character and personality, family and associates—define her. And television commercials can perform this function better and more rapidly than most other campaign tools available to the candidate and her staff. While there are countless examples of challengers running at all levels who have had some success in using commercials of this type to "define" themselves to the electorate, one who did not comes readily to mind. In the 1988 presidential campaign, challenger Michael Dukakis did not move rapidly enough after the Democratic Nominating Convention to tell the public who he was, what he stood for, what he had accomplished, and why he should be president. Consequently, the first series of ads aired by the Bush campaign immediately following the Republican Nominating Convention provided the missing definition of Dukakis. The problem for the Democratic nominee was, of course, that the Republican definition was not very flattering. Interestingly, the same thing happened to George Bush in 1992. In an examination of ads used in the presidential campaign, communication researcher L. Patrick Devlin argued that "the Bush Ad team was unable to emphasize a positive futuristic message."[19] Early in the campaign there were only negative messages. When they began the positive ads, it was too late. In his study of the 1996 presidential campaign ads, Devlin reported that Bob Dole's efforts to define his character were also flawed. For example, Dole's biographic video included a good deal of black-and-white footage of Dole's war experiences, but omitted any references to his 35 years in Congress. While his military accomplishments did make voters aware of the Senator's service to his country during World War II, it did not convince them that he was "the right person to be president." In addition, instead of focusing on a single theme or strategy, Dole's ads communicated multiple messages about Dole as a person. As a result, the Dole camp fell behind and never caught up with Clinton's lead.[20]

A second important function performed by these ads includes using commercials to develop and explain the candidate's stand or position on issues. Not only has television become the primary source of information, political commercials have become a significant source of voter information about all aspects of the campaign. As research has demonstrated, voters can learn more about a candidate's position or stand on an issue from a commercial than they can by watching the evening newscasts.[21] Moreover, ads have a cumulative effect in that their frequent repetition during the course of a campaign helps voters learn just where the candidate stands on a given issue. During the 1996 campaign, Clinton made significant use of issue ads, especially during the general election stage when 90 percent of the commercials were issue-focused. Among the issues emphasized were education (51 percent), Medicare/elderly problems (38 percent), the economy (39 percent), crime (31 percent), and children's issues (34 percent).[22]

Additional and related functions performed by spots that extol the candidate's virtues include: reinforcing the positive feelings of supporters and partisans (just watching the ad may strengthen conviction of the rightness of one's cause or choice of candidates); redefining or softening the candidate's image (in 1968 Richard Nixon's earlier image as one of "life's losers" was redefined to "statesman," in part by his television commercials; and in 1976 Gerald Ford's image as a well intentioned "buffoon" was redefined to "president" by the genius of the campaign's "I'm Feeling Good about America" spots); raising money (in 1984 Democrats used a special five-minute commercial about Walter Mondale so that they could raise money from supporters to air future ads); presenting statistical or "factual" information on issues (in 1992 Ross Perot's use of 60-second "crawls" made him appear knowledgeable and straightforward on issues important to the campaign)[23]; and focusing on shared public values (in 1996 a component of Bill Clinton's ad strategy was that "public values beat private character"—the attempt to divert attention away from character to the public values the president believed he shared with voters, such as banning cigarette ads and protecting education and the environment).[24] In short, ads whose purpose is to praise the candidate can fulfill functions important to the success of the campaign.

Ads Condemning/Attacking/Questioning the Opponent

Just as a wide variety of videostyle factors can be used in ads that emphasize the virtues of the candidate, so too can a number of different techniques be utilized in spots that focus on the opponent. For example, contemporary campaigns have used techniques such as personal witness, comparison, negative association or concept, talking head, assaultive, or cinema verité. Although the videostyle factors can vary and, therefore, alter the directness and strength of the attack, the primary purpose cannot. These are ads designed to place the opponent in an unfavorable light or in an uncomfortable position. They focus on the shortcomings (real or imagined) of the opponent rather than the attributes of the candidate. In the largest sense, the purpose of these kind of ads—no matter the variability of techniques employed—is to increase the opponent's "negatives." As such, they have received a good deal of attention from the public, as well as from journalists and scholars.

Since the introduction of televised ads whose purpose was to attack the opponent, a wide variety of formats and strategies have been employed. Some commercials have utilized humor and ridicule, others have linked the opponent with unpopular issues or negatively perceived people (guilt by association). Some have fastened labels on their opponents and then defined those labels negatively. Many have relied on fear appeals, and others have sought to create a suspicion or anxiety about the opponent's beliefs or previous actions. At times, viewers are directed to make up their own minds—that is, the attack or condemnation is implied. For example, the records of the candidate and opponent are compared and the opponent appears to have no attributes. But direct charges or conclusionary statements are not made. In other instances, the attack is direct and overt. For example, either in the narrative or by use of visual or aural symbols, viewers are told of the opponent's shortcomings. Clearly, depending on the videostyle and, of course, the intent, the commercials in this category can vary a good deal. Montague Kern has given names to two of the hardest hitting spots and distinguished between them in terms of what we think of as their videostyle strategies—primarily format and production techniques. She calls them "soft-sell" ads, which make "heavy use of lighter entertainment values, humor, self-depreciation, storytelling, or the unexpected turn of events," and "hard-sell," those which utilize "dark colors and threatening voices" and create "harsh reality advertising."[25]

Without question, the heavy use of emotionally laden attack or condemnation spots continued through the 1988 presidential election into the campaigns of the 1990s. In fact, during the 1992 presidential campaign, candidates Bush and Clinton established an advertising record: 56 percent of the Bush ads were negative and 69 percent of the Clinton spots were negative; and each had "a 50/50 positive to negative ad buying ratio."[26] It was "a new high in negative advertising by two presidential candidates."[27] However, many experts believe that negative advertising once again reached new "highs" or "lows" in the 1994 midterm election.[28] David Broder, a respected political journalist for the *Washington Post*, wrote a week before the election, "the ads are increasingly negative and personal."[29] But, even these negative campaigns were outdone by the 1996 general election campaign, which was considered "the most negative campaign in the history of presidential elections." According to Kaid, 71 percent of President Clinton's ads were categorized as negative and 61 percent of Senator Dole's were considered negative. What's more, simply looking for the inclusion of a negative attack of some kind (as opposed to categorizing the entire ad as negative) showed that 85 percent of Clinton's ads contained a negative attack and 76 percent of Dole's ads had a negative component. In total, 81 percent of all 1996 general election campaign ads contained a negative attack.[30] However, the New York Senate race in 1998 between incumbent Alfonse D'Amato and nine-term Congressman Charles Schumer may have been the "winner" of the ugliest and most expensive negative campaign in U.S. history. With attacks ranging from the mild "too many lies for too long" to name-calling (improperly using a Yiddish term to describe the opponent), the campaign was constantly criticized for consisting only of negative attacks. The combined total spent on this campaign was over $34 million.

In 1988 there were three ads used by George Bush that can serve as prototypes for the negative spots that continued to flourish in the 1990s. The three ads ("Harbor," "Revolving Door," and "Tank") were aired so frequently (the Bush campaign spent 40 percent of its budget "airing about a half-dozen of its best negative ads")[31] and had such an impact that much of the public/journalistic outcry against attack advertising may well have been fueled, at least initially, by them. An example of one of the ads, the "Revolving Door," is typical of each:

Video	Audio
A guard with a rifle climbs the circular stairs of a prison watchtower. The words "The Dukakis Furlough Program" are superimposed on the bottom of the prison visual.	Dissonant sounds are heard: a drum . . . music . . . metal stairs. An announcer states, "As governor, Michael Dukakis vetoed mandatory sentences for drug dealers.
A guard with a gun walks along a barbed wire fence.	"He vetoed the death penalty.

A revolving door formed by bars rotates as men in prison clothing walk in and back out the door in a long line. The words "268 Escaped" are superimposed. The camera comes in for a closer shot of the prisoners in slow motion revolving through the door.	"His revolving-door prison policy gave weekend furloughs to first-degree murderers not eligible for parole. While out, many committed other crimes like kidnapping and rape.
The words "And Many Are Still At Large" are superimposed.	"And many are still at large.
The picture changes to a guard on a roof with a watchtower in the background.	"Now Michael Dukakis says he wants to do for America what he's done for Massachusetts.
A small color picture of Bush appears, and the words "Paid for by Bush/ Quayle 88" appears in small print.[32]	"America can't afford that risk!"

When the 1988 election was over, many scholars and journalists believed that it had been the worst the country had ever experienced because of the harshness, lying, and distortion in the attack spots. Some argued that because advertising techniques during 1988 had built on the foundation established in the campaigns of 1984 and 1986, the public felt paralyzed about the election process and "tuned out" the election. Others maintained that the press had become so caught up in the strategy of the ads that they never discussed content or analyzed them for accuracy and fairness. David Broder argued that the press had not done its job in 1988 and challenged his colleagues to police the 1990 primaries and general election campaigns by scrutinizing attack ads for their truthfulness. He and others cautioned not to let the spots themselves serve as the news story (a practice that had occurred with much frequency in 1988). Thus, during the 1990 campaign, attack ads were frequently monitored by the media. For example, newspapers such as the *Los Angeles Times*, the *Miami Herald*, and the *New York Times* experimented with ad critiques, (in some cases, the text of the ad would be printed and the factual basis of the claims it made were probed as well as a judgment on its fairness) and another dozen or so newspapers ran what came to be know as "truth boxes" or "ad watches." In addition, three major television stations ran commentaries on the visual images contained in the ads.

While the effectiveness of the "ad cops" during the 1990 campaign continues to be debated, the fact is that it was the first time that a real effort had been made to monitor negative advertising. In 1992, ad watches were initiated by many newspapers. But in 1996, media ad watches dropped considerably; broadcast ad watch stories decreased by 68 percent and print ad watches dropped by 20 percent.[33] According to researcher Lynda Lee Kaid, ad watches are used by newspapers and newscasts to "dissect ads and point out weaknesses and misleading aspects."[34] She argues, however, that effectiveness is debatable because the analysis often does not "consider the emotional/visual aspects of the spots."[35]

For the most part, the communicative functions of attack ads are pretty straightforward. If the candidate uses them early enough in the campaign and if they are aired frequently, they can set the rhetorical agenda for the opponent who will, in some fashion, have to respond. Perhaps no better example of attack ads that seized the agenda were those used by a college professor, Paul Wellstone, in his successful 1990 campaign for the seat of Minnesota incumbent Senator Rudy Boschwitz. In a series of spots designed to paint Boschwitz as an out-of-touch, "inside-the-Beltway politician," who was concerned only with his image, Wellstone simultaneously made himself a credible candidate and taught Minnesota voters to "read Boschwitz's polished TV blitz as cynical imagemaking."[36] The spots were simple in terms of production—just the candidate and a camera. In one of the early commercials, "Looking for Rudy," Wellstone was seen "searching" for his "invisible" opponent. First he looked at Boschwitz's St. Paul Senate office where he asked to borrow a pen to leave his telephone number for the senator (one of the ideas being conveyed was the "rich" Boschwitz campaign versus the "bare-bones" Wellstone effort) and then he "searched" at the Boschwitz Minneapolis headquarters and was told by two big men in suits "that we don't like strangers walking around here."

To some extent, the Wellstone commercials had an even greater impact than they might have had in other campaign years. Not only did they attract attention because they were different from those used by other candidates, the press effort to scrutinize political messages resulted in media discussion of the ads and, consequently, of Wellstone's issues.

A second function of attack ads is that they may well cause a defensive posture—even in a challenger—and therefore reduce the time, thought, and money that can be allocated to presenting a positive image. Similarly, and perhaps most apparent in recent campaigns, the use of attack or condemnation ads (if the charges against the opponent take hold in the public mind) can make, by comparison, even a mediocre candidate look better than the opponent. In other words, in the parlance of the consultants, candidates attempt to reduce their negatives and build their positives by increasing their opponents' negatives. The use of attack spots can also aid candidates by contributing to the perception of them as strong or decisive. This, for example, was clearly part of the 1996 strategy designed to allow Bill Clinton to run the most negative advertising campaign in the history of presidential elections and yet be perceived by voters as less negative than Bob Dole. Finally, employment of attack ads can function to divert public attention away from those issues that might threaten the incumbent or prove embarrassing for the challenger. In other words, they can serve to keep the focus of the campaign on areas of strength, avoiding areas of vulnerability. Clearly, many of these functions can block or prevent meaningful campaign dialogue.

Ads Responding to Attacks or Innuendos

Until recently, little has been written about this final category of televised advertising. But as is the case with the other two types, a wide variety of videostyles can be and has been employed by candidates as they attempt to answer charges or attacks that have been leveled against them. The only "rule" or "law" that appears to be consistent in regard to these ads is that they must occur and occur very rapidly, as well as repeatedly, after the initial attack. In fact, most media consultants believe that some kind of a response to a televised attack spot must be aired as soon as possible after the initial attack because people are influenced by attacks (many are disposed to believing the worst about politicians anyway). Some theorists believe that the only instance in which a candidate can get away without responding to an attack is when the attack has been made by a weak candidate (someone with "low name recognition, no prior electoral experience, inadequate funding").[37] Perhaps, however, it was the legacy of the 1984 senatorial campaign in Kentucky that made clear the immense peril of the unanswered charge. When the campaign began, incumbent Senator Walter Dee Huddleston's approval rating was 68 percent. His challenger, Mitch McConnell, was given no real prospect of winning. However, McConnell's media adviser, Roger Ailes, designed a series of humorous ads in which he used hound dogs searching for the missing Huddleston (the senator had missed some Senate votes while he was earning speaking honorariums). The ads were humorous, but they focused attention on McConnell and his campaign. More important, Huddleston never responded to the allegation that he had a "sorry record."

While response commercials may take a variety of forms, the most frequently used are those that employ a refutation strategy (a direct rebuttal to the attack), a counterattack strategy, (instead of refuting the charge, the candidate launches an attack on the character/issue positions/motives/actions of the attacker), or a humor/ridicule/absurdity strategy. For example, in 1982 a "Talking Cows" ad was used by Senator John Melcher to respond to charges that he was too liberal for Montana (Melcher was one of the incumbents the conservative political action committee NCPAC had targeted for defeat). In one response, cows were talking and warned voters about outsiders in Montana who "have come to Montana to 'badmouth Doc Melcher' " and how the "cow pasture was full of material like NCPAC's."[38] There have been a number of successful response spots and with each election campaign their use becomes more frequent—growing, obviously, in direct proportion to the increasing use of attack spots.

During the 1990, 1992, and 1996 elections, response ads not only became more plentiful, they were on the air more rapidly than they had ever been in the past. Consultants frequently created and broadcasted them within six hours, hastening the process by beaming the ads off satellites and sending them into television stations in specifically targeted areas. In fact, "satelliting" became a campaign "buzzword." One of the reasons for focusing on a rapid response is that consultants fear the attack ads of the opponent will control the dialogue or even set the dialogue for the campaign. Although speeches given by candidates or written position papers were once the framework for dialogue, in recent years the framework has frequently been the attack and response spot. Nowhere was this more apparent than in the 1990 election in California between the former mayor of San Francisco, Democrat Dianne Feinstein, and Republican Senator Pete Wilson. During August, Californians witnessed a month-long exchange of charges and countercharges between their two candidates for governor. He accused her of supporting quotas for appointments in state government; she denied the accusation in a counterattack. She accused him of being too close to the savings and loan industry; he countered with a charge of hypocrisy because of her husband's involvement in the industry. The only ads aired by either candidate for a solid month were attack or response.[39] In the 1992 presidential campaign, one researcher described Bill Clinton's strategy as "to let no charge stay unanswered, to let no accusation remain in the news without being refuted by Clinton, his campaign spokesman, or his ads."[40] And in the 1996 presidential election, response ads were once again a major category of Clinton ads. As the president's media producer stated, "It was our strategy to be reactive. In fact, we wanted these attacks because we wanted to rebut them so that people would grow increasingly comfortable with voting for the president."[41] Even in local races in 1998, response ads played a critical role. In the first Congressional District in Ohio, incumbent Steve Chabot successfully responded to an attack ad aired by his opponent, Cincinnati Mayor Roxanne Qualls. His response was worded in such a way as to belittle Qualls for the attack, even addressing her as "Roxanne" and not "Ms. Qualls" or "her honor, the mayor," which had the effect of making her seem less dignified.

Without question, the most important communicative functions of response ads revolve around attempting to contain damage resulting from the attack. Specifically, the candidate's response must function to deflect attention away from the subject of the attack/charge and onto the candidate's own safe ground. Similarly, the ad should ideally function to put the candidate back in an offensive or "one-up" position. Candidates who must continually assume a defensive position rarely win the election.

One thesis regarding the strategy and defense of attack advertising is offered by Michael Pfau and Henry C. Kenski in their book *Attack Politics: Strategy and Defense*. They argue that the most effective strategy candidates can use is to preempt attacks before opponents use them, "thus militating their effectiveness." Specifically, Pfau and Kenski contend that one kind of preemption, inoculation message strategy, is most effective because it not only anticipates and responds to an opponent's attack before it is initiated, it strengthens resistance to accepting or believing future attacks by exposing the voter to a "weak dose" of the attack. The "weak dose" is strong enough "to stimulate defenses but not strong enough to overwhelm him."[42]

Whether or not future candidates will take the advice of Pfau and Kenski in the use of response ads is difficult to forecast. In sum, we have attempted to present a complete yet uncomplicated view of the types of political commercials used by a wide variety of candidates in the television portion of their campaigns. We turn now to a consideration of one type of those commercials as they have been employed by one group of candidates.

TELEVISED ATTACK ADVERTISING WHEN THE CANDIDATE IS A WOMAN

One of the most studied aspects of televised political advertising during the political campaigns of the 1980s and the 1990s has been the use of attack spots by female candidates. In some respects, the fact that women running for political office employed spots that condemned opponents is not surprising. As we discussed earlier, attack advertising has been a prominent strategy for all manner of political candidates from 1952 to the present. Moreover, many candidates who employed them won. In addition, the phenomenon of increased numbers of women seeking and winning political office, a phenomenon which had begun in the 1970s, continued in the 1990s. In fact, in the 1996 elections, 98 percent of women incumbents in the U.S. House of Representatives were re-elected,[43] and by 1999, the number of women holding elected federal office was without historical precedence: nine women in the United States Senate and 56 in the House of Representatives. The number of women in statewide elective posts was 89, while the number of women who were state legislators increased to 1,652 up from 1,550 in 1994.[44]

Although even in the 1990s women continued to face obstacles to their election to office, those who were credible candidates were able to garner enough financial support to run campaigns that employed media consultants and utilized television advertising as a major campaign option. For example, even the long-standing problem of getting the nomination of their political party in an open race was lessened in 1992 when redistricting and a record number of incumbent retirements created 91 seats in the United States House of Representatives. By 1992, women with political experience similar to those of men raised slightly more money than men.[45] In fact, Dianne Feinstein ranked fourth and Barbara Boxer ranked first among all 1992 Senate candidates in the success of their fund-raising; not least, as one scholar argues, "because large numbers of women are now putting their money where their votes (and hearts) are."[46] And in 1996, Barbara Boxer ranked fourth among all Senate candidates in raising a campaign warchest, and Loretta Sanchez ranked eighth among all House candidates.[47] In 1983, there were 16 women's political action committees established nationwide. But by 1996 there were 58 PACs and donor networks "which either gave money predominantly to women candidates or had a predominantly female donor base."[48] Thus it is possible to view the use of attack commercials by female candidates as a natural progression in the evolution of their direct participation in elective politics.

On the other hand, over the years in which women have sought elective office, there has been at least one important reason why female candidates might hesitate before employing attack ads. In spite of the fact that published research has never unequivocally supported the idea that distinct differences exist in the communication behavior of women and men, to some extent, even in the 1990s, sex-role stereotypes continue to shape expectations regarding what is appropriate.[49] For example, traditional expectations regarding the communication behavior of men include characteristics such as toughness, argumentativeness, aggressiveness, and dominance. However, the expectation for the communication behavior of women is almost exactly a polar opposite. When women speak, they are expected to exhibit characteristics such as sensitivity to the needs of others, compassion, affection, politeness, and openness. They are not expected to employ harsh language or to be overtly assertive, either verbally or physically. Perhaps these stereotypes were summarized most clearly by Mary Anne Fitzpatrick when she argued that "masculine traits are instrumental and defined by competence, rationality, and assertiveness; whereas female traits are expressive and hence defined by warmth, expressiveness, and nurturance."[50]

While we know that gender-based communication stereotypes are not universally accepted, we also know that speakers who fail to conform to expected behavior risk audience rejection of their message. One of the ways in which the impact of gender expectations on perceptions of communication effectiveness can be explained is by using Michael Burgoon and Gerald R. Miller's idea of Language Expectancy Theory. According to their theory, expectations about language behaviors influence the acceptance or rejection of persuasive messages. Language that negatively violates normative expectations decreases the effectiveness of persuasive attempts while language that conforms more closely to expectations than anticipated increases persuasive effectiveness.[51] Moreover, Burgoon and Miller maintain that "most people still accord the two sexes very different roles in the social structure."[52] Thus, for example, if we consider submissiveness as one of the prescriptive generalizations about appropriate language behavior for women, our expectation is that their language will be less intense than the language of males. In fact, one of the conclusions from Burgoon and Miller's research is that "females fared better when they used language of low intensity."[53] And in 1994, linguist Deborah Tannen argued in her book *Talking From 9 to 5: How Women's and Men's Conversational Styles Affect Who Gets Heard, Who Gets Credit* that our expectations "for how a person in authority should behave are at odds with our expectations for how a woman should behave."[54] In other words, "everything she does to enhance her assertiveness risks undercutting her femininity, in the eyes of others. And everything she does to fit expectations of how a woman should talk risks undercutting the impression of competence that she makes."[55]

While expectations based on gender can create problems for all professional women, in elective politics, stereotypes are particularly troublesome because of the very real potential for a backlash effect on the campaign efforts of those women whose communication defies or even challenges normative standards. In other words, backlash may occur when a female candidate exhibits so-called masculine communication behavior and thereby violates the traditional view of women as deferential, soft, and feminine.[56]

In 1981, Ruth B. Mandel, author of *In the Running: The New Woman Candidate*, argued that the female candidate continues to contend with centuries-old ideas and biases that someone who is female does not look like a governmental leader who is deciding questions of national well-being or international security.[57] One of the ways in which these biases are manifested is in the female candidate's communication behavior. If she does not employ the language expected, she will violate the "rules," the long-held perception of the way in which women traditionally communicate.

At first glance, it may appear that the biases or stereotypes regarding women is a concern of the past because the percentage of women holding elective office has increased in recent years. However, it is important to understand that the increased percentages do not tell the whole story. The fact is that the ratio of women to men remains small, especially as the level of office increases. For the most part, the higher the level, the less likely you are to find a woman as the elected official. Even in 1999, after five election cycles in which women candidates had done well at the polls, only three of the 50 states had women governors, only nine of the 100 United States Senators were women, and only 56 of 435 members of the House of Representatives were women. Thus, even with the increased percentage of women holding elective office, the ratio of men to women suggests that the biases Mandel documented in 1981 have not yet entirely disappeared.

In 1984, for example, as the vice presidential nominee of the Democratic party, Geraldine Ferraro was questioned about her hair style and her recipes for baking pies. She was sometimes given a corsage to wear at rallies at which she was the principal speaker, and the size of her dress was apparently viewed as important enough to be included in a *Newsweek* story about her candidacy shortly after the Democratic Nominating Convention. Three years later, in recalling her brief campaign to "test the waters" during the surfacing stage of the 1988 presidential election, Congresswoman Patricia Schroeder noted that when she was talking about nuclear testing, the media asked if her "husband would donate his tuxedo to the Smithsonian Institution . . ." and that judging from the kind of coverage the media gave her it was as if the "fate of all womanhood on the planet depended on whether I wore earrings."[58] Moreover, during the midterm election of 1990, the political reporters for *Newsweek* magazine, in an article entitled "Sex Still Matters," noted that although 1990 was supposed to be the "Year of the Woman," the "so-called women's issues have slipped and the macho issues are at the top of the list" and that with the "Persian Gulf crisis, there's this instinct— among men and among women—to leave it to the men."[59] During the midterm elections in 1994, the obstacle to the campaigns of most women was the issue of rising crime. Women had to "work hard to overcome the impression that they were softer on crime than male candidates."[60]

In 1998, the Republican candidate for Massachusetts Lieutenant Governor, Jane Swift, successfully won election only weeks after giving birth to a daughter. Swift was repeatedly challenged during the campaign on whether or not she could be a full-time lieutenant governor—with one radio talk show host going so far as to ask if she would be breast feeding her baby at the office. Swift noted that her opponent's wife had just given birth, "and he got the slap on the back, and probably a couple of people gave him a cigar. But he's not having to sit down and justify his decisions to the nation."[61] And in 1999, as Republican Elizabeth Dole was exploring a campaign for the presidency, the question of whether or not her statements on the Kosovo crisis would attract more public attention than a new haircut was mentioned on at least one television news program.[62] Thus, given the continuing pervasiveness of gender-based expectations or biases as well as the increasing dominance of televised attack commercials, the tasks facing female candidates as they negotiate their way through a contemporary political campaign can be formidable. If they use attack advertising they run the risk of being viewed as too aggressive, shrill, vicious, nagging, and "bitchy"—in other words, unfeminine—thus losing the advantages of being perceived as nurturing, sensitive, and warm. On the other hand, the political danger in not using attack advertising, particularly in an environment in which attacks are being used by an opponent, has been well documented.

Most researchers believe that there are three campaign conditions that favor the use of condemnation spots: low budget campaigns, campaigns of challengers, and campaigns in which one candidate is way behind or has suddenly begun a precipitous decline in the polls. Because female candidates have frequently found themselves in one or more of these conditions, they have been inclined to use attack spots. In fact, after examining 329 ads used by 25 female candidates running for the United States Congress or state governorships between 1982 and 1986, Judith S. Trent and Teresa Sabourin concluded that 20 percent or 65 of the 329 spots were attack commercials.[63]

Given the fact that female candidates are using attack advertising, three questions seem important. First, have they ignored gender-based expectations or biases regarding their communication behavior? Second, have they in some way attempted to accommodate normative expectations even as they use televised condemnation spots? Third, if they have chosen to employ both strategies, how have their attack ads been packaged—that is, what has been their content and form? While the answers are incomplete and, we would argue, in a state of flux, research done in recent years has provided some information.

In a study reported in 1985, James G. Benze and Eugene R. Declercq compared the television commercials of 23 males and 23 females who ran for elective office between 1980 and 1983. They learned that the females were slightly more likely than males to attack the issue stance of their opponents rather than to attack their opponent's character. They also discovered that the female candidates whose ads they examined did not use the ads to project an image of "toughness or aggressiveness." Instead of toughness, there appeared to be a tendency for female "candidates to stress their strengths rather than counteract their weakness."[64]

A second study, this one an examination of the "identity-building strategies" of the first two women in American history to oppose each other in a gubernatorial general election, drew a conclusion essentially similar to the one drawn by Benze and Declercq. After analyzing the television commercials used by Helen Boosalis and Kay Orr during the 1986 Nebraska gubernatorial campaign, researchers David E. Procter, Roger C. Aden, and Phyllis Japp concluded that both women attempted to "blend soft, 'womanly' images with more 'male' images of experience and leadership."[65] The authors argued that a major component of Kay

Orr's victory was that, even using attack advertising, she was able to build an image that projected compassion as well as toughness, thereby avoiding the appearance of being perceived as too strident or abrasive. In other words, the 1986 Orr campaign sought the advantages of both feminine and masculine communication stereotypes.

In an examination of the content and form of 65 attack ads used by women competing for elective office between 1982 and 1986, Judith Trent and Teresa Sabourin found a clear effort to use elements of stereotypical or expected feminine communication behavior within the confines of attack advertising. The candidates blended aspects of the female communication stereotype with masculine communication stereotypes to indicate that they were not too nurturing nor too compassionate to be successful in the office sought. To project the masculine image of strength, competence, and qualifications, the ads were infused with male voiceovers, discussion of experience or competence, and the visual picture of a candidate dressed in a highly professional/business manner. However, to maintain the feminine image, and thus preserve at least some normative expectations, candidates used strategies such as attacking issues and not character, making comparisons as opposed to harsh attacks, talking about social welfare issues, using music, picturing children or senior citizens, or ending the ad with a positive discussion of the candidate rather than continuing the attack on the opponent. In other words, attacks on opponents were embedded within a set of secondary strategies designed to mitigate against the potential negative impact of the ad on the candidate herself.[66]

In a study published in 1993, Trent and Sabourin extended their earlier research by comparing a sample of ads of male congressional and gubernatorial candidates with those of the female candidates running for the United States Congress or state governorships. They found that the spots used by males contained harder attacks, more frequently pictured the opponent, showed the candidate in strictly business attire, and did not typically feature the candidate live (however, when live he would be shown in close-ups generally and in every case he was shown in a close-up when the attack was delivered). Trent and Sabourin concluded that the negative ads of male candidates are opponent-centered. In other words, the "candidate may be distanced from the ad but the attack is 'hard and fast' and its primary focus is the opponent."[67] However, the ads used by female candidates had more variety in terms of the type of negative ad, did not picture the opponent, showed the candidate in professional clothing less frequently and was less likely to show the candidate in a close-up at the time of the attack. The female candidates were also "more likely than males to use other people in the ad (both men and women), and to physically touch someone."[68] In other words, the negative ad style of the female candidates were candidate-centered and opponent-centered in that the focus of the ads were not only the " 'negatives' of the opponent but the 'positives' of the candidate."[69] Trent and Sabourin concluded that the results reinforced their earlier study—that the negative ads of female candidates are composed of a blend of masculine and feminine strategies. They speculated that such blending allows female candidates to "accommodate gender-based stereotypes of femininity even while using a campaign tool that is inherently aggressive, confrontational, argumentative, or, in other words, stereotypically masculine."[70]

A study reported in 1994 by Montague Kern and Paige Edley argued that not only is the 30-second political spot a male-dominated structure but that it is one in which women must tread their way carefully. They must, for example, in one 30-second ad, illustrate their tough or masculine qualities, their caring or feminine qualities, and feminine and masculine policy issues. The authors contend that the portrayal of these multiple characteristics and issues takes more time than just 30 seconds. Thus, they argue that the 30-second format is assaultive, even violent, for female candidates because it interrupts the development of characterological consistency by forcing choices about which qualities (feminine or masculine) or which policy issues (feminine or masculine) will be portrayed. In other words, it becomes too difficult for the female candidate to show in one 30-second spot that she is strong, she is competent, and she is caring. Kern and Edley predicted, therefore, that female candidates will begin developing formats to use in addition to negative ads.[71]

In a study of the television commercials of 38 candidates who were running for the United States Senate between 1984 and 1986, it was learned that in both their candidate-oriented and opponent-oriented commercials, female candidates spent more time on social issues such as education and health care and male candidates spend more time on economic issues.[72]

A seventh study compared the videostyles (presentations of self through verbal, nonverbal, and production strategies) of female and male United States Senate candidates in 1992. It was learned that similarities as well as significant differences existed in the candidates' use of verbal, visual, and production strategies. Males and females equally emphasized stereotypical "feminine" and "masculine" issues and image characteristics and used about the same percentage of negative ads. Females, however, generally used verbal strategies such as invoking change, inviting action, and attacking their opponents on their records. They also used more language intensifiers, made more eye contact, smiled more, dressed more formally, spoke more often about themselves in the ads, pictured themselves and their opponents, appeared "head on" and used a "sound-on" candidate live audio. But males were more likely than females to stress trustworthiness, picture themselves and others, look serious or attentive, dress casually, use testimonials and other people to appear in the ads, speak on their behalf, and utilize a variety of spot lengths.[73]

In a study published in 1996, Barbara Walkosz used Language Expectancy Theory in an examination of 124 political advertisements of male and female candidates. She found that differences existed in how male and female candidates presented their image to voters. Female candidates were found to use less intense language, less humor, fewer direct attacks, and more prosocial strategies than male candidates. However, no differences were found in how males and females referred to autonomy or to their use of opinionated language. Analysis of the candidates' nonverbal strategies revealed that the female candidates had more pleasant voices and used more immediate and dominant kinesic cues. The study found no differences in the emphasis of trait characteristics or issues mentioned in the advertisements.[74]

In her 1997 doctoral dissertation, Cady Short-Thompson examined televised ads, speeches, and campaign literature of the nine major party female gubernatorial candidates and the nine male major party candidates who opposed them in the 1994 election. She found limited support for the idea that gender influenced the construction of televised spots. Although there were some differences in communication styles (women smiled more frequently than men, pictured their families less frequently, used fewer language intensifiers, and dressed more formally), there were a number of similarities. One of the most important commonalities was that both women and men used so-called "masculine" and "feminine" communication behaviors. In other words, the ads of these gubernatorial candidates were not limited to those communication behaviors or production strategies that have been traditionally associated with gender.[75]

There is, however, some research in which results suggest contradictory conclusions. For example, in a study in which the negative ads of men and women running in gubernatorial and United States Senate races in 1990 were compared, little evidence was found that gender influenced choices made in constructing the ads. In fact, David Procter, William Schenck-Hamlin, and Karen Haase concluded that gender was not a significant variable in terms of ad format, type of support, or presentation.[76]

Thus, our review of research on women's use of negative advertising suggests that results are mixed. There is clearly some evidence that women's ads vary in verbal, visual, or production strategies from those of men. But there is also increasing documentation that there has been a blending of what have been called "masculine" and "feminine" strategies or communication behaviors. Clearly more research needs to be done before anything approaching a definitive answer can be given.

The more interesting question regards public/voter response to attack ads used by female candidates. Does a woman risk more backlash than her male counterpart? The evidence here is sparse, but there are instances in which the ads of even well-known female candidates have been viewed as too aggressive, too tough, and too nasty (too masculine?). Theodore Sheckels, Jr., for example, after analyzing the 1986 United States Senate race between Barbara Mikulski and Linda Chavez, concluded that there may be a point at which ads that are perceived as particularly vicious work against a female candidate. His research suggests that in 1986, Linda Chavez's attack ads could well have created a type of backlash because they did not produce many pro-Chavez votes.[77] In 1992, during the New York primary campaign, some political observers believe that Elizabeth Holtzman ruined her political career (and lost the primary) because of her harsh commercials against Geraldine Ferraro. Holtzman, herself, blamed her loss on the larger society and said that those who disagreed with her negative ad strategy were "simply not ready to accept a woman who campaigns like a man. Being on the cutting edge sometimes means you will be misunderstood."[78] And in 1994, during the reelection campaign she lost, Governor Ann Richards was said to have occasionally gone "too negative," that her "sharp wit had turned acid."[79]

Whether attack or condemnation advertising is used by male or female candidates, it, more than any other strategy in the contemporary campaign, seems to have captured public, media, and scholarly attention. In the final section of this chapter we will discuss the most frequently asked question regarding this option.

A FINAL QUESTION

Questions and concerns about the use of televised attack advertising in political campaigns have risen almost as dramatically in the last decade as has the employment of the genre itself. Out of all of the dialogue, whether from journalists, consultants, political communication scholars, or even the public, we believe one important question emerges that has not been specifically addressed in this chapter: Do televised attack ads work? Although there remain areas of uncertainty, we believe that the bulk of the information available indicates that the answer to the question is "yes." But explanation is clearly in order.

Do Televised Attack Ads Work?

The fact that since the 1984 election there has been a fairly consistent increase in the use of attack advertising by candidates at all levels suggests to us that political consultants who at least influence, if they do not make, the strategical choices in a campaign believe they are effective.

Although consultants acknowledge the existence of some risks in using the option, clearly the frequency of their choice to "go negative" suggests more advantages than disadvantages.

One of the most discussed disadvantages in employing attack ads is that they will "turn voters off" or away from the election itself. However, in spite of the fact that only a third of those eligible to vote actually do, there is really no direct evidence to indicate that people are ignoring their voting responsibilities because candidates employ attack advertising. In fact, the results of a 1990 study conducted, at least in part, to test the effect of attack advertising on the political process indicated that there is no real evidence that negative advertising has any effect on voter involvement. In fact, on the basis of their findings, the researchers observed that "perhaps negative advertising turns off some voters, yet motivates others to vote."[80]

The second concern regards what researchers and practitioners call the backlash effect.[81] Because consultants and candidates fear such an effect, attack ads are frequently sponsored by a group that is technically not a part of the campaign, frequently a political action committee.[82] However, in many of the campaigns since 1984, consultants and candidates appear to have decided that the risk of backlash is acceptable because of the research that indicates that "over time voters tend to forget the origins of political messages while retaining their content."[83]

In spite of the potential risks, most consultants believe that the advantages of using attack ads outweigh the disadvantages. And the preponderance of research suggests that voters are more influenced by attack ads than by nonattack ads, that they pay more attention to them, recall them more accurately, and remember them for a longer period of time.[84] Thus, we conclude that there is one very good reason for the increased use of attack commercials: They work.

CONCLUSIONS

In this chapter, we have examined an increasingly important element of contemporary campaigns, televised advertising commercials. In so doing, we have briefly discussed their historical development in presidential politics and defined three types of commercials in terms of the overall communication functions they perform in contemporary campaigns.

Finally, we considered televised attack advertising and televised advertising by female candidates. While we found mixed results, because stereotypes regarding the appropriate communication behavior of women and men still exist, candidates who are women appear to be combining traits of "femininity" and traits of "masculinity" in their television advertising.

NOTES

1. Kathleen Hall Jamieson, *Packaging the President: A History and Criticism of Presidential Campaign Advertising* (New York: Oxford University Press, 1984), p. 97.

2. Kathleen Hall Jamieson, "The Evolution of Political Advertising in America," in *New Perspectives on Political Advertising*, ed. Lynda Lee Kaid, Dan Nimmo, and Keith R. Sanders (Carbondale and Edwardsville: Southern Illinois University Press, 1986), p. 15.

3. Ibid., p. 17.

4. Edwin Diamond and Stephen Bates, *The Spot: The Rise of Political Advertising on Television*, 3d ed. (Cambridge, Mass.: MIT Press, 1992), pp. 128–29.

5. Ibid., pp. 205–7.

6. Ibid., pp. 328–29.

7. Montague Kern, *30-Second Politics: Political Advertising in the 1980s* (New York: Praeger, 1989), pp. 23–24.

8. Ibid.

9. Lynda Lee Kaid, "Political Advertising in the 1992 Campaign," in *The 1992 Presidential Campaign: A Communication Perspective*, ed. Robert E. Denton, Jr. (Westport, Conn.: Praeger, 1994), p. 118.

10. Lynda Lee Kaid, "Videostyle and the Effects of the 1996 Presidential Campaign Advertising," in *The 1996 Presidential Campaign: A Communiction Perspective*, ed. Robert E. Denton, Jr. (Westport, Conn.: Praeger, 1998), p. 149.

11. Diamond and Bates, *The Spot*, pp. 293–345.

12. L. Patrick Devlin, "An Analysis of Presidential Television Commercials, 1952–1984," in *New Perspectives on Political Advertising*, ed. Lynda Lee Kaid, Dan Nimmo, and Keith R. Sanders (Carbondale and Edwardsville: Southern Illinois University Press, 1986), pp. 21–54.

13. Kern, *30-Second Politics*, pp. 51–54.

14. Richard Joslyn, "Political Advertising and the Meaning of Elections," in *New Perspectives on Political Advertising*, ed. Lynda Lee Kaid, Dan Nimmo, and Keith R. Sanders (Carbondale and Edwardsville: Southern Illinois University Press, 1986), pp. 139–183.

15. Jamieson, in Kaid, Nimmo, and Sanders, *New Perspectives on Political Advertising*, pp. 17–19.

16. Arthur H. Miller and Bruce E. Gronbeck, eds., *Presidential Campaigns and American Self Images* (Boulder, Colo.: Westview Press, 1994), p. 67.

17. Lynda Lee Kaid and Dorothy K. Davidson, "Elements of Videostyle: Candidate Presentation through Television Advertising," in *New Perspectives on Political Advertising*, ed. Lynda Lee Kaid, Dan Nimmo, and Keith R. Sanders (Carbondale and Edwardsville: Southern Illinois University Press, 1986), pp. 184–209.

18. Devlin, in Kaid, Nimmo, and Sanders, *New Perspectives on Political Advertising*, p. 32.

19. L. Patrick Devlin, "Contrasts in Presidential Campaign Commercials of 1992," *American Behavioral Scientist* 37 (November/December 1993): 282.

20. L. Patrick Devlin, "Contrasts in Presidential Campaign Commercials of 1996," *American Behavioral Scientist* 40 (August 1997): 1067.

21. Devlin, "Contrasts in Presidential Campaign Commercials of 1992," p. 23.

22. Kaid, in Denton, *The 1996 Presidential Campaign*, pp. 149, 151.

23. Devlin, "Contrasts in Presidential Campaign Commercials of 1992," p. 288.

24. Devlin, "Contrasts in Presidential Campaign Commercials of 1996," p. 1060.

25. Kern, *30-Second Politics*, p. 94.

26. Devlin, "Contrasts in Presidential Campaign Commercials of 1992," p. 287.

27. Ibid.

28. Robin Toner, "Bitter Tone of the '94 Campaign Elicits Worry on Public Debate," *New York Times*, November 13, 1994, pp. A1, A14.

29. David Broder, "Negative Costs," *Washington Post National Weekly Edition*, October 31–November 6, 1994, p. 4.

30. Kaid, in Denton, *The 1996 Presidential Campaign*, pp. 148–49.

31. L. Patrick Devlin, "Contrasts in Presidential Campaign Commercials of 1988," *American Behavioral Scientist* 32 (March/April 1989): 406.

32. Ibid., p. 389.

33. Courtney Bennett, "Assessing the Impact of Ad Watches on the Strategic Decision-Making Process," *American Behavioral Scientist* 40 (August 1997): 1161.

34. Lynda Lee Kaid, "Political Advertising in the 1992 Campaign," in *The 1992 Presidential Campaign: A Communication Perspective*, ed. Robert E. Denton, Jr. (Westport, Conn.: Praeger, 1994), p. 123.

35. Ibid., p. 124.

36. Charles Trueheart, "The Incumbent Slayer from Minnesota," *Washington Post National Weekly Edition*, November 26–December 2, 1990, p. 10.

37. Michael Pfau and Henry C. Kenski, *Attack Politics* (New York: Praeger, 1990), p. 36.

38. Ibid., p. 22.

39. Robin Toner, "90's Politics Seem Rough as Ever Despite Criticism of Negative Ads," *New York Times*, September 9, 1990, pp. A1, A25.

40. Devlin, "Contrasts in Presidential Campaign Commercials in 1992," p. 275.

41. Devlin, "Contrasts in Presidential Campaign Commercials in 1996," p. 1063.

42. Pfau and Kenski, *Attack Politics*, p. xiv.

43. "Women in Elective Office 1998," Center for the American Woman and Politics, National Information Bank on Women in Public Office, Eagleton Institute of Politics, Rutgers University, 1998 (available at http://www.rci.rutgers.edu/~cawp/cand.html).

44. "Women in Elective Office 1999," Center for the American Woman and Politics, National Information Bank on Women in Public Office, Eagleton Institute of Politics, Rutgers University, 1998 (available at http://www.rci.rutgers.edu/~cawp/cawpfs.html).

45. Clyde Wilcox, "Why Was 1992 the 'Year of the Woman'? Explaining Women's Gains in 1992," in *The Year of the Woman*, ed. Elizabeth Ardell Cook, Sue Thomas, and Clyde Wilcox, (Boulder, Colo.: Westview Press, 1994), p. 11.

46. Sue Tolleson Rinehart, "The California Senate Races: A Case Study in the Gendered Paradoxes of Politics," in *The Year of the Woman*, ed. Cook, Thomas and Wilcox, p. 39.

47. "Top 50 Senate/House Receipts," Federal Election Commission, 1998 (available at http://www.fec.gov/finance/hserec97.htm).

48. "Women's PACs and Donor Networks: A Contact List," Center for the American Woman and Politics, National Information Bank on Women in Public Office, Eagleton Institute of Politics, Rutgers University, 1998 (available at http://www.rci.rutgers.edu/~cawp/pacs.html).

49. Constance Courtney Staley and Jerry L. Cohen, "Communicator Style and Social Style: Similarities and Differences Between the Sexes," *Communication Quarterly* 36 (Summer 1988): 192–202.

50. Mary Anne Fitzpatrick, *Between Husbands and Wives: Communication in Marriage* (Newbury Park and Beverly Hills, Calif. and London: Sage Publications, 1988), p. 93.

51. Michael Burgoon and Gerald R. Miller, "An Expectancy Interpretation of Language and Persuasion," in *Recent Advances In Language, Communication, and Social Psychology*, ed. Howard Giles and Robert N. St. Clairs (London: Lawrence Erlbaum, 1985), pp. 199–229.

52. Ibid., p. 209.

53. Ibid., p. 210.

54. Deborah Tannen, *Talking from 9 to 5* (New York: Morrow, 1994).

55. Marjorie Williams, "He Says 'You're Fired,' She Says 'I Have to Let You Go,' " *Washington Post National Weekly Edition*, November 14–20, 1994, p. 35.

56. We would be remiss if we failed to note the very real "double bind" facing all female candidates. Not only must a woman avoid appearing "too tough," she must also avoid appearing "too soft" or "too caring" for fear that such emphasis will make her appear weak.

57. Ruth B. Mandel, *In the Running* (New Haven, Conn. and New York: Ticknor and Fields, 1981), p. 62.

58. Nadine Brozan, "Schroeder and Politics: The Problems of Gender," *New York Times*, November 23, 1987, p. B12.

59. Eleanor Clift, John Taliaferro, John McCormick, Mark Starr, and Nonny de LaPena, "Sex Still Matters," *Newsweek*, October 29, 1990, p. 34.

60. Judi Hasson, "Women Projected to Win in Record Numbers," *USA Today*, October 28, 1994, p. 2A.

61. Lynn Sherr (Reporter), "Great Expectations." *20/20*, October 30, 1998, American Broadcasting Company.

62. "Hardball with Chris Matthews," CNN, April 22, 1999; feasibility of Elizabeth Dole as a presidential candidate [online transcript] (available at http://www.lexis-nexis.com/universe), May 4, 1999.

63. Judith S. Trent and Teresa Sabourin, "When the Candidate Is a Woman: The Content and Form of Televised Negative Advertising," paper presented at the Organization for the Study of Communication Language and Gender Conference, Cincinnati, 1989. The paper was subsequently published in *Communication and Sex-Role Socialization*, ed. Cynthia Berryman-Fink, Deborah Ballard-Reisch, and Lisa H. Newman (New York: Garland Publishing, 1993), pp. 233–68.

64. James G. Benze and Eugene R. Declercq, "Content of Television Political Spot Ads for Female Candidates," *Journalism Quarterly* 62 (Summer 1985): 283.

65. David E. Procter, Roger C. Aden, and Phyllis Japp, "Gender/Issue Interaction in Political Identity Making: Nebraska's Woman vs. Woman Gubernatorial Campaign," *Central States Speech Journal* 39 (Fall/Winter 1988): 201.

66. Trent and Sabourin, "When the Candidate is a Woman: The Content and Form of Televised Negative Advertising."

67. Judith S. Trent and Teresa Sabourin, "Sex Still Counts: Women's Use of Televised Advertising During the Decade of the 80's," *Journal of Applied Communication Research* 21 (February 1993): 36.

68. Ibid.

69. Ibid.

70. Ibid.

71. Montague Kern and Paige Edley, "Women Candidates Going Public: The 30-Second Format" (unpublished manuscript, Rutgers University, Eagleton Institute of Politics, Spring 1994).

72. K. F. Kahn, "Gender Differences in Campaign Messages: The Political Advertisements of Men and Women Candidates for U.S. Senate," *Political Research Quarterly* 46 (1993): 481–501.

73. Dianne G. Bystrom, "Candidate Gender and the Presentation of Self: The Videostyles of Men and Women in United States Senate Campaigns" (unpublished Ph.D. dissertation, University of Oklahoma, 1995).

74. Barbara Jean Walkosz, "A Micro Level Analysis of Communication Strategies Utilized in the Television Advertisements of Male and Female Candidates" (unpublished Ph.D. dissertation, University of Arizona, 1996).

75. Cady Walker Short-Thompson, "Gender and Gubernatorial Candidates in 1994: A Study of Political Communication Styles and Strategies" (unpublished Ph.D. dissertation, University of Cincinnati, 1997).

76. David E. Procter, William J. Schenck-Hamlin, and Karen A. Haase, "Exploring the Role of Gender in the Development of Negative Political Advertisements," *Women & Politics* 14 (1994): 17.

77. Theodore F. Sheckels, Jr., "Mikulski vs. Chavez for the Senate from Maryland in 1986 and the 'Rules' for Attack Politics," *Communication Quarterly* 42 (Summer 1994): 317.

78. Craig A. Rimmerman, "When Women Run against Women: Double Standards and Vitriol in the New York Primary," in *The Year of the Woman*, ed. Elizabeth Ardell Cook, Sue Thomas and Clyde Wilcox (Boulder, Colo.: Westview Press, 1994), p. 115.

79. Sue Anne Pressley, "Being Colorful and Well-Known May Not Be Enough," *Washington Post National Weekly Edition*, October 17–23, 1994, p. 17.

80. Gina M. Garramone, Charles K. Atkin, Bruce E. Pinkleton, and Richard T. Cole, "Effects of Negative Political Advertising on the Political Process," *Journal of Broadcasting and Electronic Media* 34 (Summer 1990): 308.

81. Gina M. Garramone, "Voter Responses to Negative Political Ads," *Journalism Quarterly* 61 (Summer 1984): 250–59. Also see Gina M. Garramone, "Effects of Negative Political Advertising: The Roles of Sponsor and Rebuttal," *Journal of Broadcasting and Electronic Media* 29 (Spring 1985): 147–59. Also see Lynda Lee Kaid and John Boydston, "An Experimental Study of the Effectiveness of Negative Political Advertisements," *Communication Quarterly* 35 (Spring 1987): 193–201.

82. Ibid.

83. Pfau and Kenski, *Attack Politics*, p. 158.

84. Ibid., p. 4.

Part II

Practices of Political
Campaign Communication

Public Speaking
in Political Campaigns

This chapter will focus on what is perhaps the most fundamental communication practice in any campaign, public speaking. In the first section, we will examine the factors that enter into a candidate's decision to speak. Decisions on where and when to speak and what to say to a given audience are not made randomly but are often the result of considerable thought and planning on the part of candidates and their staffs. In the second section, we will inspect the use of two types of stock speeches. Virtually all candidates utilize some type of stock speech to help them meet the massive speaking demands typically placed on them. In the third section, we will discuss the practice of political speechwriting. Candidates are using speechwriters more today than ever before; any examination of public speaking practices in political campaigns must consider the use of speechwriters. Similarly, many candidates today are making extensive use of advocates or surrogates. These "substitutes" for the candidate may be heard in person by as many people, if not more, than those who actually hear the candidate. Hence, any examination of public speaking practices in contemporary campaigns that does not consider the use of surrogate speakers would be less than complete.

THE DECISION TO SPEAK

Perhaps the most important resource available to any campaign is the time of the candidate. That time must be used wisely. Decisions to use the candidates' time for public speeches are made out of self-interest, as the candidates attempt to influence the maximum number of voters. Hence, it is vital that candidates and their staffs do an effective job of analyzing voter audiences to best utilize the candidates' time. Essentially candidates face two tasks: first, to determine whom they should address and, second, to determine what messages should be presented to those they address.

Audiences

Since 1946 when Jacob Javits, then running for a seat in the House of Representatives, employed the Elmo Roper Organization to take opinion polls of his constituency to determine better what issues he should develop in his campaign,[1] political campaigns have increasingly relied on two tools to assist them in analyzing audiences. The first is studies of past voter statistics, and the second is the public opinion poll. As we have seen in earlier chapters, these tools have blossomed in recent years because of improvements in computer technology.

Local and national candidates make use of past voter statistics to analyze audiences. Yet these statistics play a more vital role in the campaigns of local candidates than they do in the campaigns of national or major statewide contenders. Indeed, there is no more valuable campaign aid to the local candidate than accurate voter statistics. Though voter statistics may serve many potential purposes, their chief function is to pinpoint, on a precinct-by-precinct basis, where candidates should be concentrating their efforts. This knowledge enables candidates to determine what speaking invitations should be accepted and in what areas of the district their staffs should attempt to arrange speaking opportunities and otherwise concentrate.

Though the same principles apply for national figures and local figures, in practicality major national or statewide figures are rarely able to aim their speeches or campaign materials to a specific precinct. The size of their constituency and the extensive media coverage they receive often prohibit tailoring a given speech to a specific precinct, as can the local candidate dealing with a smaller constituency. The local candidate, far more than counterparts seeking national or statewide office, must know precisely, down to the precinct, the nature of the constituency. Because their constituencies are smaller, in many instances the local candidate can knock on every door in the district, or at least on every door in those precincts that are deemed most valuable. When a statewide candidate like "Walking Joe" Teasdale, former governor of Missouri, walks across his state he is doing so primarily for media coverage.

Local candidates, however, will not receive the media exposure of the gubernatorial candidate. Rather, their walks in the district can put them face-to-face with a large percentage of their constituency. The act is real rather than symbolic. To be effective, the local candidate must know which areas of the district in which to walk, speak, and otherwise campaign. Accurate voter statistics are an acute concern for local candidates, who can meet a substantial portion of their constituency, can express their concern for voter problems face-to-face, and whose limited financial resources must be used with maximum effect.

Typically, candidates direct their efforts primarily toward precincts where their party traditionally runs well, those where elections are likely to be close and those where ticket-splitting commonly takes place. It is in these areas that candidates should concentrate the majority of their speaking efforts. That may even mean actively soliciting speaking engagements in these areas when none are forthcoming. It means consistently giving preference to these regions when simultaneous speaking opportunities arise in two or more sections of the district. Local candidates can think in precinct terms. National or statewide candidates use the same process but must think more in media market and electoral vote terms.

Utilizing past voter records and computers to help analyze the data, state and local political organizations will often provide candidates with a precinct-by-precinct breakdown of their district. The materials a candidate receives might be similar to the two examples shown in Table 1. These examples are modeled after materials available to Republican candidates in Cincinnati, Ohio, during recent elections. Using the table provided, can you determine whether a Republican candidate should speak in these precincts?

The first precinct is one in which a Republican candidate should actively speak and campaign since it is a heavily Republican precinct. Note that 10 of the 11 Republicans on the ballot in the last two elections have won. The only Republican who failed to win in this district was the 1994 U.S. Senate candidate, who lost to the enormously wealthy Joel Hyatt. As you can see in column ten, that candidate drew only 47 percent of the vote and lost by 17 votes. No other Republican candidate has received less than 64 percent of the vote and in 1996 the Republicans averaged 73 percent of the vote in this precinct, while two years earlier they averaged 64 percent of the vote. Among the 418 precincts in the city of Cincinnati, in 1996 this precinct had the 16th highest average Republican percentage, and in 1994 it had the 33rd highest Republican percentage.

Moreover, Republicans in this district are not excessive ticket-splitters, although at first glance they may seem to be. In 1994 it ranked 129th of the 418 precincts in ticket-splitting, but that was because of the senatorial candidate who lost, thus creating a ticket-splitting figure of 30 percent. Without that candidate on the ballot, only 20 percent of the Republican voters would have been ticket-splitters. In 1996, when all five Republicans won, the incredibly popular incumbent congressmen drew a staggering 81 percent of the vote. This was 15 percent more than the

Table 1
Prior Election Results

SAMPLE PRECINCT 1: CITY OF CINCINNATI—WARD 1 PRECINCT E

1996	U.S. Pres.	U.S. Hse.	St. Sen.	St. Hse.	Cty. Com.	1994	St. Gov.	St. Att. G.	St. Aud.	U.S. Sen.	U.S. Hse.	St. Hse.
Rep.	294	322	280	245	286		147	148	123	119	198	185
Dem.	113	76	106	130	92		80	74	94	136	69	55
Other	5											
Total	412	398	386	375	378		227	222	217	255	268	240
R. pct.	72	81	73	66	76		64	67	57	47	74	77
D. pct.	27	19	27	34	24		36	33	43	53	26	23
Diff.	181	246	174	115	194		67	74	29	-17	129	130

	Avg. R. %	Rank	Total Vote	Rank	Ticket R. %	Split Rank
1996	73	16	412	107	15	289
1994	64	33	268	129	30	135

SAMPLE PRECINCT 2: CITY OF CINCINNATI—WARD 5 PRECINCT G

1996	U.S. Pres.	U.S. Hse.	St. Sen.	St. Hse.	Cty. Com.	1994	St. Gov.	St. Att. G.	St. Aud.	U.S. Sen.	U.S. Hse.	St. Hse.
Rep.	205	204	192	169	184		130	137	117	99	153	112
Dem.	174	149	172	162	170		114	96	109	132	90	99
Other	4											
Total	383	353	364	331	354		244	233	226	231	243	211
R. pct.	54	58	53	51	52		53	59	53	43	63	53
D. pct.	46	42	47	49	48		47	41	47	57	37	47
Diff.	31	55	20	7	14		16	41	8	-33	63	13

	Avg. R. %	Rank	Total Vote	Rank	Ticket R. %	Split Rank
1996	53	159	383	142	7	354
1994	54	134	244	138	10	278

TOTAL PRECINCTS: CITY OF CINCINNATI—418

Column 1:

Rep.—The Republican vote in the precinct for a particular office.

Dem.—The Democratic vote in the precinct for a particular office.

Other—The vote for all other party votes in the precinct for a particular office.

Total—The total vote in the precinct for a particular office. Obtained by adding the Republican, Democratic, and other vote.

R. pct.—The Republican percentage in the precinct for a particular office. Obtained by dividing the Republican vote by the total vote in the precinct.

D. pct.—The Democratic percentage in the precinct for a particular office. Obtained by dividing the Democratic vote by the total vote in the precinct.

Diff.—The difference between the Democratic and Republican vote for a particular office. A minus sign (–) indicates Republican vote is less than Democratic vote.

Columns 2–6: 1996 election results.

Columns 7–12: 1994 election results.

Column 13: Average R. %—This is the average Republican percentage in the precinct.

Column 14: Rank—This is the rank order number of the particular precinct in terms of Republican percentage in the total district. The precinct with the highest Republican percentage in the district is number 1.

Column 15: Total Vote—This is the maximum number of votes cast in the precinct since 1992.

Column 16: Rank—This is the rank order number of the precinct in the district in terms of total votes cast.

Column 17: Ticket Splitting R. %—This is the percentage of ticket splitting in the precinct. It was calculated by subtracting the lowest Republican percent from the highest Republican percent in the precinct.

Column 18: Ticket Splitting Rank—This is the rank order number of the precinct in terms of ticket splitting. The precinct with the highest percentage of ticket splitting in the district is number 1.

Total Number of Precincts: City of Cincinnati Legislative Report—418

177

lowest Republican, the State House of Representatives candidate, who it should be remembered won, with an impressive 66 percent of the vote. If the incumbent congressmen had not been on the ballot, only 10 percent of Republican voters would have been ticket-splitters. Thus, although on first glance it seems that this precinct is marked by a high incidence of ticket-splitting, a close examination of the figures indicates that the precinct is generally consistent in giving Republicans substantial victories of well over 60 percent, and the apparent high ticket-splitting is largely a function of aberrant races.

The second precinct is also one in which a Republican candidate should actively speak and otherwise campaign. It too is Republican, although not nearly so heavily as the first. The average Republican received 53–54 percent of the vote in the last two election cycles. Examining the difference figures indicates that although Republicans have consistently won this precinct, again losing only the 1994 Senate race to Joel Hyatt, three of the 1994 races were won by 16 votes or less. Moreover, though all five Republicans won in 1996, three of them did so by 20 votes or less. This is clearly a precinct where close elections abound. A shift of only 11 votes would have changed the outcome of six of the last eleven elections in this precinct.

This precinct is not marked by excessive Republican ticket-splitting. In 1996, 7 percent of the Republican voters split their ticket. In 1994 that figure was 10 percent. In both years this precinct ranked well within the bottom half of the district in ticket-splitting. Nevertheless, given the multitude of close elections, ticket-splitting can have an impact in this precinct. Given that the Democrats won the 1994 Senate race in this precinct, and that Democrats have frequently come within 20 votes of winning elections here, this is a precinct that is "in play" in most elections. That is, it could be won by a candidate from either party. It is likely to be targeted by both parties.

Using figures such as these, local candidates determine where they wish to speak. Typically, they will write off about 30 percent of the district as hopeless. The first precinct we just analyzed, for example, would be targeted by Republicans, but ignored as a hopeless precinct by Democratic contenders. Candidates then target the remaining 70 percent, those precincts where their party runs strong, where a close election is likely, or where ticket-splitting is common. Precinct two, for example, might well be targeted by both Republican and Democratic candidates during 1998. Though Republican, Democrats have frequently come within 11 votes of winning it, and both sides might reasonably expect close elections in this precinct. Additionally, both of these precincts are relatively large. The vote totals rank both precincts well into the top half of the district.

National and statewide candidates operate on the same premises. They too target about 70 percent of their constituency. Typically, presidential candidates target states and media markets within states, rather than precincts, and choose to speak and campaign accordingly.[2]

Messages

The second primary tool of audience analysis is the public opinion poll. Polls help candidates develop their messages. But polls are utilized differently by local and major candidates. Accurate voter statistics down to the precinct level are of acute concern to the local candidate but often of lesser concern to the major candidate. However, the public opinion poll is of more concern to major candidates but often of lesser concern to the local candidate. Typically, the explanation for this different emphasis on the use of polls involves two distinctions between local and major candidates. First, the major candidate can normally afford a polling service and may also be helped by national polls such as those of the national television networks and national newspaper chains. Candidates for Congress and statewide and national offices all utilize polling services. Most state legislative candidates and contenders for local offices in larger urban districts also use polls.

Candidates for lesser local offices, such as sheriff, county or city recorder, clerk, or engineer, particularly in less populated communities, often cannot afford polling services. Many polling consultants themselves suggest that a campaign that is budgeted at $100,000 or less probably should think twice about using a poll. Typically, the most basic benchmark poll will cost a candidate in excess of $12,000. Most pollsters themselves would suggest that when polling eats up over 10 percent of the campaign budget, such an expense will likely reduce the ability of the campaign to communicate with the public.[3]

Second, even if the local candidate could afford polls, the essentially administrative nature, rather than policymaking nature, of most local offices tends to minimize the distinctions between the viewpoints of local candidates. Issues of policy, which sharply divide candidates for major office, often are not at stake in local elections. This is not to say that there is no opportunity for policymaking at the local level. Rather, it is to suggest that while major campaigns almost invariably involve clashes over policy issues, many local campaigns are waged for positions with comparatively little policymaking responsibilities. For example, county sheriffs and recorders are not primarily engaged in making policy. Rather, they are primarily engaged in enforcing policies set by legislatures, city councils, and similar policymaking organizations. Hence, there is often little distinction between candidates on the basis of issues and less need for polls.

Issue polls are designed to determine what concerns are uppermost in the minds of the voters. They serve major candidates as a topoi, or topics, system. In addition to suggesting topics upon which to speak, they indicate voter opinions and beliefs. As we have noted earlier, candidates rely on polling services when they develop positions on issues.

Using polls to determine important issues makes good sense. Using polls instead of solid study, research, and good judgment to determine what to say about the public's concerns is a questionable procedure. Writing in 1954, when polling was first developing as a major campaign tool, former President Harry Truman asked:

I wonder how far Moses would have gone if he'd taken a poll in Egypt? What would Jesus Christ have preached if he'd taken a poll in Israel? Where would the Reformation have gone if Martin Luther had taken a poll? It isn't polls or public opinion of the moment that counts. It is right and wrong leadership—men with fortitude, honesty, and a belief in the right—that makes epochs in the history of the world.[4]

Most political candidates agree with the implications of Truman's remark that although the polls can help determine what absorbs the public's attention, they should not be used to dictate the candidate's approach to an issue.

Typically, the candidate's polls will be able to rank order issues of concern among specific constituencies such as older voters, women voters, or middle-income voters. The degree to which the polling data are broken down and analyzed depends on the candidate's needs and the finances available. A national campaign will break down the polling data extensively, determining, for example, what issues are of concern on such bases as geography, income, race, religion, and party. As candidates speak, they can vary their subject matter to insure they are addressing the major concerns of the groups to whom they are speaking.

Polls also provide candidates with indirect feedback on messages. Candidates often reposition their stands on issues as a consequence of that feedback.

Competency and Format

Nearing the end of his fabled career, Texas Rangers pitcher Nolan Ryan once observed, "I would love to be governor of Texas, . . . as long as I didn't have to speak in public."[5] Most individuals who run for major public office can't pitch as well as Nolan Ryan, but unlike the great pitcher, most candidates for public office feel comfortable in front of an audience.[6] Most have had extensive prior public speaking experience, and many have also had both formal and informal training.[7] If prospective candidates are apprehensive about the speaking demands of their races, they might well prepare by seeking the advice of competent professionals. Many candidates utilize the services of speech coaches who specialize in training political speakers. Students of speech communication will be familiar with much of the advice offered by such individuals.[8] Additionally, the Republican and Democratic national committees, as well as many state and local party committees, provide speech training in their candidates' schools.

If candidates are uncomfortable with some speaking formats, they and their staffs might attempt to place them in formats where they do not feel uncomfortable. If, for example, they are uneasy delivering formal speeches, perhaps their formal speeches could be kept brief and be followed by extensive question-and-answer periods. The type of training and formats utilized by candidates varies on an individual basis but should not be ignored. A frank and realistic assessment of the candidate's speaking abilities, no less than assessments about where and when to talk and what to talk about, must enter into the candidate's decisions to speak.

THE SPEECH

During the 1980 primaries, the *New York Times* wrote that the presidential candidates of both major parties

make hundreds of speeches in their campaigns, speeches that vary in content depending on where they are given and the audience addressed. But every candidate has a body of material, usually presented in every speech that varies little from audience to audience. This material represents the heart of his message to the voters as he moves around the country.[9]

The *Times* was describing what political speakers call their "stock speeches," and what their speechwriters might also call their "module speeches." The great demand to speak that is placed on contemporary political figures has caused many of them to resort to the use of stock or module speeches. This is particularly true of candidates, such as major national and statewide candidates, who address diverse audiences often interested in policies that involve a wide variety of topics.

A second type of stock speech, used more by candidates for lower-level offices, especially administrative offices that do not involve a wide variety of topics and policies, are variations of the "Why I Am Running" Speech. The demand to speak is also one of the principal reasons used by candidates to justify the use of speechwriters. In this section, we will examine the use of both types of stock speeches, and in the next section we will examine the practices of political speechwriters.

Need and Justification

Speechmaking is fundamental to political campaigning. The politician cannot reasonably expect to campaign without continually facing audiences. Even the candidate for city council in a small community must constantly speak. Typically, such a candidate is called upon to make several major speeches during the campaign at such events as the local League of Woman Voters "Meet The Candidates Nights" or at the Rotary Club's monthly meeting. Moreover, these candidates must be continually speaking, often three or more times an evening throughout the final weeks of the campaign, to smaller groups of citizens. Campaign coffees, teas, church socials, and similar activities crowd the calendars of most candidates. It is not unusual for local candidates to find themselves confronting the prospect of a hundred or more speeches during the last four to six weeks of a campaign. Similarly, as we will see in the next section, candidates for more important local, state, and federal offices face situations where they must speak 30 or more times a week. Because of these demands, most candidates make use of a stock speech and, if possible, the services of speechwriters.

Stock Speeches: Utilizing Speech Modules

Although the phrase "stock speech" has entered the vocabulary of most politically aware citizens, it is a misnomer. We tend to think of it as a speech that is delivered time and time again with little change. We think of it as unvarying, set, well established. Yet if you read the *New York Times* description of stock speeches that opened this section carefully, you may recall that the *Times* noted that stock speeches "vary in content depending on where they are given and the audience addressed." They are not altogether set and established. Candidates do not give the identical speech time after time after time, regardless of the audience, occasion, or the actions of their opponents. Rather, they adapt to these factors.

How do the candidates adapt, given the heavy demands on time? They do so by making use of "speech modules." A speech module is a single unit of a speech. Typically, candidates will have a speech unit, or module, on each of the 10 to 20 issues on which they most frequently speak. Each module is an independent unit that can be delivered as a two-to-seven minute speech on the issue. The length of each can be varied simply by adding or subtracting examples, statistics, illustrations, or other support materials. Typically the organization of each module is similar and will be readily recognized by many students of public speaking.

Each module opens with some attention-gaining device, and then candidates quickly move to a discussion of a problem. Having sketched the problem, they then present their policies as an appropriate solution to the problem. If more time is available, they might then vividly describe or visualize what would happen if they are elected and their policies carried out. Thus the typical speech module is designed to: (1) gain attention, (2) describe a problem, (3) present a solution, and (4) visualize the solution.[10] The first three of these steps are characteristic of virtually every speech module the candidate presents. The final step may not be necessary. It may be implicit from the discussion of the problem and the solution and hence not warrant explicit treatment. The following is typical of a speech module used by Bill Clinton during the 1992 campaign.[11]

The American health-care system costs too much and does not work. It leaves 60 million Americans without adequate health insurance and bankrupts our families, our businesses, and our federal budget. Instead of putting people first, Washington favors the insurance companies, the drug companies, and the health-care bureaucracies. The most advanced health-care system in the world is being strangled.

Attention: Startling statement.

Startling statistic.

Startling statements.

(These statements both gain attention and start to present the problem.)

Dramatic language.

And working Americans are paying the price. Since 1980 the average cost of individual health insurance rose from $1000 to $3000 a year. Today health-care costs are the number one cause of labor disputes, bankruptcies and growth in the federal deficit. People can't change jobs because insurance companies will deny them coverage claiming preexisting conditions. Small businesses are caught between going broke and doing right by their employees. Drug companies raise prices three times faster than inflation. Working men and women are forced to pay more while their employers cover less.

Problem: Statistics and examples to indicate the magnitude of the problem and personalize it for audience members.

Health care should be a right not a privilege. And it can be. We are going to preserve what's best in our system: your family's right to choose who provides care and coverage, American innovation and technology, and the world's best private doctors and hos-

Plan: Elect Clinton and make health-care a right not a privilege.

Good features of Clinton plan.

pitals. But we will take on the bureaucracies and corporate interests to make
health care affordable and accessible
for every American.

We can't afford four more years without a President with a plan and the
will to guarantee affordable quality
health care for every American. The
United States is the only advanced
country in the world without a national health-care plan.

Reminder that Bush has no health-care
plan.

In the first year of a Clinton-Gore Administration that will change. We will
send a national health-care plan to
Congress, and we will fight to pass it.
No American family should have to go
from the doctor's office to the poor-
house.

Visualization: Audience invited to visualize Clinton battling Congress, finally securing an elusive health-care
plan.

In this module, we see an independent speech unit or module on the
health-care issue. The passage stands by itself. It also could be linked
very easily into another module with a simple transition. For example,
at this point Clinton might claim "that negligent as George Bush has
been about our nation's health care, he has been even more negligent
about our nation's environment." At this point Clinton could present his
modular on the environment.

Health-Care Module
Attention
Problem
Plan
Visualization

Transition

Environment Module
Attention
Problem
Plan
Visualization

These happen to be two modules Bill Clinton used frequently during
the 1992 election. Because health care and the environment are issues

that vitally affect all citizens, they were appropriate to use with most audiences. But let us imagine for a moment that Clinton was speaking at a Boeing Aircraft plant in Seattle, Washington. He might reasonably expect, and his polls might suggest, that the conversion of defense industry plants to accommodate the changing realities of a world where our most formidable potential foe, the Soviet Union, had collapsed was uppermost on the minds of his immediate audience and the community in general. Having already prepared a module on defense conversion, it would be a rather minor adjustment for Clinton to present his initial module, for Boeing workers and Seattle residents, like all Americans, were concerned with health care. Then, adapting to his audience he might choose to speak about defense conversion, not the environment. He could do so by:

Health-Care Module
Attention
Problem
Plan
Visualization

> *Transition*: As negligent as George Bush has been about our nation's health care, he has been even more negligent about our nation's plans for defense conversion.

> > *Defense Conversion Module*
> > Attention
> > Problem
> > Plan
> > Visualization

Most candidates will develop key modules at the outset of the campaign, occasionally adjusting them as the need arises. Additionally, they will add modules as the need arises. Then, depending on the audience, the occasion, and any other relevant factors, they will determine what modules to use for a given speech. Often, as with Clinton and health care, the same module is used in many speeches. Yet each speech is in fact tailored to the specific audience and occasion.

Speechlike Opportunities and Modular Speeches

One of the principal advantages of developing a basic speech through modules is that the modules can then be used by the candidate in many speechlike situations. Often candidates desire to appear on interview shows such as *Meet the Press* or talk shows such as *Larry King Live*. With the recent prolifieration of all-news cable stations such as the Fox News Channel, MSNBC, CNBC, and similar channels, the opportunities for such appearances have increased dramatically for major candidates. Opportunities such as these must be weighed like any other opportunity to speak. However, because they do offer free exposure, many candidates, especially those operating on a limited budget, attempt to utilize them. Moreover, almost every media market has local radio and television talk shows. Hence, these decisions are not unique to national contenders.

If candidates have already prepared speech modules on most major topics, they are likely to do well on these shows. The module, which can be varied in length, lends itself to use in these formats. Candidates can accept such invitations with a minimum of preparation and be confident that they are unlikely to be caught ill-prepared. Moreover, they can be certain that their remarks will be consistent with those they have made throughout the campaign.

Occasionally, if a module is done especially well, it can also be turned into an effective commercial or used for other purposes. Since the module can stand alone and its length can be varied by the addition or deletion of support material such as statistics and examples, it is easy to adapt to a commercial. Often media advisors wish to show their candidate in "the real world," talking to "real people." The speech module lets them do just that. Every Republican presidential candidate since Richard Nixon in 1968 has made use of modules excerpted from their acceptance address in precisely this fashion.[12]

Stock Speeches: The "Why I Am Running" Speech

A second approach to the development of a stock speech, most commonly utilized by candidates for local administrative offices, is to utilize "Why I Am Running" speeches of varying lengths. Political consultant and commentator Ron Faucheux suggests that many candidates can meet most of their speaking demands by preparing three speeches. He recommends that the first be about two minutes in length, the second should be about five minutes in length, and the third should be about 20 minutes in length. In each speech, candidates should explain, in as much detail as the time allows, why they are running.[13]

Based on sound research on the demographic makeup of the district, the prevalent beliefs in the district, the distinctions between the candidate and the opponent, and any other pertinent information, Faucheux advises candidates to develop "a sentence or short paragraph that summarizes the reason why the voters should elect you, keeping in mind your strengths, the opposition's weaknesses, and your points of inoculation."[14] This short statment is, in effect, the essence of the candidate's message throughout the campaign. Once crafted, it should be repeated consistently throughout the campaign.

For example, Faucheux claims that in 1992 Clinton's message was

Bill Clinton will bring change and an improved economy. He understands average people and their need for new hope. Bush-Quayle doesn't. That is why he will work for a middle class tax cut, expanded opportunities for the disadvantaged (working women, African Americans, gays, and the poor) and affordable health care for all.

This brief statement could be elaborated upon as Clinton saw fit. Depending on his audience and the time available, Clinton could discuss the principal economic changes he advocated. He could indict the Bush-Quayle economic policies. He could detail the nature of his tax cut. He could discuss his programs for women, African Americans, gays, and the poor. He could discuss his plans for health care.

Similarly, in 1996 Clinton might have developed a brief version of the "Why I Am Running" speech which might have read something like:[15]

Four years ago you voted for me on the basis of my promises. Now I have a record which warrants reelection because in the past four years we have created ten and a half million jobs, reduced crime, reformed welfare, and maintained the peace. In the next four years I will continue to do all of these things while protecting Medicare, Medicaid, education, and the environment.

Again, depending on the audience and the time available, Clinton could elaborate upon virtually any part of this justification for his candidacy. He could review the economic accomplishments of his administration. He could review his administration's successes in cutting crime, or reforming welfare, or maintaining the peace. He could discuss his plans for protecting Medicare and Medicaid. He could discuss his plans for improving education. He could discuss his plans for improving the environment.

Once a candidate has developed a concise answer to the question "Why I Am Running," such as the two Clinton examples, Faucheux offers several questions that can be used to evaluate and amend the answer.[16] First, Faucheux suggests asking if "from a geographic, ethnic, partisan, social, and demographic perspective, will this message appeal to the groups necessary for my winning coalition?" Utilizing the 1996

Clinton example, notice that his message should appeal directly to Democrats, those concerned with the economy, crime, welfare, Medicare, Medicaid, education, and the environment. Given that Clinton's basic constituency would be Democrats, a party which tends to consist disproportionately of citizens in the lower and middle economic classes, citizens who are black, and citizens who are female, virtually all of the points made in this message would be appealing. Clinton had particularily targeted women, the so called "soccer moms" in 1996. Polls suggested that this critical group of voters responded particularly well to the crime, health care, and education issues mentioned in the statement above.

Second, Faucheux suggests that the "Why I Am Running" speech should "zero-in" on both your strengths and your opposition's weaknesses. It should take full advantage of mirror opposites if they exist. Certainly this statement would do that. Dole, for 30 years a member of Congress, could not point to tangible accomplishments as could an incumbent president. Moreover, Dole's record on Medicare and Medicaid seemed weaker than Clinton's. Moreover, Dole and the Republican party had advocated such policies as eliminating the Department of Education and restricting environment laws. Though Dole could offer cogent rationales for these policy differences, clearly a "Why I Am Running" speech such as the one above would allow Clinton to "mirror" or stress the distinctions between himself and Dole.

Third, Faucheux suggests that the "Why I Am Running" speech should be unique. It should not be so broad that other candidates could use essentially the same speech. The sample "Why I Am Running" speech offered above could not be delivered by any other candidate in 1996. The first half of the speech points to the accomplishments of the Clinton administration. It applies only to the incumbent. Fourth, Faucheux suggests that the "Why I Am Running" speech should be "big enough." That is, it should treat major issues. Clearly, the above speech does that by treating the economy, crime, welfare, health care, education, and the environment.

Fifth, Faucheux observes that the candidate must be a credible speaker for this message. Given Clinton's record, to which the first half of the message speaks, and his efforts to improve health care, education, and the environment, he would be a credible candidate for this message. Finally, Faucheux suggests that candidates should ask whether their "Why I Am Running" speech would "inoculate" them on points where they are weak and subject to attack. The 1996 Clinton speech presented above does that in several ways. First, the stress on creating jobs, cutting crime, and reforming welfare takes away issues that traditionally have been ones where Democrats do poorly and Republicans do well. Clinton's use of these issues makes it difficult to portray him as a typical liberal who is out of touch with the daily concerns of Americans. Similarly, his inclusion of Medicare and Medicaid as areas that he would protect would likely help him overcome attacks on his ill-fated attempt to overhaul the nation's health-care system. In sum, the 1996 "Why I Am Running" speech presented above would meet the basic tests for such speeches. Hence, it would likely be an effective way for Clinton to have met many of the speaking opportunities presented to him during the 1996 campaign.

POLITICAL SPEECHWRITING

The use of speechwriters by political figures dates back to ancient Greece and Rome when men such as Julius Caesar and Nero received aid in preparing their speeches. In the United States, the use of speechwriters has been a feature of our politics since our nation's inception. George Washington had at least four different speechwriters, including Alexander Hamilton. Amos Kendell, a former editor of the *Kentucky Argus* newspaper and a close personal confidant of Andrew Jackson, was called by one of Jackson's critics, "the President's thinking machine, and his writing machine, ay, and his lying machine."[17]

Abraham Lincoln frequently called upon his secretary of state, William Seward, for advice on public speeches. Lincoln's successor, Andrew Johnson, had grown up on the frontier and did not learn to read and write until meeting and courting his wife, a teacher. Not surprisingly, he too sought a speechwriter. This rough-hewn president found his man in George Bancroft, perhaps the most erudite and distinguished historian of the day.

Although both presidents Calvin Coolidge and Herbert Hoover made use of the same speechwriter,[18] it was not until the administration of President Franklin Delano Roosevelt that the public at large became fully aware of the pervasive use of speechwriters by political figures. Roosevelt used a variety of individuals to provide him with aid in preparing speeches. Typically, Roosevelt drew upon both subject matter experts, often cabinet members, and stylists, such as authors Robert Sherwood and John Steinbeck. Among the most famous individuals to have ever been a speechwriter was President Dwight David Eisenhower who, early in his military career, served as a speechwriter for General Douglas MacArthur.[19] While the press on occasion reported on the use of speechwriters, it was not until Richard Nixon that an American president publicly acknowledged that individuals in his employ were in fact employed primarily to help write speeches.[20]

Justification and Implications of Political Speechwriting

Since Roosevelt, the public has been aware that political figures often use speechwriters. Today no national or statewide campaign is run without them. The vast majority of candidates running for Congress utilize speechwriters and so do many candidates running for lesser office. Incumbents, whether presidents, members of Congress, mayors, state representatives, or town council members, almost invariably delegate some of their speechwriting chores to paid staff members. The staff member's title may be "assistant to," or "press secretary," but part of the job responsibility is speechwriting. Similarly, challenger candidates normally hire a "wordsmith" to help with speeches, press releases, and similar tasks right after hiring a campaign manager.

Though the public has accepted leaders who make use of speechwriters, somehow we remain vaguely troubled by the thought that those who aspire to lead us often do so by mouthing the words of others. Traditionally, there have been two basic justifications for using speechwriters.

First, candidates face such extensive demands on their time that it is impossible to fulfill those demands without speechwriters. In 1948 while governing the nation and running for reelection, President Harry Truman delivered 73 speeches in one 15-day period.[21] In 1952, during the final months of the campaign, the Republican and Democratic presidential and vice presidential candidates delivered a combined total of nearly 1,000 speeches.[22] In 1960 John Kennedy delivered 64 speeches in the last seven days of the campaign.[23] In 1976 Jimmy Carter delivered 2,100 speeches while running for president.[24] In that same year, President Gerald Ford delivered a speech on average every six hours.[25] In 1992 Bill Clinton delivered so many speeches that he literally lost his voice and was reduced to speaking almost in a whisper toward the end of the campaign. In 1996, Robert Dole utilized a final 96-hour speech blitz, which saw him fly 10,534 miles and deliver scores of speeches in 20 states. Like Clinton in 1992, in 1996 Dole closed the campaign virtually unable to speak.[26]

These demands are not unique to presidential candidates. In 1954 Orville Freeman, running for governor of Minnesota, found himself facing over 120 speaking situations for which he felt the need for advanced preparation.[27] This number does not include the many countless situations in which he spoke with little preparation. In 1970 Nelson Rockefeller delivered over 300 speeches in his campaign for the governorship of New York.[28] A recent survey of candidates for Congress indicates that they spoke approximately four times a day.[29] Thus candidates at all levels simply cannot prepare for the many speeches they must make, while simultaneously fulfilling other responsibilities as candidate, breadwin-

ner, and family member, without the help of a speechwriter. This justification is a compelling one.

Though the public is aware of speechwriters and understands the time
demands that justify their use, it remains slightly troubled by the practice
of one person writing the words of another. A second reason candidates
use speechwriters is because they believe the writer will produce a good
speech. Speechwriters possess unique skills. If their skills can be mar-
shalled on behalf of the candidate, the result will be a stronger speech,
and to that extent, an increased likelihood of election. But this justification raises troubling questions.

One critic has suggested that "the essential question is how much borrowing is ethical?"[30] There is, he suggests, a continuum of help that one
can provide to a speaker. On one end of the continuum, few people
would find anything wrong if a candidate had a spouse or an aide listen
to the rehearsal of a speech, or perhaps review drafts of a speech, in each
instance making occasional suggestions to improve the language or organization. On the other end, most people might object to finding that
speeches were written entirely by speechwriters who did not consult
with the candidates, who in turn had no idea about what they were
going to say until the moment they started to deliver the speeches that
had been written for them. Where on this continuum does one draw the
line between honest and dishonest borrowing and collaboration? This is
an especially vexing question when speakers are using speeches to present themselves as competent to serve in a leadership position in their
community, city, state, or nation.

Communication scholar Ernest Bormann finds that the point on the
continuum where one must draw the line is

where the speech changes character. The language becomes different from what
it would have been had the speaker prepared the speech for himself with some
aid in gathering information and some advice from friends and associates about
parts that he should consider revising. At some point the ideas are different, the
structure of the speech is different, the nuances of meaning change from what
they would have been had this speech really been "his own."[31]

When this happens, the speech cannot achieve what should be one of its
chief goals, portraying the speaker accurately to the audience, and the
public clearly has reason to be troubled.

Thus, voters accept the use of speechwriters. However, we remain
vaguely troubled, because the speechwriter is a skilled artisan who produces a polished product, and this too causes the candidate to hire him.
To the extent that the speech reflects the writer and not the speaker, the
public has cause for concern.

The very nature of political speechwriting prevents us from knowing how often "the speech changes character," becoming more a creation of the speechwriter than of the candidate. However, an examination of the job demands imposed upon political speechwriters suggests that this is probably not as frequent an occurrence as many may think. Fortunately for free societies, the demands of political speechwriting coincide with the needs of the public.

Job Demands

A veteran of over 25 years of political speechwriting for a wide variety of Democratic candidates, Josef Berger, claims that the most important part of a speechwriter's work is "to know his man, to know the man's ideas, not only his general philosophy and background but his thoughts on the issues that he's talking about if he's clear enough on them."[32] Similarly, virtually every political speechwriter who has commented on the job reaffirms the absolutely critical importance of knowing the candidate for whom they are writing because they seek to create a speech that is essentially that of the candidate, accurately portraying the candidate to the audience. Speechwriters must be thoroughly acquainted with the candidate's value system. For speechwriters must not present what they believe is the best justification for the candidate's policy but must present the candidate's justification for a policy. William F. Gavin, a veteran political speechwriter who served on the staff of Representative Robert Michel when Michel was Minority Leader of the United States House of Representatives, has observed that a speechwriter should never "think he is writing speeches for himself. If you are doing that, then you're in the wrong business," he comments.[33] Moreover, speechwriters must do so using language with which the candidate will feel comfortable, language that is an accurate reflection of the candidate. George Bush's principal speechwriter during the last years of his presidency watched videos of Bush speeches and news conferences, talked to Bush as much as he could given the demands on a sitting president's time, and even watched impressionists of Bush, such as comedian Dana Carvey, in order to develop an ear for how Bush sounded.[34] Thus the primary demand placed on speechwriters is to gain an intimate familiarity with the candidate for whom they are working. That familiarity should include a thorough knowledge of the candidate's position on major questions, value systems, the way the candidate thinks through questions and makes decisions, as well as the candidate's manner of using language.

This information will enable the writer to produce a speech that accurately reflects the candidate. The speechwriter owes that to the public so that it might fairly judge the candidate. But what we often forget is that the speechwriter owes it to the candidate as well.

If the speechwriter does not accurately portray the candidate, the speech is likely to be a failure for several practical reasons. First, the candidate may choose to stray from the speech or ignore it altogether. In either case, the speechwriter will probably be fired for writing a speech with which the candidate felt uncomfortable or could not use. Second, if the candidate does choose to use a speech that is an inaccurate portrayal, there will likely be trouble in delivery. Unfamiliar with the basic lines of argument, the evidence, and the language, the candidate cannot be expected to do a good job in presenting the case. Third, candidates are likely to experience discomfort and nervousness in a public situation where they are liable to make some type of error as a consequence of that discomfort. Fourth, they may repudiate parts of the speech in a question-and-answer session or in subsequent public appearances. This inconsistency could create an opening for criticism. Hence, the demands on the political speechwriter to produce a speech useful to the candidate creates a speech that is an accurate reflection of the candidate's policies, thought processes, values, and language. Two recent examinations of the speechwriters' craft by experienced practitioners stress the importance of being faithful to the candidate and suggest that perhaps the principle function of the speechwriter is to polish the language a candidate might use, while remaining faithful to the candidates policies, thought processes, values, and for the most part language as well.[35] In so doing, the interests of the speechwriter and candidate coincide with the interests of the public in securing accurate information about the candidate.

In addition to knowledge of the candidate, speechwriters need at least two other types of knowledge. First, they must know the subject. Occasionally, a political figure is concerned with a specific issue and calls on someone to help with speeches because of that individual's expertise on the issue. Throughout the 1980s and even since the collapse of the Soviet Union, Senator Jesse Helms has taken strong anticommunist positions on a host of foreign policy issues. Thus, it is not surprising to find a foreign policy specialist with a highly conservative bent, Dr. James Lucier, on Senator Helm's staff. A U.S. senator, with a large staff, particularly concerned about one issue and perhaps having as many as six years before his next election can afford a subject-matter specialist. However, most political speechwriters are generalists because most candidates need generalists.

Campaign speechwriters must be versatile. The speechwriter for a Missouri congressional candidate in a recent election was asked to write speeches in a one-month period on such diverse topics as international terrorism, the importance of engineering technology to the St. Louis business community, abortion laws, a federally funded lock and dam project on the Missouri River, Israel and Middle East affairs, and National Fire Prevention Week. Thus speechwriters invariably are widely read, often in literature as well as politics and current events. Moreover, they know how to do research. If they do not know about the topic, they know where to learn about it.

The final knowledge required by the good speechwriter is information regarding the audience and occasion. Speechwriters must know which audiences in the candidate's district are essential for victory. Moreover, they must know what message or impression the candidate wishes to leave with these target audiences. Is this speech being delivered exclusively to the audience in the room? If so, what is the nature of that audience? What are their interests? Is the immediate audience of secondary importance to the audience that will be reached by press accounts of this speech? How can the interest of those two audiences and the candidate be reconciled in an appropriate speech for this particular occasion? Answering these questions and then operationalizing the answers to produce a speech demands many kinds of information. It demands knowledge of the candidate's ideas, value system, reasoning process, and use of language. It demands knowledge of the subject matter, the audience(s), and the occasion.

A final demand placed on speechwriters is the trying circumstances in which their knowledge must be utilized. As one speechwriter expressed it when commenting about the type of person hired to help, "we looked for the capacity to work under harsh and often preposterous time pressures. When a speech for a particular evening calling for a ban on leaded gasolines has been co-opted by your opponent that morning, swiftness, along with eloquence, is routinely expected of the writer in coming up with a substitute."[36]

Speechwriting Teams

As the previous section has indicated, the job demands of political speechwriting are formidable. These demands grow in proportion to the office contested. Although the types of knowledge we have discussed are required by every political speechwriter, they are normally felt to a greater degree by the speechwriter working for a major national candidate because of such factors as the need to coordinate the candidate's speaking with the radio and television messages of the campaign, the need to respond to an opponent who is also constantly speaking and using media, and the constant interjection into the campaign of new issues. Hence, speechwriting in most major campaigns is done by speechwriting teams characterized by a sharper division of labor than is found in the small campaign. Additionally, the team may perform functions that are not performed in smaller campaigns.

Firsthand accounts by members of the campaign staffs of Franklin Roosevelt, Harry Truman, Adlai Stevenson, Orville Freeman, Nelson

Rockefeller, John Kennedy, Richard Nixon, Robert Michel, Gerald Ford, Hubert Humphrey, George McGovern, Jimmy Carter, Ronald Reagan, Michael Dukakis, George Bush, Bill Clinton and a wide variety of other gubernatorial, senatorial, and congressional candidates suggest that speechwriting teams exhibit a similar division of labor in most larger campaigns. Craig Smith, who has been a part of several such teams and has studied many others, finds that typically speechwriting teams in larger campaigns are composed of three groups: the researchers, the stylists, and the media or public relations advisors.[37]

All these individuals should be familiar with the policies, values, and decision-making processes of the candidate. In practicality it may not be possible for each member of these teams to acquire that knowledge. Rather, key figures in each group acquire it.

The research group does basic library research. Prior to the 1990s, this was a group that frequently employed college students who were familiar with library research techniques. Pre-law students, college debaters, or other students interested in campaigns and with good research backgrounds often got their first experience in larger campaigns as part of the research force. While that continues to happen, more and more since 1990, well-funded candidates have turned to professional opposition research firms. The information explosion of the 1990s, fueled in part by the computer explosion, has given rise to the rapid growth of consulting firms that specialize in opposition research.[38]

The second group, the stylists, is normally composed of experienced speechwriters. They are often hired on the basis of recommendation and/or writing samples. These individuals must be able to write in any easy conversational style with which the candidate feels comfortable. They must be sensitive to the candidate's ability to tell a story, show righteous indignation, tell a joke, or use a particular jargon or group of metaphors. They use the materials presented by the researchers to produce a speech that meets high rhetorical standards and with which the candidate feels comfortable.[39]

The final group, the media and public relations consultants, are particularly concerned with the audience. More than the other groups, they tend to be familiar with survey research techniques. Their suggestions are designed to make the speeches consistent with the other messages the audience is receiving from the campaign, and given their surveys of the audience/public, to make sure that the candidate's speeches are perceived favorably by the audience.

Thus the demands put on speechwriters in large campaigns do not differ greatly from the demands put on speechwriters in smaller campaigns. The basic differences are not so much in the demands of the task, but rather in the division of labor employed to accomplish the task. Additionally, since a larger campaign is providing the audience/public with a great number of messages, most larger campaigns involve media and public relations consultants who focus on the speech from an audience's perspective, seeking to make the speech consistent with other messages the audience is receiving from the campaign.

Methods of Political Speechwriting

The literature of speech communication, as well as an examination of newspaper reports, biographies of the principals, and similar material, indicate that most speechwriters and speechwriting teams operate in a similar manner.[40] In this section we will examine the basic steps involved in campaign speechwriting.

First, the speechwriter(s), the candidate, and in some instances subject matter experts will confer. In this initial conference, the purpose of the speech will be agreed upon. The candidate will indicate positions and rationales, "talking through" the speech. Many speechwriters have noted that often the conference will be taped or a stenographer would be present. If not, the speechwriter would take copious notes. The record of the candidate's remarks would constitute a first rough draft. From the very inception, the ideas of the speech are those of the candidate. The justification and reasoning within the speech are those of the candidate. Often, some of the language used in these conferences by the candidate is worked into later drafts and remains intact in the final speech.

At this point the speechwriters, armed with a clear understanding of what the candidate wants, do their research. If the campaign has a research staff, it is brought into the development of the speech. If the campaign is small, the research is done by the speechwriter. One of the advantages of incumbency is that incumbent office holders can often put the resources of government to work on their behalf. A speechwriter for the president might draw on the expertise of a cabinet member or someone in the appropriate department. Similarly, congressional speechwriters' efforts might be supplemented by the Legislative Reference Service of the Library of Congress, acting on a legislator's request.

At this point a draft is developed. In larger speechwriting teams, this draft is typically done by one staff member whose work may be reviewed by other speechwriters and altered. In a small operation, an equivalent process takes place as the speechwriter prepares a draft and then revises it, perhaps drawing on the suggestions of staff members or advisors who know the candidate well but have no responsibilities for speechwriting. It is not uncommon for the original draft to undergo three or more revisions as speechwriters revise their own work and incorporate the suggestions of others. If possible, the candidate is shown successive drafts for input. However, this is rarely possible with every draft in larger campaigns. Nevertheless, at some point the candidate is again brought back into the process.

Depending on the candidate's reaction, several actions can be taken with the version that the speechwriter believes to be close to final. Often the candidate accepts it as final, normally continuing to make minor changes, primarily stylistic, during free moments up until the time of delivery. If the speech is basically sound, but the candidate has more than stylistic concerns, these may be indicated in marginal notes or in a meeting. Subsequent drafts, better conforming to the candidate's wishes, can then be developed and resubmitted. The candidate may have an objection to one section of the speech or perhaps to some aspects of organization. Frequently when reading over the speech, the candidate may be concerned that the material will run too long or too short for the allotted time. If the speech is to be delivered over the radio or television, the media consultants will normally enter the speechwriting process during the final few drafts. Their suggestions will be geared to insuring that the speech is appropriate for the allotted time and contains portions that can be used for brief spots on the news shows. These spots normally contain vivid and startling language that exemplifies the point the candidate wishes to make. In smaller campaigns, media consultants will not be available, but a conscientious speechwriter will strive to include potential media "spots" in the speech in case of press coverage. Additionally, such spots, even in smaller campaigns, might be submitted to the media in the hope they will be used.

With slight variations to accommodate their own circumstances, this process is an accurate characterization of speechwriting in the vast majority of political campaigns where speechwriters are employed.[41] Several key points result from this description.

First, throughout this process the candidate is a major writer/editor/collaborator in the creative process. The final speech is a clear reflection of the candidate. The candidate accepts responsibility for what is said. It is for this reason that, as one speechwriter has noted:

I don't think it occurs to the general public that a speech is ghostwritten. Even if someone in the audience has read somewhere that Congressman X has a ghostwriter and he knows it as the man speaks, he forgets it. He's listening to the man, and he's holding him responsible, and he's responding to him for everything that is said.[42]

Second, though the speechwriter has also contributed to the final product, the speech belongs to the person who utters it. It is the candidate, not the speechwriter, who will receive praise or blame for the speech. Thus, it is easy to understand why one experienced political speechwriter has commented that "if there is any prerequisite to ghostwriting for political figures, I suggest that it is a willingness to sublimate one's self to the figure for whom one works."[43]

Third, major campaign addresses undergo many drafts. A recent study of members of Congress indicates that they typically draft major campaign speeches at least three times.[44] The speeches Peggy Noonan wrote for Presidents Reagan and Bush routinely underwent five or more drafts.[45] President Clinton frequently makes final changes in his major addresses almost up to the point of delivery. And though few presidents are as notorious for using the seven or more speech drafts that Franklin Roosevelt demanded for his major speeches, every president and presidential candidate of the last 50 years has made extensive use of draft speeches prior to delivering a major address.

SURROGATE SPEAKERS

Even though most candidates make use of speechwriters, speech modules, and variants on the "Why I Am Running" speech to help them meet the demands on their time, inevitably they find that they simply cannot be in two places at once. Hence, even in smaller campaigns, it is not unusual to see surrogate or substitute speakers filling in for an absent candidate. In large national campaigns, hundreds of people serve as surrogates for the candidate, many of whom have been trained by the campaign staff.

Selection of Surrogates

The selection of surrogate speakers is not left to chance. Candidates seek surrogates who meet certain requirements. First, they should have a proven record of competence as public speakers. In smaller campaigns, the skilled college debater, a lawyer, teacher, or anyone else with speaking experience may be called upon. In larger campaigns, public officials with extensive speaking experience might be used. In a governor's race, for example, members of the state legislature might serve as surrogates for their party's nominee. At the presidential level those cabinet members, members of Congress, and family members, who are good speakers are often utilized as candidate surrogates.

Second, the surrogate should have some clearly identifiable connection to the candidate. It is for this reason that we so often see the relatives of candidates speaking. During the 1992 presidential race, all of the adult children of George Bush, several of the adult children of Ross Perot, as well as the spouses of the four principal candiates—Clinton, Bush, Gore, and Quayle—were on the campaign trail.

During the 1996 campaign, Elizabeth Dole, wife of the Republican presidential candidate, was often referred to as the stronger speaker of the two.[46] Her ability as a surrogate advocate caused her husband's campaign to earmark 30 staff members, a $1.5 million budget, and a 14-seat jet largely in support of her speaking efforts.[47] Relatives are perceived as being close to the candidate, as are cabinet members and legislative allies.

If surrogate speakers do not have an obvious connection to the candidate, they should make their connection clear to the audience early in the speech. Perhaps they grew up with the candidate, previously worked with the candidate, or have simply been long-time supporters of the candidate. In 1976 Jimmy Carter made heavy use not only of his relatives but also of many other long-time supporters from Georgia who became known as the "Peanut Brigade." In 1996 many of Senator Robert Dole's surrogates, members of previous Republican cabinets and colleagues of Dole in the Senate and House, could speak of their direct association with him as a senator and their opportunity to witness his conduct in office. Similarly, President Clinton's surrogates, including his cabinet and a wide variety of other Democratic officeholders, could speak of their direct association with him as president.

Third, the surrogate should have some clearly identifiable connection to the audience. Since the substitute is just that, a substitute, the candidate or the staff should select a substitute who is appropriate for the audience. In local campaigns, the surrogate may be a member of the organization sponsoring the speech or a native of the geographic area. In national campaigns, the surrogate may be the cabinet member with responsibilities for the area of government that most affects the sponsoring group, as when the secretary of labor represents the president at union affairs. Again, surrogates should make clear reference to this connection early in their speeches if it is not obvious.

Since the candidate is not present, it is clear that whomever is speaking on the candidate's behalf is not the audience's first choice. Hence, that individual may have to overcome the resentment of the audience. It is for this reason that the speaker should be able to stress a connection to the candidate. In effect, the surrogate is saying "I'm the next best thing" and reminding the audience that, like Hallmark cards, this candidate cares enough to send the very best.

Utilization of Surrogates

Surrogates should have attempted to familiarize themselves with the candidate's positions. Indeed, one reason that some candidates like to use their speechwriters for surrogates is that they are uniquely adept at putting themselves in the candidate's shoes. Nevertheless, two rules should govern every presentation. First, surrogates must acknowledge why the candidate is not there. Most people understand the demands placed on a candidate, and a frank statement of where the candidate is will be better received than an attempt to hide the fact that the candidate has chosen to speak elsewhere. Depending on the audience being faced, most surrogates can indicate why their principal is not present in a tactful or humorous way. One rather rotund surrogate we are acquainted with often opened his after-dinner or after-luncheon addresses by saying that his candidate wanted to maintain his weight, and it was difficult to do so during the campaign when he was constantly attending breakfast meetings, luncheons, dinners, coffees, teas, beer busts, and the like.

So he's out rounding up some votes tonight in _____ where they are not serving food. Since I am the one member of the staff who clearly does not have a weight problem, he sent me here to guarantee that your food would be appreciated. Well, I certainly appreciated this fine meal, and I hope that when I am finished this evening you will have a better appreciation of why _____ ought to be elected to the Congress.

An introduction like this one acknowledges that the candidate is campaigning elsewhere but does so in a humorous and tactful fashion, which reduces the audience's resentment.

Second, surrogates should not hesitate to remind the audience that they are not the candidate. Hence, they may not know all of the answers or precisely what the candidate thinks. If the surrogate is well prepared, there should not be many occasions for this to happen. However, the speaker may confront a difficult question. When this occurs, the surrogate should simply acknowledge that to be the case rather than guess; arrangements should then be made for the candidate or staff to respond later.

Benefits of Surrogates

The use of surrogate speakers can provide a variety of benefits to campaigns. In some instances the surrogate may be a more credible speaker for a given audience than the candidate. Additionally, surrogates can say things that the candidate feels uncomfortable saying. Finally, surrogates can often aid candidates in fund-raising.[48]

Surrogates who have a unique connection to the audience may, on occasion, be more effective with that audience than the candidate. In 1996 both Hillary Clinton and Elizabeth Dole spoke to many groups that had more in common with them than with their husbands. For example, Hillary Clinton, known for her advocacy on behalf of children, spoke to many groups that were involved with children and education in settings such as maternity wards and computer learning centers that reinforced her involvement with children.[49]

Frequently, candidates may wish to say something but find that it is not politically expedient. A surrogate may be able to make the statements for the candidate. For example, in 1992 Bush surrogate Mary Matalin, who served as deputy campaign manager and political director for the Bush–Quayle campaign, gave speeches and interviews in which she suggested that Clinton was "a philandering, pot-smoking, draft dodger." She referred to some of Bush's critics as "sniveling hypocritical Democrats." Matalin, not Bush, referred to the Clinton staff member assigned to refute and minimize the charges of Clinton's womanizing as being "in charge of dealing with bimbo eruptions."[50] Similarly, it was Clinton surrogate, Congresswoman Maxine Walters, not the candidate himself, who called George Bush "a racist."[51] Typically, surrogates deliver the harshest criticism of the foe. Surrogates, like Matalin and Walters, can deliver the candidate's message, but they are not the candidate. Hence, surrogates may be able to make remarks that are not politically expedient for the candidate to make.[52]

Finally, surrogates are often able to help candidates raise money. Many candidates feel that it is unbecoming for them to personally ask for money. Three recent examples illustrate the use of surrogates for this purpose. In February of 1994 George Bush, no longer an officeholder and having previously announced his retirement, broke his self-imposed year-long silence on political matters by addressing a major fund-raising dinnner held on behalf of one of his former White House aids, Representative Rob Portman of Ohio. Bush raised $120,000 with that one address for Portman.[53] In 1996 the Clinton campaign scheduled many of Hillary Clinton's speeches to highly sympathetic audiences where she proved to be among the most successful fund-raisers of all of President Clinton's surrogates.[54] In 1998, perhaps recalling the success he had experienced by utilizing Bush four years earlier, Representative Portman invited Bob Dole to keynote a major fund-raising event. Dole's appearance sold out and his speech on behalf of Portman raised over $150,000 for the Ohio Congressman's reelection bid.[55] Many political figures feel that it is unbecoming for them to ask for money personally. Surrogates are not embarrassed or compromised because the money is not for themselves.

In sum, the use of surrogate speakers can provide many benefits. Their primary function is to spread the candidate's messages to audiences that might otherwise not hear them. However, as Martha Kessler stresses, this is by no means the only advantage to using surrogates.[56] Indeed, the benefits of using surrogate speakers are so important in larger campaigns, where candidates cannot possibly address all the audiences that wish to hear them, that most national and many state and regional campaigns actively recruit surrogate speakers, provide them with training, and schedule them through a speaker's bureau.

CONCLUSIONS

Although, as we have seen in Chapter 4, the media have grown to play an increasingly important part in contemporary political campaigns, the public speaking of candidates and their surrogates nevertheless is at the core of any campaign. In small campaigns, public speaking may be virtually the only means of persuasion utilized. In this chapter, we have seen that the decisions to speak are not left to chance in well-managed campaigns. Rather, the campaign identifies the audiences to whom it wishes to speak and the messages it wishes to send and then arranges situations that conform to those wishes. Moreover, we have observed how candidates make use of speech modules and variants on the "Why I Am Running" speech to create a basic speech that can be used, with some adjustments, repeatedly during the campaign. Additionally, we have examined the reasons for the growing use of speechwriters, the demands placed on such individuals, and the methods they use to meet those demands. Finally, we have observed the use of surrogate speakers, focusing on the criteria for selecting such speakers, the techniques such speakers commonly employ, and the benefits surrogate speakers provide to a campaign. In spite of changes that have occurred in technology and the way campaigns are managed, all candidates, whether incumbents or challengers, whether they speak at a rally, a press conference, on television or radio, utilize the ideas we have discussed in this chapter. Clearly, public speaking remains a fundamental practice of political campaigns.

NOTES

1. Jacob Javits, "How I Used a Poll in Campaigning for Congress," *Public Opinion Quarterly* 11 (Summer 1947): 222–26.

2. See Martin Schramm, *Running for President: A Journal of the Carter Campaign* (New York: Pocket Books, 1977), pp. 428–31 for insight into a national campaign's targeting strategies.

3. See Robert V. Friedenberg, *Communication Consultants in Political Campaigns: Ballot Box Warriors* (Westport, Conn.: Praeger, 1997), pp. 42–43.

4. Quoted in "Out of the Past," *People*, February 16, 1981, p. 74.

5. Ryan is quoted in "Off the Record," *Campaigns and Elections* 15 (December/January 1994): 82.

6. Perry Sekus and Robert Friedenberg, "Public Speaking in the House of Representatives: The 97th Congress Speaks" (unpublished study, Miami University, 1982), pp. 2–4.

7. Ibid.

8. See, for example, Jeanette Alexander, "Presentation Makes the Difference," *Campaigns and Elections* 14 (October/November 1993): 53–54; and Mary G. Gotschall, "The Lost Art of Speechmaking," *Campaigns and Elections* 14 (June/July 1993): 48–49.

9. *New York Times*, February 29, 1980.

10. Organizing a persuasive message by gaining attention and then presenting a need, satisfying the need, and visualizing that satisfaction are recommendations that date at least as far back as the earliest editions of Allan Monroe's classic public speaking text *Principles and Types of Speech Communication*, which first appeared in 1935. Yet those very terms are currently utilized by political speech coaches. See Michael Shadow and Greg Peck, "Politically Speaking," in *Campaigns and Elections* 12 (May 1991): 54.

11. This text was taken from Clinton's book, *Putting People First* (New York: Time Books, 1992), pp. 107–8. It is highly representative of how he treated this issue orally and indeed this book, as will be observed later in the text, is little more than a collection of Clinton's speech modules and position papers.

12. In 1992 Democratic candidates Clinton and Gore put together a book based on their module speeches. See Bill Clinton and Albert Gore, *Putting People First* (New York: Time Books, 1992).

13. Ron Faucheux, "Public Speaking and Doing Press Interviews," presentation to *Campaigns and Elections* 12th Annual National Campaign Training Seminar and Trade Show, Washington D.C., June 17, 1995. Also see Ron Faucheux, "The Message," *Campaigns and Elections* (May 1994): 46–49.

14. Faucheux, "The Message," p. 49.

15. It is likely that most major candidates such as those for the presidency use speech modules. One such module might be a version of the "Why I Am Running" speech. We have choosen to illustrate this type of speech utilizing a national figure such as Clinton simply because more of our readers are likely to be able to identify with the issues involved in such a campaign, rather than use the campaign of a local figure with whom few of our readers could identify.

16. The next few paragraphs utilize the questions that Faucheux suggests. See Faucheux, "The Message," p. 49.

17. Quoted in William Norwood Brigance, "Ghostwriting Before Franklin D. Roosevelt and the Radio," *Today's Speech* 4 (September 1956): 11.

18. Robert Bishop, "Bruce Barton—Presidential Stage Manager," *Journalism Quarterly* 33 (Spring 1956): 85–89.

19. Discussed in Peggy Noonan, *What I Saw at the Revolution: A Political Life in the Reagan Era* (New York: Random House, 1990), p. 92.

20. Bernard K. Duffy and Mark Royden Winchell, " 'Speak the Speech, I Pray You': The Practice and Perils of Literary and Oratorical Ghostwriting," *Southern Speech Communication Journal* 55 (Fall 1989): 105.

21. Irwin Ross, *The Loneliest Campaign* (New York: New American Library, 1968), p. 89.

22. Walter J. Stelkovis, "Ghostwriting: Ancient and Honorable," *Today's Speech* 2 (January 1954): 17.

23. John F. Kennedy, *The Speeches of Senator John F. Kennedy: Presidential Campaign of 1960* (Washington, D.C.: Government Printing Office, 1961), pp. 840–1267.

24. Jimmy Carter, *A Government as Good as Its People* (New York: Simon and Schuster, 1977), p. 7.

25. George F. Will, "A Weird Sincerity," *Newsweek*, November 13, 1995, p. 94.

26. Dole used a tea called "Throat Coat" to help him through the last two

days of his final four-day marathon. See Evan Thomas and *Newsweek's* Special-Projects Team, "Victory March," *Newsweek*, November 18, 1996, p. 124.

27. Donald K. Smith, "The Speech-Writing Team in a State Political Campaign," *Today's Speech* 4 (September 1956): 16.

28. Joseph Persico, "The Rockefeller Rhetoric: Writing Speeches for the 1970 Campaign," *Today's Speech* 20 (Spring 1972): 57.

29. Sekus and Friedenberg, "Public Speaking," p. 9.

30. Ernest Bormann, "Ethics of Ghostwritten Speeches," *Quarterly Journal of Speech* 47 (October 1961): 266.

31. Ibid., pp. 266–67.

32. Thomas Benson, "Conversations with a Ghost," *Today's Speech* 16 (November 1968): 73.

33. Quoted in Martin Medhurst and Gary C. Dreibelbis, "Building the Speechwriter-Principal Relationship: Minority Leader Robert Michel Confronts His Ghost," *Central States Speech Journal* 37 (Winter 1986): 242.

34. "The Man Behind the President's Lips," *Cincinnati Enquirer*, April 28, 1991, p. A1.

35. See Melvin Helitzer, "Political Speeches," in *The Practice of Political Communication*, ed. Guido H. Stempel (Englewood Cliffs N.J.: Prentice-Hall, 1994), pp. 71–88. Helitzer's discussion of political speeches focuses around characteristics of language that facilitate good delivery. Peggy Noonan, in pehaps the most informative recent discussion of the craft of speechwriting, stresses that political speechwriters are dealing with policy. But her discussion of her years in the Reagan White House indicate that as a speechwriter she largly followed the policy directives of others and made her most important contributions by providing Reagan with language that helped persuade audiences to support his policies. Especially see Chapter 5, "Speech! Speech!" in Peggy Noonan, *What I Saw at the Revolution*, pp. 49–67.

36. Persico, "Rockefeller Rhetoric," p. 58.

37. Craig R. Smith, "Contemporary Political Speech Writing," *Southern Speech Communication Journal* 42 (Fall 1976): 52–68; Craig R. Smith, "Addendum to Contemporary Political Speech Writing," *Southern Speech Communication Journal* 43 (Winter 1977): 191–94.

38. See Friedenberg, *Communication Consultants in Political Campaigns*, pp. 72–73.

39. On the matter of candidate comfort with the writer and the speech particularily, see Medhurst and Dreibelbis, "Building the Speechwriter-Principal Relationship," pp. 242–46.

40. The speech communication literature utilized in this section includes Robert F. Ray, "Ghostwriting in Presidential Campaigns," *Central States Speech Journal* 8 (Fall 1956): 8–11; Benson, "Conversations with a Ghost," pp. 71–81; Persico, "Rockefeller Rhetoric," pp. 57–62; Howard Schwartz "Senator 'Scoop' Jackson Speaks on Speaking," *Speaker and Gavel* 5 (November 1968): 21–31; Robert Friedenberg, "The Army of Invisible Men: Ghostwriting for Congressmen and Congressional Candidates," *The Forensic* 62 (May 1977): 4–8; Sara Arendall Newell and Thomas King, "The Keynote Address of the Democratic National Convention, 1972: The Evolution of a Speech," *Southern Speech Communication Journal* 39 (Summer 1974): 346–58; Smith, "Political Speech Writing," pp. 52–68; Smith, "Ad-

dendum," pp. 191–94; Lois J. Einhorn, "The Ghosts Unmasked: A Review of Literature on Speechwriting," *Communication Quarterly* 30 (Winter 1981): 41–47; Medhurst and Dreibelbis, "Building the Speechwriter-Principal Relationship," pp. 239–47; Robert V. Friedenberg, "Jesse Alexander Helms: Secular Preacher of the Religious Right," *Speaker and Gavel* 24 (Fall/Winter/Spring 1987): 60–68; Lois J. Einhorn, "The Ghosts Talk: Personal Interviews with Three Former Speechwriters," *Communication Quarterly* 36 (Spring, 1988): 94–108; Duffy and Winchell, " 'Speak The Speech I Pray You,' " *The Southern Communication Journal* 55 (Fall, 1989): 102–15. Also see Noonan, *What I Saw at the Revolution*, pp. 68–92.

41. An extremly brief description of the ghostwriting process, which coincides with this one, can be found in Einhorn, "Ghosts Unmasked," p. 42. Also see Medhurst and Dreibelbis, "Building the Speechwriter-Principal Relationship," pp. 242–45.

42. Benson, "Conversations with a Ghost," pp. 79–80.

43. Friedenberg, "Army of Invisible Men," p. 4.

44. Sekus and Friedenberg, "Public Speaking," p. 6.

45. Noonan, *What I Saw at the Revolution*, p. 74.

46. Indeed, as this is being written in the Spring of 1998, Elizabeth Dole is being touted in some circles as a viable candidate for the 2000 Republican nomination, largely as a consequence of the positive impression she made in 1996 as a surrogate for her husband.

47. Denise M. Bostdorff, "Hillary Rodham Clinton and Elizabeth Dole as Running 'Mates' in the 1996 Campaign: Parallels in the Rhetorical Constraints of First Ladies and Vice Presidents," in *The 1996 Presidential Campaign: A Communication Perspective*, ed. Robert E. Denton, Jr. (Westport, Conn.: Praeger, 1998), p. 210.

48. On the functions of surrogates, see Martha Stout Kessler, "The Role of Surrogate Speakers in the 1980 Presidential Campaign," *Quarterly Journal of Speech* 67 (May 1981): 148–50.

49. One such group was the Washington Interfaith Network, which Clinton addressed on May 29, 1996. The transcript of her address is available from The White House, Office of the Press Secretary. Typically, Clinton talks about the need, in the city of Washington, to keep schools open from 3:00 P.M. until 6:00 P.M. so that children will have a place to play and work between the end of school and when their parents arrive home from work. This type of argument was one that she could make more credibly than her husband, given her authorship of a book, *It Takes a Village*, on children in contemporary America, and her long-standing interests in child care and educational reform. See Bostdorff, "Hillary Rodham Clinton and Elizabeth Dole as Running 'Mates' in the 1996 Campaign," p. 215, for a discussion of Clinton's use of speech settings.

50. See Jack W. Germond and Jules Witcover, *Mad as Hell: Revolt at the Ballot Box, 1992* (New York: Warner Books, 1993), pp. 419–21. Also see "Unleashing the Campaign Attack Dogs," *Newsweek*, August 17, 1992, p. 30.

51. Walters is quoted in "Unleashing the Campaign Attack Dogs," p. 30.

52. On several occassions in the final days of the 1992 presidential campaign George Bush took to calling Bill Clinton and Al Gore "a couple of bozos" and tried to suggest Gore was overly concerned with the environment by calling him "Ozone." Bush suggested that "if I want foreign policy advice, I'd go to Millie [his dog] before I'd go to Ozone and Governor Clinton." These types of com-

ments, far more characteristic of surrogates than principals, particularly sitting presidents, according to some Clinton advisors hurt Bush more than anything Clinton was saying at that time. See Germond and Witcover, *Mad as Hell*, pp. 496–500.

53. *Cincinnati Enquirer*, February 9, 1994, p. B2.

54. George J. Church, "Hillary Clinton—Hushed on the Stump" (available at http://allpolitics.com/analysis/time/9610/07/hillary/index/shtmlh).

55. *Cincinnati Enquirer*, March 4, 1998, p. B1.

56. Kessler, "The Role of Surrogate Speakers in the 1980 Presidential Campaign."

Chapter 7

Recurring Forms of
Political Campaign Communication

In his classic article, "The Rhetorical Situation," Lloyd Bitzer defined a rhetorical situation as "a complex of persons, events, objects and relations presenting an actual or potential exigence which can be completely or partially removed if discourse, introduced into the situation, can so constrain human decision or action as to bring about the significant modification of the exigence."[1] Bitzer's work has served as the basis for many studies of rhetoric that are based on the premise that comparable rhetorical situations produce comparable rhetorical responses.[2] While such studies have been subject to criticism, we find that the basic premise that some rhetorical situations are relatively analogous and hence produce relatively analogous discourse is a valuable premise for the study of much political campaign communication. In this chapter, we shall suggest that most political campaigns tend to produce several similar, comparable, or analogous situations. Moreover, these situations tend to produce similar, comparable, or analogous discourse. Four such comparable situations, found in most campaigns, are the rhetorical situations created by:

1. the need of candidates to announce formally their candidacies to the public
2. the need of candidates to accept publicly the nomination of their party
3. the need of candidates to seek media coverage of their views
4. the need of candidates to make public apologies for their statements or behavior

In this chapter, we will examine the discourse to which these situations traditionally give rise: announcement speeches, acceptance addresses, press conferences, and political apologies. We will study these recurring forms first by describing the situations that create the need or exigence for their use. Second, we will discuss the purposes that these four recurring forms of political campaign communication traditionally serve. Third, we will dicuss the strategies most frequently and successfully employed by candidates delivering these four recurring forms of political campaign communication.

ANNOUNCEMENT SPEECHES

Candidates normally announce that they are seeking public office through a formal address to the public. However, this formal address is rarely the first act of the campaign. Rather, it has been preceded by considerable work. The effort that candidates and their associates have engaged in during the surfacing stage helps to shape the rhetorical situation in which the announcement address is made.[3]

Preannouncement Situation

At least three activities typically precede any announcement address, regardless of the office being sought or the candidate who is announcing. First, an assessment must be made of the likelihood of winning. This will include an assessment of the candidate's ability to attract sufficient voter support, to gain sufficient financial support, and to develop an organization capable of winning the office. The results of this analysis may enter into the announcement address itself. In any event, it gives the candidate a clearer understanding of the situation.

Second, most candidates tend to inform key individuals personally, prior to their public announcement. Typically these are politically, financially, or personally significant individuals whom the candidate wishes to flatter. If the office being contested is statewide or national in scope, often the candidate may inform a small group of individuals personally and then send a personal letter of announcement, in advance of the candidate's public statement, to several dozen, hundreds, or even thousands of others. The point is that these individuals are significant, and the candidate wishes to flatter them.[4]

However, the advance announcement in person to a few key figures fulfills a second purpose. It serves as a means of providing the candidate with feedback regarding the rhetorical situation to be faced. These key, well-placed individuals may be able to help shape strategy, better understand the concerns of the constituency, or identify possible obstacles. For example, a judge with a group of six family members and close friends decided to run for Congress. After having assessed his opportunity for winning, the judge personally set about contacting 25 key individuals whom he wanted to inform of his decision to run. He anticipated that all would be encouraging and would pledge their support. Among those contacted were three elected officials, several party leaders, five prospective financial contributors, the director of a prominent local political action committee, three journalists who were contacted entirely off the record, and officers of several organizations whose members the judge felt might be sympathetic to his candidacy. While those contacted pledged their support, over half indicated that they believed the incumbent would prove much more difficult to defeat than the judge's initial planning group had anticipated. Many pointed to aspects of the judge's record that might work against him in an election. Moreover, they pointed out characteristics of the incumbent that would make him much harder to defeat than he had been two years earlier, when he won election by under 5,000 votes. Thus, through a tentative exploration of candidacy with key individuals, the judge became more aware of the situation that confronted him.

Finally, the announcement should conform to any preconceived expectations that the public might have about it. Hence, the third preliminary activity of the candidate is to determine public expectations about the announcement. For example, have prior candidates conditioned the public to expect that an announcement of candidacy for the office sought should be made from the state capitol rather than from the candidate's home? Does the public have any expectations about what the candidate should say? Does the public have expectations about the qualifications necessary for this position that might be mentioned in the announcement speech?

Clearly, the rhetorical situation for every announcement address differs. Yet, typically, the candidate has first to analyze prospects for the campaign, second to share impending candidacy with a group of significant associates, and third to consider public expectations concerning the announcement address.

Purpose of Address

The announcement address should serve several purposes. Depending on the situation that the candidate confronts, one or more of the purposes discussed here may be minimized or underplayed, while others are stressed. Nevertheless, a sound announcement address may serve several purposes. First, it clearly signals the candidate's intention to run. Second, it may serve to discourage the competition. If the announcement address alludes to the candidate's strengths, such as the ability to articulate the issues, raise money, or wage an aggressive campaign, it may discourage other potential candidates from contesting for the party nomination or the office itself. As we will see in our discussion of strategies, typically the content of the address must be accompanied with actions that successfully discourage the competition. Nevertheless, one of the purposes of an announcement address, particularly if there is liable to be a primary, may be to discourage potential competition.

The third purpose announcement addresses often serve is to indicate why the candidate is running. Candidates may want to stress what they can bring to the office that others cannot—how they can uniquely serve the public. California Governor Pete Wilson was the last Republican to announce his candidacy for the presidency in 1996. This enabled him to clearly contrast himself with his foes for the Republican nomination. Governor of the largest state in the nation (a state which, if an independent nation, would have a larger budget than all but a handful of nations), Wilson claimed that none of his foes could match his executive experience because most of them were legislators, not administrators. "Members of Congress can abstain from voting, but governors can't abstain from leadership," he claimed.[5]

A fourth purpose frequently served by the announcement address is to initiate the themes of the campaign. As the candidate's first major campaign address, it is appropriate to initiate any important themes that may run throughout the campaign. For example, Lamar Alexander launched his 1996 presidential race by claiming that the one central challenge facing Americans was rolling back the federal government. "In every neighborhood in America, the government in Washington is stepping on the promise of American life," claimed Alexander. Calling Washington "arrogant" six times, Alexander asserted that he would shift $200 billion worth of federal spending back to the states. Everything about his announcement, including his clothing, a red flannel shirt rather than a business suit, and it's setting outside of the county courthouse in his hometown of Maryville, Tennessee, was designed to help Alexander portray himself as the candidate who was running against the federal government in Washington.[6]

At the time of Alexander's announcement, the only other announced candidate for the Republican nomination was Senator Phil Gramm of Texas, and most speculation centered around the likely candidacies of Senators Arlen Specter, Richard Lugar, and Robert Dole. Clearly former Tennesse governor Alexander was far less identified with the federal government than any of these likely foes, and the major theme of his announcement was to stress his anti-Washington attitudes. In sum, the announcement address may serve several purposes in addition to the obvious one of officially signaling the candidate's intent to run. It may serve to discourage possible competitors, indicate why the candidate has chosen to run, and initiate major campaign themes.

Strategies of Address

In preparing to announce their intention to run, a variety of choices confront candidates. They must consider the timing, location, who should be with them, speech content, and finally the means by which they follow up on their announcement.

Timing the announcement speech may be difficult. Often the first candidate to announce receives more coverage, and by virtue of being first, may be perceived as being more serious, credible, or legitimate. Though an early announcement may attract media coverage, content of the coverage might well focus on the candidate's potential to win, the funds raised, and the staff that has been recruited. Obviously, by announcing early to gain coverage, the candidate runs the risk that the announcement will not be taken seriously because there are few other overt trappings of a campaign.

Timing is also vital because of the effect that it may have on others who are politically important, both other candidates and potential supporters. There is evidence to suggest, for example, that Michael Dukakis was not anxious to run for the presidency in 1988 but was forced to do so because he feared that in 1992 Massachussets Senator Edward Kennedy would be a presidential candidate.[7] By running in 1988, Dukakis could start with the support of his own home state, which could not be taken for granted if he delayed until 1992.

The importance of timing may have been best illustrated in 1976. Had either Governor Jerry Brown of California, the most populous state in the union, or Senator Frank Church of Idaho, chairman of the Senate Foreign Relations Committee, chosen to announce their campaigns much earlier, perhaps they would have attracted much of the early support that went to former Georgia Governor Jimmy Carter, the first Democratic candidate to announce his candidacy for president that year.[8] Rather, both Brown and Church delayed announcing their candidacies, allowing Carter to build a strong organization and raise funds without having to compete against them. In races for lesser offices, timing of the announcement can also be important. Obviously it may not receive the publicity that is associated with a presidential candidate's announcement, but it will be noticed and considered by other crucial decision makers in the constituency: potential opponents, potential contributors, volunteers, staff members, or supporters.

Where to deliver the announcement address is a second strategic consideration that candidates must confront. In so doing, they must consider voter expectations and tradition, as well as the issues they hope to develop in the upcoming campaign.

In 1992, as Bert Gross has observed, all of the Democratic challengers, running as outsiders and seeking to indict Washington as the source of our national problems, announced their candidacies outside of Washington.[9] Paul Tsongas and Iowa Senator Tom Harkin announced in locations that had personal meaning for them and reflected campaign themes. Similarly, stressing that they were not Washington insiders, but nevertheless knew how to make government work, Virginia Governor Douglas Wilder, Arkansas Governor Bill Clinton, and Nebraska Senator Robert Kerry all announced from their respective statehouses. Former California Governor Jerry Brown, claiming that our political system was being held captive by the wealthy and "corrupted by the powerful forces of greed," chose to announce his 1992 candidacy for the presidency from a site that would remind Americans that government once did, and in the future again could, work for them—Independence Hall in Philadelphia.

In 1996 many Republican presidential aspirants chose to announce their candidacies for the presidency from locations that had symbolic meaning and reflected their themes. This was most noticable in the announcement site selected by California Governor Pete Wilson. Wilson traveled across the country to kick off his campaign in New York City's Battery Park where he spoke with the Statue of Liberty serving as a backdrop. "To understand America," Wilson claimed, gesturing toward the Statue of Liberty, "is to see it through this lady's eyes. She promises freedom—not a free ride. She promises fairness—not favoritism. She promises unlimited hope—not a guaranteed result." He then laid out his vision of freedom, fairness, and hope, which included balancing the budget, overhauling welfare, halting illegal immigration, and ending affirmative action.[10]

Similarly, the location of the announcement address is important in lesser campaigns. The local candidate who is making improved road conditions a prominent issue might well deliver his announcement address from a major road repair site. Most communities have buildings and locations that have unique connotations. Candidates who announce their intention to run at such locations are at least symbolically identifying themselves with the persons or events that have given this location its uniqueness. Additionally, if the site is visually attractive, the candidate may be increasing the limited likelihood of receiving television coverage of the announcement address. Long-term Cincinnati City Councilwoman Bobbie Stern has on occassion announced her candidacy while standing in front of the William Howard Taft statue in downtown Cincinnati's Lytle Park. Thus, she associates herself with one of the city's most esteemed figures and assures herself of a stimulating visual background that enhances the probability of television coverage.[11]

A third question candidates consider when making their announcement addresses is with whom they might wish to share the spotlight. That is, who else should be present and in a prominent position? Traditionally, most candidates have announced their candidacies while surrounded by family, close friends, admirers, and supporters. However, exactly who should be invited, who should sit with the candidates, and who might also make a few brief remarks are questions that must be answered by candidates as they plan their announcement event. Often the presence of prominent individuals in the community, city, or state, supportive remarks from party leaders, and similar visible signs of support for the candidate at the very outset of the campaign can help establish credibility and discourage potential competitors for the nomination or the office itself.

In 1960 John Kennedy's staff was in close contact with Ohio Governor Michael DiSalle. The Kennedy announcement was made with the full knowledge that immediately thereafter Governor DiSalle would be the first governor to endorse Kennedy. In doing so, DiSalle could guarantee that the large Ohio delegation to the Democratic Convention was committed to Kennedy.[12] DiSalle's actions, immediately after the Kennedy announcement, made it clear to prospective challengers that the Kennedy campaign was not to be underestimated and may well, as the Kennedys hoped, have slowed down or discouraged the challenges of other possible contenders.

In contrast, in 1996 virtually no one besides his wife Gayle was on the podium with Governor Pete Wilson. This fact was observed and commented upon in press reports. It was utilized to suggest that Wilson had little support. For example, the widely syndicated *New York Times* account of Wilson's announcement observed that "he faces a tough fight . . . in New York state, for instance, most major party leaders have endorsed Dole. So Wilson appeared alone Monday on the podium, except for members of his family and a few friends."[13]

The announcement address itself is yet a fourth strategic consideration with which candidates must deal. The content of this speech is, in part, dictated by its purposes. Typically, three themes are present in most announcement addresses. Candidates announce that they are, in fact, running. Additionally, they typically offer an explanation of why they are running. Finally, they also suggest the likelihood of their victory.

Unless candidates can provide some cogent reasons for running, their candidacy may end very early. Senator Edward Kennedy experienced this difficulty in 1980 when he announced his intention to run for the presidency. In his announcement speech and in the speeches and interviews that followed, he had difficulty in offering cogent reasons for running. He chose to challenge an incumbent president of his own party. Yet, analysis of his positions on major issues, compared to those of President Carter, revealed very few significant differences at the outset of the campaign.[14] Kennedy's failure to offer a clear explanation of why he was running hurt his candidacy. The public expects candidates to have rational reasons for running and to share those reasons at the outset of the campaign. Candidates who fail to provide them in the announcement speech, or very shortly thereafter, tend to generate public distrust of their motives.

In contrast to Kennedy, in 1996 Republican candidate Bob Dole used his announcement address to indicate the differences he perceived between himself and President Clinton. He presented an overall philosophical difference, claiming that Clinton was a "clever apologist" for big government while "my mandate as President would be to rein in the Federal government."[15] He then went on to indicate specific differences between himself and the president. Dole advocated four distinct changes in tax policy that distinguished him from the president. He indicated that he would eliminate two cabinet level departments, Education and Housing and Urban Development. He indicated that the Department of Energy should be absorbed by the Department of Defense. He indicated that he felt that "half of what the Department of Commerce does has nothing to do with commerce or trade," and that the Department unnecessarily duplicates the work of 71 other governmental departments, agencies and offices." But Dole would hardly stop with eliminating major departments of government that Clinton had supported and funded in his budgets.

Dole advocated eliminating a host of government programs that the Clinton administration supported. They included the Endowment for the Arts and Humanities, The Corporation for Public Broadcasting, and affirmative action programs. Moreover, he advocated turning welfare programs over to the states and eliminating federal participation in welfare. Finally, he claimed that the Clinton administration often subordinated American foreign policy interests to the United Nations. As president, Dole vowed, "American policies will be determined by us, not by the United Nations."[16] In sum, Dole used his announcement speech to draw a host of distinctions between himself and the incumbent.

In recent years some incumbent officeholders have not made formal announcement addresses to indicate that they are running for reelection. Rather, they have simply used press releases. Moreover, in 1996 President Clinton chose not to make any address whatsoever. No president has had as thorough a "permanent campaign" as Clinton, who campaigned continually from the White House during his first term. Though the Clinton camp engaged in all the activities necessary to launch his reelection bid, most notably working diligently to scare challengers from the field during the Democratic primaries, Clinton himself never announced that he would be a candidate for reelection.[17]

In announcing candidacy, most office seekers also stress the likelihood of their victory. In so doing, they often focus on their strengths and on the weaknesses of potential opponents. Implicit in this discussion is their fitness for the office. The candidate claims to be better able to manage the office, better able to represent the constituency, and of course better able to attract funds and wage an effective campaign than anyone else.[18] In sum, the actual content of the candidate's announcement address varies with the situation. However, most candidates, perhaps conditioned in part by public expectations, will formally declare their candidacy, attempt to explain why they are running, and suggest that they will win.

The strategies involved in the announcement address must also include the immediate follow-up to the address. The candidate should not simply announce that he is running and then seemingly disappear from public view. Rather, the timing of the address, perhaps its location, the other people invited to the announcement, and the discourse itself might all contribute to and be climaxed by the means by which the candidate follows up on the announcement. For example, in recent years many cash-starved candidates have followed up on their announcement addresses with a practice introduced by Florida Senator Richard Stone, but forever associated with Missouri Governor "Walking Joe" Teasdale. Immediately upon concluding their announcement addresses these candidates start on a walking tour of their district or state. Such a method of following up may allow the candidate to stress key issues and begin to live up to announcement address promises. It enables the candidate to express concern for all constituencies within the district, evidencing ability to unify people. At various points in the walk, the candidate can be greeted by prominent supporters, discuss the campaign with them, and of course get extensive media coverage of all this.

Regardless of the specific method used—a walk, follow-up mailings, the endorsement of prominent citizens, announcing staff appointments, or the like—it is sound strategy to coordinate the announcement address with some type of follow-up activity illustrating that the candidate is serious about seeking office and is already gaining support. Perhaps the most notable follow-up activity of any of the 1996 presidential candidates was the fund-raising dinner of Texas Senator Phil Gramm. Within days of his February 24th announcment, Gramm's campaign raised $4.1 million at a single dinner. He used the occassion to utter one of the more memorable lines from the Republican primary period, claiming that "I have the most reliable friend you can have in American politics and that is ready money."[19]

In sum, the announcement address is not as simple as it may at first appear. Considerable thought must be given to the timing of the address, to its location, to the other parties who may share the spotlight with the candidate, to what the candidate will actually say, and to how the candidate will immediately follow up on the announcement. The announcement address is the centerpiece of a rhetorical situation created by the candidate's need for formally announcing candidacy to the public.

Though the address may be the first public indication of candidacy, it should not be the first political activity the candidate attempts. Rather, the announcement speech should be preceded by considerable thought and preparation to ensure that the candidate's campaign is opened effectively.

ACCEPTANCE ADDRESSES

In the 1830s, national candiates nominated by the Democratic party began to respond to their nominations with letters of acceptance. By the 1850s, Democratic candidates began to respond to their nominations with informal speeches. In 1868 Horatio Seymour delivered the first formal nomination acceptance address, but like most such addresses in the latter portion of the nineteenth century, it was a perfunctory speech indicating gratitude at receiving the nomination and promising a full formal letter of acceptance. It was not until 1892, when Grover Cleveland accepted his nomination for the presidency by speaking at a large public meeting in Madison Square Garden, that acceptance addresses began to assume their current importance. Cleveland, William Jennings Bryan in 1896, and subsequent national candidates have used acceptance addresses as a means of thanking their supporters, seeking party unity, and dramatizing the issues. In 1932 Franklin Delano Roosevelt flew to the Democratic National Convention and became the first presidential candidate to accept personally his nomination at the convention.[20]

Situation during Address

The situations faced by candidates delivering acceptance addresses have often varied, but typically they share several key characteristics. Most importantly, candidates have successfully attained their party's nomination for office. This success may be the consequence of running in primaries throughout the nation, as it is with current presidential candidates. It may be the consequence of persuading a majority of party voters in a statewide or local primary. It may be a consequence of persuading a majority of key party officials in a local, regional, or state party caucus or committee. It may even be a consequence of default because no one else chooses to run. Regardless of how it is achieved, the important point is that candidates have obtained the nomination of their party and the legitimacy and attention accompanying that nomination.

Acceptance addresses are given to audiences as varied as the massive television audience that watches the major party presidential nomination conventions or a small group of highly partisan political activists who form the Republican, Democratic, or third party central or executive committee for a small town. The acceptance address may be given after a long, exhausting, and bitter fight, or it may be given after a placid and uncontested nomination. Clearly the nature of the audience and the nature of the struggle preceding the nomination are situational factors that must be accounted for in the candidate's acceptance address.

A final situational factor that heavily affects acceptance addresses is the fact that they must be considered as part of what a variety of scholars have called "a legitimation ritual."[21] In full view of those who have nominated them, candidates lay claim to their nomination and attempt to justify their supporters' faith and belief. Both their nominators and the public have come to expect such a ritual. Both nominators and the public will judge the candidate's effort and begin to accord the nominee legitimacy in part based on their judgments of the candidate's success at fulfilling the demands of acceptance address ritual.

Purpose of Address

Acceptance addresses should satisfy four closely related purposes. First, the address is the means through which the candidate publicly assumes the role of a candidate/leader of the party. Second, the address should generate a strong positive response from the immediate audience. Third, it should serve to unify the party. Finally, it is a partisan political address, which in some instances may be the most important such address the candidate makes thoughout the campaign. Hence, it should also serve as a strong persuasive message.[22]

The candidate typically spends very little time formally assuming the role as a party leader. In their 1996 acceptance addresses to the Democratic and Republican National Conventions, Bill Clinton and Bob Dole took 36 and 161 words respectively to acknowledge and accept their nominations. These perfunctory remarks, made at the outset of lengthy speeches, nevertheless, are vital.[23] The public has come to expect that candidates are grateful to be nominated and expects such ritualistic signs of that gratitude as acknowledgement and thanks. For many state and local offices, convention delegates believe that they are doing an important job. They have come to expect that the candidate ritualistically acknowledge their efforts by formally accepting the fruit of their work, the nomination. Even at the national presidential nominating conventions, where the delegates are essentially simply ratifying the decisions made in the primary elections, delegates expect the candidate to acknowledge their efforts. Audiences would find something lacking, something incomplete, something unfulfilling if these rituals were not observed. The rhetorical situation demands that the candidate acknowledge obtaining the party's nomination.

The immediate audience for acceptance addresses is normally composed of those individuals who have affirmed the candidate's nomination. Hence, it is imperative that they respond positively to the candidate's remarks. These individuals, be they national, state, or local party officials, should constitute a nucleus of solid and vigorous support for the candidate in the forthcoming election. A second major purpose of the acceptance address is to arouse these individuals and properly motivate them for the responsibilities that will be falling upon them as the campaign progresses. This may be particularly difficult if large numbers of them have supported other candidates for the party nomination.

The third major purpose of acceptance addresses is to reaffirm, and if necessary reestablish, party unity. If the most active members of the party (its delegates to local, state, and national nominating conventions) leave the proceedings divided and with mixed attitudes toward the candidate, the base that most candidates count on for election—their party support—is of little value. In acceptance addresses that have been delivered by candidates who won bitterly contested nominations, it is not uncommon to see major segments of the acceptance address aimed at restoring party unity. Finally, the acceptance address is a partisan political speech. David Valley has pointed out how each new advance in communications technology has brought national presidential acceptance addresses to larger and larger audiences.[24] Similarly, the acceptance address of state and local figures, delivered at state and local nominating proceedings, are often read or heard by a large portion of the public. Consequently, acceptance addresses present the candidate with a unique opportunity to speak not only to party partisans but also to the general public. Valley concludes that as early as 1896 William Jennings Bryan was tailoring his acceptance address not to the immediate audience but to the hundreds of thousands of citizens who might read his speech.[25] Similarly, even state and local candidates must consider that their acceptance addresses may be carried in full, or quoted in part, by the newspapers. Moreover, segments of the address may be quoted in radio and television reports. Through such accounts and reports, even local acceptance addresses acquire broad audiences, while the audiences for the acceptance addresses of national figures number in the tens of millions. Hence, acceptance addresses serve partisan political purposes.

Strategies of the Address

A variety of strategies have been uitilized by campaigners to satisfy the purposes associated with acceptance addresses. Traditionally, acceptance addresses are characterized by:

1. simplified partisan statements
2. laments about the present and celebrations about the future

3. stress on the crucial nature of this election
4. attempts to seek support from the entire constituency.

In recent years, as the importance of political parties has declined, and as decision making has shifted from nominating convention delegates to the will of party voters as expressed in primary elections, the functions of acceptance addresses have changed. As communications scholar Kurt Ritter has argued, candidates giving acceptance addresses today "face a voting public who will judge them not so much on the basis of their political party as on their personal appeal on television." As a consequence, Ritter continues, acceptance addresses "must persuade audiences who are less inclined to vote on the basis of party affiliation, and more inclined to vote on the basis of the individual candidate and his or her general orientation as liberal, moderate or conservative."[26] Hence, Ritter suggests that acceptance addresses are now less distinct from other campaign speeches and exhibit two additional characteristics not readily apparent in such addresses earlier. First, candidates are increasingly utilizing their biographies as "important sources of material for acceptance addresses." Second, acceptance addresses are increasingly "likely to reflect a personal comparison between the leading candidates."[27]

Which of these six strategies will dominate an acceptance address is largely a function of the specific situation in which that address is being delivered. All six strategies are common in current acceptance addresses.

In an attempt to attain a strong positive response from the immediate audience, as well as deliver a frankly partisan political address to the large secondary audience, candidates often use simplified partisan statements. Such statements characteristically suggest that the nominees and their parties are necessary to solve any problems confronting the constituency and/or that opponents and their parties will exacerbate any problems confronting the constituency. Typically, in harsh and uncompromisingly partisan language, candidates suggest that there is no real choice in this election, that their position and party are clearly right, and that their opponents are clearly wrong. Though simplified partisan statements are still common in acceptance addresses, Ritter cogently argues that as party affiliation becomes less important to voters such statements are likely to be found less and less in acceptance addresses.[28] A comparison of the 1992 and 1996 acceptance addresses of the Republican and Democratic candidates suggests that Ritter is correct in claiming that simplified, harsh partisan statements are growing less important in these addresses.

In his 1992 acceptance address, George Bush reviewed the soul searching decisions he made as commander in chief during the Persian Gulf conflict and then asked, "Well, what about the leader of the Arkansas

National Guard, the man who hopes to be commander in chief? Well, while I bit the bullet, he bit his nails." He spoke of Clinton as a "con man," and claimed that, as governor, Clinton had raised taxes "128 times and enjoyed it every time."[29] Similarly in his 1992 acceptance address Bill Clinton claimed that the Bush administration had "hijacked" government for the "privileged, private interests." He went on to claim that the Bush administration represented "forces of greed," and that the Bush administration was "brain-dead."[30] Both Bush and Clinton used harsh and uncompromising language to suggest that there was no real choice.

In his 1996 acceptance address, Bob Dole called the Democrats "the party of government," and told his audience that "you now work from the first of January into May just to pay your taxes so that the party of government can satisfy its priorities with the sweat of your brow, because they think that what you would do with your own money would be morally and practically less admirable than what they would do with it." Moments later he described the Clinton administration as "a corps of the elite who never grew up, never did anything real, never sacrificed, never suffered, and never learned." Obviously these are partisan statements, but they seem less intense than those of Bush. Moreover, Dole even went so far in his speech as to observe that Clinton is "my opponent—and he is my opponent, not my enemy."[31]

Similarly, in 1996 Clinton was not as harsh as he had been in 1992. There are no passages whatsoever in Clinton's 1996 address comparable to his 1992 claims that the Bush administration had "hijacked" the government, represented the "forces of greed," and was "brain-dead." Rather, Clinton acknowledged "that Bob Dole, Jack Kemp, and Ross Perot love our country, and they have worked hard to serve it." The harshest language Clinton used was to call Dole's tax proposals a "scheme" that would "explode the deficit." Indeed, like Dole two weeks earlier, Clinton made a point of referring to the senator as "my opponent."[32]

Though it might well be argued that the reduction in partisan statements is unique to these two candidates in this particular election, it seems more likely that what we saw in 1996, as Ritter claims, is a recognition on the part of the candidates that harsh partisan attacks are not likely to be well received by contemporary audiences that have less party affiliation than ever before. It seems likely that the more temperate language of 1996 reflects the rational choices of candidates. Though simplified partisan statements, which in the past caused one critic to call acceptance addresses the "apotheosis of political oratory,"[33] are likely to remain a characteristic of these speeches, it is also likely that their prominence is declining.

The recent work of communication researchers William L. Benoit, William J. Wells, P. M. Pier, and Joseph R. Blaney also points to yet another manifestation of the reduction of purely partisan statements. These researchers find that since 1980 the acceptance addresses of major party presidential candidates have focused far more on candidates than on parties. In the five earlier campaigns they studied (1960–1976), Benoit and his colleagues found that acceptance addresses acclaimed or attacked individual candidates almost exactly as often as they did the parties. However, since 1980, over four times as many remarks were aimed at candidates than were aimed at parties.[34] Clearly, acceptance addresses are partisan statements, but in recent years the diminishing stature of parties and the growing candidate-centeredness of campaigns has produced a corresponding shift in the targets of that partisan rhetoric.

A second strategy characteristic of acceptance addresses is that they tend to lament the present, while celebrating the future. As Kurt Ritter has illustrated, challengers lament the present, claiming that incumbents have abandoned the abiding principles of the American Dream, and hence, have contributed to the nation's problems. Challengers offer to lead the people back to fundamental American values, thereby resolving our problems, and thus giving rise to a bright future.[35] In 1996 Dole accused Clinton of ignoring the nation's defense, abandoning the war on drugs, overtaxing citizens, and ignoring the needs of children in favor of the demands of their teachers. All of these actions were portrayed as departures from our national tradition. But, Dole concluded, "we recognize America preeminently as a country of tomorrow." Dole claimed that his proposals, outlined in his speech, would bring America back. Hence he concluded, "tonight I stand before you, tested by adversity, made sensitive by hardship, a fighter by principle and the most optimistic man in America."[36] In so concluding, Dole was inviting his audience to join him in recovering from adversity, overcoming hardship, fighting for principle, and ultimately restoring America.

While lamenting the past and celebrating the future appears to be a strategy uniquely suited to challenger nominees, Ritter points out that it is also used, with slight adaptation, by incumbents:

The "in-party" version of the acceptance speech places the speaker at the later stages in the sequence of the rhetorical form. Instead of citing immediate difficulties, the incumbent cites the national decline immediately prior to his arrival at the White House. The incumbent typically describes the sorry state of America when he took office and then points out how he has brought the nation back to its historic purpose. . . . Each incumbent is quick to add that our work is not yet done. In fact, the opposing party threatens the restoration.[37]

Hence, this strategy of lamenting the past and celebrating the future is one that incumbents may also utilize in their acceptance addresses. In his 1996 acceptance address to the Democratic National Convention, Bill

Clinton lamented the past economic policies of Republican party leaders. He spoke of the Republican recession of 1991 and 1992. He spoke of the debt run up in the 12 years Republicans were in the White House prior to his administration. He proudly observed that his administration had righted the nation's economy and could be counted on in the future to continue to create jobs, raise wages, and enact policies that would sustain the nation's prosperity.[38]

A third common strategy found in acceptance addresses is to stress the urgency and crucial nature of this election. In his study of presidential acceptance addresses, David Valley reports that 74 percent of all the words in the acceptance speeches of Democratic nominees he studied "have been used to discuss contemporary issues."[39] Ritter similarly concludes that "although incumbent and challenging candidates have found different lessons from the American past, they all find that their election represents a key moment in American history."[40] In his 1996 acceptance address, Bill Clinton concluded by observing that

68 nights from tonight, the American people will face once again a critical moment of decision. We're going to choose the last president of the 20th century and the first president of the 21st century. But the real choice is not that. The real choice is whether we will build a bridge to the future or a bridge to the past, about whether we believe our best days are still out there or our best days are behind us, about whether we want a country of people all working together or one where you're on your own. Let us committ ourselves this night to rise up and build the bridge.[41]

Clinton hoped his audience recognized the critical nature of this election, and would choose him and his policies to lead them into the new millennium. Dramatizing the importance of this election, whether it be for county sheriff, state senator, congressperson, or president, is an acceptance address strategy designed to mobilize support.

A fourth strategy characteristic of acceptance addresses is to call on all audience members, immediate and secondary, to unify behind the nominee to secure victory in the upcoming general election. Calls of this sort may be exceptionally important if the nomination has been bitterly contested. In 1980 because of the highly divisive primary campaign between Senator Edward Kennedy and President Carter, the latter made a special point of including a passage in his acceptance address in which he addressed Kennedy by name:

Ted, your party needs—and I need—you and your idealism and dedication working for us. There is no doubt that even greater service lies ahead of you—and we are grateful to you and to have your strong partnership now in the larger cause to which your own life has been dedicated. I thank you for your support. We'll make great partners this fall in whipping the Republicans.[42]

Carter was trying to unify his party by beckoning to his Democratic opponent and inviting his support.

Candidates typically solicit not simply the support of their party colleagues but also use their acceptance addresses to reach out beyond the immediate audience of party members, to solicit unity and support from others who might be listening, watching, or reading. Bill Clinton implemented this strategy in his 1992 acceptance address when he stated:

> But I cannot do it alone. No President can. We must do it together. It won't be easy and it won't be quick. We didn't get into this mess overnight, and we won't get out of it overnight. But we can do it—with our commitment and our creativity and our diversity and our strength. I want every person in this hall and every citizen in this land to reach out and join us in a great new adventure to chart a bold new future.[43]

In passages like this, candidates seek to move beyond their own party, which has already granted them the nomination, and establish identification and unity with other members of the village, city, state, or in the case of presidential candidates, nation.

The final two strategies that are commonly utilized in acceptance addresses are outgrowths of the increasingly candidate-centered nature of campaigning. We have already noted that the candidate centered nature of campaigning has affected the target of partisan remarks. Additionally, largely as Ritter and Wayne Fields have argued, the candidate-centered, rather than party-centered, nature of recent campaigns is reflected in acceptance addresses by the stress recent candidates have placed on elements of their own biography.[44] Additionally, it has caused candidates to compare themselves with their opponents to a greater degree than ever before. These two candidate-centered strategies were clearly evident in the 1996 acceptance addresses of Bob Dole and Bill Clinton.

After perfunctorily accepting his party's nomination, Dole introduced the first major section of his speech by asking, "And who am I that stands before you tonight?" Dole then launched into an extensive answer to that question which stressed the impact upon him of his upbringing in Russell, Kansas, and the values he learned growing up in Russell. Similarly, when he turned to a discussion of the policies a Dole administration would pursue, he often supported them by pointing to aspects of his own life.

Clinton, with perhaps less need to acquaint the national audience with the details of the formative experiences of his life, given that his audience had heard many of them in the 1992 campaign, nevertheless wove elements of his biography into his discussion of policies. When he discussed his desire to reduce the use of drugs in the United States, Clinton spoke about the strain on his family that had been created by his brother's drug usage. When he discussed policies to strengthen American families, he spoke about the example that his own single mother had presented to him.

Both men also concluded on a biographical note. Dole concluded with oblique references to his humble upbringing and serious war injury by claiming that "my life is proof that America is a land without limits." Clinton concluded with a reference to his birthplace. "My fellow Americans, after these four, good, hard years, I still believe in a place called Hope, a place called America."

Throughout their addresses, both Dole and Clinton compared and contrasted themselves with the other. In so doing, they attacked each other. Along with the growth of personal campaigning, one of the most discussed characteristics of American campaigns in the last twenty years has been negative advertising. Candidates "go negative" not simply in their ads but also in their speeches. The tendency of candidates to "go negative" in their acceptance addresses has been well illustrated by Benoit, Wells, Pier, and Blaney.[45] In their study of the acceptance addresses of every major party candidate since 1960, they conclude that 27 percent of the statements found in acceptance addresses were attacks that portrayed the opposing candidate or party in an unfavorable light. Benoit, Wells, Pier, and Blaney found that Republicans tended to attack more than Democrats in these addresses, largely because the only presidential candidate who totally eschewed attacks was a Democrat, Hubert Humphrey. Not unsurprisingly, Benoit, Wells, Pier, and Blaney also found that challenger candidates used their nomination acceptance addresses to attack to a greater extent than incumbents. Moreover, these researchers also found that 60 percent of the attacks were directed specifically at the opposing candidate, 27 percent were directed at the opposing party, and 13 percent were directed toward both.

In 1996, Dole used both implicit and explicit attacks on Clinton. For example, he claimed, "And it must be said: Because of misguided priorities, there have been massive cuts in funding for our national security. I believe President Clinton has failed to adequately provide for our defense. And for whatever reason his neglect, it is irresponsible." Passages such as these were clear, explicit attacks on Clinton.

However, much of Dole's attack was implicit. As he claimed that "greatness lies not in what office you hold, but in how honest you are, how you face adversity, and in your willingness to stand fast in a hard place," he was virtually inviting his audience to compare his record with that of Clinton. His remark was likely designed to cause listeners to think about the way Clinton had handled adversity during the Vietnam era, the way Clinton had so quickly abandoned his liberal agenda after the 1994 elections and quickly reversed himself to support and sign dramatically more conservative legislation in 1995 and early 1996, and the ongoing investigations of several Clinton administration figures for alleged illegal activities. When Dole claimed that "the fundamental issue is not of policy, but of trust," he was implicitly asking the audience whether they trusted Clinton's explanations of such things as his draft dodging, his alleged sexual activities, and the oft-ridiculed explanation of his marijuana usage. Thus Dole, both explicitly and perhaps more effectively, implicitly, compared and contrasted himself to Clinton. Clinton claimed of his opponents that "I will not attack: I will not attack them personally, or permit others to do it in this party if I can prevent it." Given his checkered personal history, it is understandable why Clinton would want to avoid personal attacks. Hence, Clinton did not engage in any comparisons of personal characteristics as did Dole.

Rather, he limited his attacks to explicit attacks on Dole policies. He called Dole's economic proposals "a risky, $50 billion tax scheme" and made the contrast stark by observing that it was a worse proposal than the one "I vetoed last year." He praised his administration's efforts to curtail smoking and contrasted himself with Dole by observing "that battle [over antismoking legislation] is far from over and the two candidates have different views. I pledge to America's parents that I will see this effort all the way through." He drew a sharp contrast with Dole, the former Senate majority leader, when he claimed that when "the leaders of this Congress invited the polluters into the back room to roll back 25 years of environmental protection that both parties had always supported, I said no." He contrasted himself yet again to the Republican Congress in which Dole had served when he itemized several crime fighting proposals that Congress had rejected. "We need," claimed Clinton, "in short, the laws that Congress refused to pass. And I ask them again: Please, as an American, not a partisan matter, pass these laws now."

Thus, in their 1996 acceptance addresses, both major party candidates compared themselves to each other. Dole tended to utilize implicit comparisons, enabling him to tactfully stress personal characteristics. Clinton deliberately attempted to avoid comparisons of personal characteristics. Rather, he focused on explicit policy comparisions.

In sum, acceptance addresses are often among the most important speeches of a campaign. They are responses to a unique rhetorical situation that serve a variety of purposes beyond simply accepting a nomination and that may utilize at least six common strategies to fulfill those purposes.

NEWS CONFERENCES

Candidates universally complain of their lack of media coverage. But some events or statements that occur during the campaign are perceived by candidates and their staffs as uniquely important and especially deserving of media coverage. Such occasions often cause the candidate to call a news conference.

Situation for News Conferences

News conferences are normally occasioned by events or statements that the candidate feels warrant special attention. Ostensibly, they provide a means of making statements that will be passed on, through the media, to the public at large. The manner in which candidates communicate with the public at large underwent substantial change in 1992. Though the phenomena of bypassing the press and going directly to the public primarily through television talk shows such as *Larry King Live, Donahue, Oprah, Nightline, Good Morning America, Today, Tonight,* and others was most evident in the presidential campaign, widespread use of local television and radio shows in lower level races was also common. Again in 1996 candidates often went directly to the people through television talk shows. By 1996 the growth of 24-hour news/talk stations such as MSNBC, CNBC, Fox News, and others provided candidates more opportunities than ever before. Hence, the traditional importance of press conferences may be diminishing, as new technology and programming formats facilitate candidates' bypassing the press to speak directly to the public.

Nevertheless, though their importance may be diminishing somewhat, news conferences remain an important and recurring means of campaign communication. Part of that importance is derived from the fact that though the public is one audience in the news conference situation, at least four other audiences also exist: the candidates' rivals, their own staffs, political elites, and journalists. These five potential audiences exist for every news conference.[46] Moreover, on occasion, the candidate's remarks at a news conference are not meant primarily for the general public but for one or more of the other four audiences. It is through a news conference, ostensibly held for the public, that the candidate may also choose to address these other audiences.

News conferences are an exceptionally effective means of addressing an opponent. Candidates can exchange challenges, promises, or threats in private and by using third parties. But, if such messages are conveyed through a news conference, they take on a different dimension. A message to one's rival made publicly in the midst of a news conference clearly implies a degree of commitment that the same message conveyed privately lacks. By deliberately going on public record and calling unusual attention to the message, the candidate is telling the opponent that this is no idle challenge, promise, or threat, but rather a deadly serious message. The use of a news conference, more than virtually any other form of communication, conveys that seriousness and hence is occasionally used by candidates as a means of addressing one another.

Candidates may also use news conferences as a means of addressing their own staffs. As political scientist Leon Sigal has observed, "campaign organizations tend to combine decentralization at the bottom with inaccessibility at the top."[47] The decentralized group of supporters at the bottom of the campaign have infrequent and short contact with the candidate. A news conference presents the candidate with a forum to which the campaign organization will no doubt be attentive. Hence, messages aimed primarily at the candidate's organization may be transmitted through the news conference.

News conferences also serve the candidate by providing a means of addressing political elites. In prior years, as discussed in Chapter 1, campaign decisions were often made by relatively few individuals, often in private meetings to which the public had little access. The decline of political parties and changes in campaign financing have tended to increase the number of politically elite. In the past, candidates might have used a few meetings and phone calls to put out the word that they needed money, had dramatically spurted in the last poll, or had found a new campaign issue. Today, it would be difficult to contact all of those with whom a candidate might want to share this news. Hence, candidates may choose to use news conferences as a means of reaching political elites with information.

The use of news conferences to reach multiple audiences can be seen in the joint press conference held by then Vice President George Bush and Dan Quayle on August 17, 1988, the day after Bush announced that Quayle was his choice for vice president. Though many of questions and answers were predictable in this exceptionally well attended and covered conference, the exchanges on campaign tactics suggest Bush and Quayle's awareness of multiple audiences.

Question: I'd like to ask both of you gentlemen about the growing speculation Senator Quayle that you are going to lead the charge against the Democrats. And words like pit bull have been used and so forth. Without using those words, is that true? Are you going to be leading the charge against the Democrats?

Quayle: Well, that's a new description. I am going to be working with the Vice President in campaigning and articulating a very positive agenda of the future of the family and preserving our freedoms and preserving our hope and opportunity. Now obviously I intend to point out what would happen if the party of McGovern, Carter, Mondale and Dukakis would somehow get back in power. I think it would be a disaster.

Bush: Let me add since you addressed it to both of us. We're going to tell the truth and it's going to seem like they've engaged a couple of pit bulls because that's the way it's going to be. . . . And we will be telling the truth about where we want to lead this country, spelling out my priorities and Dan speaking to the issues. And trying to challenge the Democrats to do the same thing. Competence is important but ideology is very important and we're going to be talking on both.[48]

In this exchange Quayle immediately links Dukakis to McGovern, Carter, and Mondale. This linking might well have helped to galvanize the Republican campaign staff and Republican political elites into action. Though Bush could have no doubt simply gone on to the next question, he also choose to respond to this question. Significantly, he picked up on Quayle's response and extended it, claiming that this campaign would involve not simply competence, as Dukakis had asserted in the Democratic convention several weeks earlier, but more importantly, ideology. Like Quayle, Bush may have been speaking not only to the public at large but also to activist Republicans, and in this instance, perhaps to Dukakis as well. In their responses Quayle and Bush were serving notice that the Republican ticket would have a hand in framing the issues of this campaign and that those issues would involve ideology as well as competency. Each time in this press conference that Bush or Quayle was asked about campaign tactics they invariably claimed that this was a campaign of issues and ideology. This emphasis on issues and ideology was important for the public, but Bush and Quayle surely recognized that in stressing it they were also sending a message to their staffs, other Republican political elites, such as large contributors, Republican candidates, and campaign staffs, and perhaps to Dukakis as well.

Finally, candidates use news conferences as a means of influencing journalists. Those journalists who attend the news conference comprise the immediate audience. The candidate clearly seeks to influence what they disseminate and by so doing influence the many secondary audiences already discussed. Additionally, many news organizations may choose not to be represented at the news conference and fail to cover it. If candidates are newsworthy at the conference and if their remarks get good play in the media that is represented at the conference, the likelihood of increased media coverage of their campaign will be enhanced.

In sum, rhetorical situations in which candidates perceive the need to seek media coverage of their views for the purpose of better expressing them to the public, to rivals, to their own staffs, to political elites, and to journalists may frequently give rise to news conferences.

Purposes of News Conferences

News conferences serve three basic purposes. First, they are an avenue by which the candidate can get the attention of a variety of audiences. News conferences often serve this purpose better than alternatives, such as news releases. However, they should not be abused. National candidates and major regional and state candidates can often be assured of reasonable media attendance at any news conference they call, simply because of the importance of any statement being made by a potential president, senator, or governor. Incumbents also have an advantage in attracting the media, simply because news organizations routinely assign someone to cover state senators, state representatives, members of city councils, and administrative offices. Other candidates frequently have trouble getting media coverage of their campaigns. There are three reasons why properly used news conferences can increase coverage.

The first reason is novelty. The conference must be a reasonably unusual event. Candidates who are not overly newsworthy cannot expect the media to respond to daily announcements of press conferences. On the other hand, if they call conferences only a few times during the campaign, the very novelty may cause some news organizations to send representatives. Second, the conference should be called with a clearly newsworthy issue in mind. News organizations should be made aware of what the candidate will discuss. Unless the candidate has hard news and hopefully the data to support statements, news organizations may choose to ignore the conference. But if candidates are prepared to really make news that will be of interest to the readers, listeners, and viewers of the news organizations in their area, the news conference may be well covered.

For example, a recent congressional candidate, concerned about excessive government spending and what he believed to be unfair government intervention in strikes, linked these two issues together when a major employer in his district was struck during the campaign. He pointed out that federal government benefits would be given to these strikers. He noted that the strikers all had well-paying, skilled labor jobs and that they had voluntarily, by their own vote, given up those jobs to strike. The candidate questioned whether people who were voluntarily unemployed should be subsidized by the government. He cited federal employees and federal laws to explain in detail the benefits that these strikers would receive from the federal government, noting that it could well approach half a million dollars. This portion of his presentation was made with visually interesting aids for the benefit of television. He contrasted the government help that these strikers were receiving with the benefits received by people of his district who were physically disabled, could not work, and hence also received government aid. He claimed that the physically disabled should receive more money since they clearly needed it, while those who had voted to strike should not receive any government subsidy. Unlike the physically handicapped, they had well-paying jobs to which they could return at a moment's notice. He concluded by criticizing his opponent who had voted for much of the legislation that provided help to strikers.

This news conference was one of only three that the candidate called throughout the campaign. It was directly related to an important news story, a large strike that affected thousands of families in the district. It related this strike to a major difference in the position of the two candidates. Moreover, the candidate provided hard information by way of facts and figures on government programs, quotes from government officials, and the voting record of his opponent. The material was presented orally but also with an awareness of the needs of television. The novelty and newsworthiness of this conference resulted in extensive coverage for the candidate.

A final reason why news conferences can effectively serve to focus widespread attention on the candidate's message is that reporters consider them reliable. Reporters often express doubts about the reliability of press releases. But the reliability of news conferences, witnessed by many reporters, with the candidate's statements captured on both audio and video tape, cannot be doubted.

Thus the news conference can serve as an avenue through which the candidate is able to reach many audiences. Even candidates whom news-gathering organizations judge to be unworthy of much attention can gain some attention if they use news conferences properly.

A second important purpose served by news conferences is to allow the candidate to focus attention on one issue or a limited number of issues. As we discussed in Chapter 2, a major function of the press is to help set the campaign agenda. But the candidate also wants to help shape the agenda. By focusing remarks on one issue, the candidate is able to influence strongly what issue the media will cover. Using a press conference, but focusing the issues treated and stressed in that conference, is an effective means utilized by many candidates to help set the campaign agenda.

A final purpose served by news conferences is to establish and improve relationships between the candidate and individual members of the media. The more efficiently run the conference is, the more prepared and responsive the candidate is, the easier the job of the reporter becomes. Press conferences are one means by which candidates can make the job of reporters easier and in so doing improve relationships between themselves and the media. The chief purpose of news conferences—to allow candidates to bring their views to the attention of many audiences—may be readily apparent, but we should not ignore the other purposes served by press conferences: to allow the candidate to focus attention on one or a limited number of issues, presumably selected by the candidate to be of advantage to the candidate, and to enhance candidate-press relationships.

Strategies of News Conferences

Candidates attempt to use news conferences to their own advantage. One of the reasons they are used by candidates is to foster the illusion that candidates are not in control. C. Jack Orr has suggested that presidential news conferences can be thought of as "counterpoised situations" in which the reporters have competing obligations. They must both confront the president, and they must give deference to him.[49] To a lesser extent, the same counterpoised situation exists when reporters interview any office seeker. The candidate must be shown some deference as a responsible individual running for a responsible job. Moreover, the conference is, after all, the candidate's proceeding. Yet, reporters also may seek to confront, challenge, and criticize.

The candidate's control extends beyond the deference that may be extended by reporters. The control is real. The candidate decides when and where to hold a news conference. The candidate decides what format will be used. The candidate decides who will ask questions, and of course the candidate provides the answers. Scholars who have examined news conferences, such as Robert Denton and Dan Hahn, have concluded that while the situation may appear to be one in which the press has considerable control, ultimately it is the skilled respondent who controls the news conference.[50] Candidates exercise their control by utilizing one or more of at least 10 common strategies.

Since it is the candidates who call news conferences, they will do so to suit their own needs. Decisions by the candidate about the timing of news conferences are important, and determining when to call a conference is the candidate's first strategic decision. As indicated earlier, typically the fewer conferences called, the more attention the press will extend to those that are called. Calling a news conference to deal with a topic is a clear means of signaling not only that the candidate attaches major importance to this topic but also of increasing the treatment it receives in the media.

In addition, the candidate must consider the media that will attend and the deadlines with which they operate. Typically, candidates vary the time of day that they hold press conferences so that they are not slighting any of the media organizations serving their constituency. However, this too is a strategic decision. The candidate, by determining the time of day to hold the conference, can play favorites with the media.

A second consideration is where to hold it. Candidates may make their conferences visually interesting to audiences and hence especially appealing to television news organizations by holding them in visually appealing settings. The candidate who has promised to repair the roads and eliminate dangerous potholes might choose to hold the conference at the site of a recent fatal accident caused by poor roads.

Although George Bush held relatively few press conferences during the 1988 election, he used site selection to the utmost advantage when he attacked Michael Dukakis. For example, in his attempt to claim that Dukakis was weak on environmental issues, Bush visited the most polluted harbor in the nation, which just happened to be Boston Harbor, Dukakis's home city. Similarily, Bush subsequently discussed the environment and pollution with the press while visiting the New Jersey coast, off of which Governor Dukakis had proposed dumping sewage from Massachussets. By selecting these sites, Bush provided the media with visually appealing settings and focused the media's attention on the weaknesses of his opponent.

Candidates should keep in mind that sometimes a site might be highly visual, lending itself to television news, but it might be difficult and time consuming to reach. Such sites may cause radio and print media representatives to feel that a news conference is hardly worth their effort. Typically, candidates seek to balance their news conference site selections. Some are held with television in mind, while others are held in the campaign headquarters or some highly accessible central location. Whatever decision is made, the candidate can use the selection of a news conference site strategically to help fulfill overall purposes.

These first two strategic concerns involving news conferences, where and when to hold them, relate primarily to the candidate's goal of increasing news coverage. The second group of strategies can help focus the topic of the conference on the areas that the candidate wants covered and stressed in the media.

Candidates utilize at least five strategies to guarantee that the agenda-setting function of the media works in their favor when news organizations cover their press conferences. Perhaps the most commonly used of these strategies is to make an opening statement at the outset of the conference. Based on her studies of presidential press conferences and her experience as director of political coverage for ABC News, Carolyn Smith has suggested that opening statements are an exceptionally effective means of setting a press conference agenda if they are used at the outset of press conferences that involve reacting to a single major event or treating a single major policy.[51] Though this tactic seems commonplace today, Dwight Eisenhower was the first president who regularly made opening statements at his news conferences.[52] The opening statement should, in itself, be newsworthy. If it is, it will generally prompt questions on the issue it treats and be the focus of most reports of the news conference. Moreover, as Catherine Collins has illustrated in her examination of former Secretary of State Henry Kissinger's press conferences, if the interviewee assumes the role of the expert, defines the topic of immediate concern, develops a perspective from which events should be viewed, utilizes data to depict the event, and warns the media that other perspectives will not be considered acceptable, the chances are greatly increased that the interviewee's perspective will be reflected clearly in media accounts of the conference.[53]

Similarly, candiates may not only present opening statements, but they may also restructure questions. In restructuring a question, candidates are again generally attempting to focus attention onto key issues, from certain perspectives, in order to make their points better.

A third strategy frequently utilized by candidates to insure that news conferences focus on their agenda is to follow the advice of Republican political consultant Roger Ailes who recommends that candidates use the formula $Q = A + 1$ when responding to questions. Ailes explains that when asked a question (Q) his clients "reply briefly and directly with an answer (A). Then if it will help, add a point or points (+1) preferably from your agenda." One of his clients, Ailes continues,

a congressman, was asked by a reporter, "You were pressured by the big chemical companies not to introduce that legislation weren't you?" That's the question. The congressman answered, "I met with everyone involved in the issue, including the environmentalists, the consumer groups and the companies." Then he added [+1] "Based on these discussions, all the parties agreed that the industry would set new standards rather than Congress passing a law."[54]

A fourth strategy utilized to make sure candidates are able to focus the conference on their topics and from their perspective is to plant questions. This tactic was commonplace in the presidential press conferences of Eisenhower and Johnson.[55] It has been used by many candidates for public office. Typically, a staff member approaches a reporter and suggests a question that might be asked, noting that it will no doubt produce a newsworthy response. Obviously, many reporters may not choose to be used in this fashion. But others will, perceiving the suggested question as a means of drawing attention to something that is newsworthy, which is just what the candidate also wants. The ethics of restructuring questions and planting questions is certainly open for debate. But clearly they are strategies that are utilized by many interviewees, including political candidates, who wish to limit the focus of news conferences.

The final strategy, utilized primarily to focus the news conference, is selective recognition of reporters. Candidates recognize those who question them, but they can fail to recognize those who wish to question them. Most of the time, recognition is haphazard. But it can also be done in a deliberate fashion. A survey of the White House press corps found that "the random selection of questioners by the President" was among the most serious problems associated with White House news conferences.[56] News conferences held by candidates for lesser office will not draw the massive number of reporters that a White House news conference attracts. But any conference that draws a reasonable sample of the media is one in which a candidate might selectively recognize reporters.

Candidates normally hold news conferences when they seek extensive coverage of their views. Typically, they have a limited number of issues on which they wish to focus in the news conference and that they hope the public will learn of through the efforts of the journalists in attendance. To insure that these topics are clearly the centerpieces of the news conference, candidates often assume the role of the expert, utilizing an opening statement that spells out their position on issues and indicates the perspective on the issue that they find satisfactory. They may also choose to restructure questions, consistently add comments from their agenda to answers ($Q = A + 1$), plant questions, and selectively recognize reporters. All these strategies are done primarily to enable candidates to stress their issues and prevent the conference from dealing with other issues. However, as Smith points out, reporters attend press conferences to address their own agendas of what is newsworthy, not to serve as a foil for the individual holding the conference. [57]

Three final strategies can be utilized by most candidates in news conferences. First is to prepare. Candidates differ in the manner of their preparation for news conferences. However, most attempt to anticipate questions that might be asked and prepare responses. Presidents, such as Truman and Kennedy, typically rehearse for news conferences by reviewing 40 to 75 possible questions that might arise in their press conferences.[58] Most candidates follow similar procedures. They rely on their staffs to generate possible questions and then prepare responses.

Second, if the conference starts to go bad, the candidate can filibuster. Typically, press conferences are called for specific time periods. The press has deadlines and the candidate has a full schedule. Hence, if their conferences are going poorly, some candidates will take considerable time in answering questions, particularly those that they are comfortable with and deal with topics they wish to address. By so doing, they reduce the opportunity the press has for further questioning.

Finally, candidates often attempt to appear vulnerable in press conferences. Given the many controls and strategies available to candidates who utilize news conferences, it may be easy to forget that there are other actors in this situation. President Carter's television advisor noted that even though the news conference is in effect a theater in which the president called upon reporters to play their supporting roles, "it is important that the President appear vulnerable."[59] Similarly, most candidates wish to appear vulnerable in news conference situations. The desire to appear vulnerable often motivates the use of the news conference. It is one of the reasons why candidates will utilize "risky" news conferences, rather than safer press releases, audios, or other forms of communication with the public. The appearance that the candidate is taking a chance and is vulnerable is one that most candidates believe the public admires. The news conference situation suggests openness and honesty, as well as confidence in one's ability, that candidates are rarely able to attain through the use of other forms of communication.

The symbiotic relationship that exists between candidates and journalists is, perhaps, nowhere more evident than in the news conference. News conferences are called by candidates seeking widespread coverage of their views. They are attended by representatives of news organizations who sense that the conference may produce newsworthy material. Both candidates and reporters have an interest in aiding one another. But candidates are not only desirous of creating news, they are also desirous of influencing and persuading. Hence, most candidates utilize a variety of strategies attempting to insure that their conferences are indeed covered and that the conferences focus on those issues that the candidates wish to focus upon. Moreover, though they prepare in order not to be vulnerable and weak, they recognize that a format that suggests their vulnerability may be desirable.

APOLOGIAS

An increasingly recurring form of speech that many candidates have recently found necessary to deliver is the apologia. In this section, we will examine the situations that create apologias and in so doing perhaps also gain an understanding of why they have been on the increase in recent years. We will also examine the major purposes of such speeches and the strategies utilized to attain those purposes.

Situation for Apologias

Apologias are speeches made by candidates who find it necessary to apologize for some statement or behavior. Typically, the statement or behavior implies a serious flaw in the candidate's character, one that if widely accepted by the public would prevent the candidate from winning office. In 1984 Jesse Jackson's anti-Semitic remarks, characterizing Jews as "Hymies" and New York City as "Hymietown," were offensive not simply to Jews but also suggested that Jackson could not equitably and fairly govern a racially, ethnically, and religiously diverse nation such as the United States.

Similarly, in 1992 Bill Clinton was the subject of widespread rumors that he engaged in numerous affairs while governor of Arkansas, the most infamous of which was alleged to have lasted for 12 years and been with a former Little Rock newswoman, Gennifer Flowers. If such rumors and accusations proved true, Clinton, at that point in time simply one of several candidates for the Democratic party nomination, was in grave trouble. With relatively few people familiar with Clinton and his candidacy, charges of this sort would suggest to many that Clinton lacked the integrity, honesty, and other qualities of character desired in national leaders.

Apologias have become an increasingly more common feature of recent campaigns for two reasons. First, the news media seem more prone then ever before to report on the candidate's weaknesses and flaws. Gone are the days when Franklin Delano Roosevelt could dictate that he never be photographed in leg braces or being carried by his aides. Gone are the days when the candidate's private life was not discussed. The press is far more unsparing of candidates today. Additionally, one of the legacies of Watergate has apparently been to sensitize the public to the personal integrity of candidates. During the Clinton administration the President's personal integrity has come under frequent attack. Clinton has acknowledged inappropriate sexual behavior and has also been held in contempt of court. He has been accused of perjury, obstruction of justice, and violating campaign finance laws. Though he remains in office after being impeached by the House of Representatives and undergoing a Senate trial, Clinton's difficulties have likely resensitized both press interest and public interest in the personal character of political figures.

Purposes of Apologias

Apologias serve to enable the candidate to explain some statement or behavior that casts doubt on the candidate's suitability for office. To accomplish this explanation, with the least amount of damage to their image, candidates often have three purposes in mind when they deliver apologias.

First, they hope to explain the behavior or statement in a positive light. In so doing, they hope to minimize damage to their character and image. If the incident that triggered the need for the apologia cannot be explained positively, the second purpose of the apologia may be considered. The candidate can at least justify behavior. Again, by so doing, the candidate hopes to minimize damage to character and image.

The final purpose of an apologia is to remove the topic from public discussion. Ellen Reid Gold has pointed out that, at least with major national figures, frequently reporters repeat the charges against a candidate so often that it is difficult for the candidate not to appear guilty.[60] Day after day, the candidate is seen denying the charge. The proliferation of media has compounded this problem. With a host of relatively new 24-hour-a-day cable news networks, the growth of 24-hour-a-day talk radio stations, and a host of new politically oriented publications, the "feeding frenzy" of the press is greater today than ever before. To the extent that an apologia can put an end to questioning and allow the campaign to move on to other issues, it has served a vital purpose.

Strategies of Apologias

Rhetoricians have identified six strategies commonly utilized by speakers delivering apologias. Not every strategy can be used in every apologia, but all six have been used frequently. First, apologias are often best delivered in settings where individuals other than the candidate seem in control.[61] Many early apologias were delivered in settings where the candidate seemed to be in complete control. For example, Richard Nixon's 1952 Checkers address, following charges that Nixon benefited from a slush fund set up by wealthy supporters, and Ted Kennedy's 1969 Address to the People of Massachusetts, following the incident at Chappaquiddick, in which Kennedy's car went off a bridge and a young woman died, were both made by men who had purchased air time and were in complete control of what was said. However, as Sherry Butler points out in contrasting these two addresses, by 1969 mass media viewers were "more sophisticated, less likely to place automatic belief in the magic power of the television tube, more likely to question."[62] Additionally, the legacies of Vietnam, Watergate, and the Clinton scandals include voter disenchantment with less than honest officials. Both of these facts, growing voter sophistication in using media, and growing voter disenchantment with public figures, have contributed to changes in the early apologia, typified by Richard Nixon's Checkers address.

Rather than an address such as Nixon's in which the candidate is in complete control of the setting, candidates today often deliver their apologias in settings that appear to be controlled by others. For example, the best known political apologia of recent years is no doubt that delivered by Bill Clinton in response to the accusations that he had conducted a 12-year affair with Gennifer Flowers. Significantly, Clinton's apologia was delivered on a special edition of CBS's *60 Minutes*, one of the nation's most respected investigative TV shows. Viewers no doubt were aware that Clinton and his wife were not in control of the situation as they responded to questions from correspondent Steve Kroft, who appeared to control the interview. When Clinton saw the broadcast, he is reported to have been "furious," claiming that the interview was "a screw job."[63] As Clinton's appearance on *60 Minutes* illustrates, appearing in a setting where one does not have complete control involves risk. However, many contemporary candidates choose to take this risk, believing that public sophistication with media and alienation from leaders make this an acceptable risk that must be taken if their message is to be appreciated.

A second strategy utilized by candidates delivering apologias is to simply deny the "alleged facts, sentiments, objects, or relationships" that give rise to the charge.[64] If the candidate cannot deny the substance of the charge, one can deny the intent, arguing that the statement or action has been misunderstood.[65] Kroft opened his *60 Minutes* interview by observing that Gennifer Flowers "is alleging and has described in some detail in a supermarket tabloid what she calls a 12 year affair with you."[66] As Kroft finished his statement Clinton jumped in. "That allegation is false." He went on to suggest that though as a public figure in Little Rock he had known Flowers when she was a TV reporter in the same city, her story was a total fabrication, which she no doubt made up for the payment she received from the tabloid.[67] As the interview progressed Kroft again offered Clinton an opportunity to deny the alleged affair. "I am assuming from your answer," said Kroft, "that you are categorically denying that you ever had an affair with Gennifer Flowers." The camera showed Clinton nodding his head affirmatively as Kroft spoke and then declaring "I said that before."

Though Clinton clearly denied having an affair with Gennifer Flowers, he did not deny the possibility of other infidelities. At one point he acknowledged that "I have caused pain in my marriage." Kroft responded by stating, "Your answer is not a denial is it?" Clinton responded: "Of course it is not." Thus, while Clinton's denial might resolve the charges of Gennifer Flowers, he did not attempt to deny all of the rumors about his infidelity. Clinton's response to the broader issue of infidelity utilized several additional strategies common to apologias.

A third strategy frequently used in apologias is what B. L. Ware and Wil Linkugel characterize as "bolstering strategies." Bolstering strategies are attempts by the candidate to identify "with something viewed favorably by the audience."[68] Clinton made use of bolstering when he attempted to make a virtue out of his inability to totally deny the accusations of marital infidelity. "I have acknowledged wrongdoing. I have acknowledged causing pain in my marriage. I have said things tonight and to the American people from the beginning that no American politician ever has." Repeatedly Clinton and his wife claimed that they had "leveled" with the American public and had been "candid" with the American public. Clearly Clinton was attempting to bolster his case by claiming to display character traits viewed favorably by the audience—candor and honesty. To the extent that Clinton might make his candor and honesty in dealing with charges of infidelity the focus of audience attention, rather than the infidelity itself, he was likely to successfully bolster his case.

Clinton's apologia was unusual because of the presence and statements of a second individual, his wife, Hillary. Throughout the interview the couple was seated side-by-side, and as one spoke, the camera, for the most part, remained focused on both of them. Both Hillary Clinton's presence at her husband's side and her statements in defense of him may have fulfilled bolstering functions for the governor. Mrs. Clinton's presence and active defense of her husband suggested a solid marriage that had endured stress. Clinton observed that "my wife and I are still in love with each other, we have a stronger marriage than most people who have never had to survive the trials and tribulations of a challenging marriage. As most married Americans will acknowledge, marriage is a hard institution. But it is a better alternative to divorce that is prevalent in our society." To the extent that Americans associated the Clinton's with people who had successfully resolved troublesome issues in their marriage, they bolstered their own case by identifying themselves with a second set of qualities typically admired by most Americans, the determination and ability to work through a troubled relationship, rather than abandon it.

A fourth strategy frequently used in political apologias is differentiation. Ware and Linkugel define differentiation strategies as "separating some fact, sentiment, object, or relationship from some larger context within which the audience presently views that attribute."[69] As Gold notes, "in political campaigns, the candidate may try not only to redefine the larger context for the audience, but to separate himself symbolically from the accusation by attacking the source."[70]

Attacks on the source have become increasingly common in political apologias. Kathryn M. Olson offers an incisive explanation of why this tactic has become widely used, though as she observes, it is a "strategy near last resort."[71] Olson claims that in recent years, in part because of the growing dominance of television as a news media, the blending of journalism and entertainment, and the economic realities of the contemporary news media, journalists have faced growing tension between "objective" reporting, and "adversarial" reporting. Candidates can exploit that tension to their advantage by utilizing what Olson has characterized as role imbalance attacks. That is, candidates can suggest that journalists have crossed the line between objective reporting and treated them in a harshly adversarial fashion, thereby exacerbating, exaggerating, or otherwise inappropriately reporting the charges against the candidate.

Repeatedly the Clintons utilized differentation and role imbalance attacks as they attempted to differentiate the questions of infidelity from the context of Clinton's fitness for office and place it within the context of the right to privacy. If the public viewed infidelity as an issue pertinent to the right of privacy, rather than one pertinent to presidential fitness, then Clinton's role imbalance attacks on the press were also pertinent and potentially persuasive.

Olson claims that for role imbalance attacks to succeed the accused "must not appear totally self-serving" and hence must suggest "that the news media's role imbalance has negative implications for someone in addition to him- or herself." Clinton's strongest attempt to do this is his last remark in the interview. He claims that "this will test the character of the press. It is not only my character that is being tested." Clearly he is suggesting that the press coverage of him is really a test of the press's objectivity and that both the press and the entire public will suffer if the press continues it's unobjectively imbalanced adversarial treatment of him.

Similarly, Olson claims that for role imbalance attacks on the press to succeed the accused must indicate that press coverage "threatens the democratic system and/or hurts innocent individuals." Both Clinton and his wife made accusations of this type during their interview. Clinton claimed that "the press has to decide if it is going to engage in a game of 'got you' " and went on to add that the excessively imbalanced adversarial attacks he had already endured made it impossible for him to defend himself. "No matter what I say," asserted Clinton, "to pretend the press will then let this die, we are kidding ourselves. This has become a virtual cottage industry." Clinton portrayed the press as engaging in unfair, imbalanced adversarial reporting from which it profited. His wife suggested that many innocent individuals, not simply the Clintons, would suffer if the press continued in this type of behavior, observing that "I think it is real dangerous in this country if we don't have some zone of privacy for everybody."

Thus, the Clintons used differentiation strategies to move questions about his maritial infidelity out of the context of presidential fitness and into the context of the right of privacy. Placing the charges against him in the context of the right of privacy then facilitated the Clinton's use of role imbalance attacks on the press.

The fifth type of strategy found·in political apologias is what Ware and Linkugel have called the transcendental strategy. This kind of strategy "cognitively joins some fact, sentiment, object, or relationship with some larger context within which the audience does not presently view that attribute."[72] Such strategies "psychologically move the audience away from the particulars of the charge at hand in a direction toward some more abstract, general view of his character."[73] The combined effect of the Clinton's strategies, if successful, would serve this purpose. That is, if the Clintons were able to get the public thinking about the courage they had in appearing on *60 Minutes*, their candor and honesty in "leveling" with the American public about the difficulties they had experienced in their marriage, their perserverance in working through the troubles of their marriage, and the press abuses of their rights to privacy, then these more abstract general issues, not Clinton's character, as reflected specifically in charges of infidelity, would be the focus of attention.

The final strategy that political figures have utilized in their apologias is to confess. If the candidate is guilty, a quick confession may put the unwinnable issue generating the apologia behind the candidate and let the campaign progress to other issues. In 1984, Jesse Jackson's attitudes toward Jews became the focal point of 14 days worth of news coverage about his campaign, at the very outset of the critical first primary in New Hampshire. Finally, on the fourteenth day, rejecting the advice of his staff, Jackson spoke to a Jewish audience at Temple Adath Yeshurun in Manchester, New Hampshire, confessed to making the derogatory statements that had given rise to the controversy, and observed that "however innocent and unintentional, it was insensitive and it was wrong. In part, I am to blame, and for that I am deeply distressed."[74] With that confession, Jackson was finally able to put the controversy behind him and return to other issues. Moreover, the issue never surfaced in Jackson's 1988 campaign.

Similarly, though Clinton denied a long-standing affair with Gennifer Flowers, he never flatly denied having had extramarital affairs. Most Americans, including moderator Steve Kroft interpreted his remarks about having caused "pain" in his marriage essentially as a confession of infidelity.[75] Having so confessed, there was little more that the press could pursue on this story. Moreover, combined with the other attempts discussed earlier to put the most favorable light on his extramarital affairs, and combined with his criticism of the press, this confession helped caused this story to drop out of the campaign early in the Democratic primaries.

The situation Clinton faced in 1998, when he was accused of having had an affair with a 21-year-old White House intern, Monica Lewinsky, was substantially more complex than the situation that typically gives rise to a campaign apologia. First, the accusations were not made in the context of a political campaign. Clinton was president at the time of the affair and much of the affair took place in the White House. Second, campaign apologias rarely involve statements or behavior that can provoke legal action. Clinton, who ultimately acknowledged lying about his affair, was alleged to have done so under oath, while testifying in the sexual harassment case brought by Paula Jones. The legal dimensions of this situation distinguish it from most occasions that give rise to campaign apologias. Third, many of the strategies associated with apologias presume that the candidate is innocent, or that at the least there is doubt about the candidate's guilt. Those strategies were essentially denied to Clinton with the presence of physical evidence of his affair in the form of Monica Lewinsky's famed semen-stained dress and his subsequent statements on August 17, 1998 acknowledging his actions. In at least these three critical respects, this situation differs sharply from those that normally give rise to campaign apologias.

In sum, apologias seem to be characterized by the use of one or more of six strategies. Increasingly, candidates are making their apologias in situations over which they do not have full control. Moreover, they are using denial, bolstering, differentiation, transcendental and confessional strategies to carry out their apologias.

Apologias did not seem to have been a common form of political speech until relatively recently. Contemporary stress on the character of candidates and the aggressiveness of contemporary journalists seems, in recent years, to have created far more situations calling for apologias than ever before. It is likely that apologias will be a feature of American political rhetoric for years to come.

CONCLUSIONS

In this chapter, we have observed that most campaigns are marked by similar, comparable, or analogous situations that require a rhetorical response. The responses to four such situations take the form of announcement of candidacy speeches, nomination acceptance addresses, news conferences, and apologias. We have examined the situations that give rise to these types of presentations, the purposes of such presentations, and the major strategies employed in each type of presentation.

NOTES

1. Lloyd Bitzer, "The Rhetorical Situation," *Philosophy and Rhetoric* 1 (January 1968): 6.

2. Karlyn Kohrs Campbell and Kathleen Hall Jamieson, "Form and Genre in Rhetorical Criticism: An Introduction," in *Form and Genre: Shaping Rhetorical Action*, ed. Karlyn Kohrs Campbell and Kathleen Hall Jamieson (Falls Church, Va.: Speech Communication Association, 1977), p. 15.

3. Judith S. Trent, "Presidential Surfacing: The Ritualistic and Crucial First Act," *Communication Monographs* 45 (November 1978): 281–92.

4. See for example, Hamilton Jordan, "Memo of August 4, 1974 to Jimmy Carter," in *Running for President: A Journal of the Carter Campaign*, ed. Martin Schram (New York: Pocket Books, 1977), p. 416.

5. B. Drummond Ayres, "Wilson in Presidential Race," *Cincinnati Enquirer*, August 28, 1995, p. A2.

6. Ronald Brownstein, "Casual Alexander Makes '96 Bid Formal," *Cincinnati Enquirer*, March 1, 1996, p. A2.

7. Shortly before Dukakis announced his 1988 candidacy, *Boston Globe* political columnist David Nyhan claimed that Kennedy might well be ready to run for the presidency again in 1992 and that Massachussetts' junior United States Senator, John Kerry, was looking to 1996. If one believes this scenario, and certainly Dukakis and his advisors were aware of it, then 1988 loomed as the only year in which Dukakis could run and be assured of the unified support of the Massachussets Democratic organization from the outset. See *The Winning of the*

White House, ed. Donald Morrison (New York: Time Incorporated, 1988), pp. 125–26.

8. Trent, "Presidential Surfacing," p. 284.

9. Bertram W. Gross, "The Announcement Speeches of Democratic Candidates for the 1992 Presidential Nomination," paper presented at the Speech Communication Association Annual Convention, October 29, 1992, p. 25.

10. Ayres, "Wilson in Presidential Race," p. A2.

11. Friedenberg interview with Dorothy Christtenson, Administrative Assistant, Councilwoman Bobbie Stern, January 19, 1983.

12. Kenneth P. O'Donnell and David F. Powers, *Johnny, We Hardly Knew Ye* (New York: Pocket Books, 1977), p. 416.

13. Ayres, "Wilson in Presidential Race," p. A2. This article was written for the *New York Times* which then syndicated it to other papers such as those in Cincinnati.

14. See the Kennedy and Carter responses in *The Candidates 1980: Where They Stand* (Washington, D.C.: American Enterprise Institute, 1980). Also see Robert V. Friedenberg, "Why Teddy Wasn't Ready: An Examination of the Speaking of Senator Edward Moore Kennedy During the 1980 Presidential Primaries," paper presented at the Ohio Speech Association, October 1980, pp. 3–4.

15. These quotations and the discussion of this address in these paragraphs are based on Robert Dole, "Campaign Announcement Speech, Topeka, Kansas, April 10, 1995." Dole's announcement speech was posted on the Internet in a variety of sources including ElectionLine and the Dole for President home page.

16. Dole, "Campaign Announcement Speech."

17. The Clinton campaign worked assiduously during 1995 and early 1996 to prevent a primary challenge to Clinton. Harold Ickes headed the campaign's efforts, which were directed primarily at Jesse Jackson and secondarily at Senators Bill Bradley and Bob Kerry. Ickes worked to dry up the contributor base for any challenger candidate among the normal Democratic constituency and to secure the endorsements of what might have been Jackson's core supporters, America's big city black mayors. The success of this effort was startling, given Clinton's weakened position in the wake of the health-care debacle and the Republican landslide in the 1994 elections. Thus, many of the purposes for delivering an announcement address did not apply to Clinton in the primary months, and his campaign simply decided an announcement address was unnecessary, given that all the other trappings of his reelection campaign were in place. See Roger Simon, *Showtime: The American Political Circus and the Race for the White House* (New York: Random House, 1998), pp. 135–54.

18. Perhaps because of a sense that the public expects modesty from candidates, often this theme is not as directly stated as the other two. Rather, candidates speak of "our administration," as though they have already been elected. They speak of the inspiration they have received from their families, their supporters, the people, and God. In so doing candidates obliquely suggest that no opponent could defeat them. See Robert V. Friedenberg, "Form and Genre in Announcement of Candidacy Addresses," paper presented at the Temple University Fourth Annual Conference on Discourse Analysis: Form and Genre in Political Discourse," March 1983, pp. 13–14.

244   POLITICAL CAMPAIGN COMMUNICATION

19. Gramm is quoted in Joe Klein, "They're Back," *Newsweek*, March 6, 1995, p. 26.

20. For a thorough history of Democratic acceptance addresses, see Chapters 2 and 3 of David B. Valley, *A History and Analysis of Democratic Presidential Nomination Acceptance Speeches to 1968* (Lanham, Md.: University Press of America, 1988). A more concise history can be found in Valley's "Significant Characteristics of Democratic Presidential Nomination Acceptance Speeches," *Central States Speech Journal* 25 (Spring 1974): 56–60.

21. Thomas B. Farrell, "Political Conventions as Legitimation Ritual," *Communication Monographs* 45 (November, 1978): 293–305; and Kurt W. Ritter, "American Political Rhetoric and the Jeremiad Tradition: Presidential Nomination Acceptance Addresses, 1960–1976," *Central States Speech Journal* 31 (Fall 1980): 153–71.

22. For discussions of these purposes see Robert O. Nordvold, "Rhetoric as Ritual: Hubert H. Humphrey's Acceptance Address at the 1968 Democratic National Convention," *Today's Speech* 18 (Winter 1970): 34; Valley, "Nomination Acceptance Speeches," p. 60; and Ritter, "American Political Rhetoric," p. 155.

23. See the first paragraphs of their respective acceptance addresses. Robert Dole, "Acceptance Address to the Republican National Convention," August 15, 1996. This and all subsequent references to and quotations from Dole's acceptance address are taken from the transcript available at http://www.politicsnow.com/news/Aug96/15/apol85doletext/#top. Bill Clinton, "Acceptance Address to the Democratic National Convention," August 29, 1996. This and all subsequent references to or quotations from Clinton's address are taken from the transcript available at http://www.msnbc.com/specials/newsarchive/convention/26249.asp.

24. Valley, "Nomination Acceptance Speeches," p. 61.

25. Ibid.

26. Kurt Ritter, "The 1996 Presidential Nomination Acceptance Addresses: What Do the Speeches by Dole and Clinton Tell Us about the Genre of Acceptance Speeches?" paper presented at the annual meeting of the Speech Communication Association, San Diego, November 1996, p. 2.

27. Ibid., p. 1.

28. Ibid., pp. 1–3.

29. George Bush, "Transcript of Bush Accepting the Nomination for Another Four Years," *New York Times*, August 21, 1992, p. A14.

30. Clinton and Gore, *Putting People First*, pp. 218–22.

31. Though Dole hoped to campaign, in part, on his integrity and character, at the very time he was preparing this address rumors concerning the nasty treatment he had shown his first wife at the time of their divorce began to circulate. Dole may have felt it inappropriate, considering the possible "skeletons" in his own closet, to be harshly critical. Moreover, throughout his career he had evidenced an ability to compromise with Democrats including Clinton. Additionally, throughout the campaign he attempted to show respect for the office of the president. All of these factors likely contributed to his avoiding harsh attacks.

32. During his first administration Clinton had worked with Dole frequently and found him more cooperative than the other Republican congressional leader with whom he had to work, Congressman Newt Gingrich. The relationship be-

tween the men, and Dole's refusal to engage in harsh attacks in his acceptance address, made it easier for Clinton to do the same when he addressed the Democratic convention two weeks later.

33. Nordvold, "Rhetoric as Ritual," p. 34.

34. William L Benoit, William J. Wells, P. M. Pier, and Joseph R. Blaney, "Acclaiming, Attacking, and Defending in Presidential Nominating Acceptance Addresses, 1960–1996," *Quarterly Journal of Speech* (in press): 21–23. The authors wish to thank Benoit and his associates for providing us with an advance copy of this work. The pagination cited in this and other references to this work refer to the advance copy.

35. Ritter, "American Political Rhetoric," pp. 157–64.

36. Dole, "Acceptance Address."

37. Ritter, "American Political Rhetoric," pp. 161–62.

38. Clinton, "Acceptance Address."

39. Valley, *A History and Analysis of Democratic Presidential Nomination Acceptance Speeches to 1968*, p. 60.

40. Ritter, "American Political Rhetoric," p. 162.

41. Clinton, "Acceptance Address."

42. Jimmy Carter, "Acceptance Speech, Democratic National Convention, August 14, 1980," in *The Pursuit of the Presidency 1980*, ed. Richard Harwood (New York: Berkley Books, 1980), p. 402.

43. Clinton and Gore, *Putting People First*, pp. 229–30.

44. Wayne Fields, *Union of Words: A History of Presidential Eloquence* (New York: Free Press, 1996), p. 72.

45. Benoit, Wells, Pier, and Blaney, "Acclaiming, Attacking, and Defending in Presidential Nominating Acceptance Addresses, 1960–1996." The information discussed in this paragraph is drawn from pp. 16–17 and 21.

46. This analysis of news conference audiences is adapted from Leon V. Sigal, "Newsmen and Campaigners: Organization Men Make the News," *Political Science Quarterly* 93 (Fall 1978): 466–67.

47. Ibid., p. 466.

48. "Transcript of Debut News Conference by Bush-Quayle Ticket," *New York Times*, August 18, 1988, p. A22.

49. C. Jack Orr, "Reporters Confront the President: Sustaining a Counterpoised Situation," *Quarterly Journal of Speech* 66 (February 1980): 17–21.

50. Most such examinations have focused on presidential news conferences, but the rationales for the conclusions, as well as the conclusions themselves, seem appropriate for most political candidates. See Robert E. Denton and Dan F. Hahn, eds., *Presidential Communication* (New York: Prager, 1986), p. 252; Michael Grossman and Martha Kumar, *Portraying the President: The White House and the News Media* (Baltimore: Johns Hopkins University Press, 1981), pp. 243–44; Orr, "Reporters Confront the President," pp. 31–32; and Delbert McQuire, "Democracy's Confrontation: The Presidential Press Conference," *Journalism Quarterly* 44 (Winter 1967): 638–44.

51. Carolyn Smith, *Presidential Press Conferences: A Critical Approach* (New York: Praeger, 1990), p. 81.

52. Peter M. Sandman, David M. Rubin, and David B. Sachsman, *Media: An*

Introductory Analysis of American Mass Communications (Englewood Cliffs, N.J.: Prentice-Hall, 1972), p. 344.

53. Catherine Ann Collins, "Kissinger's Press Conferences, 1972–1974: An Exploration of Form and Role Relationship on News Management," *Central States Speech Journal* 28 (Fall 1977): 190–93.

54. Roger Ailes, *You Are the Message: Secrets of the Master Communicators* (Homewood, Ill.: Dow Jones–Irwin, 1988), pp. 154–55.

55. Grossman and Kumar, *Portraying the President*, p. 248.

56. McQuire, "Democracy's Confrontation," p. 640.

57. Smith, *Presidential Press Conferences*, p. 89. Though Smith's observations deal directly with presidential press conferences, many of her comments on agendas seem entirely appropriate for press conferences held in the course of political campaigns.

58. A. L. Lorenze, Jr., "Truman and the Press Conference," *Journalism Quarterly* 43 (Winter 1966): 673–75; and Harry P. Kerr, "The President and the Press," *Western Speech* 27 (Fall 1963): 220–21.

59. Barry Jogoda quoted in Grossman and Kuman, *Portraying the President*, p. 243.

60. Ellen Reid Gold, "Political Apologia: The Ritual of Self Defense," *Communication Monographs* 45 (November 1978): 311–12.

61. Ibid., p. 311.

62. Sherry Devereaux Butler, "The Apologia, 1971 Genre," *Southern Speech Communication Journal* 37 (Spring 1972): 283.

63. The morning after the interview broadcast, Clinton is reported to have claimed that "It was a screw job. They [*60 Minutes* producers/editors] lied about how long it was going to be. They lied about what was going to be discussed. They lied about what the ending would be. It couldn't have been worse if they had drawn black X's through our faces." Quoted in "How He Won: The Untold Story of Bill Clinton's Triumph," *Newsweek* (Special Election Issue dated November/December 1992), p. 34.

64. B. L. Ware and Wil A. Linkugel, "They Spoke in Defense of Themselves: On the General Criticism of Apologia," *Quarterly Journal of Speech* 59 (October 1973): 25.

65. Gold, "Political Apologia," p. 308.

66. This and all other direct quotes drawn from this *60 Minutes* episode have been transcribed directly from the videotape of the *60 Minutes* broadcast of January 28, 1994.

67. Flowers was reported to have received $150,000 for her story from the *Star*.

68. Ware and Linkugel, "They Spoke in Defense of Themselves," p. 277.

69. Ibid., p. 278.

70. Gold, "Political Apologia," p. 308.

71. This and all subsequent references are to Kathryn M. Olson, "Exploiting the Tension between the News Media's 'Objective' and Adversarial Roles: The Role of Imbalance Attack and Its Use of the Implied Audience," *Communication Quarterly* 42 (Winter 1994): 36–56.

72. Ware and Linkugel, "They Spoke in Defense of Themselves," p. 280.

73. Ibid.

74. Quoted in Jack Germond and Jules Witcover, *Wake Us When It's Over: Presidential Politics of 1984* (New York: Macmillan, 1985), p. 159.

75. In January of 1998, giving a sworn deposition in the Paula Jones case, Clinton acknowledged having had a sexual relationship on one occasion with Gennifer Flowers. Clinton's defenders observed that in 1992 he had denied a 12-year affair and claimed that his statement made under oath did not contradict his 1992 claim.

Chapter 8

Debates in Political Campaigns

In the summer of 1858, one of the most remarkable local political campaigns in U.S. history was being waged on the plains of Illinois. The 1858 Illinois Senate race was remarkable for many reasons. Few races, regardless of office, bring together two such outstanding public servants as those competing for the Senate seat from Illinois in 1858. Few races, regardless of office, have had as profound an impact on our national history as did the race for the Illinois Senate seat in 1858. Few races have produced such masterpieces of campaign oratory as those produced on the plains of Illinois in the summer of 1858. For in that year, Abraham Lincoln and Stephen Douglas vied for the Senate seat from Illinois.

On July 24, Lincoln challenged Douglas to a series of debates. Douglas accepted. As the front-runner in what was anticipated to be a close election, Douglas dictated the terms. He suggested seven debates and demanded the opportunity to both open and close four of the debates. Lincoln would open and close only three. Lincoln accepted, and thus ensued what the *New York Tribune* called "a mode of discussing political questions which might well be more generally adopted."[1]

Though the Lincoln–Douglas debates were the first significant political campaign debates in U.S. history, as Jamieson and Birdsell remind us, they were not the first American political campaign debates.[2] Moreover, unlike their successors, they were real debates rather than joint speeches or joint press conferences. Most authorities would agree with J. Jeffery Auer when he argues that there are five essential elements for a true debate. "A debate," claims Auer, "is (1) a confrontation, (2) in equal and adequate time, (3) of matched contestants, (4) on a stated proposition, (5) to gain an audience decision."[3] Auer points out that "each of these elements is essential if we are to have a true debate. Insistence upon their recognition is more than mere pedantry, for each one has contributed to the vitality of the debate tradition."[4]

The Lincoln–Douglas debates were not followed by many other debates. It was not until a century later, in 1960, that we next had "Great Debates" of comparable significance. However, the 1960 presidential debates between Senator John F. Kennedy and Vice President Richard M. Nixon gave rise to political debating as we now know it in the media age.

Yet, most contemporary political debaters, including Presidents Carter, Reagan, Bush, and Clinton, have not engaged in political debates. Based primarily on the Kennedy–Nixon model of 1960, most contemporary political debates can be characterized as "counterfeit debates."[5] This is not to say that contemporary political debating is, like a counterfeit bill, of little value. As we will see later, contemporary political debates are extremely valuable. But in large part because of the influence of media, they involve different formats and strategies than those of the Lincoln–Douglas era.

Perhaps the counterfeit nature of contemporary political debates can best be understood by using Auer's five essentials of debate to compare the Lincoln–Douglas debate with the prototypic contemporary media political debate, that of Kennedy and Nixon in 1960.

First, the Kennedy–Nixon debate and most political debates since do not involve direct confrontation. Lincoln and Douglas confronted one another. They met on the same platform, questioned one another, and refuted one another. Indeed, the highlight of the seven debates came in the second debate, at Freeport, when Lincoln confronted Douglas with a series of four questions to set up what became known as "The Freeport Dilemma."

Lincoln claimed that Douglas had to repudiate the Supreme Court's Dred Scott decision (which made it illegal for voters to prohibit slavery in the territories and hence was enormously popular in the South) or repudiate his own program of popular sovereignty. As chairman of the Senate Committee on Territories, Douglas had argued that each of the Western territories should be allowed to choose by popular vote if it would enter the Union free or slave. Repeatedly in the debates after Freeport, Lincoln confronted Douglas with this dilemma. Lincoln demanded that Douglas choose between a fundamental tenet of U.S. democracy—the sanctity of Supreme Court decisions—or his own proposal. If Douglas supported the Dred Scott decision, he was admitting that he had labored in the Senate on behalf of a policy that was illegal. If he supported popular sovereignty, he was admitting Supreme Court decisions were not the highest law of the land and was isolating himself from the Southern wing of the Democratic party. Lincoln confronted, questioned, followed up, and harangued Douglas. Douglas responded, claimed the dilemma was false, and argued that Lincoln ignored a third alternative.

In contrast, it was not Richard Nixon but a journalist who suggested to John Kennedy that "you are naive and at times immature." Nor was it John Kennedy but rather a journalist who suggested to Richard Nixon that his experience as vice president was as an observer not as a participant or initiator of policy.[6] Kennedy and Nixon did not talk to each other, as did Lincoln and Douglas. Kennedy and Nixon did not question and pursue one another, nor did they respond to one another. Rather, if Kennedy, Nixon and most political debaters since are confronted at all, it is by the media not by one another.[7]

Second, the Kennedy–Nixon debate, and most political debates since, did not involve equal and adequate time. The key, of course, is adequate time. Lincoln and Douglas dealt almost exclusively with one issue, the future of slavery in the territories. Each man spoke for one and a half hours in each of seven debates. Kennedy and Nixon each spoke half an hour in each of four debates. The subject matter for the first Kennedy–Nixon debate was domestic affairs, for the last foreign affairs, and no restrictions whatsoever existed for the middle two debates. It is entirely fair to say that Lincoln and Douglas spent up to 21 hours debating one issue, while Kennedy and Nixon spent eight minutes on any one issue. Formats like the Kennedy–Nixon format typically allow candidates three to five minutes to deal with an issue.[8] Kennedy and Nixon, and most political debaters since, did not have adequate time to deal with major public issues.

Political debates do typically meet the third criteria for debates. The contestants are closely matched. If one contestant is vastly brighter, more fluent, more poised, more knowledgeable, and better prepared, no real debate can take place. Typically, this is not the case in political debates, where both candidates must agree to debate and hence are probably able debaters, having merit enough to secure major party nominations to the office.

However, political debates frequently do not meet the fourth criteria of debates. The Kennedy–Nixon debate and most political debates since did not involve one stated proposition. Rather, depending on format, ten or more topics are discussed in a single debate. In the first Kennedy–Nixon debate, the two men dealt with such diverse questions as who was most fit and prepared to lead the country, how would each man handle the farm subsidy programs, what policies each would advocate for reducing the federal debt, what would each man do about improving the nation's schools, what policies would each pursue with respect to medical aid to the aged and with respect to a comprehensive minimum hourly wage program. Moreover, each was asked how serious a threat to national security he believed communist subversive activity in the United States was and how he would finance public school construction. In sum, Kennedy and Nixon had under an hour to deal with nine totally diverse topic areas.

Finally, the Kennedy–Nixon debates did not really gain an audience decision on the issues. Debates, as Auer suggests, are "clashes of ideas, assumptions, evidence, and argument."[9] They secure from audiences a decision on the issues. In 1858 the Lincoln–Douglas debates revealed the inadequacies of Douglas's program of popular sovereignty for the territories and the inconsistency of that program with existing institutions. It was because he illustrated the inadequacies and inconsistencies of Douglas's position, while justifying and defending his own belief in restricting slavery's spread into the territories, that Lincoln emerged from the debates a national figure, and Douglas's national aspirations were shattered. Those debates were a true clash of ideas, assumptions, evidence, and argument. In 1960 the Kennedy and Nixon debates did not facilitate the audience's making a decision about the issues. Contemporary political debates that are heavily oriented toward the broadcast media audience are not in the tradition of issue-oriented debates.

Political debating is widespread in this country. It is almost a ritualistic aspect of campaigns for one candidate to challenge the other to a debate. Yet, as we have seen, contemporary media-oriented debates, regardless of what office is sought, are vastly different from the first political debates in our nation's history. Though they typically involve matched candidates, they rarely if ever entail direct confrontation, equal and adequate time, one stated proposition, and a clear decision on the issues. In the next section, we will trace how political debates evolved from the Lincoln–Douglas debates to the media-oriented debates we have today.

HISTORY OF POLITICAL DEBATES

During the the nineteenth century, debating was an important aspect of campaigning, though perhaps not as widespread as it is today. However, a few debates of local or statewide interest did take place.[10] Although Lincoln and Douglas had gained national attention, figures of comparable stature did not engage in campaign debates in the years that followed. Rather than debating their opponents, in the nineteenth century many candidates utilized surrogate debaters. This practice was especially widespread in nineteenth century presidential elections.[11] Nevertheless, relatively few nineteenth century debates received attention beyond their own constituencies, and none attained national prominence.[12]

By the mid-1920s, due to the growth of radio, national debates began to seem feasible. In 1924, testifying before a congressional committee investigating broadcast regulations, William Harkness, an executive of the American Telephone and Telegraph Company, made what is generally believed to be the first suggestion for broadcasting political debates.[13] At the time of Harkness's suggestion, such a broadcast would have probably been local or regional in scope, but within two years, with the birth of the National Broadcasting Company in 1926, nationwide political broadcasts became feasible. NBC's first programs were carried over a 24-station hookup serving 21 cities from the East Coast as far west as Kansas City. Other networks soon followed.

The implication of national radio networks for political campaigns was not lost on Congress. In 1927 Congress included a section in its radio broadcast regulations dealing with political broadcasts. Those regulations were modified in 1934, and section 315 of the Communications Act of 1934 affected political broadcasts for years. This "equal time" provision required that if any licensed radio or television station allows a legally qualified candidate for any public office to use its station, it must "afford equal opportunities to all other such candidates for that office in the use of such broadcasting station."[14] This provision, designed to provide equal access to the public's airwaves to all candidates, tended to inhibit political debates. It required that if major party candidates received airtime from a station, that station would have to provide airtime to every other candidate, regardless of the extent of their following. Few broadcasters were willing to make time for the many minor party candidates, and hence little time went to any campaign activities. Although this act was modified in 1959 to insure that broadcasters could cover the normal newsworthy activities of major political candidates without being subject to harassment by lesser candidates,[15] throughout the period 1934–1976, section 315 inhibited political debates in any race where more than two candidates were involved.

Nevertheless, political debating did not come to a complete standstill during this period. On October 17, 1936, during the presidential election between Governor Alfred Landon and President Franklin Roosevelt, Republican Senator Arthur Vandenberg of Michigan produced a "fake" debate over the CBS network by editing recordings of Roosevelt's speeches. The live Vandenberg naturally bested the edited Roosevelt. The nature of this debate was not made clear to stations until shortly before the broadcast. Of the 66 stations scheduled to broadcast the debate, 23 did so without interruption. Clearly Vandenberg had edited Roosevelt's speeches to produce a partisan one-sided program. However, perhaps more than anything that had preceded it, this program focused attention on the possibilities of nationally broadcast political debates between major figures.[16] Four years later, in 1940, Republican Wendell Wilkie opened his campaign by challenging President Roosevelt to debate. Polls found the public almost evenly divided in their response to Wilkie's challenge.[17]

Apparently much of the opposition stemmed from the public's perceptions of the risks that might be involved in having an incumbent president debate. Roosevelt suffered no significant political consequences in declining to debate.

In 1948 the first broadcast debate between two major presidential candidates took place. The candidates were Governor Harold Stassen of Minnesota and Governor Thomas Dewey of New York. They were seeking the Republican nomination to challenge President Harry S. Truman. In the midst of the Oregon primary, Stassen challenged Dewey to debate. Dewey accepted but specified the terms. As Dewey wished, the debate was held in private, with only a small audience of journalists. Stassen had suggested that it might be held in a ballpark with a large public audience. Dewey spoke last, as he wanted. Dewey selected the topic: that the Communist party should be outlawed in the United States. Moreover, Dewey chose to defend the negative. The debate was broadcast nationally by all four major radio networks and was well received by audiences and political observers.[18] Among the first suggestions that 1952 presidential candidates General Dwight David Eisenhower and Illinois Governor Adlai Stevenson engage in a televised debate were those made by Michigan Senator Blair Moody and Democratic media specialist J. Leonard Reinsch.[19] Both NBC and CBS immediately offered to provide the airtime, if Congress would suspend or revoke the equal time provision. However, nothing came of the network's offer, since both Eisenhower and Stevenson were reluctant to debate.[20] Not so reluctant were the two Massachusetts senatorial candidates, Henry Cabot Lodge and John F. Kennedy, who debated that year in Waltham, Massachusetts.

By 1956 virtually the entire country had access to television. Televised political programs of every sort were commonplace. Candidates at all levels—presidential, senatorial, congressional, as well as scores of local candidates—were routinely appearing on television. But with one significant exception, broadcast debates between political candidates were not seen on the nation's television screens.

In 1956 the contest for the Democratic presidential nomination became a fight between Tennessee Senator Estes Kefauver and Adlai Stevenson. Kefauver had become a well-known political figure in 1951 when, as chairman of the Senate Crime Investigating Committee, he had presided over nationally televised hearings investigating organized crime. Kefauver challenged Stevenson to debate during the primaries. Stevenson, reluctant to debate Eisenhower in 1952, was again reluctant. However, after losing the Minnesota primary, Stevenson agreed to debate Kefauver in the Florida primary. The debate was nationally televised, and though it apparently helped Stevenson, he came away unimpressed with political debates.[21] As in 1952, in 1956 neither Stevenson nor Eisenhower wished to be involved in broadcast debates during the general election.

In 1960 John Kennedy was challenged to debate in the primaries by Senator Hubert Humphrey. During the West Virginia primary, both men agreed to a televised debate. Observers agreed that Kennedy did well in the debate, which was televised throughout the East Coast as well as throughout West Virginia. Perhaps this experience and his 1952 debate with Lodge contributed to Kennedy's acceptance of an NBC offer for free time during the general election if he would agree to a series of joint appearances with the Republican nominee. This offer had been made feasible by a joint resolution of Congress suspending the equal time law until after the election. Like Kennedy, Richard Nixon quickly accepted the NBC offer but noted that since the other networks had issued similar invitations the networks should coordinate their proposals. The networks had lobbied earlier in the year to suspend the equal time law for just this opportunity. They perceived televised presidential debates as providing them with enhanced credibility as a news medium. As we will see in more detail in the next section, 1960 was one of those years when the selfish interests of both candidates seemed best served by involvement in political debates. Hence, in 1960, for the first time since 1858, the United States was absorbed by a political debate or at least a joint appearance, national in scope and significance.

Political debates at the presidential level were not held for the 16 years following the Kennedy–Nixon debate, for reasons that will be discussed in the next section. However, they became commonplace in campaigns for almost all other offices. In the years immediately following the Kennedy–Nixon debate, there were political debates between candidates for statewide office in Michigan, Massachusetts, Connecticut, Pennsylvania, and California. Races for lesser offices frequently included debates. For example, two short years after the Kennedy–Nixon debates, debates were held between the candidates for all six congressional seats in Connecticut.[22] Although presidential candidates frequently utilized debates during the primaries that were held after 1960, it was not until 1976 that presidential debates were held during the general election. However, unlike their presidential counterparts, local, regional, and statewide candidates made increasing use of debates during the 1960s and 1970s. One such debate, which took place between the two candidates for governor of Tennessee in 1970, indirectly led to the 1976 presidential debate between Governor Jimmy Carter and President Gerald Ford and resolution of the impediment to political debates caused by the equal time provision.

In 1970 Winfield Dunn, Republican, and John J. Hooker, Jr., his Democratic opponent for the governorship of Tennessee, decided to debate. Aiding Dunn was a University of Virginia law student, Stephen A. Sharp, who found several Tennessee stations reluctant to carry the debates for fear that they would have to provide equal time to all other minor candidates for the governorship. Sharp's involvement in the Tennessee race caused him to prepare a law school paper on the history and interpretation of section 315. He found that political debates between major candidates might well be considered "bona fide" news events under the 1959 changes to section 315. If so, they could be reported on by stations as normal newsworthy activities, and those stations would not be subjected to providing equal time to all other candidates.

Sharp was subsequently hired by the Federal Communications Commission (FCC) where his work with section 315 became known. The FCC had previously ruled that candidate appearances not "incidental to" other news events were not newsworthy and hence not exempt from the equal opportunities requirement. Political debates by major candidates that were not incidental to any other activity were not exempt. But a political speech incidental to a rally or a dinner was exempt.

After considerable legal maneuvering by a variety of interested parties, including the Aspen Program for Media and Society, the Columbia Broadcasting System, and others, the FCC ruled in 1975 that debates that were covered live and in their entirety and not sponsored by broadcasters (and hence presumably legitimate news events that would take place with or without the press) could be covered without fear of having to provide time to all minor candidates.[23]

This 1975 FCC ruling, known as the Aspen decision, made nationally televised presidential debates feasible from the network's standpoint. But debates do not take place without willing debaters. In 1960 Kennedy and Nixon had both been willing to debate for reasons that will become evident in the next section. Republicans and Democrats in Congress, following the lead indicated by their presidential candidates, had suspended section 315. After the Aspen decision, an act of Congress was no longer necessary for presidential debates, but willing debaters were.

The League of Women Voters, responding to the Aspen decision, took it upon itself to become the sponsoring organization for presidential debates in 1976. In 1976 both major candidates perceived that their own self-interest might be well served by political debates. We will examine in detail what motivates candidates to accept or reject an invitation to debate in the next section. However, in every election since 1976 both major presidential candidates were willing to debate. Today, political debates are widespread at all levels.

DECIDING WHETHER TO DEBATE

At virtually every level of politics, candidates and their advisors strategically address themselves to six questions in determining whether to engage in political debates.[24] At the presidential level public expectations have grown steadily stronger since 1976 that serious candidates for the nation's highest office will be willing to debate their ideas. Today, presidential candidates risk the possibility of severe backlash if they decline to debate. Candidates for lesser office are not likely to face as much public aversion to their failure to debate. Consequently, since 1976 these factors have grown less important for presidential candidates, though they remain factors for consideration in most other races.

1. *Is this likely to be a close election?* Expectations about the outcome of the election are vital to the decision to engage in debates. If the election seems as though it will be close and both candidates are in doubt about the outcome, the likelihood of political debates is greatly increased. If either candidate has a strong conviction that they can win the election without engaging in debates, the likelihood of debates taking place is dramatically reduced.

2. *Are advantages likely to accrue to me if I debate?* No candidate willingly engages in counterproductive activity. Consequently, both candidates must have good reason to expect that the debates will be advantageous to them. As we will see in the next sections, the advantages a candidate perceives may come as much from the act of debating as from the actual debates themselves. Nevertheless, unless both candidates can anticipate advantages, political debates are unlikely to be held.

3. *Am I a good debater?* No candidates willingly put themselves in a position where their foe will clearly appear to be stronger. Consequently, when measuring themselves against their opponents, candidates must be confident about being good debaters.

4. *Are there only two major candidates running for the office?* Typically, our political system produces two serious candidates for each office. On those occasions where a third candidate seems to have a possibility of drawing a respectable share of the vote, it is highly unlikely that political debates will take place. Third party candidates are not predictable. They are not bound by the same "rules" as candidates who anticipate election. Often they speak to make a point or to dramatize an issue, rather than to win an election. Moreover, the presence of a third candidate provides the possibility that two candidates may "gang up" on one. These variables reduce the likelihood that political debates will take place in races where a third candidate is on the ballot and appears to have a possibility of drawing a respectable share of the vote.

5. *Do I have control of all the important variables in the debate situation?* Candidates cannot be expected to place themselves in postions where they cannot reasonably anticipate what will happen. Consequently, each candidate must feel comfortable with all the major variables in the debate situation: the dates, location, formats, topics, and other participants (moderators and questioners). Unless every candidate feels in control of all the major variables in the debate, they are unlikely to consent to debating.

6. *Is the field clear of incumbents?* If either candidate is an incumbent seeking reelection, the probability of debate taking place is reduced, especially for lower level races. Incumbency is a greater obstacle to political debating in lower level races than it is in upper level races for at least four reasons.

First, most incumbents reason that their credibility is unquestioned by virtue of prior service. The credibility of their opponents is often an issue in the campaign. This is more apt to be true in lower level races where challengers may be virtually unknown than in more prominent races where challengers have probably held other offices, or attained prominence in their choosen fields.

Second, incumbent officeholders are frequently better able than challengers to make their views known to the public. Hence, they are reluctant to provide their opponents with a platform from which to be heard. Again, this is more apt to be true in lower level races, where the overall press coverage of the race is not as great as the coverage for major races and challengers have an especially difficult time of getting coverage.

Additionally, almost any incumbent will necessarily be placed on the defensive in a political debate. The incumbent's record will probably be a major topic of discussion. Typically, no incumbent will hand an opponent the opportunity to attack vigorously, much less in a well-publicized situation. Again, this is more apt to be true in a lower level race. In major races challenger candidates have generally held offices and established political records that may lend themselves to attack by an incumbent, but in lower level races challengers may not have held office in the past and may not have an established political record for an incumbent to attack.

Finally, since 1976, when President Ford became the first incumbent president to engage in a debate, the public has grown to expect candidates for major office to engage in debates. By 1984, public expectations had grown so strong, that some have argued that incumbent Ronald Reagan, holding a commanding lead in all the polls, nevertheless risked debating because he felt that not to do so would create a greater problem for him than any possible error he might make in debating.[25] In recent years incumbents have come to fear that their failure or obvious reluctance to debate will be interpreted extremely negatively by the public to mean that they are weak and unable to defend their own positions and policies.[26] Candidates for lower level offices do not generate quite the same expectations in the public and hence are unlikely to suffer as greatly if they fail to debate. The public is often unfamiliar with the positions and policies of such candidates, largely uninterested in them, and relatively unconcerned about debates between them.

APPLYING THE CONDITIONS REQUISITE FOR
POLITICAL DEBATES

Below the presidential level, few political debates will occur unless the conditions implicit in these questions exist to the satisfaction of both candidates. The importance of these conditions can be illustrated by analyzing virtually any campaign. However, in the next few pages we will examine three presidential campaigns to better illustrate the ways in which candidates and their managers determine whether they should debate. We have chosen to focus on select presidential campaigns because they are especially instructive and also because readers are probably more acquainted with the circumstances and events of presidential campaigns than with those of any other campaigns. However, keep in mind that public expectations that presidential candidates will debate have grown so strong since 1976 that today for a major presidential candidate to refuse would likely be a serious mistake. Such a refusal would likely have nowhere near as damaging an effect in most other campaigns. Thus, though presidential campaigns are somewhat unique, the same principles are used by all candidates, particularly those contesting lower offices. Candidates do not choose to debate by chance. Rather, their decisions are based on self-interest.

1960: Kennedy–Nixon Debates

From the outset, most observers expected a close election.[27] As the campaign progressed, public opinion polls confirmed expectations. Neither candidate ever led by more than six points in the major polls. Clearly, both camps anticipated a close election.

In 1952 vice presidential candidate Richard Nixon gave one of the most successful political speeches in U.S. history. Using the new medium of television, he had saved his position on the ballot as Dwight Eisenhower's running mate with his Checkers speech. His 1960 advisors considered him a "master" of television.

His own extensive background as a college debater and his recent "kitchen" debates with Soviet Premier Khrushchev also contributed to Nixon's confidence in his ability to debate Kennedy. Nixon's strategists were so confident that their candidate would gain in the debates that they initially argued for only one debate. They believed that Nixon could virtually eliminate Kennedy in one debate and that it would be disadvantageous to give Kennedy any opportunity to recover. Clearly, Nixon's camp believed that advantages would accrue to him from debating and that he was a good debater.

The optimism of the Nixon camp was curious in light of the fact that in 1947 Nixon and Kennedy had debated to a standoff. In 1947 Pennsylvania Congressman Frank Buchanan had been asked to bring two outstanding young political figures to McKeesport, Pennsylvania, a town in the midst of the Pennsylvania steel belt, to debate the controversial Taft–Hartley labor bill. Buchanan had asked freshmen Congressmen Richard Nixon and John Kennedy. They accepted. Nixon had defended the bill, and speaking to an audience which included many who were sympathetic to labor, argued that big labor had grown too powerful. Kennedy had acknowledged merit in the bill but felt it was unnecessarily restrictive on labor. Perhaps foreshadowing 1960, Nixon seemed to have won the debate itself, but Kennedy seemed to have won the audience.[28]

Moreover, while many observers recalled Nixon's successful 1952 Checkers speech, few 1960 observers recalled what most of Kennedy's inner circle best remembered about 1952. John Kennedy ran for the Senate against a heavily favored, vastly more experienced incumbent Republican, Senator Henry Cabot Lodge. Kennedy debated Lodge at Waltham, Massachusetts. From that point forward, Lodge's assertions about his superior experience, maturity and judgment—the same issues Nixon was using in 1960—were no longer viable. At least two of Kennedy's inner circle, his brother Robert and close advisor Kenneth O'Donnell, anticipated that the Kennedy–Nixon debates might well be a "rerun" of the Lodge debate. Clearly, Kennedy's strategists felt that their man was an able speaker and that his presence on the same platform as Nixon, as well as what he said, would prove advantageous. Thus, both candidates felt that they were good debaters and hence would be advantaged by debates.

Kennedy and Nixon were the only major candidates for the presidency. After 15 negotiating sessions, which included discussions of virtually every detail of television production—camera angles, staging, lighting, and backdrops—both camps felt that no unexpected variable would confound the situation.

Thus, Nixon and Kennedy had every reason to debate. It was no accident that they became the first presidential candidates to engage in an extensive series of public debates. It was at their bidding that both Republican and Democratic members of Congress voted to suspend section 315 of the Communications Law to allow national coverage of the debates.

1992: Clinton–Bush–Perot

In 1987, at the recommendation of a variety of experts, a nonprofit, nonpartisan corporation was established to sponsor presidential and vice presidential debates. The Commission on Presidential Debates sponsored all of the 1988 debates. In the years since 1988 the Commission has worked with a variety of organizations, including the National Communication Association, to promote and study political debates. Charged with developing a schedule and format for the 1992 debates, the Commission ultimately proposed a series of three presidential debates and one vice presidential debate for 1992. Importantly, the Commission proposal was for 90-minute debates to be conducted by a single moderator.[29]

Democratic candidate Governor Bill Clinton accepted the Commission proposal, but incumbent Republican President George Bush did not. The Bush campaign was widely reported to object to the single moderator format, preferring instead the use of a panel of questioners, as had been used in his 1988 debates with Governor Michael Dukakis. The single moderator format had been offered by the Commission as the format most conducive to follow-up questions and probing of the candidates. It was widely believed to be the format that best provided viewers with information.

This seemingly simple detail of format, the use of a single moderator or a panel of questioners, almost prevented debates in 1992. The date of the Commission's proposed first debate, September 22, came and passed with no debate. With one debate canceled and the election only six weeks distant, the Commission on Presidential Debates offered the candidates another proposal. Clinton again immediately accepted. The Bush campaign refused, observing that it had sent a proposal for debates directly to the Clinton campaign and awaited a response.

Bush no doubt favored the format in which a group of reporters rotated in asking questions for several reasons. First, it was the format in which Bush had excelled four years earlier. Second, it was likely to yield questions on a wide variety of topics. If the debate remained focused on one or a limited number of topics, as might happen with a single moderator asking a series of follow-up questions on a limited number of issues, the Bush economic record was most assuredly going to be discussed at length, with little discussion of Clinton or his policies. However, the use of a panel of reporters might facilitate questions about many of Clinton's often vague promises, as well as the controversial aspects of his life, such as his reputed womanizing and draft dodging.

Bush's refusal to accept the offers of the nonpartisan Commission on Presidential Debates, in light of Clinton's acceptance, continued to cause Bush discomfort. Clinton's attacks on Bush for not debating were resonating well with the public and by late September and early October Bush himself was getting fed up with the negative image his refusal to debate was creating, telling his staff that "I'm tired of looking like a wimp."

With time running short, hoping to change growing negative public opinion about his refusal to debate, Bush challenged Clinton to a series of six debates. The Bush challenge quickly resulted in direct negotiations between the two campaigns. After extensive discussions, the campaign staffs announced their agreement. A series of four debates, three presidential and one vice presidential, would be held. The sponsoring organization would be the Commission on Presidential Debates. The overall package of formats for the four debates was an equitable settlement of the major format differences between the two campaigns.

Thus, after resolving the issues between the candidates regarding the important variables in the debate situation, both candidates were willing to debate. Though Clinton held a lead in all the polls, the president's natural advantages as an incumbent and the continued attacks on Clinton's character suggested the likelihood of a close election. Both candidates saw advantages to debating. The debates offered Bush what many thought might be his last strong opportunity to catch up. For Clinton, they offered the opportunity to go before the entire American public and prove himself worthy of the office, dispelling many of the charges raised about him during the primaries and early campaigning. Both men perceived of themselves as good debaters. Bush had successfully debated as both a vice presidential and presidential candidate. Clinton had been successful throughout the Democratic primary season.

Though Bush was an incumbent, the public expectation that presidential candidates debate was so great that Bush was suffering in the polls for his failure to debate. Indeed, Bush's own tracking polls indicated that he was paying a price in public opinion for this failure. Hence, though an incumbent, Bush was willing to debate.

Though the details of debates were worked out by negotiators representing only President Bush and Governor Clinton, at the very time the Clinton and Bush camps were negotiating the details of the debates, wealthy businessman H. Ross Perot, candidate of the "United We Stand, America" movement, reentered the race. Typically, as we have seen, the presence of a third party candidate discourages political debate. Perot had entered the race, initially captured the sympathy of support of upwards of 30 percent of the voters, and then withdrawn. Now, six weeks later, he again entered the race.

The Commission on Presidential Debates, recognizing that within days of reentering Perot seemed to be attracting the support of 7–10 percent of the public, that during the spring he had actually at one point been the front-runner when his support surged to about 30 percent, and that he would be waging an exceedingly well-financed campaign, determined that he warranted an invitation to debate. Neither the Clinton nor the Bush campaigns wanted to offend the Perot supporters by keeping their candidate out of the race. Both major party candidates hoped that eventually the Perot support would fade and turn to them. Consequently, neither objected to the Commission's invitation to Perot. Typically, third party candidates reduce the likelihood of debates. Though neither Clinton nor Bush were likely to be happy with the presence of Perot in the debates, neither felt that they could afford to engender ill will from the Texas businessman or his supporters.

1996: Clinton–Dole

In anticipation of the 1996 debates, and wishing to avoid a situation such as it experienced in 1992 when it had to make a determination about including Ross Perot on short notice, in 1995 the Commisson on Presidential Debates developed two sets of recommendations that it hoped to apply to the 1996 presidential debates. First, the Commission created a schedule and format for presidential debates. The Commission advocated a series of three presidential debates and a vice presidential debate. These debates would be held on four consecutive Wednesday evenings starting with the last Wednesday of September. Each would last 90 minutes and be conducted by a single moderator.[30]

The second set of recommendations that the Commission had developed during 1995 focused on determining which candidates would be allowed to participate in the debates. No doubt responding to the situation involving Ross Perot in 1992, on September 19, 1995, a full year prior to the expected 1996 presidential debates, the Commission approved a criteria for determining who they would invite to the 1996 debates.

The Commission determined that only candidates with "a realistic chance of being elected the next President of the United States and who properly are considered to be among the principal rivals for the Presidency," would be invited to debate.[31] The Commission elaborated on this statement by indicating that it would use evidence of a national organization, signs of national newsworthiness, signs of national competitiveness, and indicators of national enthusiasm and concern to determine if a candidate had a "realistic chance of being elected."[32]

With the nominations of President William Clinton and Senator Robert Dole, there was never any doubt that the two major contenders for the presidency would meet in debates. However, by September 25, the date that the Commission had set for the first debate, representatives of the Clinton and Dole campaigns were unable to agree on the number and format of their debates. Each side held out for debates that would advantage their own candidate. The Clinton campaign argued for two presidential debates, each lasting two hours. They proposed that Reform party candidate Ross Perot be included in the first debate, but excluded from the second debate. They argued that the first debate should follow the traditional format of candidates responding to questions from a moderator. They felt that the second debate, without Perot, should utilize the town hall format with questions coming from the audience. The Clinton

campaign also argued that the entire sequence of two presidential debates and a vice presidential debate all be held within one week. They
suggested that the entire sequence be done between October 6 and October 13.[33]

The Clinton proposal would have included Perot in the first debate.
Perot was widely believed to draw votes primarily from Dole, thus advantaging Clinton. The Clinton proposal would have utilized Clinton's
favorite format, the town hall format with audience questioners, again
advantaging the president. Moreover, by compacting all three debates
into one week, the Clinton proposal would have prevented the public
and the press from focusing extensively on any errors made in the first
two debates, since attention would turn within one or two days to the
next debate. This schedule would also have advantaged Clinton. Ahead
by 15 points or more at the time of these negotiations, Clinton's schedule
would have effectively prevented the nation from focusing on any errors
he or Vice President Gore might make in the first two debates since the
next debate would be literally only one or two days later.[34]

In contrast to Clinton's proposal of three debates, the Dole campaign
proposed a series of six debates, four between the presidential candidates
and two between the vice presidential candidates. Moreover, the Dole
campaign argued that there should be a one-week break between each
debate, facilitating analysis and discussion of the statements made in
each debate. Dole's negotiators were flexible on the format of the debates.
However, they were unyeilding in their demand that the Reform party
candidate be excluded from the debates. Former South Carolina governor Carroll Campbell, Dole's primary negotiator, asserted that "Perot is
not something we're discussing."[35]

On September 17 the Commission on Presidential Debates ruled that
Perot had not met its criteria for inclusion in the debates. The Commission had turned to an advisory board, headed by Professor Richard
Neustadt of the Kennedy School of Government at Harvard University,
to apply their criteria to the Perot candidacy. After reviewing a considerable amount of material about the Perot campaign and speaking to a
wide variety of political scientists and political journalists, the advisory
board concluded that

at this stage of the campaign, Mr. Perot has no realistic chance of popular election
in November or of subsequent election by the House of Representatives, in the
event no candidate obtains an Electoral College majority. None of the expert
observers we have consulted thinks otherwise. . . . Therefore, the Advisory Committee unanimously concludes at this time that only President Clinton and Senator Dole qualify for admission to the CPD's debates.[36]

Neither Clinton nor Dole wished to risk public displeasure by being
perceived to be unwilling to debate. Hence, the two leading candidates

ultimately compromised their differences. The Clinton camp secured a tight schedule in which both of the presidential debates as well as the vice presidential debate were held in a 10-day period between October 6 and 16. Moreover, one of the two debates would utilize the town hall format in which Clinton had excelled in 1992. Dole got the chance to confront Clinton as he wished, one-on-one, without the distraction of Ross Perot or any other third candidate.

POLITICAL DEBATE STRATEGIES

Political debate strategies can best be understood if we recognize that they involve three stages. First are those strategies that take place prior to the debate itself. Second are those the candidate attempts to implement during the debate. Finally are those following the debate. Each is important. A political debate can be won or lost before it takes place, as it takes place, or after it is held. In this section, we will examine political debating strategies.

Predebate Strategies

That a candidate is perceived to have won the debate is often a function of what people expected. Hence, many candidates seek to lower public expectations of their performance. If prior expectations are low, then it may not take a strong effort on the part of the candidate to appear to have done well. Moreover, if a candidate is expected to be outclassed but does well, it may be perceived as a major victory.

Goodwin F. Berquist and James L. Golden have noted that the media tend to establish public expectations regarding the probable outcome of political debates.[37] Observing the 1980 Reagan–Carter debate, Berquist and Golden point out that prior to the debate the media alerted the public to what might take place by discussing expected candidate strategies, interviewing campaign staffs, and presenting guidelines for successful debating to which the candidates might adhere.[38]

The interaction between the candidate and campaign staff on the one hand and the media on the other can be crucial during the predebate period. As the media go about their job, they will seek comments from the campaigners. Campaigners will normally tend to downplay the potential outcome of the debate. By minimizing expectations, campaigners feel they are putting themselves in the best possible position to capitalize on a strong performance and to rationalize a weak one.

Typically, it is easier for a challenger to minimize expectations than it is for an incumbent. The incumbent already commands respect and has fulfilled the job responsibilities for several years. Incumbents may have debated about the demands of this very office being contested just a few years earlier. To the extent that the debate contributed to that victory, incumbents are perceived as good debaters.

In their analysis of the 1984 presidential debates, Craig Allen Smith and Kathy B. Smith observed that at the outset of the first debate expectations for incumbent Ronald Reagan were exceptionally high.[39] Much of his success in the 1980 election was attributed to his strong showing in his debate with President Carter. Moreover, throughout his Senate career, challenger Walter Mondale had always been characterized as a relatively lethargic speaker who came across to audiences as rather boring. Expectations were extremly high for the incumbent president and extremely low for his challenger. However, Mondale exceeded all expectations, and Reagan failed to meet the expectations placed on him. Hence, Mondale was judged the winner, Reagan the loser.

Exactly two weeks later, when they debated a second time, the results of the first debate had contributed to reversing expectations. If the president had been overconfident and overrated prior to the first debate, reaction to that debate suggested that Reagan faced an uphill struggle in the second debate. It was widely speculated that his age was beginnning to take its toll on his abilities. Moreover, Mondale was now perceived as a far more formidable debater than previously believed. Hence, public expectations for the second debate were far higher for Mondale and considerably reduced for Reagan. Facing far lower expectations, it was generally agreed that Reagan won the second debate. Facing far higher expectations, it was generally agreed that Mondale lost the second debate. Reagan had no difficulty in meeting the lowered expectations of his abilities, while Mondale was unable to match the inflated expectations of his abilities. As the 1984 Presidential debates well illustrate, candidates, regardless of the office being contested, the size of the constituency, or the extensiveness of media coverage, have good reason to seek to lower public expectations of their likely debate success.

In 1996 both Clinton and Dole, as well as their staffs, attempted to lower expectations. Clinton did so largely by suggesting that the demands of the presidency had prevented him from preparing well. Some news reports indicated that Clinton felt that his preparation for the upcoming Mideast summit, was preventing him from preparing for the debates with Dole.[40]

Closely related to this first predebate strategy is the second—setting up an opponent. Again often utilizing the press to effect public perceptions, candidates typically emphasize two themes in dealing with their opponents. First, they attempt to heighten expectations of their opponents. Lauding their opponents as experienced debaters and speakers who may be quick on their feet (a skill not required for the office, which demands considerable thought), candidates attempt to set difficult standards for their opponents to meet. In 1996 Bob Dole claimed that Clinton was such a good debater and that most observers had such low expectations for Dole that he would do well against Clinton just by showing up.[41] Similarly, Dole's running mate, Jack Kemp, pointed out that he always had trouble providing short answers to questions, such as those that would be necessary in the debate. Moreover, he observed that he had never been involved in a high-pressure televised debate, while Gore had gained such experience in his 1988 presidential race, his 1992 vice presidential race, and most recently in 1993 when he debated Ross Perot on the merits of the North American Free Trade Agreement (NAFTA).[42]

The second theme a candidate will stress in setting up an opponent is to stress the anticipated shortcomings of that opponent so that the press and public will be especially attentive. In predebate interviews, the candidate will ask if audiences might finally hear the opponent's plan to revitalize the economy or conserve natural resources. A candidate will continually remind audiences prior to the debate of the opponent's penchant for talking in simple terms, or flip-flopping on issues, or failing to be specific. All of these remarks are meant to focus the public's attention on an opponent's anticipated weaknesses. Thus the second predebate strategy is to set up an opponent by heightening the expectations placed on the opponent and by alerting the press and public to the opponent's expected shortcomings and demanding that the opponent be held accountable.

The third predebate strategy is to determine clearly the target audience. Political debates, as will be illustrated in the next section, typically draw the largest audiences of any single communicative event of the campaign. The candidates must determine who their target audiences are for the debate. Typically, they will be the same as the normal campaign target audiences. However, due to the unusual size of the audience, it is possible that the candidate may choose to go after a new target group of voters during a debate. The debate may be the first time that this group has been exposed to the candidate. Most practitioners would not suggest using the debate to attract massive numbers of new and different voters to the candidate. But the unusual nature of debate audiences—their size, the presence of many adherents of the opponent, the propensity of both the college-educated and women to attend debates—means that the candidates must clearly determine whether they wish to maintain their campaigns' targeted audiences for the debate or whether they wish to make some changes, normally in the form of adding a targeted group.

Finally, with a clear conception of targeted audiences in mind, candidates must work out answers to possible questions and practice them. This is the fourth predebate strategy. The firsthand reports of many participants in political debates suggest several successful approaches to practice.[43] First, in a relaxed atmosphere the candidate and a limited number of aides should work through possible questions and answers, consistently keeping in mind overall themes and target audiences. Second, the candidate should practice the answers in a situation as similar to the real one as possible. For nationally televised presidential debates, this has meant simulating the television studio or auditorium to be used and often utilizing a stand-in for the opponent. Some candidates have reviewed the speeches and tapes of their opponent's past performances. In the case of opponents who have debated in the past, an examination of their past debates has proven helpful.[44] Preparing for a debate may well mean curtailing other campaign activity for several days, but given the attention normally focused on debates, this sacrifice would seem worthwhile. In 1996 all four participants in the presidential and vice presidential debates took time out from their schedules to engage in mock debates and other methods of preparation.[45]

Debate Strategies

As the debate progresses, candidates must constantly respond to specific questions on the issues of the day. While those issues vary from campaign to campaign, most successful political debaters have been able to integrate the specific issues into an overall framework. For example, when Senators John Kennedy and Hubert Humphrey debated in the 1960 West Virginia primary, Kennedy developed the overall thesis, just as he did months later when debating Nixon, that while the United States was a great nation, it could and should be greater. As he dealt with specific issues concerning West Virginia and the nation, he integrated many of them into his overall thesis that the United States could do better.[46] Similarly, in 1988 George Bush's overall thesis was that he was responsibly conservative whereas Michael Dukakis was too liberal for America. Repeatedly, his answers returned to this theme.

Prior to 1992 and throughout much of the early campaign, Bill Clinton was often charged with being a "policy wonk," who responded in such detail to questions that he confused and bored his listeners. Consequently, the goal of his debate preparation was to develop "an overarching theme with which to frame all his debate answers."[47] Clinton stated his overarching theme with the first sentences out of his mouth. "The most important distinction in this campaign is that I represent real hope for change, a departure from trickle-down economics, a departure from tax-and-spend economics to invest in growth."[48] Clinton hewed to this theme, that he best represented change, particularly economic change, all evening. Hence, the first debate strategy is to utilize issues by relating them to an overall theme.

The skilled political debater will first present his overall theme in his introductory statement, if the opportunity to make such a statement is allowed in the debate format being used. Then he will reinforce it with his answers to as many specific questions as possible. Finally, he will return to it in his concluding statement.

In the 1988 presidential debates the format did not include opening statements. However, George Bush concluded the first debate by observing that "it gets down to a question of values. . . . We've got a wide array of differences on those [values]. But in the final analysis, in the final analysis, a person goes into that voting booth, they're going to say, who has the values I believe in?"[49] Bush felt his conservative values were more acceptable to the nation that Dukakis's liberal values, and he used his concluding statement, as well as his responses to many questions, to emphasis this thesis. Similarly, in the final debate between the two men, it was not an accident that Bush concluded by addressing three issues: taxes, crime, and military preparedness.[50] These issues were clearly among those that best distinguished Bush's conservative values from Dukakis's more liberal values.

In 1996 Clinton and Gore seemed more coordinated than any two debaters in the history of national political debating. Indeed, they utilized virtually identical language in presenting their overall thesis. In his opening statement of the first debate, Clinton claimed that if reelected, he and Gore would "balance the budget and protect Medicare, Medicaid, education and the environment." Gore claimed that "we have a plan to balance the budget while protecting Medicare, Medicaid, education and the environment." Both men repeated this refrain throughout their debates.[51]

Issues serve skilled debaters by allowing them to develop an overall thesis. We know that most people forget much of what they hear in as little as 24 hours. Any response to an opponent or a panelist on a specific issue is liable to be forgotten by most of the audience. But by making the response to a specific issue part of a theme that is consistently repeated, issues can be used to best advantage. Strategies on specific issues, of course, cannot be generalized. They vary depending on the candidate and the situation. But developing an overall thesis, which can be presented in opening and closing statements and repeatedly reinforced by the responses to many specific issues, is a highly effective strategy employed by many political debaters.

Issues are one of the two major concerns of the candidate during the debate. The other is image. As Robert O. Weiss has argued, in political debates "issues and images are in practical fact overlooked and . . . they intertwine in all manner of convolutions and mutually affect one another in countless ways."[52] Weiss calls this relationship the "issue-image interface."[53] Though issues and images are closely intertwined, there are several image strategies that can be employed in political debates.

The principal image strategies that can be utilized in political debating include the development of a leadership style, personification, and identification.[54] As Dan Nimmo points out, political figures can develop an activist leadership style or a passive leadership style. The activist is just that. In a debate, activists consistently refer to their actions, their initiatives, their effect on events. Passive leaders are cautious. They do not speak of their initiatives, but rather portray themselves as reacting to events.

In 1992 both Clinton and Perot portrayed themselves as activists seeking change. Bush attempted to do so as well, but was less successful. Clinton repeatedly claimed, "I've worked hard.... I've gotten experience.... I've touched more people.... My plan triggers in ..." Similarily, Perot made frequent references to his activist nature, evidenced by his past successes. In contrast, though Bush made similar efforts, he frequently seemed passive and powerless. The very first words out of his mouth, "Well, I think," suggest hesitancy. He observed that "the way we're going to get it [his economic program] done is we're going to have a brand new Congress," suggesting that it would be Congress, not Bush, that would get things done. Amazingly, in the first debate he frequently returned to this idea, that a new Congress would enact his agenda for America's renewal, implying that it was Congress that would act and that he was relatively powerless until they did so.

The weaknesses in Bush's responses in the first debate illustrate an image problem he had trouble dealing with throughout the debates and indeed the entire campaign. On one hand he was the incumbent president. As such, Congress notwithstanding, Bush was the most ready target for those who were dissatisfied with government policies. His incumbency required that Bush offer some defense of his four years of leadership. He did so in part by blaming the Democratic Congress for having contributed to the nation's economic problems. Hence, when he attempted to portray himself as an activist with an agenda for economic renewal, he had to acknowledge that he needed congressional cooperation, undermining the very activist image he was attempting to portray. It is for reasons such as these that debates are often thought of as vehicles for challengers, not incumbents.

In 1996, with Congress in Republican hands, and hence in a situation analogous to that Bush faced in 1992, President Clinton simply ignored the need for congressional cooperation and portrayed himself as an activist. In his opening two-minute statement of the first of his debates with Dole, Clinton cited 11 different accomplishments of his first term and indicated that he would extend those accomplishments in his second.[55] He clearly portrayed himself as a dynamic activist.

The second image strategy that lends itself to political debating is personification, the effort of the candidate to personify a definite role. For example, the candidate may work to be perceived as a nice guy or an efficient manager. In 1980, concerned about President Carter's attempts to characterize him as a warmonger who might have an itchy trigger finger on the nuclear button, Ronald Reagan worked to counter that image in the debate. He did so in part by personifying a kind, statesmanlike, religious family man seeking peace. For example, at various points in the debate he observed that "I believe with all my heart that our first priority must be world peace. . . . I am a father of sons; I have a grandson. . . . I'm going to continue praying that they'll come home [the Iranian hostages]."[56] In sum, Reagan was attempting to personify himself, to play a role, as a kindly, statesmanlike, religious family man. This personification would be most distant from the image of warmonger.

The final image strategy is identification. Debaters attempt to identify themselves with what they believe are the principal aspirations of their audience. Governor Clinton was exceptionally effective at this throughout the 1992 campaign as he identified himself with the nation's aspirations for economic improvement. In 1996, in a strategy no doubt geared to one of his principal target audiences, women, Clinton accented his education policies at the end of his opening statement. Clinton was skillfully appealing to that most basic of human aspirations, the desire to pave the way for great success by one's children. Clinton sketched a picture of 8-year-olds reading, 12-year-olds surfing the Internet, and 18-year-olds in college.

As these examples make clear, there is a close relationship between a candidate's response to specific issues and the image that the candidate projects. Nevertheless, as the debate is in progress, the candidate should have a clear idea of an overall issue strategy or thesis to which specific answers can be related. Moreover, candidates should be cognizant of the image they may be projecting and develop appropriate strategies, such as a leadership style, personification, and identification, to create the persona they want.

Postdebate Strategies

Political debates are not over when the last word is uttered. Who won? Who made a grievous error? Who seemed best in control? Questions like these immediately follow the debate, and their answers are often as important as the debate itself. After all, it is what the audience perceives to have happened in the debate that is of consequence. Therefore, the well prepared campaign will be ready to try to influence audience perceptions of the debate as soon as it concludes.

The importance of postdebate strategies was dramatized in the second Ford–Carter debate of 1976, perhaps best remembered because President Ford seemed to be unaware of the Soviet domination of Eastern Europe.

Yet, at the time that Ford made his unfortunate statement, it was barely noticed. It was not until the next day, after continual publicity of his remark, that Ford was perceived as having erred badly. Frederick T. Steeper studied this debate and concluded:

The volunteered descriptions of the debate by the voters surveyed immediately after the debate included no mentions of Ford's statement on Eastern Europe. Not until the afternoon of the next day did such references appear, and by Thursday night they were the most frequent criticism given Ford's performance. Similarly, the panelists monitored during the debate gave no indication of an unfavorable reaction at the time they heard Ford's Eastern European remarks. The conclusion is that the preponderance of viewers of the second debate most likely were not certain of the true status of Eastern Europe, or less likely, did not consider Ford's error important. Given the amount of publicity given Ford's East European statements the next day by the news media and the concomitant change that took place it is concluded that this publicity caused the change.[57]

Most students of political debate believe that the effects often lag behind the debate itself. Frequently, audience members do not reach final judgment until they have discussed the debate with others and have observed the media reaction.[58] It is during these hours, when interpersonal influence and media influence are often operating, that the campaign engages in the postdebate strategy of favorably influencing perceptions of the debate.

The principal postdebate strategy is to provide a massive and well-coordinated surrogate effort. Tom Rosenstiel, media and political correspondent of the *Los Angles Times* illustrated the extent of these efforts in 1992.

Ten minutes before the second presidential debate of 1992 ended, the Clinton campaign's high command gathered in a holding room beneath the University of Richmond Athletic Center for a conference call. On one end of the line was Clinton's Little Rock headquarters. On the other, in Virginia, were Clinton's top strategists. Also listening were the chairmen from Clinton's fifty state offices. The Democrats had to get their story straight.

This debate was over the moment a woman in the audience asked George Bush how the deficit had affected him, and Bush said he didn't get the question, campaign manager David Wilhelm explained. That was a metaphor for the whole election, campaign chairman Mickey Kantor suggested. This President doesn't get it. He doesn't understand what the economy is doing to people.

That would be the main point the Democrats would make about this debate, said Wilhelm. And Bill Clinton does get it. He was in touch. . . . It didn't matter that the truth was grayer than Wilhelm made it sound. It was irrelevant that the woman confronting Bush had probably meant to ask how the recession had affected Bush rather than the national debt, and that her imprecision, not the economy, was what had stumped the less-than-nimble President.

What mattered was the black outline of recollection: A citizen asked Bush about the economy and he didn't understand her question. The moment reinforced exactly what was driving the election—that Bush was out of step. If Clinton's team could get the press to repeat their talking point and replay the video of that moment over and over in the days after this October 15 debate, they would define what this moment came to mean and trap Bush with his own words.

Within minutes Clinton campaign headquarters in Little Rock had written up the "Talking Points" and faxed them to both the group in Virginia and the fifty state offices to use. The document began, "I'm not sure I get it," said George Bush.[59]

As Rosenstiel illustrates, the Bush campaign staff was also working arduously to have its own interpretation of the debate become the dominant media story. Both camps made their spokespersons available to the media to put the proper "spin" on the debate. A massive and coordinated surrogate effort means that in the crucial postdebate hours, viewers and media representatives are hearing many respected figures present a cogent rationale of why their candidate did well in the debate. Often these interviews are widely reprinted and broadcast and may serve to influence audience perception of the debate. Learning from Ford's problem after the second debate in 1976, almost every major campaign since has made prominent spokespersons available to the media following their debate.[60]

In 1996 the two presidential debates and the vice presidential debate, which was sandwiched between those of the presidential candidates, were all held within 10 days. Unlike the 1976 debate where analysis of the debate was a major story through several days worth of news, in 1996, almost as soon as a debate was over, the press focused on the upcoming debate. Hence, the presidential campaigns had less opportunity to influence the public by "spinning" their versions of what happened. Moreover, the news media, perhaps smarting some from criticism directed at it for allowing partisan political advocates to dominate their postdebate shows, reduced their use of candidate spokespersons after the debates. Rather, they tended to rely on their own staffs and academic experts to provide postdebate analysis.[61] Nevertheless, the campaign "spin doctors" were ready to go with their interpretations of the debate even before it was over.[62]

The use of prominent spokespersons to present a positive view of the debate is the most common postdebate strategy.[63] It is used in all levels of campaigns. Other strategies are less common and often depend on the circumstances and formats of the specific debate. Often, if an audience is present, campaign staff members will work to "load" the audience with partisans. Not only will these partisans provide positive responses during the debate, but as they are interviewed later, they may well do the same thing. Community leaders, known to be sympathetic to the candidate, can be urged to write letters to the editors of local papers, commenting favorably upon the candidate's performance. In every instance, postdebate strategies such as the use of surrogates, audience members, and letters are designed to influence public perception in the crucial hours and days that immediately follow.

EFFECTS OF POLITICAL DEBATES

Any discussion of the effects of political debates must be tempered with an awareness that it is difficult to draw strong conclusions about them. This difficulty arises for several reasons. First, each debate is different. It involves different candidates, different offices, different issues, different audiences, different press coverage, different formats, and a host of other differences. Hence, to talk about the specific effects of debates is virtually impossible, for no two will be identical, nor will their effects be identical.

Second, debate effects cannot be isolated from the effects of all the other communication that voters receive during the campaign. Individuals may be exposed to a dozen messages about the candidates on the very day of the debate. Distinguishing the effects of the debate from all the others is difficult.

While there have been scores of political debates in the last 30 years, by and large, researchers have only studied the presidential debates in detail. Hence, our discussion of effects must necessarily be limited to a consideration of the effects of presidential debates. We cannot be certain that the effects of nationally televised political debates are similar to those of the vast majority of political debates held in campaigns for lesser offices. Most debates are not nationally televised. They are not well publicized in advance. They are not subjected to endless speculation, examination, and evaluation for days afterward. However, while findings concerning the effects of presidential debate are not necessarily valid for other debates, there is reason to suspect a broad similarity in the pattern of effects produced by political debates. But, we cannot be absolutely certain.

Finally, unlike laboratory experiments, scientists cannot control political debates. Hence, those debates that have beeen examined are often subject to studies that, of necessity, are prepared under less than ideal conditions, including little advance planning and an inability to control fully all of the variables in the study.

Despite each of the above problems, at this time there appear to be some striking findings about the effects of political debates, which are subject to revision as debating becomes an even more widely studied communication event.

Effect 1: Increased Audiences

Political debates, even at the local or state level, attract large audiences. Debates create conflict, the essence of drama. Hence, it should not surprise us that presidential debates attract huge audiences. Similarly, we might well hypothesize that debates attract larger audiences than virtually any other activity that takes place during the typical campaign. While research on audiences for nonpresidential debates is not yet widely available, the basic element of conflict exists and might operate as it evidently does in presidential debates—to attract a large audience.

In 1960 CBS estimated that over 100 million people in the United States watched at least part of the Kennedy–Nixon debates.[64] Numerous other surveys also suggested that the Kennedy–Nixon debates drew an immense national audience. In fact, the debates drew the largest audience for any speaking event in history, up to that time.[65] Similarly, every measure of audience size conducted in connection with the 1976 debates also suggests a massive audience. Most measures of the 1976 debates claim that over 70 percent of the nation watched at least part of the first Carter–Ford debate. While viewing fell off somewhat as the series of debates progressed, it never fell below 60 percent.[66] In 1960 and again in 1976, debates between presidential candidates were novelties. However, such debates have been a feature of every election since. Moreover, debates between the vice presidential candidates have also become common. This may, in part, account for the fact that between 1980 and 1996 the audiences for national political debates diminished slightly. In 1984, for the first time, slightly less than half the nation watched the presidential debates between Reagan and Mondale. By 1988 that figure is estimated to have shrunk to about 40 percent. Nevertheless, even the least watched of national political debates, the 1988 confrontation between vice presidential candidates Dan Quayle and Lloyd Bentsen, drew an audience estimated at 60 million people. [67]

Audiences for the 1992 presidential and vice presidential debates consistently exceeded their 1988 counterparts. The two 1988 presidential debate ratings indicated that 39 percent of the nation's TVs were tuned to the debates. In 1992 the first of the three presidential debates drew a rating of 43 percent and the last two drew ratings of 50 percent. It should be noted that in 1992, for the first time in history, one of the three major networks, CBS chose not to show one of the debates. Rather than show the first debate, CBS honored its contract with major league baseball and showed the American League Championship playoff game. In 1996 presidential debate viewership dropped slightly from 1992 levels. Nevertheless, approximately 70 million people watched each of the presidential and vice presidential debates. [68] Though the public seems to have become accustomed to debates between presidential candidates, and though in 1996 there was little drama to a race in which an incumbent president was consistently ahead in the polls by 15 percent or more, even in 1996, political debates drew by far the largest audiences of any campaign activity.

Effect 2: Audiences Reinforced

Comedian Lenny Bruce unwittingly summarized a host of research studies about the effects of political debates when he observed that

everybody hears what he wants to hear. Like when they were in the heat of the 1960 election campaign I was with a group who were watching the debate and all the Nixon fans were saying "Isn't he making Kennedy look like a jerk?"— and all the Kennedy fans were saying "Look at him make a jerk out of Nixon." Each group really feels that their man is up there making the other man look like an idiot.

So then I realized that a candidate would have had to have been that blatant— he would have had to look at his audience right in the camera and say, "I am corrupt. I am the worst choice you could ever have for President."

And even then his followers would say, "Boy there's an honest man. It takes a big guy to admit that. That's the kind of man we should have for a President."[69]

As Bruce's comment suggests, most research has concluded that political debates tend to reinforce the positions of a candidate's partisans. After the 1960 debates, most researchers did not find substantial shifts of voter opinion. Rather, they found that Kennedy and Nixon partisans became more strongly committed to their candidate. As *Newsweek* reported, the debates "merely stiffened attitudes."[70]

Research since the 1960 debates tends to confirm these early findings. Examining data pertinent to all of the presidential debates held prior to 1987, George Gallup, Jr. claims that "presidential debates in all years have tended to reinforce the convictions of voters who were already committed. They have caused few people to change their minds."[71] Similarly, the debates held since 1988 seem to have served primarily to reinforce existing attitudes.[72] The reason for this effect is explained by Sears and Chaffee, who claim that "the information flow stimulated by debates tends to be translated by voters into evaluations that coincide with prior political dispositions. They perceive their party's candidate as having 'won' and they discuss the outcome with like-minded people." Sears and Chaffee continue, noting that since the Democratic party is substantially larger than the Republican, the net effect of the cumulative reinforcement stimulated by the debates probably benefits Democratic candidates.[73] The Democratic party is no longer as substantially larger than the Republican as it was when Sears and Chaffee first wrote. However, their reasoning remains valid. The logical outgrowth of these conclusions applied to local campaigns would be that debates, because they tend to reinforce prior political dispositions, generally work to the advantage of the party that is dominant in the district, city, or state.[74]

Effect 3: Shifting Limited Numbers of Voters

Political debates do not normally result in massive shifts of votes. As indicated above, most audience members have their existing predispositions reinforced by the debate. However, some voters may shift. In a close election, the number who shift as a consequense of debates might be decisive.

The Kennedy–Nixon debates were widely perceived at the time as having affected massive numbers of voters. President Kennedy helped foster this impression by attributing his election to the debates. Yet, evidence on this point suggests that, while they may have been decisive due to the extremely close nature of the election, the debates did not shift massive numbers of votes. The highest estimate of voter shift is pollster Elmo Roper's guess that 4 million voters, about 6 percent of the vote, changed as a consequence of the debates.[75] However, most researchers are far more cautious. Katz and Feldman, after examining 31 studies of the 1960 debates, typify the conclusions of most when they write, "Did the debates really affect the final outcome? Apart from strengthening Democratic convictions about their candidate, it is very difficult to tell."[76] Evidence on the 1976 presidential debates,[77] as well as those of 1980 tends to confirm this limited effects paradigm.[78]

In their perceptive analysis of the effects of the 1984 presidential debates, Smith and Smith observe that, although some polls reported that Walter Mondale had clearly beaten Ronald Reagan in their first debate, this victory did not translate into a shift in votes.[79] A Lou Harris poll, for example, found that 61 percent of the respondents felt Mondale won the debate while only 19 percent felt that Reagan had won. Yet that same poll reported that President Reagan's support had only dropped from 54 percent prior to the debate to 53 percent after the debate, while Mondale's support had only risen from 42 percent prior to the debate to 44 percent after the debate. This degree of movement is negligible for such a one-sided victory, and given the amount of polling error reported, even this degree of movement is suspect.[80]

In 1988 Michael Dukakis was judged to have won a close debate in the first of his confrontations with George Bush.[81] However, as Elizabeth Drew points out, "he was unable to capitalize on this victory."[82] Dukakis's debate victory did not seem to appreciably affect the preferences of many voters. Similarly, in 1992 and 1996, polls and analysts concurred in finding that Clinton seemed to have bested his foes in the debates. Yet, in 1992 the polls continually showed Clinton leading with 45–47 percent of the vote, Bush second with 35–38 percent of the vote and Perot trailing with 9–12 percent of the vote.[83] Moreover, in 1996 Clinton continually polled 51–53 percent of the vote shortly before, during, and shortly after, the debates. During this same period, Senator Dole remained consistently at 34–36 percent and Ross Perot trailed with 12–14 percent.[84]

Effect 4: Debates Help Set Voters' Agenda

As we have discussed in Chapter 4, much recent research has stressed the importance of the agenda-setting function of mass communication. In essence, this research holds that "we judge as important what the media judge as important. Media priorities become our own."[85] If the considerable body of evidence that supports the agenda-setting function of mass media is correct, then it would stand to reason that those issues stressed in mass media political debates and mass media coverage of those debates should also become issues of high priority for voters who watch the debates and attend to the media coverage of them.

Swanson and Swanson offer strong evidence in support of the agenda-setting function of political debates.[86] They attempted to determine whether those issues of primary concern to voters changed as a consequence of watching political debates. Based on research done at the University of Illinois during the 1976 campaign, they concluded that "the first Ford–Carter debate exerted an agenda-setting effect on our subjects who viewed it, although that effect was tempered by enduring personal priorities of subjects."[87] As Swanson and Swanson subsequently observed, "to the extent that citizens base their voting choices on their assessment of campaign issues, this is surely an effect of some political importance."[88] The agenda setting function of political debates seems to remain strong. However, as campaigns become more and more sophisticated and candidates attempt to work into their debates the very lines that permeate their speeches and paid advertising, regardless of the questions asked by the panelists, it grows increasingly difficult to isolate the agenda-setting effects of political debate from the overall agenda-setting effects of media coverage of the entire campaign.

The importance of the potential agenda-setting effects of debates was implicitly acknowledged in the format of the second 1992 debate. Held in Richmond, Virginia, this debate allowed an audience of undecided Richmond voters to question the candidates. Allowing voters, rather than journlists, to question the candidates was, in part, an attempt to provide that the public's agenda was served by the debates. Similarly, in 1996 the second presidential debate utilized an audience of undecided voters from the San Diego metropolitan area.

Effect 5: Debates Increase the Voters' Knowledge of Issues

A wide variety of studies have attempted to determine whether political debates increase the voters' knowledge of the issues. These studies seem to point to three conclusions. First, voters do seem more knowledgeable as a consequence of watching political debates. Second, debates are particularly helpful to voters in local elections. Tempering these conclusions is the final conclusion: often voters do not learn about the very issues that most concern them.

That voters clearly learn about the issues as a consequence of watching debates seems to have been well established by research.[89] Moreover, it would appear that debates serve as a more important source of information in local elections, which receive comparatively little media coverage, than for major national or statewide races. One study suggests that 80 percent of the viewers of debates between local candidates report that they learned about the candidates by viewing the debates, whereas only 55 percent made the same claim about the presidential debates.[90]

Although voters apparently learn about issues by watching debates, often they do not learn about the issues that most concern them. Michael Pfau has cogently argued that "a political debate ought to match—to the extent possible—the agendas of the candidates and the public." However, after studying several presidential debates he concluded, "the journalists' questions have virtually ignored the public's agenda."[91] The problem is well illustrated in the remarks of one of the journalists who helped to set the agenda of the 1980 debates with her questions. She claimed that she "felt under enormous pressure to try forming a single question that would somehow catch the well-briefed candidates by surprise on a subject of importance."[92] More appropriately for the public, she might have attempted to ask a question dealing with those issues that were of greatest public concern. But far too often, the public's concerns are not reflected in the journalists' questions.[93] Indeed, one critic of the 1988 debates has characterized many of the questions asked in that year's presidential debates as "trite."[94]

Significantly, virtually every program of reforms suggested for political debates includes a reduction or total elimination of the panel of journalists that helps to set the debate agenda.[95] Even the panelists themselves acknowledge that they are intrusive and the public might be better served by reducing the role of journalists or eliminating them altogether and having the candidates directly question one another without any third party intrusions.[96] It should be recalled that in 1960, when the precedents that have since been largely followed were established, the impetus for a panel of journalist/questioners came from the candidates, not the press.[97] Hence, for a variety of reasons, not the least of which is the intrusion of journalistic panels, the public agenda is frequently ignored in political debates. As we saw in the last section, at least one of the several formats used in the 1992 and 1996 debates was, to some degree, an attempt to address this concern. Additionally, in 1996 the traditional use of a panel of journalists was abondoned. Rather, one journalist, Jim Lehrer of the Public Broadcasting System, served as the moderator and questioner. The use of only one questioner was designed to allow follow-up questions. Multijournalist panels tended to skip from one topic area to the next, as each of the journalists asks a question about a different topic. The use of one questioner meant that Lehrer could repeat a question and follow up on evasive answers, thus providing greater information to the public.

In sum, while debates do increase the voters' knowledge of issues, particularly debates in local campaigns, their formats often prevent them from being as informative as the public might wish.

Effect 6: Debates Modify Candidate Images

Debates apparently affect the images of candidates. In their evaluation of the impact of the 1976 debates, Hagner and Rieselbach suggest that debates affect candidate images primarily when the candidate is not well known and hence the candidate's public image is not well developed.[98] When the public is unfamiliar with the candidate, perception of the candidate's general character, personality attributes, and general competency seems to be affected by political debates and their subsequent media coverage.

Most accounts of the 1960 debates note that Kennedy, the comparative unknown, improved his image as a consequence of the debates. He was able to convey a sense of competency and familiarity with major issues, as well as a charming personality. Similarly, Sears and Chaffee summarize a number of studies of the 1976 debates and conclude that the public's image of the candidates was affected by the debates.[99]

In his perceptive study of the 1976 vice presidential debates, Kevin Sauter observed that both Walter Mondale and Robert Dole hoped to impress the voters with their presidential potential. Sauter concluded that Mondale was successful in this effort and his strong image contributed appreciably to his subsequent nomination to the presidency. Conversely, Sauter finds that a variety of circumstances, many beyond his control, contributed to Dole's failure to impress the voters with his presidential potential. His failure in 1976, Sauter suggests, may have contributed to Dole's difficulty in obtaining the Republican nomination, for which he was a candidate repeatedly prior to his 1996 nomination.[100]

In 1992 the least known figure on any of the tickets was James Stockdale. Though many in the public were aware that he was the senior American officer captured in Vietnam and had been an inspiration to other American prisoners while suffering enormously at the hands of his Vietnamese captors, comparatively little else was known about him. The vice presidential debate afforded him an opportunity to allow America to become acquainted with him. Yet, the image he projected was remarkably unpresidential. Often unable to answer questions and frequently admitting his lack of knowledge, Stockdale projected an image of incompetence. Moreover, in contrast to the much younger Gore and Quayle, his hearing difficulties and limp, both largely a consequence of his treatment while a prisoner of war, no doubt concerned voters who were evaluating his ability to step into the presidency if the need arose. Though in many respects the most praiseworthy of the three vice presidential candidates, Stockdale projected the least presidential image. He appeared unable to grasp the complexities of many public issues. He appeared passive and frail. He was characterized in the press as "clueless," "an embarrassment," and "not ready for prime time."[101] Given that Stockdale had a distinguished career as both a military figure and as a scholar, but that his accomplishments were little known by the public, it is clear that the debate created a dramatically negative image of him. In sum, debates can affect public perception of a candidate's image—general competency, personality attributes, and character traits. The potential for affecting image seems to be inversely related to public knowledge of the candidate. The better known the candidate, the less likely the debate will greatly affect that candidate's image. Hence, the potential for improving one's image is generally greater for the lesser-known candidate. Moreover, it is likely that in races for lesser offices, among lesser-known candidates, the impact of a debate on the image of the candidates is potentially great.

Effect 7: Debates Freeze the Campaign

The timing of the 1992 debates, all four of which came in a 12-day period, and those of 1996, all three of which came in a 10-day period, emphasized a previously little noticed effect of debates. As Dan Hahn has observed, once debates are announced, "there will be an electoral flat-line until after the debates."[102] Once debates are announced, most voters tend to harden their positions until after the debates. Partisans see no reason to consider changing until after the debates, and as we have observed earlier, the debates rarely provide them with sufficient cause to change. Undecided voters tend to reserve judgment in the days immediately preceding the debates and throughout the debates, preferring to utilize the debates in making their judgment.

This effect of debates, to largely freeeze the campaign in place until their conclusion, works to the advantage of the leading candidate. It makes the leader more difficult to catch by effectively shortening the time the trailing candidates have to catch up.

Effect 8: Debates Build Confidence in U.S. Democracy

A wide variety of studies have attempted to evaluate the effects of political debates on American political institutions. Do debates result in greater confidence and support of political institutions and officeholders? Do debates facilitate political socialization? While individual studies differ, and continued research will no doubt shed greater light on questions such as these, current research does offer some tentative answers.

First, as Kraus and Davis argue, debates are consistent with democratic theory, which stresses the importance of rational decision making by an informed electorate.[103] Second, as Becker, Pepper, Weiner, and Kim point out, debates provide voters with greater exposure to information about candidates, which "probably resulted in a certain degree of commitment to the election process and to the candidate selected through that process."[104] Third, as Chaffee illustrates, debates apparently have a positive impact on people's confidence in government institutions and play a positive role in political socialization or the recruitment of new members into the body politic.[105]

In sum, it appears that political debates contribute to voter satisfaction with the democratic process. Though much has been written about growing voter apathy, growing voter disenchantment with the political process, and growing voter skepticism of politicians, it would appear that this overall trend of disaffection with the political process is not fostered by debates. Quite to the contrary, as Sidney Kraus has claimed, "televised presidential debates may be unparalleled in modern campaigning as an innovation that engages citizens in the political process."[106] Indeed, current research suggests that political debates might be a step in the direction of remedying current disaffection.

CONCLUSIONS

In sum, it would appear that political debates have at least eight distinct effects. Typically, they attract large audiences. Second, they seem to reinforce many of the preexisting attitudes and beliefs of audience members. Third, they seem to shift a limited number of voters. Though the number of voters whose opinions are shifted by the debates is limited, it should be kept in mind that, as discussed earlier in this chapter, debates are much more likely to be held in close elections, where the shift of a limited number of voters might well prove crucial to the outcome. Fourth, debates help to set the political agenda. Fifth, debates contribute to the education of audience members. Voters who watch the debates apparently are more knowledgeable as a consequence of their watching. This educational benefit of debates must be tempered somewhat by the recognition that current debate formats often preclude the viewers really learning about the issues that most concern them. Sixth, debates seem to affect the images of candidates. The image of the lesser-known participant is normally affected more by a political debate. Seventh, debates tend to freeze the campaign in place until their conclusion. Finally, debates seem to contribute to the public's confidence in government institutions and leaders.

NOTES

1. Quoted in *The Lincoln–Douglas Debates*, ed. Robert W. Johannsen (New York: Oxford University Press, 1965), p. 3.

2. Kathleen Hall Jamieson and David S. Birdsell note that as early as 1788, when two future presidents, James Madison and James Monroe, debated for a seat in the new House of Representatives, debates have been a part of American election campaigns. See their *Presidential Debates: The Challenge of Creating an Informed Electorate* (New York: Oxford University Press, 1988), p. 34.

3. J. Jeffery Auer, "The Counterfeit Debates," in *The Great Debates: Kennedy vs. Nixon, 1960*, ed. Sidney Kraus (Bloomington: Indiana University Press, 1962), p. 146.

4. Ibid.

5. This term was first used by Auer in his essay, "The Counterfeit Debates," to describe the 1960 debates. It has since been used to describe many political debates, most notably by Lloyd Bitzer and Theodore Rueter in their work *Carter vs. Ford: The Counterfeit Debates of 1976* (Madison: University of Wisconsin Press, 1980).

6. The statements in this paragraph were made by panelists Robert Flemming and Stuart Novins during the opening minutes of the first Kennedy–Nixon debate. See *The Joint Appearances of Senator John F. Kennedy and Vice-President Richard M. Nixon: Presidential Campaign of 1960* (Washington, D.C.: Government Printing Office, 1961), p. 78.

7. See Bitzer and Reuter, *Carter vs. Ford*, especially Chapter 3, for an excellent analysis of the adversary nature of the press in the 1976 debates. The adversary nature of the press remains a characteristic feature of campaign debates. Susan A. Hellweg and Anna M. Verhoye, "A Comparative Verbal Analysis of the Two 1988 Bush–Dukakis Presidential Debates," paper presented to the Speech Communication Association, Chicago, Ill., November, 1989, pp. 17–18 details the extent of adversary questioning in the 1988 presidential debates. The only contemporary national political debate that afforded the candidates an opportunity to directly question and clash with one another was the 1992 vice presi-

dential debate between Senator Albert Gore and Vice President Dan Quayle. With this lone exception, all other contemporary national political debates have utilized journalists to stimulate clashes.

8. Formats of the presidential debates are fairly well known. For examinations of the formats used in presidential primary debates, see Susan A. Hellwig and Steven L. Phillips, "Form and Substance: A Comparative Analysis of Five Formats Used in the 1980 Presidential Debates," *Speaker and Gavel* 18 (Winter 1981): 67–76; Michaael Pfau, "A Comparative Assessment of Intra-Party Debate Formats," paper presented at the Speech Communication Association Convention, Chicago, Illinois, November 1984. Examinations of debate formats at the non-presidential level can be found in Jack Kay, "Campaign Debate Formats: At the Non-Presidential Level," paper presented at the Speech Communication Association Convention, Anaheim, California, November 1981; and Michael Pfau, "Criteria and Format to Optimize Series," paper presented at the Speech Communication Association Convention, Anaheim, California, November 1981. Ironically, Patrick Caddell noted that the 1980 presidential debate format used by Reagan and Carter, which allowed for nine to ten minutes of discussion on a single topic, was "exhaustive." See his "Memo of October 21, 1980," reprinted in Elizabeth Drew, *Portrait of an Election: The 1980 Election* (New York: Simon and Schuster, 1981), p. 426.

9. Auer, "Counterfeit Debates," p. 148.

10. Perhaps the debate with the most significance for the subsequent development of political debating was the one held between the Tennessee gubernatorial candidates in 1886. For an explanation of the subsequent impact of this debate, see Herbert A. Terry and Sidney Kraus, "Legal and Political Aspects: Was Section 315 Circumvented?" in *The Great Debates: Carter vs. Ford, 1976*, ed. Sidney Kraus (Bloomington: Indiana University Press, 1979), pp. 44–45.

11. See Jamieson and Birdsell, *Presidential Debates*, pp. 35–36 for a discussion of this feature of nineteenth-century campaigns.

12. When debates were held, they were frequently the centerpieces of the campaigns. For an expecially informative example of this, see Cal M. Logue, "Gubernatorial Campaign in Georgia in 1880," *Southern Speech Communication Journal* 40 (Fall 1974): 12–32.

13. Samuel L. Becker and Elmer W. Lower, "Broadcasting in Presidential Campaigns," in *The Great Debates: Kennedy vs. Nixon, 1960*, ed. Sidney Kraus (Bloomington: Indiana University Press, 1962), p. 29.

14. Quoted in Sidney Head, *Broadcasting in America* (Boston: Houghton Mifflin, 1976), p. 331.

15. For a full discussion of these changes, see Edward W. Chester, *Radio, Television, and American Politics* (New York: Sheed and Ward, 1969), pp. 247–65. Also see Head, *Broadcasting in America*, pp. 330–32.

16. Chester, *Radio, Television, and American Politics*, p. 37. Also see Becker and Lower, "Broadcasting in Presidential Campaigns," p. 35.

17. Chester, *Radio, Television, and American Politics*, p. 42.

18. An excellent description of this debate can be found in Robert F. Ray, "Thomas E. Dewey: The Great Oregon Debate of 1948," in *American Public Address: Studies in Honor of Albert Craig Baird*, ed. Loren Reid (Columbia: University of Missouri Press, 1961), pp. 245–70.

19. Lee M. Mitchell, *With the Nation Watching* (Lexington, Mass.: D.C. Heath, 1979), p. 28 claims that Moody made his suggestion while being interviewed on the CBS radio network show *The People's Platform* in July of 1952. J. Leonard Reinsch, a media consultant to Presidents Roosevelt and Truman also made an early effort to get Stevenson and Eisenhower to debate. See Goodwin Berquist, "The 1976 Carter–Ford Presidential Debates," in *Rhetorical Studies of National Political Debates: 1960–1988*, ed. Robert V. Friedenberg (New York: Praeger, 1990), p. 29.

20. In 1952 neither man felt comfortable with the idea of televised debates. Both candidates were also advised not to debate.

21. Mitchell, *With the Nation Watching*, p. 30.

22. Chester, *Radio, Television, and American Politics*, pp. 133–35 provides a brief account of the stimulus that the 1960 presidential debates had on political debating.

23. For a complete and far more thorough account of this change in the equal time provisions, see Terry and Kraus, "Legal and Political Aspects," pp. 41–49.

24. This section is based primarily on two articles by Robert Friedenberg. Full citations for all quoted material and fuller explanations of all major points can be found in those two articles. See Robert V. Friedenberg, " 'We Are Present Here Today for the Purpose of Having a Joint Discussion': The Conditions Requisite for Political Debates," *Journal of the American Forensic Association* 16 (Summer 1979): 1–9; Robert V. Friedenberg, " 'Selfish Interest,' or the Prerequisites for Political Debate: An Analysis of the 1980 Presidential Debate and Its Implications for Future Campaigns," *Journal of the American Forensic Association* 18 (Fall 1981): 91–98. The authors wish to thank the American Forensic Association for permission to use those articles.

25. Reagan's 1984 advisors have been quoted as claiming that "they did not think it would be politically acceptable" for the president to refuse to debate. Apparently well in command of the election, Reagan and his strategists nevertheless evidently feared the negative reaction his refusal to debate might prompt. See J. Jeffery Auer, "Presidential Debates: Public Understanding and Political Institutionalization," *Speaker and Gavel* 24 (Fall 1986): 5. Auer cites a conversation between Reagan advisors and reporter Elizabeth Drew. Similarly, see Craig Allen Smith and Kathy B. Smith, "The 1984 Reagan–Mondale Presidential Debates," in *Rhetorical Studies of National Political Debates: 1960–1988*, ed. Robert V. Friedenberg, (New York: Praeger, 1990), p. 96.

26. On the evolution of public attitudes toward incumbent presidential debating see Robert V. Friedenberg, "Patterns and Trends in National Political Debates: 1960–1996," in *Rhetorical Studies of National Political Debates—1996*, ed. Robert V. Friedenberg (Westport Conn.: Praeger, 1997), pp. 62–64.

27. The following account of the 1960 debates is based primarily on Theodore White, *The Making of the President 1960* (New York: Pocket Books, 1961); Kenneth P. O'Donnell and David F. Powers, *Johnny, We Hardly Knew Ye* (New York: Pocket Books, 1973); and Friedenberg, "Conditions for Political Debates."

28. For a more complete account of this debate see Christopher Matthews, *Kennedy and Nixon: The Rivalry That Shaped Postwar America* (New York: Simon and Schuster, 1996), pp. 51–53.

29. The sources used for this paragraph and throughout the remainder of this

section on the 1992 debates include the appropriate sections of Peter Goldman and Tom Mathews, *Newsweek* "Election Special" edition, November/December 1992; Jack Germond and Jules Witcover, *Mad As Hell: Revolt at the Ballot Box, 1992* (New York: Warner Books, 1993) and the continuing campaign coverage of the *New York Times*, the *Washington Post*, and the *Cincinnati Enquirer* for September and October of 1992.

30. Commission on Presidential Debates, "Schedule for 1996 Debates" (available at http://www.debates 96.org/96sched.htm).

31. Commission on Presidential Debates, "Candidate Selection Criteria for 1996 General Election Debate Participation" (available at http://www.debates96.org/criteria.htm).

32. Ibid.

33. Politics Now, "Dole, Clinton Haggle on Debates" (available at http://www.politicsnow.com/news/Sept96/18/apo918debates/).

34. Gallop Poll, "3 Way Trial Heat-Selected Trend" (available at http://www.gallup.com/poll/news/960927.html).

35. Politics Now, "Dole, Clinton Haggle."

36. Richard E. Neustadt, "Text of Letter from Advisory Board to Commission on Presidential Debates," September 17, 1996 (available at http://www.debates96.org./advisory.htm).

37. Goodwin F. Berquist and James L. Golden, "Media Rhetoric, Criticism, and the Public Perception of the 1980 Presidential Debates," *Quarterly Journal of Speech* 67 (May 1981): pp. 125–26.

38. Ibid., pp. 127–28.

39. This and the next paragraph are based heavily on Smith and Smith, "The 1984 Reagan–Mondale Presidential Debates," pp. 100–116, which focuses heavily upon the role of public expectations.

40. See Kathleen Kendall, "The 1996 Clinton–Dole Debates: Through Media Eyes," in *Rhetorical Studies of National Political Debates: 1996*, ed. Robert V. Friedenberg (Westport, Conn.: Praeger, 1997), p. 13.

41. Ibid., p. 17

42. Gaut Ragsdale, "The 1996 Gore–Kemp Vice Presidential Debate," in *Rhetorical Studies of National Political Debates: 1996*, ed. Robert V. Friedenberg (Westport, Conn.: Praeger, 1997), p. 34.

43. One of the authors, Friedenberg, has been involved in a variety of political debates. Also see for examples Dale Hardy-Short, "An Insider's View of the Constraints Affecting Geraldine Ferraro's Preparation for the 1984 Vice Presidential Debate," *Speaker and Gavel* 24 (Fall 1986): 8–22; Myles Martel, "Debate Preparations in the Reagan Camp: An Insider's View," *Speaker and Gavel* 18 (Winter 1981): 34–46; Martin Schram, *Running for President* (New York: Pocket Books, 1977), pp. 326–31, 348–64, 370–89; Caddell, "Memo of October 21, 1980," pp. 410–39; White, *Making of the President 1960*, 335–55; Theodore Otto Windt, "The 1960 Kennedy–Nixon Presidential Debates," in *Rhetorical Studies of National Political Debates: 1960–1988* ed. Robert V. Friedenberg (New York: Praeger, 1990), pp. 9–10; and Judith S. Trent, "The 1984 Bush–Ferraro Vice Presidential Debate," also in *Rhetorical Studies of National Political Debates: 1960–1988*, pp. 135–36.

44. By all accounts, Ronald Reagan's preparation for his 1980 debates with John Anderson and Jimmy Carter was the most thorough in this regard. Reagan

practiced in a garage converted to resemble the actual television studios used in the debates. His staff went to great lengths to simulate and anticipate his opponents, including studying tapes of prior debates involving Anderson and Carter. Eventually David Stockman, a former administrative assistant to John Anderson, based in large part on his study of tapes, played both Anderson and Carter in Reagan's practice sessions. The 1980s proliferation of candidate forums and candidate debates during the primary season has meant that by the general election, at least at the presidential level, candidates have been in a variety of debates or debate-like situations, and an opponent will normally have access to tapes of their prior performances.

45. See the sections on debate preparation in the Kendall and Ragsdale studies cited above.

46. An informative account of this frequently overlooked precursor to the 1960 general election debates can be found in Goodwin F. Berquist, "The Kennedy–Humphrey Debate," *Today's Speech* 7 (September 1960): 2–3.

47. Walter Shapiro, "Countdown Mentality," *Time*, September 28, 1992, p. 43. Also see Jeffrey H. Birnbaum, "Bush and Clinton Work at Honing the Themes of Their Campaigns into Weapons for Debates," *Wall Street Journal*, October 9, 1992, p. A16.

48. "Transcript of First TV Debate Among Bush, Clinton, and Perot," *New York Times*, October 12, 1992, p. A14.

49. "Transcript of the First TV Debate Between Bush and Dukakis," *New York Times*, September 26, 1988, p. A19.

50. See "Transcript of the Second Debate Between Bush and Dukakis," *New York Times*, October 14, 1988, p. A14.

51. Debate transcripts for all of the 1996 presidential and vice presidential debates can be obtained through the home page of the Commission on Presidential Debates (http://www.debates96.org).

52. Robert O. Weiss, "The Presidential Debates in Their Political Context; The Issue-Image Interface in the 1980 Campaign," *Speaker and Gavel* 18 (Winter 1981): 22–27.

53. Ibid., p. 22.

54. This threefold analysis of image strategies is based on Dan Nimmo's discussion of the techniques that can be used by a political figure. The terminology and definitions are Nimmo's. See Dan Nimmo, *Popular Images of Politics* (Englewood Cliffs, N.J.: Prentice-Hall, 1974), pp. 100–102.

55. See the transcript of the first debate cited above. Both Bush in 1992 and Clinton in 1996 wanted their parties to regain control of Congress to better facilitate the passage of their own programs. However, Bush undermined his activist image by alluding to his need for a new Congress, while Clinton simply ignored the need for a new Congress and focused entirely on his own accomplishments and goals for the future.

56. Quoted passages from the 1980 presidential debate are taken from the NBC-verified transcript record of the debate found in *The Pursuit of the Presidency 1980*, ed. Richard Harwood (New York: Berkley Books, 1980), pp. 359–400.

57. Frederick T. Steeper, "Public Response to Gerald Ford's Statements on Eastern Europe in the Second Debate," in *The Presidential Debates: Media, Electoral*

and Policy Perspectives, ed. George F. Bishop, Robert G. Meadow, and Marilyn Jackson-Beeck (New York: Praeger, 1978), p. 101.

58. Ibid. Also see Roger Desmond and Thomas Donohue, "The Role of the 1976 Televised Presidential Debates in the Political Socialization of Adolescents," *Communication Quarterly* 29 (Fall 1981): 306–8; and George A. Barnett, "A Multidimensional Analysis of the 1976 Presidential Campaign," *Communication Quarterly* 29 (Summer 1981): 156–65.

59. Tom Rosenstiel, *Strange Bedfellows: How Television and the Presidential Candidates Changed American Politics, 1992* (New York: Hyperion Books, 1993), pp. 303–4.

60. In 1992 the Perot campaign did not make a "spin" effort commensurate with those of Clinton, Bush, and most presidential campaigns since 1976.

61. See the studies of the 1996 debates by Kendall and Ragsdale for discussion of the postdebate television coverage.

62. Evan Thomas, "Victory March," *Newsweek*, November 18, 1996, p. 114.

63. The use of this strategy is largely dependent upon the cooperation of the press, which must disseminate the views of the surrogate spokespersons. Steven Brydon's study of the network treatment of the 1988 presidential debates suggests that the networks are becoming sensitive to being "used" in this fashion. Negative network characterizations of candidate surrogates as "spin doctors," as well as the reduced time networks seem to be giving such spokespersons, may ultimately reduce their effectiveness. See Steven R. Brydon, "Spinners on Patrol: Network Coverage in the Aftermath of Presidential and Vice Presidential Debates," paper presented to the Speech Communication Association Convention, San Antonio, Tex., November 1989.

64. Cited in Harry P. Kerr, "The Great Debates in a New Perspective," *Today's Speech* 9 (November 1961): 11.

65. Susan A. Helleg and Steven L. Phillips, "A Verbal and Visual Analysis of the 1980 Houston Republican Presidential Primary Debate," *Southern Speech Communication Journal* 47 (Fall 1981): 24.

66. John P. Robinson, "The Polls," in *The Great Debates: Carter vs. Ford, 1976*, ed. Sidney Kraus (Bloomington: Indiana University Press, 1979), pp. 262–63.

67. The preceding audience figures are all drawn from Warren Decker, "The 1988 Quayle–Bentsen Vice Presidential Debates," in *Rhetorical Studies of National Political Debates: 1960–1988*, ed. Robert V. Friedenberg (New York: Praeger, 1990), p. 181. Decker cites a *Washington Post* article as the source of these figures.

68. The figures cited in this paragraph are drawn from The Freedom Forum Media Studies Center, *The Finish Line: Covering the Campaign's Final Days* (New York: Freedom Forum Media Studies Center, 1993), p. 40; Germond and Witcover, *Mad as Hell*, p. 480; and Kendall, "The 1996 Clinton–Dole Presidential Debates," p. 22.

69. Bruce is quoted in Kitty Bruce, *The Almost Unpublished Lenny Bruce* (Philadelphia: Running Press, 1984), p. 91.

70. *Newsweek*, October 17, 1960, p. 27.

71. George Gallup, Jr., "The Impact of Presidential Debates on the Vote and Turnout" in *Presidential Debates: 1988 and Beyond*, ed. Joel L. Swerdlow (Washington, D.C.: Congressional Quarterly Books, 1987), p. 34.

72. The debates seemed to have very slight effect in 1996. Typical of many

polls were the findings of the Gallup organization, which were conducted for several media outlets. Gallup found that during the week prior to the first debate, Clinton was favored by 52.42 percent of the voters. In the week after the last debate, Clinton was favored by 52.71 percent of the voters. In the week prior to the debates Dole was favored by 36.85 percent of the voters. In the week after the debates, Dole was favored by 34.14 percent. See "Daily Tracking Poll" (available at http://www.usatoday.com/elect/eq/eq/127.htm). The Gallup figures are highly consistent with those of other polling groups. See for example, the results of the ABC News Poll, "The Data" (available at http://www.politicsnow.com/news/Oct96/31/abc1031data/).

Walter Zakahi, Kenneth Hacker, and Nancy Baker's "The Effects of Post Presidential Debate Analysis by Network Television Journalists on Viewer's Perceptions of Debate Outcomes," paper presented at the Speech Communication Association Convention, San Antonio, Tex., 1993, p. 10 claimed that the most surprising of their findings was that even among undecided voters, whom they hypothesized would be most likely to be affected by the 1992 debate, the debate had little effect on voting intention. Similarly, journalists Jack Germond and Jules Witcover concluded that the debates did not change the dynamic of the 1992 campaign (Germond and Witcover, *Mad as Hell*, p. 480). Studies of the 1988 debates also suggest that those debates reinforced existing attitudes. See, for example, Michael Pfau and Jong Geun Kang, "The Impact of Relational and Nonverbal Communication in Political Debate Influence," paper presented to the Speech Communication Association Annual Conference, San Antonio, Tex., November 1989, p. 16.

73. David O. Sears and Steven H. Chaffee, "Uses and Effects of the 1976 Debates: An Overview of Empirical Studies," in *The Great Debates: Carter vs. Ford, 1976*, ed. Sidney Kraus (Bloomington: Indiana University Press, 1979), p. 255.

74. For a study of the 1980 debates that clearly supports these implications, see David Leuthold and David Valentine, "How Reagan Won the Cleveland Debate: Audience Predispositions and Presidential Debate Winners," *Speaker and Gavel* 18 (Winter 1981): 60–66, esp. pp. 65–66.

75. Elmo Roper, "Polling Post-Mortem," *Saturday Review* (November 26, 1960): 10–13.

76. Elihu Katz and Jacob Feldman, "The Debates in Light of Research: A Survey of Surveys," in *The Great Debates: Kennedy vs. Nixon, 1960*, ed. Sidney Kraus (Bloomington: Indiana University Press, 1962), p. 211.

77. Jack M. McLeod et al., "Reactions of Young and Older Voters: Expanding the Context of Effects," in *The Great Debates: Carter vs. Ford, 1976*, ed. Sidney Kraus (Bloomington: Indiana University Press, 1979), pp. 365–66; Paul R. Hagner and Leroy N. Rieselbach, "The Impact of the 1976 Presidential Debates: Conversion or Reinforcement?" in *The Presidential Debates: Media, Electoral, and Policy Perspectives*, ed. George F. Bishop, Robert G. Meadow, and Marilyn Jackson-Beeck (New York: Praeger, 1978), p. 178.

78. Leuthold and Valentine, "How Reagan Won," p. 62.

79. Smith and Smith, "The 1984 Reagan-Mondale Presidential Debates," p. 102.

80. Ibid.

81. For a summary of the findings of major polls taken after the first 1988

debate see Halford Ryan, "The 1988 Bush–Dukakis Presidential Debates," in *Rhetorical Studies of National Political Debates: 1960–1988*, ed. Robert V. Friedenberg (New York: Prager, 1990), p. 159. *Time*, October 10, 1989, p. 27, summarized the findings of their poll, and illustrated part of Dukakis's difficulty in translating his debate victory into votes by observing that "although voters judged Dukakis the 'better debater,' they found Bush 'more presidential and more likeable'— qualities far more likely to guide them in the voting booth." Also see Michael Pfau and Jong Geun Kang, "The Impact of Relational and Nonverbal Communication in Political Influence," p. 16.

82. Elizabeth Drew, *Election Journal: Political Events of 1987–1988* (New York: William Morrow and Company, 1989), p. 291.

83. These figures are drawn from a wide variety of sources. See, for example, "Clinton Fending Off Assaults," *The New York Times*, October 15, 1992, p. A1; *Newsweek*, Special Election Edition, November/December 1992, p. 88; L. Patrick Devlin, "The 1992 Gore–Quayle–Stockdale Vice Presidential Debate," in *Rhetorical Studies of National Political Debates: 1960–1992*, ed. Robert V. Friedenberg (New York: Praeger, 1994), p. 228; "Jabs, No Knockouts," *USA Today*, October 12, 1992, pp. 1A. "Debates Set; Will People Watch," *Boston Globe*, October 4, 1992, p. 16.

84. See "Daily Tracking Poll," and "The Data."

85. Maxwell McCombs, "Agenda Setting Research: A Bibliographic Essay," *Political Communication Review* 1 (Summer 1976): 3.

86. Linda L. Swanson and David L. Swanson, "The Agenda Setting Function of the First Ford–Carter Debate," *Communication Monographs* 45 (November 1978): 347–53.

87. Ibid., p. 353.

88. Ibid.

89. Lee B. Becker et al., "Debates' Effects on Voter Understanding of Candidates and Issues," in *The Presidential Debates: Media, Electoral, and Policy Perspectives*, ed. George F. Bishop, Robert G. Meadow, and Marilyn Jackson-Beeck (New York: Praeger, 1978), pp. 137–38; Steven H. Chaffee, "Presidential Debates—Are They Helpful to Voters?" *Communication Monographs* 45 (November 1978): 336; Jian Huazhu, J. Ronald Milawsky, and Rahul Biswas, "Do Televised Debates Affect Image Perception More Than Issue Knowledge: A Study of the First 1992 Presidential Debate," *Human Communication Research* 20 (March 1994): 302–32.

90. Allen Lichtenstein, "Differences in Impact Between Local and National Televised Political Candidates' Debates," *Western Journal of Speech Communication* 46 (Summer 1982): 296.

91. Pfau, "Criteria and Format," pp. 5–6.

92. Soma Golden, "Inside the Debate," *New York Times*, September 24, 1980, p. A30.

93. For an examination of the differing agendas of voters, reporters, and candidates, see Marilyn Jackson-Beeck and Robert Meadow, "The Triple Agenda of Presidential Debates," *Public Opinion Quarterly* 42 (Summer 1979): 173–80.

94. Ryan, "The 1988 Bush–Dukakis Presidential Debates," p. 160.

95. See, for example, Stephen Mills, "Rebuilding Presidential Debates," *Speaker and Gavel* 24 (Fall 1986): 41–51; Jamieson and Birdsell, *Presidential*

Debates, pp. 201–2; Sidney Kraus, *Televised Presidential Debates and Public Policy* (Hillsdale, N.J.: Lawrence Erlbaum Associates, 1988), pp. 144–45.

96. See J. Jeffery Auer, "Presidential Debates: Public Understanding and Political Institutionalization," *Speaker and Gavel* 24 (Fall 1986): 5–6. Auer cites a study of 11 journalists who served on debate panels and reports that five of them claimed such panels should be eliminated.

97. Windt, "The 1960 Kennedy–Nixon Presidential Debates," p. 4.

98. Hagner and Rieselbach, "Impact of 1976 Presidential Debates," p. 172.

99. Sears and Chaffee, "Uses and Effects of 1976 Debates," pp. 246–47.

100. Kevin Sauter, "The 1976 Mondale–Dole Vice Presidential Debate," in *Rhetorical Studies of National Political Debates: 1960–1988,* ed. Robert V. Friedenberg (New York: Praeger, 1990), pp. 45–68.

101. These characterizations are representative of a wide variety of press reactions cited in L. Patrick Devlin, "The 1992 Gore–Quayle–Stockdale Vice Presidential Debate," in *Rhetorical Studies of National Political Debates 1960–1992,* ed. Robert V. Friedenberg (New York: Praeger, 1994), pp. 229–30.

102. Dan Hahn, "The 1992 Clinton–Bush–Perot Presidential Debate," in *Rhetorical Studies of National Political Debates: 1960–1992,* ed. Robert V. Friedenberg (New York: Praeger, 1994), p. 208.

103. Sidney Kraus and Dennis Davis, "Political Debates," in *Handbook of Political Communication,* ed. Dan Nimmo and Keith Sanders (Beverly Hills, Calif.: Sage, 1981), pp. 273–98.

104. Samuel L. Becker et al., "Information Flow and the Shaping of Meanings," in *The Great Debates: Carter vs. Ford, 1976,* ed. Sidney Kraus (Bloomington: Indiana University Press, 1979), p. 396.

105. Chaffee, "Presidential Debates," pp. 343–45.

106. Kraus, *Televised Presidential Debates and Public Policy,* p. 123.

Chapter 9

Interpersonal Communication in Political Campaigns

This chapter examines the place of interpersonal communication in political campaigns. We perceive interpersonal communication to be transactional. When people communicate they define themselves and simultaneously respond to their perceptions of the definitions being offered by others. This transactional perspective, which we share with most communication scholars, has several implications that have unusual importance for political communication.

First, interpersonal communication is contextual. Part of the context in which any communication takes place is the other person. You behave differently when you are with your children than when you are with your employer. Each participant affects the other. Similarly, candidates behave differently when they visit with a small group of bowlers in neighborhood bowling alleys than when they visit with a few large financial contributors in someone's home. The physical setting of the two transactions, the differences in background music and noise, the differences in clothing worn by the bowlers and the contributors, the differences in the language used by the two groups, and countless other stimuli help define the bowlers and the contributors to the candidate. Simultaneously, the presence of the candidate in the bowling alley or at a contributor's home, the clothing and language of the candidate, and countless other stimuli that the candidate emits enable the bowlers and the contributors to define the candidate. As each party to the transaction shapes and refines definitions of the other, their own behavior will be affected, thus continually changing the communication context.

Second, this perspective suggests that each party to the transaction is simultaneously both a sender and a receiver of verbal and nonverbal messages. When you meet the candidate at a neighborhood coffee and criticize a local bond issue that the candidate supports, you are simultaneously watching facial expressions, observing the tightening of the candidate's fist, and noting that the candidate's face is becoming flush. As candidates emit these communicative stimuli, they are defining themselves to you. You better sense the candidate's support for this bond issue and the irritation your criticism provokes, even though the candidate may have said nothing.

Clearly, as you observe candidates listening to your criticism, they appear affected by your statements. Similarly, as you see the candidate's face flush and fist tighten, you begin to temper your criticism. You gradually lower your voice and use more moderate language. You have been affected by this communication transaction, and so has the candidate. This is the third major implication that the transactional perspective has for political communication; each participant affects and is affected by the other.

In addition to noting our transactional perspective, before beginning our discussion of interpersonal communication and political campaigning, we want to note two other characteristics of the interpersonal communication to be studied in this chapter. They deliberately narrow the expanse of interpersonal communication, limiting it to interpersonal communication utilized in political campaigns. First, one party to the interpersonal transactions discussed in this chapter is either a candidate or the surrogate/advocate of a candidate. The surrogate/advocate may be a formal representative of the candidate, such as a member of the campaign staff, or an informal representative, such as a voter who is not in any way affiliated with the candidate but nevertheless discusses the candidate. The final characteristic of the interpersonal transactions examined is that the overt, normally verbal, messages either directly or indirectly involve a campaign for public office.

In this chapter, we will discuss three crucial areas of interpersonal communication in political campaigns: interpersonal communication between the candidate and voters, interpersonal communication between the candidate and potential financial contributors, and interpersonal communication between voters.[1]

INTERPERSONAL COMMUNICATION BETWEEN CANDIDATES AND VOTERS

As indicated in Chapter 5, no resource is more vital to the campaign than the candidate's time. This is a finite resource. Once the time is lost, it cannot be replaced. Consequently, if candidates are spending time meeting individuals or small groups of individuals, they must be sure that there is an unusually high chance that these meetings will be productive. For candidates to spend three hours with two, four, or 10 people and come away with nothing is a loss that cannot be recovered. More money cannot buy lost time, nor can more volunteers produce it. Hence, decisions on where the candidates should spend time and with whom they should meet are critical.

The use of the candidate's time is especially critical in local campaigns. Over 500,000 public offices in the United States, from president to the infamous dog catcher are filled by election.[2] Lynda Lee Kaid points out that the tendency of researchers to study highly visible national and statewide campaigns has caused us often to neglect what is the most effective channel of political persuasion in vast numbers of races—the interpersonal communication of the candidate.[3] As Kaid notes, the channels of communication available to candidates in thousands of campaigns below the national and statewide levels are often severely limited.

In many campaigns, the geographic makeup of the district precludes the effective use of mass media such as radio and television. For example, the eighth congressional district of Ohio, located between Cincinnati and Dayton, includes about 95,000 residents of suburban Cincinnati. It also includes Hamilton (a town of 80,000), Middletown (a town of 60,000), all of Preble County (a prosperous agricultural county with no town over 20,000) and parts of Darke, Green, and Montgomery counties, including portions of suburban Dayton. To use traditional broadcast television effectively in this district, the candidate would have to purchase time on both Dayton and Cincinnati stations. Yet the approximately 70 percent of the district receiving Cincinnati television constitutes less than 20 percent of the Cincinnati media market. The remaining 30 percent of this district, within the Dayton media market, constitutes less than 10 percent of the Dayton media market. To cover this district adequately with broadcast television, candidates would have to pay for an audience approximately 10 times larger than the one they want. As will be illustrated in Chapter 10, in recent elections, the growth of cable television has started to facilitate the use of television in some districts such as these.

Moreover, within this single congressional district, there are hundreds of other elected public officials: county commissioners in Butler, Preble, Darke, Green, Hamilton, and Montgomery counties; county prosecutors, treasurers, sheriffs, and the like in each county; and city council members, mayors, and a variety of other officials in at least 40 communities. The point should be abundantly clear. Geographic and financial considerations make television, radio, and other mass media at best extremely costly and at worst simply impractical for hundreds of races in this area alone and for hundreds of thousands of races nationally. The targeting provided by radio, and even cable, is often simply not narrow enough for many lower ballot races. Additionally, messages on behalf of most local candidates, delivered through the mass media, are liable to be ignored or ineffective when those media are saturated with information concerning the major contests for president, governor, or senator. Although it may not be as widely appropriate as when she first wrote, Lynda Lee Kaid's conclusion that "the interplay of some or all of these limitations may create an environment in which interpersonal communication, particularly communication between the candidate and the voters, may be a crucial factor in the outcome of an election"[4] is still true for many races, particularly those for lesser offices and those in rural areas.

Given the importance of the candidate's time and given that in many races its waste cannot be offset by purchasing media time, it is essential that the candidate's interpersonal communication be utilized effectively.[5] This means that candidates must know where to campaign. Consequently, in local races especially, the most valuable materials that a campaign can have are often the precinct analysis of recent voter statistics, such as those illustrated in Chapter 6. The thoroughness of such analysis is a direct function of the amounts of money spent on obtaining them. In most states, local party organizations will prepare voter statistics for candidates. Hence, even in areas where the local organization is weak, candidates should not have trouble obtaining a complete analysis of prior voting statistics for their district. Moreover, if the various party organizations do not provide an analysis of statistics, candidates can obtain the statistics themselves and perform their own analysis, since all vote totals are a matter of public record and kept on file by the appropriate election boards.

Once they have access to prior election results, particularly a precinct-by-precinct analysis, candidates can determine which precincts are essentially Republican, Democratic, or marked by a high incidence of ticket-splitting. As we observed in Chapter 6, the candidate should direct the campaign primarily at those precincts where the party traditionally runs well and those precincts where ticket-splitting commonly takes place. It is in these precincts that most of the candidate's interpersonal communication should take place.

Far more than national figures, local candidates must know precisely where to spend their time. Because their constituencies are smaller, in many instances local candidates can knock on every door in their district or at least on every door in those precincts that are deemed most important. The door-to-door campaigning of candidates for major offices is most often done for media coverage, rather than for any direct impact. It allows the major candidate to appear in the media while walking through a ghetto or a cornfield, presumably illustrating concern for blacks or farmers. Local candidates will not receive media exposure of their door-to-door campaigning. Rather, their efforts will put them face-to-face with a large percentage of their constituency. Interpersonal campaigning is not symbolic for the local candidate, as it is for the major candidate. Rather, it is often the major thrust of the campaign, an essential means of compensating for the lack of media exposure.

It is often difficult for an inexperienced candidate or campaign staff to recognize the critical importance of targeting voters, even in interpersonal campaigning. Candidates and campaign staffs are often tempted to meet the most people, not necessarily targeted people. But just as duck hunters must go where the ducks are, regardless of where the deer or the turkeys may be, so too candidates must go where their targeted voters are, not simply where there are a lot of people. Candidates for lower ballot races especially will often want to campaign at the county fair, the little league game, the municipal pool, the factory gate, or the busy intersection. Typically, the people whom the candidate may meet in these situations are often not those targeted by the campaign. Indeed, a good deal of the candidate's precious time might well be wasted dealing with people who are not even registered to vote, or not registered in their district. The candidate's interpersonal communication should always be targeted to potential voters and supporters. If this allows the campaign to utilize the candidate or other affiliated spokespersons at the factory gate or the busy street corner, fine. But campaigns, particularly local campaigns, must keep in mind that their interpersonal communication efforts must not be aimed at communicating with the most voters, but rather at communicating with targeted voters.[6]

Though major candidates do not rely as extensively on interpersonal campaigning as do local candidates, it does often serve an important place in their campaigns. Clearly, because of the size of the constituency, major candidates, as well as many local candidates, will utilize surrogate/advocates to represent them in door-to-door canvasses of a community. The door-to-door canvass is often especially effective in the primary campaigns of major candidates. Such races typically involve substantially fewer voters than the general election. Candidates and their representatives can often reach a high percentage of those voters who are eligible to vote in the primary. George McGovern's effective use of the principles of interpersonal communication in door-to-door canvassing in small state primaries that occurred early in 1972, such as New Hampshire, Massachusetts, and Rhode Island, played a substantial role in his success that year and has been emulated by imitators in every primary season since.[7]

The most typical methods of interpersonal campaigning by candidates or their representatives are coffees and door-to-door canvasses. Each method allows the candidates or their representatives to interact for brief periods of time with a small number of voters. Done repeatedly, they may serve as an effective means of supplementing media campaigning or, as in the case of many local candidates, almost entirely replacing it.

The Coffee

Keeping in mind the precinct analysis of voters, the campaign organization will arrange a schedule of coffees. The events can be as casual or formal as the hosts wish. Some hosts will keep it very informal, serving coffee, tea, soft drinks, perhaps beer. If, as might happen on occasion, the event is also to serve as a fund-raiser, the refreshments will typically be somewhat more elaborate. But these details are for the host/hostess to arrange. Once they have agreed to host the event, the campaign may provide them guidance, but it is, after all, their party for the candidate.[8] The organization should arrange the coffees so that the candidate is able to meet with two groups. First, "those people residing in areas which are generally independent" and in which considerable ticket-splitting takes place. Second, "coffees should be scheduled in areas where the candidate and his party can be expected to run well."[9] In these areas, coffees give "the candidate an opportunity to pay personal attention to those who are working for him. It gives the campaign organization an opportunity to recruit new workers."

Keeping in mind our transactional viewpoint of interpersonal communication, we can readily see why campaigners seek to hold coffees and similar events that promote interpersonal transactions with neutral and friendly voters. Such events provide the candidate with much more than the opportunity simply to meet voters. They provide the candidate with the opportunity to establish a relationship, to affect the other parties in the transaction.

In virtually any election, but perhaps more so in local elections, candidates will often meet constituents in countless small social gatherings early in the campaign. They can then follow up on the relationships initiated at these meetings by remaining in contact with short notes, letters, and calls. People are affected by the candidates they meet this way, and subsequently those people often prove helpful to the candidates.

Conversely, candidates are also affected by interpersonal transactions such as coffees. As we have seen in Chapter 2, promises made during the surfacing and primary stages of a campaign tend to be kept more than those made later. Part of the reason for this seems to be that promises made early in the campaign are frequently made in small interpersonal contexts, where the candidate is more prone to be affected by voters. Later in the campaign, crowded candidate schedules often prohibit the types of interpersonal transactions that frequently take place early in the campaign.

Candidates "should never attend" coffees by themselves. They should

always have another person with them. The function of this other individual is to get the candidate away from the coffee gracefully if the host/
hostess fails to do so. The candidate's associate, not the candidate or the
host/hostess, can take the blame for rushing the candidate away if that
becomes necessary. The candidate should avoid making speeches at coffees. Rather, a candidate "need give only brief informal remarks." After
the candidate's brief remarks, a short question-and-answer period is appropriate.

Four rules should govern every coffee. First, "optimum size of the
gathering is twenty to thirty people." This includes the host and hostess,
candidate, and those traveling with the candidate. Second, name tags
should be provided for each guest. The affair is essentially social, and
the candidate wants to establish a first name relationship with the guests.
One consultant who has been involved in arranging a large number of
meetings of this sort advises candidates to "obtain a list of the attendees
prior to the event and become familiar with your audience."[10] The individual traveling with the candidate might also help in this regard.
Third, the host or hostess should "never permit a guest to buttonhole
the candidate or enter into arguments." Finally, it should always be remembered that the coffee "is an excuse for getting together, and the
stress should be on easy informality and comfort."

This description of an ideal coffee clearly indicates that the simple act
of being present and interacting with a number of voters is as important,
if not more so, than what the candidate actually says. A well-run coffee
maximizes the opportunities for fruitful interpersonal transactions. Time
is devoted to establishing personal friendships. The group is small
enough for the candidate to interact with everyone, and the candidate's
aide as well as the host or hostess of the coffee should facilitate the
candidate's interaction with everyone.

Laura Peck, vice president of a large political consulting firm, recommends that in situations such as these, eye contact is essential. She recommends that candidates "give your full attention, even if for just a few
seconds, to the person in front of you. If someone is anxious to meet
you, you will feel positively encouraged and reinforced. Once the connection is sealed, you can then move on."[11]

Peck also stresses the importance of handshakes. She claims that "with
a handshake, you touch your audience physically for the first time. This
tactile presentation will be remembered." She adds that "if you wish to
make the connection especially heart-felt, place your other hand on top
of the handshake."[12]

Local candidates often run for administrative positions that do not
involve issues of policy. The county recorder, engineer, prosecutor, and
sheriff, for example, provide administrative services, but they rarely set
policy. Hence, interpersonal communication opportunities, where can-

didates can establish relationships illustrating their concern, personality, and character, are vital. Given that many local races lack real issues between the candidates and that the candidates are relatively unknown, often the candidates who are best known in the district, who have visited the neighborhoods, who seem to make themselves available and accessible, and who have worked at establishing relationships are the candidates who most appeal to the voter.

Good campaigns can effectively arrange three coffees an evening for their candidates, several evenings a week, through the last months of the campaign. Such programs, particularly in local races, enable candidates to interact with a significant percentage of their constituency. Moreover, the candidate's presence in the neighborhood will be rapidly reported the next day over backyard fences, in beauty and barber shops, at gas stations, and in stores, as those invited to the coffee discuss their experience.

The Door-to-Door Canvass

The use of small social gatherings such as coffees serves primarily to foster interaction between the candidate and voters. A second major form of interpersonal communication between the candidate and voters, the door-to-door canvass, typically serves several additional purposes. Like the coffees, it should provide candidates and their representatives with an opportunity to deal personally with a large number of voters. Hopefully, as with the coffees, candidates will be perceived as accessible and concerned, leaving a positive image with the voters they meet. Presumably, the same impressions should be left with voters who meet the candidates' representatives.

The canvass can serve additional functions and is often utilized in major races, where coffees play a lesser role. When utilized in major races, most of the canvassing is done by representatives of the candidate. Regardless of who is canvassing, the canvass can identify voters who are favorable, neutral, or hostile to the candidate. Depending on their attitudes, these voters can subsequently be contacted. The canvass also is an excellent means of distributing information about the candidate. A conversation between the canvasser and the voter can provide information about the candidate. Additionally, the canvasser can leave materials, and if the voter has a specific concern, the canvasser can arrange to have additional information sent later.[13]

Important principles of interpersonal communication should be implemented by canvassers if they are doing their jobs well. The instructions given to those who canvass on behalf of a candidate "will typically exhibit sensitivity to psychological principles important in interpersonal communication."[14] Instuctions such as these are representative of what most campaigns will encourage.

1. Speak with enthusiasm and sincerity.
2. Be a good listener. Let the voters speak. Do not interrupt or argue.
3. Be open-minded. Whenever possible, express your agreement with the voter.
4. Family members make good surrogates. It impresses voters that the candidate's husband, wife, mother, father, or sibling came to their door. When unrelated strangers canvass people sometimes wonder what the canvasser is getting out of it.
5. Don't knock on doors after dark.[15]

Pennsylvania state legislator Mike Hanna adds several additional guidelines that candidates should use when they are doing the canvassing. When candidates canvass themselves, Hanna advises them to dress in normal business clothing. He observes that "people will take you seriously if you look the part of a serious candidate." Additionally, he advises that candidates always end their interaction in a canvass by "explicitly" asking for the citizen's vote. Most importantly, Hanna observes that when candidates are going door-to-door, they should avoid long conversations. "Civics lessons aside," claims Hanna, "your job is not to bring voters over to your point of view. Your objective is to show yourself at their door for a brief and shining moment and leave them with an impression that you are a nice, trustworthy person and that you care."[16]

These guidelines focus primarily on the actual canvass itself. Laura Peck adds several suggestions that campaigns might follow to prepare for the canvass. Peck suggests that prior to canvassing a neighborhood, the campaign should provide advance warning by utilizing yard signs announcing the impending canvass or sending out a mailing that lets voters know that the candidate will be visiting their neighborhood. Similarly, she suggests that candidates might utilize neighborhood residents to accompany them on canvasses and brief them on the neighborhood in which the canvass is taking place.[17] Peck also suggests that the neighborhood canvass might be made into a memorable neighborhood event by creating a miniparade. As the candidate canvasess door-to-door, one or more campaign vehicles with signs can accompany the candidate down the street, and several campaign volunteers wearing campaign shirts could also be on the street.[18]

Canvassers who follow instructions such as these can accomplish much. They can leave literature, determine voting intentions, or question for other information that the campaign desires.[19] Additionally, when done by well-prepared canvassers, particularly the candidate and members of the candidate's family, the door-to-door canvass leaves voters with a positive feeling about the candidate that will not be readily forgotten.

In sum, interpersonal communication between the candidate and the voter is, for most people, a unique event. The details of the coffee or the door-to-door canvass meeting will no doubt fade from an individual's memory. But the fact that the candidate cared enough to come to the neighborhood or send a representative or family member and followed up the initial coffee or canvass will often remain and loom far larger in the voter's mind than the specifics of what may have been said.

INTERPERSONAL COMMUNICATION BETWEEN THE CANDIDATE AND PROSPECTIVE FINANCIAL CONTRIBUTORS

Before examining interpersonal communication designed to solicit campaign contributions, we must first answer two fundamental questions about fund-raising. First, who currently contributes to political campaigns? Second, who is likely to contribute in the future?

In recent years, federal laws on campaign contributions have encouraged candidates for federal office to solicit relatively small contributions from large numbers of voters. As mentioned earlier, federal laws today place a $1,000 ceiling on the amount of money that a single individual can contribute to a candidate and a $5,000 ceiling on the contributions of political action committees. A candidate may receive such contributions in a primary election, and if the candidate goes on to the general election, a second such contribution can be made for that election. Most individual states have also imposed ceilings on the amounts that can be given to candidates for state and local office.[20] Restrictions on state and local candidates are generally not as tight as those placed on candidates for federal office. Nonetheless, the effect of these laws, passed in the 1970s in the wake of the Watergate scandal, has been to reduce the number of large contributors and the size of their contributions, while increasing the total number of campaign contributors to the official campaigns of candidates.

One unintended consequence of these laws has been to make candidates spend more and more time on fund-raising. In the late 1920s, 70 percent of the money raised by both national political parties came from contributions of $1,000 or more. It should be kept in mind that in 1928 a consumer could buy not one car, but two for $1,000. Such a contribution was affordable only by the wealthy.[21] It did not take very many large contributions of this sort to finance elections.

However, today a candidate must receive thousands, indeed, tens of thousands, of $1,000 contributions to finance a major race, which often

costs millions of dollars. The result is that candidates spend disproportionate amounts of their time and effort raising money. Former congresswoman and vice presidential candidate Geraldine Ferraro, running in
the 1998 Democratic primary for the party nomination to challenge incumbent United States Senator Alfonse D'Amato of New York, was reported, in March of 1998, to be spending six hours a day phoning
potential contributors.[22] Moreover, had she survived the Democratic primary, she would have had to start all over again to raise well over $10
million dollars she anticipated needing for the general election. Clearly,
raising money from large numbers of people is more time consuming
than raising it from a relatively few people.

A second unintended effect of these laws, based in part on court interpretations of the reform laws of the 1970s, has been the growth of soft
money. The 1996 elections witnessed an enormous growth in the use of
soft money in political campaigns. Hard money is money given explicitly
to the candidate's campaign. Soft money is money that is given to the
parties or PACs for "party building activities," such as get-out-the-vote
efforts or generic ads that endorse a party's issue position rather than a
candidate. In 1996 soft money contributions, especially to the Republican
and Democratic National Committees, dramatically increased. In the
four-year period between 1992 and 1996, the soft money given to the
Republican National Committee rose from $49 million to $141 million
and that given to the Democratic National Committee rose from $36
million to $122 million.[23] There are no limits on the amounts of soft
money that can be utilized in a campaign. So, soft money that a party
raises and then uses to run issue-oriented ads in a given congressional
district is not closely regulated.

The law does prohibit soft money expenses being coordinated with the
activities of the official campaign. As long as there is no contact between
the candidate and the candidate's official campaign and those who provide and spend soft money, current laws have not been broken. In 1996
the amounts of soft money contributed to political campaigns far exceeded all previous use of soft money. In addition to the use of soft
money by both parties, perhaps the most conspicuous use of soft money
in 1996 was the union attempt to return control of Congress to the Democrats by targeting many of the 70 Republicans who first won election
in 1994 and pumping $35 million dollars into those campaigns.

The 1996 experience of Republican Congressman Phil English of Erie,
Pennsylvania, illustrates the use of hard and soft money in a hotly contested congressional campaign. English had originally estimated that it
would cost $600,000 to win reelection in 1996.[24] He and his campaign
staff consistently revised those estimates upward, until he ultimately
raised and spent $1,200,000 in a district with very modest media costs.
His Democratic opponent, Ron DiNicola, raised and spent $468,000,

more than English had spent in 1994 to originally win the seat. But, this hard money raised and spent by the candidates was only a fraction of the overall cost of the campaign. So many special interest groups became involved in this race that the candidates were literally surprised to hear advertisements for themselves. Among the groups that spent $10,000 or more on behalf of either English or DiNicola were the American Hospital Association, the Citizen Action Fund, the Citizens for the Republic Education Fund, the Pensylvania Democratic and Republican state parties, Project 95 (later Project 96) of the AFL-CIO, and the United States Chamber of Commerce. On election eve, special interest groups ran more television advertising than either candidate. Between them, the two candidates raised and spent $1.65 million dollars. In most years, this hard money would have been virtually the entire cost of the election. But in 1996, the parties and special interest groups put at least $1.4 million dollars into this election.[25]

Although PACs may make large contributions, often in the form of soft money, many derive their own money from small individual contributors. Some organizations, such as the American Association of Retired People, the National Education Association, and many unions, have PACs that are often financed, at least in part, out of member dues. Collectively, because of the large membership, this money can be used for large political contributions on behalf of the group. It is far more difficult to track this money than to track contributions made directly to campaigns because direct or hard money contributions must be reported to the Federal Election Commission or equivalent state organizations. But soft money does not have to be reported.

Though soft money may have diminished the importance of individual contributors, nevertheless they remain a critical element in any campaign finance plan. The importance of the individual contributor is well illustrated by Frank Sorauf's analysis of the contributors to the 1990 congressional campaigns. A total of $471.2 million was raised by congressional candidates in 1990. Individual contributors provided $249.4 million, or 53 percent. Political action committees, typically more active in congressional races than in most other types of campaigns, provided $150.6 million, or 32 percent. The candidates themselves contributed $37.9 million, or 8 percent, to their own campaigns. Party organizations—national, state, and local—contributed $4.3 million, or 1 percent, to the 1990 congressional races. These four sources contributed 94 percent of all money raised for the 1990 congressional elections. The remaining 6 percent was composed primarily of loans, not contributions, and interest earned by the campaign treasuries. Thus 53 percent of all the money raised in these races (actually 61 percent of all contributions to these campaigns exclusive of those of the candidate who is not subject to the campaign contribution limits that apply to other citizens and monies obtained through loans and interest) came from individual citizens giving small amounts.[26]

The 1994 Congressional races indicate the same pattern. Individual citizens, contributing relatively modest amounts of $1,000 or less, provide the bulk of campaign funding. As Dwight Morris of the Campaign Study Group has illustrated, in 1994 the 25 senatorial candidates who received the most money in the form of small individual contributions received between $2,475,000 and $20,555,000. In contrast, the 25 senatorial candidates who received the most money from PACs received between $852,000 and $2,507,000. Similarly, the 25 congressional candidates who received the most money from individuals received between $733,000 and $2,262,000. The top 25 PAC recipients received between $571,000 and $1,158,000.[27] Though PACs play an important role in funding congressional candidates, their role is smaller in state and local races. Dwight Morris, whose Campaign Study Group has become one of the definitive sources on political financing, observes that though most people think that PACs flood candidates with contributions, "that's just not true." Rather, says Morris, "most of the money still comes from individual donors." Morris, points out that through the early portion of the 1998 election cycle, the average PAC donation was only $2,100, which is only $100 more than an individual could contribute to a candidate running in both a primary and general election.[28]

If the current election laws remain the same, the need for candidates to solict money from larger and larger numbers of small contributors will no doubt increase as the cost of campaigning spirals higher and higher. According to Federal Election Commission figures, between 1990 and 1996 the total spending of the 435 winning congressional campaigns increased from slightly over $93 million to $287 million. Thus, the average winning campaign had tripled in cost, from approximately $213,000 to approximately $640,000, in six years. Similarly, the cost of winning a Senate seat virtually tripled in the same time period. By 1996 the average winning Senate campaign was spending $3,765,000.[29] These figures include only hard contributions made directly to the candidate's campaign and subject to limitations. They do not include soft money.

Consequently, the largest single source of hard money political contributions to individual candidate campaigns is the individual citizen donor. In recent years, a pattern of campaign giving seems to have emerged. Though this pattern varies for any individual campaign and races for federal offices such as the presidency and congressional races tend to draw more PAC contributions than most other races, generally speaking about 30 to 35 percent of the money raised for political campaigns comes from individual citizens contributing $100 or less. This percentage tends to be a little higher for lesser races and a little lower for major races. About 35 to 40 percent of the money raised for political campaigns comes from individual citizens contributing $100 to $1,000. Hence, in most elections approximately 65 to 75 percent of all contributed money comes in the form of individual citizen donations in relatively small amounts. The remaining money comes in the form of aid from political and special interest groups as well as loans and interest.[30]

It is likely that the current pattern of campaign contributions will continue in the future. Surveys taken repeatedly over the last two decades indicate that in major election years 15 to 20 percent of the population is solicited for a political contribution. Of those solicited, slightly more than 40 percent make some type of contribution.[31] Currently, it is estimated that over 12 million U.S. citizens contribute to political campaigns.[32] Moreover, Gallup Poll figures suggest that about 40 percent of those not solicited for a political contribution would have made at least a $5 contribution to a political candidate if they had been asked.[33] The widespread success of direct mail since 1972, when computer technology was brought to direct mail political solicitations, further suggests that in the future most money raised for political purposes will be raised through the relatively modest contributions of large numbers of individual contributors. Moreover the prospect of continued campaign financial reform is yet another reason to expect the present pattern of campaign finance to continue or expand. The trend of reform, at the federal, state, and local levels is to lower caps on contributions. This trend will continue to heighten the necessity for a larger donor base.[34]

People do not contribute to a political campaign unless they are attracted to the candidate. Political fund-raising is largely interpersonal in nature. Typically, the candidate, finance director, and members of the finance committee seek contributions from individuals they believe would be receptive to such an appeal. Similar in conception, though obviously less personal in execution, is direct mail fund-raising. Here again, the campaign seeks contributions from individuals believed to be receptive to the candidate. Invariably, the key is to determine who would be attracted to the candidate and thus receptive to financial appeals.

Students of interpersonal communication identify at least five principles of human attraction.[35] First, we are attracted to people who are in close physical proximity to us. Second, we are attracted to people who are similar to us. Third, we are attracted to people who provide us with positive feedback. Additionally, at least two situational factors tend to heighten the likelihood of our being attracted to other people. Fourth, if we find ourselves in an anxiety-producing situation, we tend to have a greater need for human interaction and hence are more prone to be attracted to other people. Fifth, if we have already extended some type of supportive behavior to an individual, we are more likely to be attracted to that individual than if we had never provided such behavior. Each of these five principles of human attraction has major implications for conducting political fund-raising.

The first determinant of attraction is proximity. That is, all things being equal, the more closely two people are located the more likely they are to be attracted to each other. Far too often, campaigns tend to neglect this simple fact. Rather than seek fiscal support from the most likely sources—people within the district—they seek financial support out of the district. Doing so creates two potential problems. First, and most serious, it rarely works. Just as charity begins at home, just as most of us contribute to our own United Way, our own church, our own schools and colleges, most of us will be more prone to contribute to candidates who will directly affect us.

This simple fact was illustrated by the efforts of a recent congressional candidate who was a Christian Scientist and a graduate of Principia College, the only Christian Science institution of higher education in the country. The candidate made an extensive fund-raising effort among Principia alumni. But he was running for a Missouri congressional seat and Principia is in Iowa. Additionally, as the only Christian Science school in the nation, Principia has a national flavor, attracting students from throughout the country, and its alumni have settled throughout the country. The candidate's efforts failed to produce any significant results beccause so few of those he contacted were located in close proximity to him and his district. Indeed, he received a number of responses indicating that some people were annoyed by his soliciting them, since they did not live in his district.

The importance of proximity is also illustrated by the guidelines both the Republican and Democratic national committees use to determine which candidates will receive their financial support. One of those guidelines is that candidates must demonstrate fund-raising ability *within* their districts. The assumption is that if they cannot raise money among people in close proximity, they cannot raise money from anyone.[36]

The second determinant of human attraction that is of exceptional importance for political fund-raising is similarity. We are attracted to people who are similar to us. Potential donors should always be approached by people who are highly similar to them. A carefully selected and highly motivated fund-raising committee working through their own social networks or precincts (the people with whom they are most similar) and drawing on the candidate's presence when necessary is perhaps the most effective means of utilizing the concept of similarity. The key to a successful interpersonal fund-raising effort is in the selection of the individuals who will head the fund-raising effort by endorsing the candidate and seeking contributions for the candidate from their friends and associates. Political consultant Cathy Allen calls the use of these interpersonal fund-raising networks "peer pressure politics" and observes that in selecting key fund-raisers, candidates must remember that they "are soliciting an endorsement which will translate into thousands of dollars in contributions from the endorser's peers."

She observes that the key fund-raiser in each group (Lawyers for Smith, Nurses for Smith, Environmentalists for Smith, etc.) should be a highly credible and influencial member of the group. Someone, in other words, whom group members will perceive favorably in large part because of their similarity.[37] If the candidate selects good fund-raisers, each new fund-raiser in a congressional race shoud produce $5,000–15,000 from her colleagues, family, and friends.[38]

When the candidate is making the solicitation calls, the principle of similarity is still critical. Allen suggests that immediately after establishing rapport, candidates who are phoning for contributions should explain what they have in common with the prospective donor.[39] Even if the prospective donor rejects the candidate's request for money, the candidate's response should utilize the concept of similarity. Allen suggests that virtually regardless of the reason for the turndown ("I'm supporting someone else; I don't have any money right now"; "I really don't know you well"; "I want to learn about all the candidates first") the candidate should respond with "feel, felt, found." That is, the candidate should indicate similarity to the donor by observing that "I know how you feel, I've felt that way myself, but I have found that. . . ."[40] Notice, that prior to directly responding to the prospective donor's rationale for refusing a donation, the candidate attempts to establish similarity by speaking about mutual feelings.

The fund-raising efforts of former Minnosota Senator Rudy Boschwitz well illustrate the importance of similarity. Relying heavily on family and friends, Boschwitz was able to utilize "peer pressure politics" to put together what he and his staff called "The Washington Club," a group of 850 supporters who contributed $1,000 a year, payable in four equal installments, to his campaign; "The Lincoln Club," a group of supporters who contributed $100–$250 a year to his campaign; and "The Skinny-cats," a group of supporters who contributed under $100 a year to his campaign. Members of these groups received appropriate certificates and buttons from Boschwitz and no doubt had a strong feeling of being connected to him, though many of them were likely recruited by their friends, and had few if any firsthand contacts with Boschwitz. By utilizing the basic concept of similarity, Boschwitz assembled a fund-raising organization that enabled him to open his last campaign with $1.5 million dollars in the bank and earning interest.[41]

The third principle of attraction that has import for political fund-raising is that we are attracted to and respond favorably to people who like us and validate us with positive feedback. Candidates and their surrogates must keep this fact uppermost in their minds as they seek funds.

This does not mean the fund-raiser must be overly compliant. If fund-raisers feel compelled to do that, then they are not dealing with equals. They should not be attempting to get donations from persons with whom they do not feel similar and equal. Rather, it means that fund-raisers must do their research. They should be able, if the situation arises, to make reference to the potential contributor's family by name, to make reference to recent accomplishments of the potential contributor's business, schools, family, and friends. In many fund-raising meetings, it is fair to say that topics such as politics, current events, and making political contributions do not take up more than two to three minutes of a 10-minute conversation. Fund-raising situations are so patently obvious that often they do not need any belaboring. Rather, such meetings stress the similarities between the candidates, their supporters, and the prospective contributors, as the candidates or their supporters attempt to provide positive feedback to the prospective contributors. Often this is done by focusing comments on the contributor's role in mutual projects of a non-political nature, such as charitable, social, educational, or civic projects.

Once the similarities between the candidate, fund-raiser, and potential contributor have been established, the fund-raiser can make his pitch on behalf of the candidate, stressing the philosophical or issue similarities between the candidate and the prospective contributor. If the fund-raiser has done a good job of establishing similarities, his or her final pitch on behalf of the candidate should convince the contributor that the question is not so much whether to give to the candidate, but rather how much to give.

A fourth principle of human attraction enters into political fund-raising. Research suggests that we experience a heightened need for human attraction during moments of anxiety.[42] This point should be noted by the competent political fund-raiser. As the campaign develops, the good fund-raiser will keep in mind who might be made anxious by current events. As opponents make statements and develop their campaigns, the good fund-raiser will follow them closely, seeking to determine who might be made anxious by the opponents' statements and positions. And as current events take place and receive publicity, the well-run campaign will have the appropriate person seeking funds from the individuals most likely to be made highly anxious by these events, at the very moment that they may be causing anxiety. For example, in a St. Louis area congressional race, one candidate announced that he was in favor of a controversial Army Corps of Engineers construction project that involved erecting several dams and flooding thousands of acres of lowland to create a large lake and recreational area to be utilized primarily by St. Louis residents. His opponent opposed this project as an unnecessarily wasteful and extravagant use of federal funds that would prove utterly disruptive to much of the Missouri environment and wildlife. Within three days of the first candidate's announcement, the second candidate or his representatives had contacted over 120 members of the St. Louis chapter of the Sierra Club, as well as similar environmental organizations. This effort produced almost $8,000 of unexpected contributions and many new enthusiastic workers for the campaign.

The final basis of human attraction that warrants the attention of the political fund-raiser is the concept of supportive behavior. Research suggests that our own behavior greatly influences our perception of other people. If, for example, you perform a favor for another person, you tend to like that person better as a consequence.[43] Hence, good fund-raisers, if unsuccessful in getting what they want—large contributions—should always have backup requests. If the car dealer will not contribute $1,000, $500, or $100, maybe the dealer will let candidate Smith use that beautiful yellow car in the showroom for three hours during the Labor Day parade. If worse comes to worst, at least the car dealer can look over some of Smith's campaign literature.

The practice of consistently seeking some type of supportive behavior, minimal as it may be, has at least two beneficial effects. First, the tangible benefit requested will be honored. Candidate Smith does ride in the most attractive car in the parade. Second, now that the car dealer has provided some sort of supportive behavior to the candidate, the dealer is more likely to respond favorably to a second fund-raising appeal. Importantly, once people have made an initial contribution to the candidate, they are prone to make a second or third contribution. Notice, in the discussion of Senator Boschwitz's fund-raising group mentioned earlier, that those groups contributed money on a yearly basis, year after year after year. Effective fund-raisers are aware of the positive effect that supportive behavior has on subsequent behavior and consistently strive to obtain some type of supportive behavior from everyone they approach. As Robert Kaplan, president of one of the most successful political fund-raising firms in the country, has observed, "At it's core, a successful fund-raising philosophy is based on asking, asking again and asking one more time."[44]

These principles of interpersonal communication should guide candidates and fund-raisers as they seek contributions. Moreover, they clearly have implications for other forms of fund-raising. They can help determine, for example, both the mailing list and the message content of direct mail solicitation on behalf of the candidate. In sum, candidates and fund-raisers who are skillful interpersonal communicators, clearly sensitive to and aware of the determinants of human attraction, are far more prone to achieve success than those who ignore these important variables of interpersonal communication.

INTERPERSONAL COMMUNICATION
BETWEEN VOTERS

Voters talk among themselves about politics, campaigns, and candidates. Interpersonal communication between voters is an important aspect of virtually every campaign. In this section, we will try to answer three questions about interpersonal communication between voters. First, in what campaigns is it likely to be of unusually high importance? Second, what do voters typically discuss? Third, what is the relationship between interpersonal communication and mass media in political campaigns?

Importance

Interpersonal communication between voters is normally of greatest importance in those campaigns that receive little media attention. When information about the campaign and the candidates is lacking in the media, voters rely more heavily on interpersonal communication. Consequently, several types of campaigns characteristically lacking in media coverage often must rely heavily on interpersonal communication. First are campaigns for lesser offices or local offices; second are primary campaigns. Atwood and Sanders have found that communication with other people was the most credible source of information for 32 percent of the voters in a primary election, but that it was the most credible source of information for only 12 percent of the voters in a general election.[45] Though there has been little research since Atwood and Sanders on this point, and the exact figures may have changed, their basic conclusion that people learn more about primary elections from other people, where other sources of information are limited, and less about general elections, where other sources of information are more plentiful, continues to make sense. Often, as when three or more candidates seek a single office in a primary, the media coverage received by any single candidate tends to be more limited than in a general election. Moreover, the media budgets of most primary campaigns are lower than those of general elections. The reduced media coverage of individual candidates and campaigns in some primaries likely causes voters to rely more heavily on interpersonal communication in these elections than in general elections.

The third group of campaigns where interpersonal communication between voters seems to play an unusually important role are those campaigns in which the constituency has a relatively high educational level. Research on this point is limited, and much of it has been done primarily on school-age populations. Nevertheless, it does tend to suggest that voters with good educational backgrounds are less affected by the media, more prone to discuss current events, and more prone to be influenced by those discussions.[46]

Discussion Topics

Voters discuss virtually everything that is pertinent to a campaign. However, three subjects tend to dominate their conversations. First, interpersonal communication is often the means by which people initially learn of a newsworthy development in the campaign. In one of the first studies to focus on how people learn about campaign events, Wayne Danielson found that knowledge of news events in a presidential campaign was most rapidly spread throughout the population by radio and interpersonal communication. Television and newspapers, according to Danielson, did not transmit knowledge of news events as rapidly.[47] Though Danielson's findings may have since been altered by the widespread growth of television, it nevertheless seems safe to conclude that many people do frequently discuss and often first learn of news events through interaction with one another.

Second, Kimsey and Atwood found that voters tend to "talk most about the things they like least about candidates."[48] Conversations between voters are not subject to libel laws, equal time laws, and the other legal constraints that may affect the various mass media. Media coverage of the negative aspects of a candidate may be tempered by considerations such as these, but interpersonal communication is not.

Additionally, Kimsey and Atwood found that voters tend to use interpersonal communication selectively to reinforce their vote decisions.[49] This finding makes good sense because of our tendency to be attracted to and communicate primarily with those who are similar to us. Hence, we are prone to be exposed to messages congruent with our own ideas. Moreover, we do not equally attend to all the messages we receive. We are prone to selectively attend to those messages that conform to our existing attitudes and beliefs. Kimsey and Atwood's findings, that we use interpersonal communication selectively to reinforce prior decisions, seems to be very much in accord with our existing knowledge of interpersonal communication.

Thus, interpersonal communication is used by voters to deal with virtually everything that happens in a campaign. However, in contrast to other forms of campaign communication, it may be especially important as a medium of news transmission, as a medium by which negative information about a candidate is transmitted, and as a medium that serves to reinforce attitudes and beliefs.

Interpersonal Communication between Voters, Mass Media, and Voting Behavior

As early as 1948, students of mass media realized the relationship and importance of interpersonal communication. John P. Robinson provides us with a critique of the relationships between voting behavior, mass media, and interpersonal communication.[50] Robinson, like prior researchers, finds that when interpersonal communication is in conflict with media information "interpersonal sources wield greater influence."[51] The explanation for this no doubt rests in large part on the feedback and adaptation that one voter can provide to another as they discuss politics. Mass media messages cannot adapt and react to feedback, as can interpersonal communication. However, Robinson also finds that interpersonal influence attempts are not that pervasive in elections. More people seem to be exposed to media attempts to influence their votes than to interpersonal attempts to influence their votes.[52] Those people who receive media messages attempting to influence their votes, but no interpersonal messages, seem much more receptive to direct influence from the media.[53]

Recent research by Silvo Lenart, consistent with much prior research, argues for what Lenart calls "an integrated model." Lenart claims that candidates and campaigns utilize the mass media to communicate to voters but that these efforts are often affected by such interpersonal influences as the characteristics of individual voters, the one-to-one individual discussions between voters, and the group interactions that voters have. Lenart concludes that "once a campaign is underway in the media, the entire communication process is best characterized as a dynamic interplay among media, interpersonal interactions and opinion climate pressures."[54]

Though most candidates make special efforts to facilitate interpersonal communication between themselves and voters and between themselves and financial contributors, few candidates make concrete efforts to facilitate interpersonal communication between voters that might have a favorable impact on their candidacy. However, at least one formally prominent political consultant has long attempted to stimulate interpersonal communication among voters to benefit his clients. Stephen Shadegg, who advised Barry Goldwater and whose son currently serves in Congress, advises candidates to develop "social precincts" as crucial elements of their campaigns.[55] Social precincts, as Shadegg employs them, are simply enthusiastic and knowledgeable supporters of the candidate. They are not members of special organizations or groups, nor are they in any way prominent in their communities. Initially, members of social precincts are recruited from among friends and associates of the candidate, and gradually the number of members is increased. Many of these people may not even know the candidate well.

Members of social precincts are provided "inside" information. As the campaign progresses, they get key press releases a day in advance, and their opinion is solicited before the candidate makes a key speech. They are made to feel that they are insiders whose opinions and advice are valued by the candidate. And indeed they are just that. By using the mail, as well as computer networks, faxes, and other technology, the candidate is able to develop a large group of people who look upon the candidate as someone with whom they have a special relationship. Based on extensive experience with social precincts, Shadegg claims that if he can enlist 3 to 5 percent of the constituency in these social precincts, he will win the election. For if 3 to 5 percent of the constituency believe they have a special interest in a candidate, Shadegg feels that in their normal day-to-day social interactions they will prove influential on a significantly large enough number of voters to win most elections.

Shadegg's approach is one of the few clear attempts to mobilize interpersonal communication among voters on behalf of a candidate. His success with social precincts, as well as research evidence on the relationship between voting behavior, mass communication, and interpersonal communication, speaks to the importance of interpersonal communication between voters.

CONCLUSIONS

In this chapter, we have examined interpersonal communication in political campaigns. We have found that interpersonal communication between the candidate and voters is exceptionally important in local campaigns, in campaigns where the use of media may not be feasible, and in primary campaigns. In such campaigns, the interpersonal communication between the candidate and voters through programs of informal coffees and canvasses can be extremely valuable. Moreover, we have found that political fund-raising lends itself to interpersonal communication and that current interpersonal communication research on attraction has major implications for interpersonal fund-raising by political candidates and their advocates. Finally, we have examined the often neglected interpersonal communication between voters. We have seen in which campaigns such communication is most important, what voters tend to discuss among themselves, and the relationships between voting behavior, media, and interpersonal communication.

NOTES

1. For a discussion of some of the mechanics involved in implementing the first two of these types of interpersonal communication, see Robert Agranoff, *The Management of Election Campaigns* (Boston: Holbrook Press, 1976), pp. 411–54.

2. Herbert E. Alexander, *Financing Politics: Money, Elections and Political Reform* (Washington, D.C.: Congressional Quarterly Press, 1980), p. 1.

3. Lynda Lee Kaid, "The Neglected Candidate: Interpersonal Communication

in Political Campaigns," *Western Journal of Speech Communication* 41 (Fall 1977): 245.

4. Ibid.

5. The following analysis of the importance of interpersonal campaigning in local political campaigns is based heavily on Robert V. Friedenberg, "Interpersonal Communication in Local Political Campaigns," *Ohio Speech Journal* 12 (1974): 19–27.

6. Daniel M. Shea, *Campaign Craft: The Strategies, Tactics, and Art of Political Campaign Management* (Westport, Conn.: Praeger, 1996), pp. 243, 249.

7. See L. Patrick Devlin, "The McGovern Canvass: A Study in Interpersonal Political Campaign Communication," *Central States Speech Journal* 24 (Summer 1973): 83–90, for an account of some of the McGovern techniques that have been widely copied.

8. See Nancy Bocskor, "No Place Like Home," *Campaigns and Elections* (April 1998): 28–29. Bocskor stresses the fund-raising potential of coffees and similar events hosted by supporters of the candidate in their own homes.

9. This statement and all quotations in this section, unless otherwise explicitly footnoted, are drawn from "Coffee: The Campaign Beverage," a pamphlet issued by the Republican State Central and Executive Committee of Ohio to candidates for state and local offices. No date or place of publication.

10. Laura Peck, "Face to Face Campaigning: How to Work a Room," *Campaigns and Elections* (April 1996): 47.

11. Ibid.

12. Ibid.

13. See Patrick Devlin, "The McGovern Canvass," pp. 82–90, for an excellent description of a highly effective canvassing operation that served all of the functions described in these paragraphs.

14. Ibid., p. 89.

15. These guidelines are modeled after those provided to McGovern canvassers during the 1972 presidential primaries, which have been widely copied ever since, and the guidelines recommended by Pennsylvania Democratic state representative Mike Hanna whose upset 1990 election with 65 percent of the vote in a district where Republicans dominated was largely attributed to his successful utilization of door-to-door canvassing. See Devlin, "McGovern Canvass," pp. 84–85 and Mike Hanna, "The Campaign Door Knocking Game," *Campaigns and Elections*, (September 1991): 52–53.

16. See Hanna, "The Campaign Door Knocking Game," p. 52.

17. Laura Peck, "Going Door-to-Door: 10 Tips for Success," *Campaigns and Elections* (July 1996): 45.

18. Ibid.

19. See Agranoff, *Management of Election Campaigns*, pp. 411–54, for a discussion of the many purposes of canvasses as well as illustrations of the materials used in canvasses.

20. Alexander, *Financing Politics*, pp. 130–32.

21. See Frank J. Soranf, *Inside Campaign Finance: Myths and Realities* (New Haven, Conn.: Yale University Press, 1992), p. 3.

22. "Politics—Working the Phones," *Washington Times*, March 27, 1998 (available at http://www.washtimes.com/politics/inside.html).

23. Dan Froomkin, "Big Money—The Cost of Winning." This article is part one of a six-part *Washington Post* special series on campaign financing. It can be found at http://www.washingtonpost.com:campaign finance introduction, updated May 21, 1998.

24. This figure and all other details about this campaign in the next paragraphs can be found in Guy Gugliotta and Ira Chinoy, "Outsiders Made Erie Ballot a National Battle," *Washington Post*, February, 10, 1997, p. A1. This article is also available at http://www.washingtonpost.com/wp-srv/national/longterm/campfin/erie.htm.

25. Because detailed reporting does not have to be kept, this figure is an estimate, based primarily on the expense records. If anything, it is likely to be low.

26. Sorauf, *Inside Campaign Finance*, pp. 30–31.

27. Dwight Morris, "Myths and Money: Campaign Stories," available on the Internet at *ElectionLine*, Febuary 7, 1996 (available at http://www.electionline.com). These figures reflect contributions to the official campaigns of the candidates. They do not reflect soft money contributions.

28. Jeff Schear, "Weird Political Science: How Dwight Morris Cornered the Campaign Money Market," *Capitol Style* (September 1998): 25–27.

29. The precise FEC figures for 1996 and the percentage of growth can be obtained from the FEC or found in a variety of published sources. See, for example, *Campaign Insider*, January 15, 1997, p. 3. The best short study of campaign finance, which includes these figures as well as considerable other detail, is the *Washington Post*'s special report on campaign finance, most readily available at http://www.washingtonpost.com:Campaign Finance.

30. These figures have remained remarkably consistent over time. See, for example, Agranoff, *Management of Election Campaigns*, pp. 232–34, for an account of the financing of 1972 congressional races and Larry Sabato and Frank Sorauf in their more recent studies of election financing in the late 1980s and early 1990s. Moreover, Sabato notes that PACs have probably had their greatest influence on races for the United States Senate and House of Representatives. See Larry Sabato, "Real and Imagined Corruption in Campaign Financing," in *Elections American Style*, ed. James Reichley (Washington, D.C.: Brookings Institution, 1987), p. 157. See also Alexander, *Financing Politics*, pp. 45–67, for a discussion of individual donors. Virtually all researchers, including those cited in this chapter, find that candidates for federal offices tend to raise a higher percentage of their funds from PACs than state and local candidates.

Though female candidates, regardless of office, have more difficulty raising money from special interest groups, according to Ruth B. Mandel, *In the Running: The New Woman Candidate* (New Haven, Conn.: Ticknor and Fields, 1981), pp. 191–94, this situation is gradually being corrected. The emergence of EMILY'S List, a PAC devoted to raising money for liberal woman candidates, as the single largest PAC in the 1992 elections is indicative of the growing access of women to PAC monies that may soon make Mandel's 1981 observation dated.

31. The best brief examinations of political campaign contributors can be found in Agranoff, *Management of Election Campaigns*, pp. 230–34; Alexander, *Financing Politics*, pp. 62–64; and Sabato, "Real and Imagined Corruption," pp. 157–59.

32. Alexander, *Financing Politics*, p. 64.

33. Ibid., p. 63.

34. John F. Persinos, "Pushing the Envelope," *Campaigns and Elections* (June 1994): 20.

35. Many researchers have attempted to establish the major determinants of human attraction. Two of the better summaries of current research, upon which this analysis is based, are Joseph Devito, *The Interpersonal Communication Book* (New York: Longman, 1997), pp. 302–5; and Stewart L. Tubbs and Sylvia Moss, *Human Communication* (New York: Random House, 1987), pp. 66–75.

36. This guideline is a long-standing one used by Republican and Democratic national committee field staff to help determine which candidates are the most viable and hence warrant aid from their respective national committees.

37. Cathy Allen, "Peer Pressure Politics: Getting Your Money's Worth from Friends and Colleagues," *Campaigns and Elections* (June/July 1990): 49.

38. Robert P. Odell, Jr., "The Money Pit," *Campaigns and Elections* (November 1992): 51.

39. Cathy Allen, "How to Ask for Money," *Campaigns and Elections* (April 1998): 25.

40. Ibid., p. 27.

41. For a description of Boschwitz's fund-raising efforts and his other suggestions about campaigning see "A Senator's Advice: Don't Give Consent to Reelection Debate," *Wall Street Journal*, May 2, 1985, p. A1.

42. Tubbs and Moss, *Human Communication*, pp. 72–73.

43. William Wilmot, *Dyadic Communication: A Transactional Perspective* (Reading, Mass.: Addison-Wesley, 1975), pp. 73–74.

44. Robert Kaplan, "Psychology of Silence: Raising More Money by Psyching Out Donors," *Campaigns and Elections* (November 1991): 54.

45. L. Erwin Atwood and Keith R. Sanders, "Information Sources and Voting in a Primary and General Election," *Journal of Broadcasting* 20 (Summer 1976): 298.

46. John P. Robinson, "Interpersonal Influence in Election Campaigns: Two-Step Flow Hypotheses," *Public Opinion Quarterly* 40 (Fall 1976): 312; and Marilyn Jackson-Beeck, "Interpersonal and Mass Communication in Children's Political Socialization," *Journalism Quarterly* 56 (Spring 1979): 53.

47. Wayne A. Danielson, "Eisenhower's February Decision: A Study of News Impact," *Journalism Quarterly* 33 (Fall 1956): 437.

48. William D. Kimsey and L. Erwin Atwood, "A Path Model of Political Cognitions and Attitudes, Communication and Voting Behavior in a Congressional Election," *Communication Monographs* 40 (August 1979): 429.

49. Ibid., p. 430.

50. Robinson, "Interpersonal Influence in Election Campaigns," pp. 304–19.

51. Ibid., p. 315.

52. Ibid.

53. Ibid., p. 316.

54. Silvo Lenart, *Shaping Political Attitudes: The Impact of Interpersonal Communication and Mass Media* (Thousand Oaks, Calif.: Sage, 1994), pp. 110–12.

55. This discussion of social precincts is based on Stephen C. Shadegg, *The New How to Win an Election* (New York: Tapplinger, 1976), pp. 103–19.

Chapter 10

Advertising in Political Campaigns

Many campaigns are waged essentially through advertising, primarily over radio and television. These campaigns tend to be high profile races, such as those for national and statewide office. In many urban areas, lower races such as those for Congress or city offices are also waged heavily through the use of radio and television. However, in lower level races, where budgets preclude the extensive use of radio and television, or where local demographic conditions make it impractical, other forms of advertising remain dominant. Moreover, even high-profile media campaigns cannot forsake the more traditional, often preelectric media means of campaigning and advertising. If they do so, they run a serious risk of incurring consequences that so badly damage their efforts, that even a highly effective media campaign cannot win the election.

The experiences of Harriet Woods in her two Missouri campaigns for United States Senate well illustrate the complexity and problems involved in using media in political campaigns. They provide us with three lessons that serve as background to understanding the practices commonly employed in using media in contemporary campaigns.

After a long career of public service in University City, a suburb of St. Louis, in 1976 Harriet Woods began to attract statewide notice by winning election to the Missouri Senate. Once established in the statehouse, in 1982 she waged an aggressive race for the United State Senate. A distinct underdog to Missouri's popular incumbent Senator Jack Danforth, Woods seemed on the verge of upsetting Danforth. Most statewide polls showed her ahead going into the last 10 days of the campaign. At that point Senator Danforth launched an intensive statewide television blitz, which Woods did not have the finances to match, and Danforth won a narrow victory. Woods rebounded in 1984 running a successful race for lieutenant governor and becoming the first woman ever elected to statewide office in Missouri. Hence, in 1986 she and her advisors placed special emphasis on television advertising. Her 1982 experience led her 1986 campaign strategists to conclude that their number one priority in her race with two-time Missouri Governor Christopher "Kit" Bond would be to equal or exceed Bond's effort with paid television advertisments. She and her advisors were determined that she would not be beaten by television in 1986.[1] However, as the votes were tallied on election eve, it became apparent that Bond had beaten Woods. Ironically, Woods was beaten by television. However, unlike 1982, in 1986 she was beaten by her own use of television.

In 1982 Harriet Woods may well have lost because she could not mount sufficient advertising. Political advertising can be enormously expensive. Later in this chapter we will examine the expenses of advertising more closely; suffice to say at this point that for many candidates the major obstacle to successful political advertising is the lack of money. In 1986 the Harriet Woods campaign staff had estimated that to run successfully in the moderately populous state of Missouri, served by two major media markets, St. Louis and Kansas City, she would need to raise in excess of $4,600,000. As the campaign progressed that estimate was revised upward by approximately half a million dollars. Six years earlier, in 1980, Senator Thomas Eagleton had won reelection in Missouri, spending $800,000.[2] The largest single reason for this staggering increase was the increasing reliance of statewide candidates on increasingly costly television commercials. Moreover, the costs of television and other media, as we will see later in this chapter, have continued to rise dramatically since Woods was a candidate.

The experience of Missouri candidates is typical of those throughout the country. The staggering increases in the costs of campaigning are primarily a consequence of increasing reliance on television. Thus, the first lesson that Harriet Woods's campaigns teach us about political advertising is that candidates who expect to use media, particularly television, must be prepared to raise substantial amounts of money. Harriet Woods found this out the hard way in 1982.

In 1986 Woods had a difficult time in raising money, but raise it she did. However, the principal student of Woods's 1986 campaign, participant/observer Deborah Chasteen, has claimed that "although Woods was able to raise the millions of dollars necessary to remain competitive in the media, that success limited her ability to reach voters in other ways. She was unable to fund traditional voter appeals such as yard signs and bumper stickers, and had to restrict her public appearances to those which would yield either money or media coverage."[3] Chasteen notes that Woods curtailed virtually all other forms of advertising and repeatedly passed up important speaking opportunities to facilitate her media campaign. Cumulatively, the effect of her decisions, claims Chasteen, was a "unidimensional campaign."[4]

In failing to engage in the traditional forms of advertising, and in failing to appear at a variety of locally important functions, often because she deemed her time better spent at fund-raising or working on media, Woods cost her campaign the enthusiasm and energy of party workers and loyalists throughout Missouri. Understandably, though incorrectly, they often mistook her failures to appear at local events, or to provide them with such things as yard signs, bumper stickers, phone banks, and advertisements in the local press as indicative of indifference. Different media as we will see in this chapter, serve different functions. Though Harriet Woods's television commercials reached the public at large, the "unidimensional campaign" she waged made it difficult for Democratic party activists around the state to become enthusiastic about her campaign. Some media serve not only to help persuade the public but also to mobilize and encourage volunteers and staff. The second lesson that we learn from Harriet Woods's campaigns is that most strong campaigns involve a mix of media to convey their messages.

The Woods campaign is instructive for yet a third reason. Preoccupied with getting her commercials on the air, Woods's strategists failed to thoroughly consider the content and full implications of her commercials. Chasteen points out that Woods's most important decision in the campaign, to air a controversial series of advertisements that came to be known as the "crying farmer" commercials, was conceived "hastily in reaction to an eight point shift in polling numbers," was "never tested," and represented a substantial shift from the campaign's original strategy for using television commercials, worked out in cooperation with media consultant Robert Squier.[5] Moreover, Chasteen observed that the Woods campaign "did not anticipate the types of responses Bond might have . . . did no contigency planning and had no strategy for extending their arguments."[6] In sum, Chasteen concludes of the Woods campaign that "the medium for conducting their ideas took precedence over the ideas they wanted to convey."[7] Thus, the final lesson of the Woods campaigns: Though the skillful use of the medium is critical, ultimately the medium serves only as a vehicle for presenting candidates and their messages. It is the images candidates present of themselves and of one another, and the ideas they express, that are of greatest consequence.

Let us now examine some of the major practices involved in political advertising with these three lessons in mind: (1) that political advertising is enormously costly, not only in dollars, but also in time and effort; (2) that appealing as telelvision commercials may be, rarely can a campaign be waged successfully by relying exclusively on television; and (3) that advertising mediums are simply vehicles for conveying the images and ideas of candidates which are ultimately of more consequence. The remainder of this chapter will focus first on factors that affect the selection and use of various advertising media available to political campaigners. Second, we will focus on what have become key figures in many contemporary campaigns, professional political consultants, with emphasis on those who specialize in media.

DEVELOPING A MASTER PLAN FOR POLITICAL ADVERTISING

The array of advertising media that has been used in political campaigns is staggering. A partial listing includes brochures, newsletters, questionnaires, letters, billboards, yard signs, bumper stickers, newspaper advertisements, magazine advertisements, matchbooks, buttons, pencils, computer bulletin boards, faxes, Internet home pages, and of course, radio and television commercials. This list does not even include one of the author's all time favorites, cans of GOLD WATER, the delightful drink for all right thinking supporters of the 1964 Republican standard bearer! Indeed, the list is endless. Political campaigners have used virtually every technological advance in communication to facilitate getting their messages to the public. However, almost every campaigner pays homage to the adage that the good campaign dominates the dominant media. If the dominant media in the school board election is yard signs, the good campaign will have the best and most yard signs. If the dominant media in the congressional race is television, the good campaign will have the best and most television commercials.

Among the first responsibilities of any campaign is to develop a master plan for the campaign that should include a section on expected advertising. Typically such a plan should be developed 15–18 months before election day.[8] This plan should serve to coordinate all of the paid media activities of the campaign. Obviously occasions will arise when events make it necessary to deviate from the overall plan. However, well run campaigns plan their media activities early, and then stick as closely as possible to their overall plans, adjusting as events make it necessary.

The advantages of advance planning cannot be overestimated. Decisions that are made as the campaign is beginning tend to be made more dispassionately and are typically based on greater objectivity, thought, and research. Decisions made on the spur of the moment in response to campaign events are typically subject to less thought, less research, less analysis, and hence are prone to be less successful. Notice, in the campaign discussed at the outset of this chapter, Harriet Woods's decision to run the controversial "crying farmer" commercials was made hastily, in response to a campaign development. It was a marked deviation from the campaign's previously well-thought-out plan that involved using "soft" commercials to develop a positive image for Woods at this early stage of the campaign rather than "hard" attack commercials, criticizing Bond.

The many advantages of advance planning can be best illustrated by example. Let us imagine that we are involved in planning a congressional primary race. Our candidate is only moderately known in the district. However, our opponent is also known only moderately in the district. They are both vying for the nomination to succeed a popular incumbent who is retiring after 24 years in Congress. We will imagine that our candidate is a university professor who has served on local school boards and subsequently was elected mayor of a small college town of 21,000 within the district, a position she currently holds. She is also highly active in supporting the arts and has been a long-time supporter of the local symphony orchestra. Our opponent is a young lawyer who just completed his second term in the state House of Representatives, representing a district of about 80,000, located in the suburbs of a large city. His district comprises about one-fourth of the congressional district; the town in which our candidate serves as mayor comprises only about 6 percent of the district. Another 25 percent of the district is comprised of suburbs, such as the one our opponent has represented, and about half the district is rural, though the rural area includes several towns of about 15,000–25,000, such as the one our candidate has served as mayor. For the sake of illustration we will imagine that traditionally candidates wait until January before announcing their candidacy for the May 1 primary.

Using the surfacing period during the summer of the year preceding the election, we draft our first master plan. We decide to run a series of radio and television commercials for 10 days immediately after declaring candidacy in January. Moreover, we decide to take out large advertisements in the three daily papers that serve the district and in each of the district's 10 highest circulation weekly papers in the week immediately following our candidate's announcement. Our advertising master plan then calls for three direct mail efforts in February and March. The first two mailings (in February) are to target groups that may be expected to be highly supportive of the candidate. We might imagine a master plan that calls for a mailing on February 12 to individuals concerned with education, such as the members of teachers groups, PTAs, and similar organizations. The master plan then calls for a mailing on February 25 to members of a variety of groups concerned with culture and music, such as season ticket purchasers to local theater groups, symphony, and ballet. The master plan we develop further calls for a mailing on March 25 to all voters eligible to participate in the primary. In addition to mailings, we develop a master plan that calls for the distribution of 500 yard signs during the first two weeks of March, and a major push to distribute 500 yard signs on each of the last two weekends of March.

Since the primary election is scheduled for May 1, we decide that our radio advertising should start on April 1, doubling in quantity every 10 days. That is, for every commercial run between April 1–10, two radio commercials will be run between April 11–20. For every commercial run between April 11–20, two radio commercials will be run between April 20–May 1. Moreover, we decide to use a second and final round of television commercials to start on April 1, and their number is to double on April 21. Additionally, the master plan calls for running large advertisements in each of the three daily papers and in each of the 10 largest weekly papers in the district during the last phase of the campaign. Advertisements will be placed on each of the last three days in the three dailies, and in each of the last two editions for the 10 weekly papers. Finally, the master plan calls for a final mailing to all eligible voters to be sent on April 25 so as to be received by voters within three days of the election.

Notice what developing this relatively simple advertising plan has forced us to do and how it impacts upon and governs much of the rest of the campaign. The first advantage to developing this plan early is that it forces us to identify our basic goal in the campaign. In this example we have one basic goal: acquiring name recognition as a prominent member of our party. Since this is a primary, there may not be major differences between the candidates. Moreover, since this district has been won by the candidate of our party for the last 24 years, securing the party nomination may in itself be the basic step necessary for our candidate's ultimate election. In most campaigns the first advantage to developing an initial advertising program is that it forces the campaign to develop and prioritize its overall objectives or goals for the campaign.

Since our goal is recognition, we have decided to campaign vigorously from the moment of our announcement. If we are going to use newspapers, radio, and television all in the first weeks of the campaign, as our plan calls for, then clearly we need money early in the campaign. Our master plan for advertising must be coordinated with our fundraising. For example, if we cannot raise money for 10 days worth of radio and television at the outset of the campaign, what can we do? Perhaps we should curtail the radio and television and use yard signs earlier in the campaign. Yard signs, however, may call for considerable use of volunteers. Yards have to be solicited; signs have to be made and distributed. We can estimate the cost of producing commercials and buying time. We can estimate the number of volunteers needed to produce and place yard signs. The second advantage to planning our advertising campaign early is that it forces us to work closely with those involved in fund-raising and volunteer efforts, making sure the entire campaign is well coordinated.

In this example, we may conclude that, since name recognition is clearly an early problem for us, we are best served, given our limited initial finances, by using radio, billboards, and yard signs, early in the campaign. These forms of media can all be used effectively to help establish early name recognition. Moreover, they are typically less expensive than newspaper advertisements and television commercials. Hopefully, early in the campaign when we are laying out our positions we may be able to supplement advertising with free media, newspaper stories, and stories and interviews on the local radio and television shows. Later in the campaign, when we have more money, and when we may need to communicate more than our name and party, billboards and yard signs will be of little help. Using them in March as we originally planned, may not make as much sense as using them earlier, which also enables us to save money for newspaper and television advertisements that we might need later in the campaign to explain our positions. Moreover, if we use yard signs early, it forces our volunteer coordinators to amass a large number of volunteers early, and those people will be vital to our later efforts to put out a variety of mailings. Thus, as we plan early we are able to refine our advertising program in those ways that best enable us to blend with the efforts of other elements of the campaign.

Additionally, as we begin to recognize our financial problems, we may choose to divert a greater effort in that area. We may be forced, as Harriet Woods was, to have our candidate spend a great percentage of her time on fund-raising. We may have to develop extra fund-raising activities. Regardless of our situation, by giving ourselves ample time to plan we can make the most of whatever resources we have available to us. Among the factors that our advance media planning should consider are:

• Relative costs in dollars of available media

• Relative costs in candidate time/volunteer effort or other campaign resources of available media

• Ability of media to target specific audiences

• Ability of various media to accomplish specific goals of advertising

• Sequential development of advertising

• Coordinating advertising with the remainder of the campaign

We can best understand many of these factors by examining the various media that campaigners can choose to employ.

BASIC CONSIDERATIONS IN THE SELECTION OF POLITICAL ADVERTISING MEDIA

Political campaigns make use of seven types of advertising media; display graphics, direct mail, telephone, print, radio, television, and the Internet. Each of these options has virtues, and each has liabilities. Advance planning that evaluates those virtues and liabilities in relation to the factors listed above facilitates a skillfully developed campaign advertising program. Hence, this discussion will focus on each of the seven types of advertising media in relation to the factors that must be considered as the campaign's advertising program is developed.

Display Graphics

Display advertising, also called graphic advertising, most commonly includes such items as billboards, posters, yard signs, bumper stickers, and buttons. Such advertising has been a part of American campaigning virtually from our nation's inception. As technology has changed, so too has display advertising. For example, campaign buttons were virtually unknown until the late nineteenth century. But by 1896 the celluloid button process had been patented and in the 1896 campaigns of William McKinley and William Jennings Bryan, buttons assumed their place in the arsenal of the campaign persuader. In the 1920s technological changes allowed for the lithographed production of buttons on tin. This process did not allow for the elaborate artwork and use of photographs that celluloid buttons did, but brought the cost of buttons down dramatically.[9] Display advertising can be instrumental in helping (1) to create and reinforce name recognition, and (2) to give a very quick impression of the candidate. If these are among the goals of the advertising campaign, and often early in the campaign they are, the use of display advertising should be considered. Such advertising normally carries an exceedingly brief message, often no more than the candidate's name, or the name and a brief slogan. For example, in recent national elections, billboards, posters, yard signs, bumper stickers, and buttons have carried such messages as: "Forward with KENNEDY," "Nixon Now, Re-elect the President," "PRESIDENT MUSKIE Don't You Feel Better Already?," "Leaders for Change—CARTER Mondale," "The Time is Now REAGAN & BUSH," "Geraldine Ferraro America's First Woman Vice Pres.," "JACKSON for President—Follow the Rainbow," "Ross for Boss," "Clinton Gore—Out in Four," "Go Pat Go! Buchanan for President," "A Proud Tradition: Dole 96."[10] Typical of the similarly brief messages used on display media in recent state and local campaigns are messages such as: "DEWINE for OHIO," "I Gave A Buck for YOUNG for Congress," "Run RABBITT Lt. Governor," "ROCKY!", "FRANKE for

CONGRESS," "Elect CASEY Congressman," "For Mayor, OLIVAS," "Light Up Congress: Elect Dennis J. Kucincich."[11]

Display advertising such as those cited above clearly contribute to enhancing name recognition. Additionally, as several of these examples illustrate, display advertising may reinforce a major campaign theme. For example, in 1972 Richard Nixon continually stressed his incumbency and experience, hence the theme of his campaign, "Re-Elect the President." In the 1992 race for Ohio's U. S. Senate seat, Dayton area Congressman Michael Dewine argued that incumbent John Glenn was preoccupied with national issues and had neglected Ohio. Hence, "Dewine for Ohio."

Display graphics, the format of which does not allow for an extended message, can serve two additional important, yet often overlooked, functions. They are particularly useful in reinforcing partisans who are already committed to the candidate. When distributred at campaign meetings, rallies, and similar activities they often enhance the spirit of the staff and volunteers, serving as a visible link between the candidate and the worker. Indeed, many campaigns will purchase a few hundred pins, bumper stickers, or yard signs, simply to keep the moral of the staff up. One candidate of the author's acquaintance complained so badly about his lack of yard signs that the campaign manager assigned a volunteer to post 50 yard signs on the mile and a half route the candidate took into his headquarters every morning, and then to check once a week to replace any signs that had come down. The manager reported an immediate improvement in the candidate's outlook and performance! On occasion the cost for a small amount of display graphic advertising is well worth the improved staff and volunteer moral that it provides.

Finally, if handled well, display graphics can be used to impress voters with the candidate's strength and help to create a bandwagon effect. For example, most consultants would advise that yard signs or bumper stickers not be given out in a small trickle, a few every day. Rather, a well coordinated effort should be made to distribute a massive number of them simultanously. So, for example on September 9 there are virtually no yard signs in the district. All of a sudden, on September 10, there seems to be one every block. Though there is not a sign in every block, the startlingly sudden appearance of many signs multiplies their effectiveness, making the casual voter highly aware of them, and often suggesting to that voter that the candidate must have a large organization behind him to get up so many signs so quickly. Putting up massive numbers of yard signs all at once makes their impact far stronger, suggests massive support for the candidate, and helps create a bandwagon effect among casual voters. A similar effect can be achieved by distributing bumper stickers throughout the district all at once. Many campaigns will post volunteers in every high school football field parking lot one Friday night in early October, and in that fashion distribute thousands of bumper stickers simultaneously. The same effect can be achieved by using shopping mall parking lots.

In recent years the quantity and variety of display graphic advertising in political campaigns has been diminished. This is a direct function of cost. As recently as the early 1970s it was not uncommon for a voter to be able to walk into the campaign office of a candidate and be given pins, bumper stickers, and similar materials, not only of that candidate but also of other candidates of the same party. Today, the voter seeking such material is often asked to leave a contribution of 50 cents or a dollar for every button or bumper sticker they take.

Display graphics are expensive, both in terms of dollars and in terms of time and effort. Costs vary from community to community, though national suppliers that specialize in campaign materials tend to be exceedingly competitive. The cost for 1,000 2¼ inch celluloid buttons that allow the use of photographs, other elaborate art work, and a variety of colors will be about $250 or 25 cents each from most national suppliers. The same size plastic-coated metal buttons, which allow for one color printing on a standard background color, will be moderately less expensive, running about $210–$240 per thousand or 21–24 cents each. Most suppliers offer quantity discounts for orders of 2,500, 5,000, or more, which will bring the per button price down, though the discounts are not sharp. Large quantity orders will reduce the costs by about two to four cents per button.[12]

In recent years many campaigns have saved on the cost of buttons by utilizing adhesive roll stickers. These stickers or labels can be peeled off the roll and will adhere to clothing, serving the same name recognition function as a button. Unlike a button they cannot be readily reused from day to day. The current cost for 3-inch round roll labels is $95 per thousand, or 9.5 cents each. Most suppliers will offer substantial discounts for volume purchases, bringing the costs down to approximately 5 cents when 5,000 labels are ordered and as little as 2.5 cents each when 20,000 such labels are ordered.[13]

In addition to buttons or stickers, perhaps the most popular small form of display graphic is the bumper sticker. The current cost for 1,000 of the simplest standard 3 inch by 11.5 inch bumper stickers, one color printing on a standard background color, will range from $260 to $330, or 26 to 33 cents each. Most venders offer a substantial discount for volume. Thus, 2,500 of the same bumper stickers will cost $430–$550, or 18–22 cents each. An order for 5,000 of the same bumper stickers will cost $545–$900, which brings the cost down to about 12–18 cents each.[14]

A wide variety of other smaller forms of display graphics have been used by campaigns. They include such products as car litterbags, emery boards, pocket combs, refrigerator magnets, pens, pencils, and balloons—

always with the candidate's name prominently displayed. Prices for these smaller forms of display advertising vary, but most can be obtained for between $130 and $190 per thousand.[15]

Larger forms of display advertising such as billboards and yard signs are also costly. In Cincinnati, Ohio, the twenty-eighth largest media market in the nation, the 1998 cost of renting sufficient billboard space to provide that 25 percent of the Cincinnati population will see your message at least once daily was $9,360 a month.[16] Additionally, the printing cost for those boards will normally run approximately $1,400. Thus, the total cost for a modest billboard effort running only one month in duration would be approximately $10,700.[17]

Yard signs are also costly. Their price will vary depending on such factors as the size and quality of material used. However, because they are designed to remain outside, the posterboard used must be of good quality, and many campaigns prefer to use a high grade thick laminated paper. The current cost for 1,000 professionally printed yard signs, measuring a standard 22 inch by 28 inch size, printed on a thick laminated paper stock or polyethylene-coated cardboard, using one color printing on a standard background color with the same copy and color on both sides, ranges from $1,100 to $1,360 from national suppliers.[18] It should also be remembered that typically some expense will also be incurred in purchasing stakes for the signs and in transporting them throughout the district.

In recent years printed cardboard or polyethylene-coated cardboard signs have been replaced or supplemented in over 1,200 campaigns— including the 1996 Clinton, Dole, and Perot campaigns—by poly-sleeve yard signs. These signs are printed on a heavy-duty polyethylene plastic sleeve or bag that fits over a wire frame, provided and included in the cost. Patriot Signage, the leading supplier of this alternative to traditional yard signs, prices a 26 by 16 sign utilizing one color plus white at $1,910 per thousand. Purchases in larger quantity will result in a substantial price reduction.[19] Though this cost is greater than that of cardboard or polyethylene cardboard, the more traditional signs also have to be assembled, which costs volunteer time, and stakes and staples must be purchased. Hence, the discrepancy in cost is not as great as it may appear at first glance.

Direct Mail

Direct mail advertising provides campaigns with one enormous advantage that cannot be readily duplicated by any other form of political advertising. It allows the campaign to be highly selective in targeting audiences. The wise use of radio and television commercials or of newspaper and magazine advertisements also allows for some degree of targeting. However, direct mail allows the campaign to target an audience more precisely than virtually any other form of advertising. The only comparable media, in terms of precise targeting, is the telephone.

Unlike many other forms of campaign communication, direct mail can be considered "high interest, low backlash communication." That is, a direct mail piece can be tailored to reflect the interests of a specific constituency. For example, the candidate's views on the United States and NATO (the North Atlantic Treaty Organization) might be featured in a mailing sent to a large section of the district where most residents are of European extraction. However, the candidate's views on Latin American policy can be featured in a mailing sent to an immediately adjacent few square blocks in the district where most residents are of Latin American extraction. Such mailings focus on topics of high interest to the recipients. However, they create low backlash. If the candidate spoke about NATO or Latin America on radio or television, or in the print media, it is likely that many viewers or readers would have little interest in these topics and hence react negatively to the candidate for boring them by failing to address their concerns.[20] By using direct mail to target audiences, the likelihood of high recipient interest is increased and the risk of backlash is largely eliminated.

Not only does direct mail allow for precise targeting of audiences, but it allows for an extended message. It is a vehicle that enables the candidate to fully express herself on a given issue. It is not uncommon for candidates to use letters and mailings that run four or more pages in length to treat one specific issue or a group of closely related issues. For example, a candidate may wish to fully explain her position on social security and compulsory health insurance, topics that are of special interest to older Americans. To do so might require considerable radio and television time or considerable newspaper space and hence be extremely expensive. However, by using a mailing piece directed at older voters, the candidate can explain her position more fully than would be possible by using other media and actually save money.

Because it allows for precise targeting, and because it can be used to convey a long message, political campaigns have used direct mail both to persuade voters and to raise money from contributors. In the 1970s direct mail became the principal means of fund-raising for a variety of candidates, most notably George McGovern, who harnessed the direct mail team of Morris Dees and Tom Collins to find approximately 250,000 supporters who financed his presidential campaign largely by responding to his repeated direct mail solicitations.[21] Since that time direct mail has served as the principal means of fund-raising for at least two other presidential campaigns, the 1980 campaign of independent candidate John Anderson and the 1980 Republican campaign of Congressman Philip Crane. Some specialists in the use of direct mail suggest that it is most effective in raising funds among older voters and hence is best suited to use with contributor lists that are oriented toward older voters.[22] Though direct mail is an expensive way of raising funds, with 60–70 percent of every dollar raised often going to offset the cost of the mailing, it has been the principal means of fund-raising for a host of lesser candidates.[23]

The dollar costs of direct mail are difficult to talk about because mail pieces can be as simple as a mimeographed flyer or as elaborate as a multicolor, multipage letter and brochure with pictures produced on high quality stock. As with most display graphics, quantity orders yield considerable discounts. One major national distributor, for example, will offer a prefolded 9 inch by 11 inch four color mailer on high quality glossy coated paper as inexpensively as seven cents each when a million or more are ordered. That same mailer would cost over 30 cents in quantities of 10,000 or less.[24] While costs for the mailing piece itself normally diminish as the number of pieces purchased increases, the larger the mailing the larger the costs of postage and the larger the costs in the use of volunteer time or payment to a direct mail house that arranges the mailing.

By controlling the costs of the mailpiece itself, as well as the size of the mailing, the cost of direct mail can generally be managed to conform to the campaign's needs, enabling most campaigns to use mailings. Direct mailings are the major form of campaign advertising in many lower level races. Often, the advertisements that the lower level campaign might use in newspapers or on radio and television are likely to be lost in the large number of political advertisments that flood those media in the weeks before election. Moreover, often the costs of purchasing sufficient radio or television time are simply beyond the ability of small local campaigns. Direct mail, which can be made to fit most campaign budgets, can be targeted to specific voter blocs, and allows candidates to explain themselves thoroughly, is often critical in lower level races.

Indeed, while most lay persons think first of television as the principal medium of political campaigns, more money is actually spent on direct mail than on any other campaign medium. When every race from the bottom of the ballot to the top of the ballot is counted, and when all the expenses involved in direct mailings (including list rentals, database management, labeling, printing, and of course postage) are included, political candidates and their committees spent more money on direct mail—over $3 billion—than on any other advertising medium in the 1994 and 1996 election cycles.[25] In the wake of the campaign finance scandals of 1996 and calls to reduce the costs of campaigning, it has been pointed out that, ironically, the largest single recipient of money spent on campaigns is the United States Postal Service.[26]

As with any form of campaign communication, there are principles that have proven successful in the use of direct mail. Hal Malchow, creative director of The November Group, a well-respected political direct mail firm, has recently suggested a variety of guidelines for designing direct mail. They include:

1. Throw away the envelopes. Malchow claims that envelopes cost extra money and serve no useful purpose. To gain immediate attention, he recommends using oversized post cards, unusual shapes, and folded pieces that look nothing like either a letter or a traditional campaign brochure. Such a mailpiece gains immediate attention.

2. Give the voter a reason to read your mailing. Begin the mailpiece in a dramatic and compelling way. The opening panel of the mailpiece should be designed to attract attention through the use of a dramatic headline or an interesting photograph.

3. Localize your message. Because direct mail facilitates very precise targeting, it should be used accordingly. If a neighborhood in your district is concerned about a school issue or a proposed highway be sure that the mail sent to that community reflects your interest in their concern and does not ignore local issues in favor of simply treating issues of more general concern throughout your constituency.

4. Use the 20-second test. Malchow claims that the average voter will give a mailpiece between 20 and 60 seconds. "They will look at the cover, the headlines, the pictures and often the captions under the photographs. But few people will actually read your literature." Thus, he claims that "to be effective, you have to tell your story in a 20 second glance. Can someone in 20 seconds read the headlines, look at the pictures and maybe read the captions and come away with the basic points of your message? If not, you have not designed a good piece of campaign literature."

5. Use a lettershop. Malchow is an advocate of using a professional mailing organization. He claims that "we all want to save money, but don't be a dunce. A lettershop is cheaper than pizza and beer for your volunteers." Malchow has found that for two to five cents per piece, a lettershop will automatically label your pieces, sort and bag the mail, and fully prepare it for the post office in a manner that qualifies for full postal discounts for presorted mail. He claims that "even the poorest campaign should avoid" hand labeling and sorting third-class mail. He finds such a task to be both so difficult and so time consuming that the costs of having it done professionally are well worth the expense.[27]

Telephone Contact Services

Growing sophistication in the application of computer technology to campaigning has resulted not only in the growth of direct mail but also in the growth of telephone contact services. Companies providing such services, in many instances, will work from voter lists that they have prepared and will sell or lease to candidates as well as from lists that the campaign itself provides. Campaigns will use telephone contact for a variety of purposes. Most commonly, it will be used to deliver persuasive messages, raise money, and to get out the vote on election day.

When used for persuasion, voters can be targeted by demographic characteristics and a persuasive message can be scripted for members of each group being called. Similarly, fund-raising solicitations can also be narrowly targeted and a precise script developed to use with various types of potential contributors. Telephone contact, like direct mail, allows for precise targeting. Telephones are frequently used on election day to get out the vote. As the day progresses, voters previously identified as supportive can be contacted to remind them, and if necessary help them, to get to the polls.

Telephone contact firms will provide several services to a campaign. First, they will often script the phone conversation. Second, they will provide professionally trained callers to actually make the calls. Third, they will provide state-of-the-art equipment to facilitate efficient use of the phone. Predictive dialing systems, used by most major national telephone contact services, which utilize sophisticated dialing equipment and computer software, can provide the campaign with major savings in time and cost. Typically, by filtering out all busy signals, answering machines, disconnected lines, and other useless responses, such systems allow the campaign to deliver as many as 30–35 messages of 90 seconds in length each hour from each phone being used. Noncomputerized phone banks will average about 15 calls per phone, per hour, of the same length. Moreover, these systems can reduce the per call cost of reaching voters by 30 percent or more, often bringing the costs down to under a dollar a call for persuasive messages and as little as 35 cents or less for election day "get out the vote" calls. In addition, a sustained effort can reach a large number of voters. With good equipment, a 50-line phone bank, using a 90-second script, operating three hours an evening, can place approximately 5,000 calls per night.[28]

Print Advertisements

Print advertisements in newspapers and magazines have been a part of American campaigns from our nation's inception.[29] Newspaper and magazine advertisements, the two types of print advertisements upon which this section will focus, offer political advertisers several advantages. First, they provide for timeliness. Not only can the campaign plan well in advance to determine precisely when they want an advertisement to run, but normally the campaign can make changes, both in the advertisement content and in the advertisement size, relatively quickly.

Consequently, utilizing the daily paper may be an effective means of quickly countering an opposition argument.

Typically, if advertisement space has been purchased in advance, the copy can be changed on short notice in most metropolitan dailies. Additionally, a new advertisement can be purchased on short notice.[30] Since skilled writers can normally produce a political advertisement extremely quickly, the daily paper is an efficient means of responding to opponents. Radio commercials offer a similar advantage, but television is normally not as advantageous. Though television stations can accommodate changes in commercials, it normally takes a greater effort to produce a television commercial than to produce a newspaper or radio spot, making it more difficult for the candidate to respond rapidly through television. This is not to say that television commercials cannot be changed, for frequently they are. However, typically, the process is either slower or works considerably more hardship on the campaign.[31]

Newspaper and magazine advertisements also offer the opportunity for candidates to express themselves more fully than do most other types of paid advertising. Candidates can present a considerable amount of material about themselves in a full page, or even a half or quarter page advertisement. Speaking at the normal rate of speed, a 60-second radio or television commercial forces the campaign to reduce its message to 150 words or less.[32] By adjusting the size of both the advertisement and the type used in the advertisement, candidates can easily present a print message that is three times longer or more, and still create a physically appealing advertisement. If the message being sent is complex and needs considerable explanation, newspapers and magazines are often exceptionally good vehicles for getting the message to voters.

The liabilities of print advertising involve targeting and cost. First, according to most estimates, over 12 percent of adult Americans are functional illiterates.[33] Clearly this substantial group of citizens cannot be effectively reached by print media. Second, it is frequently difficult to target specific audiences with newspaper and magazine advertisements.

However, in recent years targeting messages to specific magazine and newspaper audiences has become easier. Many larger daily papers that have readerships located in large geographic areas have special sections or editions that are used in the appropriate geographic area. For example, both of the daily papers in Cincinnati, Ohio, have special northern Kentucky editions. While the paper is largely the same, the northern Kentucky editions focus the local news coverage more heavily on Northern Kentucky than on Ohio. These editions are distributed to Kentucky subscribers and used on newsstands in Kentucky, facilitating some geographic targeting. The use of special editions aimed at specific geographic segments of the market has become commonplace for many larger metropolitan papers.

Smaller newspapers, because their circulation is limited, may also lend themselves to targeting. Candidates running for offices that include the entire voting populations of smaller towns may do well to advertise in the weekly papers that service most smaller communities or suburban communities. Candidates who have targeted a specific religious, ethnic, or occupational group might also do well to consider advertising in the smaller, often weekly, newspapers that are aimed at these audiences.

Additionally, today many magazine advertisements can also be bought on a regional or even a zip code basis. This type of magazine purchase facilitates rather precise targeting. For example, a congressional candidate might choose to advertise in a special interest magazine that she feels is read heavily by a group she has targeted. Moreover, the candidate can limit her purchase to subscribers who live in those zip codes within her congressional district.

An additional advantage to this type of purchase is that it may give a local, regional, or statewide candidate additional stature to be associated with a national publication. The degree to which specific magazines can accommodate this type of advertising varies, as of course does price. In recent years, primarily as a function of the growth of computerization within the newspaper and magazine industry, the use of magazines and newspapers for targeted audiences has become more feasible. However, they are still considered "mass media" and cannot be as narrowly focused as direct mail.

Precisely because they are "mass media," read by hundreds of thousands of people, newspaper and magazine costs are often high. For example, a full page weekday black and white advertisement in the *Cincinnati Enquire*, the dominant daily paper in the twenty-eighth largest market in the country, currently costs $15,232. Smaller advertisements are sold at the rate of $118.08 per column inch and their costs are calculated using 129 column inches to the page. A similar ad, run on a Sunday, when the other daily paper in Cincinnati does not print, costs $19,840. The costs of smaller Sunday advertisements are calculated at the rate of $153.80 per column inch.[34]

Radio

Radio is an often underestimated vehicle for political advertisements. Surveys suggest that the typical American household has four radios, not including those in cars.[35] Radio also allows for a moderate degree of targeting. While not as precise as direct mail, the wide variety of radio stations found in most areas tends to segment the audience and provides campaigns with the means to target some audiences.

For much of the first half of the twentieth century, radio was ranked with the print media as the dominant form of political advertising. However, beginning in the 1950s, radio was utilized less and less frequently. The 1952 presidential campaign between General Dwight David Eisenhower and Governor Adlai Stevenson was the last national campaign in which expenditures on radio advertising were roughly equal to those on television.[36] Since 1952 television has superseded radio as the dominant electronic media.

Nevertheless, radio retains an important place in the arsenal of political advertising weapons available to candidates. In 1968, after managing Richard Nixon's successful presidential campaign, John Mitchell claimed that if he were to manage the campaign over again the only significant change he would make would be to utilize more radio.[37] The reasons that radio retains considerable popularity among campaign professionals are at least threefold.[38] First, radio lends itself to advertisements that can vary greatly in length and hence can serve a variety of functions. Second, radio can be targeted. Third, radio is not perceived as an expensive medium.

Radio commercials can be bought in a variety of time lengths, ranging from 10 or 15 seconds, through the more common 30- and 60-second spots, to longer time slots, such as five minutes, 15 minutes, or half an hour. Consequently, radio can serve a variety of functions. For example, a 10-second spot might consist of nothing more than a brief jingle in which the candidate's name is repeated several times. Constant use of this jingle can quickly help to establish name recognition. A five minute commercial allows the candidate to present a reasonably complete analysis of one or perhaps more questions. Purchasing such time slots on television is often either costly or impractical.

Radio can be targeted because certain stations tend to attract certain demographic groups. Easy listening stations, religious stations, foreign language stations, hard rock stations, newstalk stations, oldies stations—all appeal to different demographic groups. Radio gives the campaign an opportunity to target specific audiences and prepare messages aimed at those audiences. It is impossible to say whether radio allows for better targeting than, for example, newspapers and magazines. Every campaign has to evaluate the media available to it and the audiences it wishes to target. Nevertheless, in many communities radio can be used to reach targeted audiences and often lends itself to this use better than many other forms of advertising.

Radio is often perceived as an inexpensive advertising medium. Most political campaigns seek to advertise during drive times—5:00 A.M. to 9:00 A.M. and 2:00 P.M. to 6:00 P.M.—when commuters on their way to and from work help to create the largest radio audiences. During the 1998 elections, a one-minute political commercial during drive time on the most popular talk radio station in Cincinnati cost $75.[39] While the specific target audiences of a given campaign will help to dictate the choice of stations used, newstalk stations tend to be popular with political campaigns because of the perception that they attract knowledgeable audiences who are more likely to vote than the audiences attracted to many other types of stations. For example, the same commercial run on a popular music station that attracts younger voters sells for $60.[40] Though there are slight differences in audience size, the demographics of these two stations also enter into their relative attractiveness to political advertisers.

One-minute advertisements on popular nationally syndicated radio talk shows, such as those of Dr. Laura Schlesinger, cost $90 in the Cincinnati market, while a one-minute advertisement on the most popular radio talk show, that of Rush Limbaugh, costs $150.[41]

As will become evident in the next section, in some areas the cost of a single television commercial on a local nightly news program may be the equivalent of a week's worth of drive-time radio advertising on a highly rated station, or two weeks or more of drive-time advertising on a station that may not attract a broad audience but that appeals to a group targeted by the campaign.

Radio is particularly popular among political advertisers who are campaigning in rural areas and those who are campaigning for lesser offices. Rural areas may be reliant upon papers from larger nearby cities or on small town weekly papers. Similarly, they are normally reliant upon more urban areas for television. Advertising in the larger paper or on television forces the campaign to purchase an audience that cannot vote in its election. This is often simply not cost-effective for the rural election. Utilizing the small town paper provides an appropriate audience but that audience can only be addressed once per week. Hence, many rural campaigns find local small town radio stations an attractive option to include in their media mix. Similarly, lower level elections, often poorly financed, and often covering a smaller geographic area than that served by television stations and large circulation metropolitan area papers, find radio a viable option.

Indeed, in some areas radio stations have been forced to put a limit on the number of political commercials they will accept. Typically, such stations limit political campaigns to two drive-time advertisements each morning and two each afternoon during the work week.[42] Such limits are often necessary because the demand of political advertisers during the few weeks preceding the election are often so great that stations could not accommodate their normal advertisers and honor their long-term advertising contracts to those advertisers if they accepted all of the political commercials that campaigns wish to air.

Though radio has many virtues as a vehicle for political commercials, it also has drawbacks. Chief among them is the fact that, among all of the major forms of media, radio demands the least amount of attention.

Most radio is listened to by individuals simultaneously engaged in other activities. Consequently, campaigns are paying for audiences that are not giving them full attention.

Television

Television offers the political advertiser a variety of advantages. First, it is the only advertising medium that appeals to two of our senses, sight and hearing. As a consequence, television is able to convey more in a short time, and typically has a greater impact on the viewer who is getting "twice the message."

Second, of all the mass media, television is often able to produce the largest audiences. The viewership for a popular show often exceeds the readership for the largest circulation papers in a community. If the candidate seeks widespread exposure, television is unmatched as an advertising medium. However, many television programs attract audiences that are politically apathetic, thus somewhat diminishing their value. Because news programs tend to attract audiences that are attentive to current events and more prone to vote, political advertisers normally seek to place their advertisements on news programs and other shows such as *Prime Time Live, Dateline, Today,* and *Good Morning America,* that attract individuals with an interest in current events. Somewhat related to the fact that television can provide a large audience is the third advantage of television. In our media-oriented society, television lends a degree of credibility. Imagine, if you can, how serious a presidential candidate would be taken if he never used television. Indeed, this was one of the problems that Jesse Jackson faced in 1984. In part because his campaign did not make extensive use of television, he was not viewed as a viable candidate. The legitimacy that television conveys to a campaign has also been recognized by candidates running for lesser offices. Today, in many areas, it is not uncommon to see television commercials on behalf of candidates for every federal and statewide office, and for many local offices such as mayor, city councilman, county prosecutor, judge, or sheriff. Candidates for offices that voters have come to associate with television commercials run a real risk of losing credibility if they do not include television in their media mix.

A final advantage of television is that it does allow for some degree of targeting. As indicated above, certain shows tend to attract audiences composed of individuals who are concerned with current events and prone to vote. Other shows attract audiences that are heavily weighted toward a given demographic group that the campaign may have targeted. For example, a sporting event is more prone to attract a heavily male audience, while *General Hospital* is more prone to attract a heavily female audience. Even local news shows often attract audiences with different demographic appeals, often depending on the nature of the anchor persons.

In sum, television has become the dominant media of political advertising for a variety of reasons. Because it allows the viewer to use two senses, it is often able to convey more than other media. Television can provide wide exposure, helping the unknown candidate become known rapidly. Moreover, it lends a sense of credibility to candidates and allows for some degree of targeting. However, like all political media, television is not without its liabilities.

The most obvious disadvantage of television is the enormous expense associated with it. For the growing number of campaigns that utilize television, it almost invariably is the principal expense that these campaigns incur. Many campaigns budget 75 to 80 percent of their money for television.[43] In 1974 the average incumbent member of the United States House of Representatives spent $54,000 to win the election. In 1996, an average campaign for a seat in the House of Representatives cost $640,000. This figure includes only hard money. Perhaps another way of dramatizing the escalating costs of campaigns is to observe that to raise that amount of money, a candidate had to raise $876 every day for two years.[44] And, of course, these figures have continued to increase. Virtually every explanation for this staggering increase in the cost of campaigning focuses partially, if not primarily, on the increased costs of television.[45]

Several examples will make clear how quickly television costs escalate. In 1998 a single 30-second political spot on highly rated news-like morning shows such as *Today* cost $750 in the medium-sized market of Cincinnati. Lesser rated competitors such as *CBS This Morning* commanded $300 for the same 30-second spot.[46] Shows such as this tend to attract audiences concerned with current events who are prone to vote. Hence, they are popular with political advertisers. The cost of a 30-second spot on a syndicated talk show, many of which are broadcast throughout the morning on the network affiliates in Cincinnati, ranged from $150 for a poorly rated show such as *Maury* to $500 for a top-rated talk show such as that of Jerry Springer. A 30-second spot on the afternoon soap operas, whose demographics make them appealing to campaigns that are targeting women, cost $250 in the Cincinnati market.[47]

A thirty second ad on a syndicated early evening quasi-news show such such as *Entertainment Tonight* cost $625 in the Cincinnati market during the 1998 election cycle. A political advertiser on Cincinnati's top-rated show at the same time, also a syndicated quasi-news show, *Hard Copy*, paid $1,000 for a 30-second ad. These shows are often popular with political advertisers since they command large audiences as they lead into the prime evening viewing hours.

During 1998, a 30-second spot in the Cincinnati market on a highly rated prime time news-oriented show such as *60 Minutes* cost $4,000. In 1998 a single 30-second spot on the most popular prime time shows, such as *Seinfeld*, cost $14,000 or more in the Cincinnati market.[48] Representative of the costs of a single 30-second political spot on other relatively popular prime time shows are *Touched by an Angel*, which cost $2,600; *3rd Rock*, which cost $3,800; and *Frasier*, which cost $5,500.[49] In 1998 a single 30-second spot on the second-rated late evening local newscast in the Cincinnati market cost $1,200.

Thus, in 1998 a very limited television campaign consisting of a daily 30-second spot on a soap opera, a daily 30-second spot on an early evening quasi-news show such as *Hard Copy*, two prime time ads in an entire week on shows such as *Touched by an Angel* and *Frasier*, and a single daily spot on the second-rated late evening news would cost slightly over $20,000 a week. Keep in mind, this would be an exceedingly limited advertising campaign. It includes only three regularly scheduled commercials a day, and then they are only scheduled for a five-day week. These daily commercials are supplemented with only two commercials a week on modestly priced prime time shows. Moreover, Cincinnati is not among the largest 25 media markets in the nation. A campaign that advertised on two or more newscasts, which is common in political campaigns, or that advertised in the morning, as many campaigns seeking to target older voters and women commonly do, or that included several more prime time commercials, or that advertised on weekends, as most campaigns do, or was waged in a larger media market would quickly escalate the costs. Clearly, the costs of television advertising can be expensive.[50]

In addition to the cost of purchasing time, television involves more elaborate production costs than other media. Most political consultants who specialize in television currently suggest that a good rule of thumb is to estimate the cost of television production at 5–10 percent of the cost of air time. Many political spots are produced for $10,000 or less. The more expensive political spots rarely exceed $30,000 in production costs. While this is substantially higher than the production costs for other forms of political media, it is exceedingly modest when compared to the production costs of other television commercials.[51]

A second difficulty with television is one that is a function of geography. In many parts of the nation, targeting with television is difficult and candidates may be forced to pay for audiences that cannot vote in their elections. For example, the media markets served by stations in such cities as St. Louis, Kansas City, Philadelphia, New York City, Louisville, Washington D.C., and Boston, just to name a few, are composed of residents of more than one state. Thus, candidates running for any local office, and even state offices, are forced to pay for audiences that cannot participate in their election. While this problem also exists for other media serving communities such as these, the expenses of television heighten the problem.

A third potential problem with television is that many candidates do not project well using television. Though some candidates like Ronald Reagan and Jessie Helms entered politics after first working in radio and television, and others such as former New York Congresswoman Susan Molinari and former Cincinnati Mayor Jerry Springer had such an affinity for televison that when they left elected office they became television personalities, many candidates are not comfortable with television. This does not by any means preclude the use of television, but it does mean that a realistic assessment of the candidate's abilities must be made and that if the candidate is found wanting the campaign may have to change its advertising strategy.[52]

In sum, just as with any other advertising medium, television offers political candidates both advantages and disadvantages. Though campaigns have grown increasingly reliant upon television, the experiences of candidates like Harriet Woods reminds us that candidates cannot win most elections by relying almost exclusively on television. Television commercials often have a strong impact on viewers who must utilize two of their senses as they attend to the commercials. Television can also provide a massive audience for the campaign's messages, contribute to the candidate's credibility, and allow for limited targeting. However, the costs of television are extremely high, especially in many races where candidates find themselves paying for audiences that cannot participate in the election. Moreover, production costs for television are also high, and many candidates do not perform well on television. All of these factors must be weighed as the campaign develops its own unique media mix.

Videocassettes and Cable Television

By 1994 over 92 million VCRs could be found in over 75 million American households. Over 90 percent of the the households that included regular voters owned a VCR.[53] Political campaigns, always on the cutting edge of technology, have not ignored the explosive growth in VCR popularity.

Traditionally, the use of a customized videocassette to distribute the candidate's message has been perceived as either excessively expensive or ineffective. But improved technology in the production of the cassettes themselves, as well as improved methods of packaging and mailing, has brought the cost of a customized videocassette to under $2 each, including mailing costs.[54] Cost figures of this sort, which might also include accompanying literature and a mailer that typically has a printed message on it, are gradually making customized videos price-competitive with direct mail. Improved technology, and the economies of size suggest that though customized cassettes will likely remain more expensive than most mailpieces, the gap will continue to diminish in the near future.

Moreover, evidence suggests that customized videocassettes are exceptionally effective. According to some studies as many as 40 percent of those who receive an unsolicited video will watch it, a far higher rate than unsolicited mail typically generates. Moreover, studies suggest that the response rates, whether the video is simply seeking voter support or seeking volunteers and/or money, typically run 20 percent higher than direct mail.[55] As discussed in the preceding section, television is a powerful medium. Moreover, a cassette typically provides the candidate with more time to persuade and inform the voter than the normal 30 to 60-second television spot. Cassettes can be better targeted to specific voters than typical television spots. Moreover, customized videos can be adapted for a variety of uses. They can be shown as part of a coffee or tea, both in place of the candidate or as a supplement to the candidate's message. They can be used with surrogate speakers. They can be used for both persuading voters and seeking contributions.

Like customized videocassettes, the use of cable television also allows political figures to capitalize on the power of television as medium, while providing better targeting than can typically be done through the use of network and local affiliate programming. As recently as 1988, political campaigns made virtually no use of cable television. In 1992, a mere four years later, cable billings to political campaigns totalled $4.5 million. In 1996, some estimates suggest that 3–6 percent of political media budgets was spent on cable and approximately 80 percent of all congressional candidates used cable.[56]

The rise of the cable industry, whose sales forces have been aggressive in seeking political business, and the decline in network viewership are altering the political time-buying strategies of many campaigns. The availability of national advertising on the cable networks, local advertising on cable networks and local cable shows, and even regional advertising on "cable interconnects," which link cable systems into regional networks, facilitates voter targeting. Moreover, the fact that audience research suggests that cable voters tend to be 24 percent more likely to vote than the average TV viewer is yet another strong impetus driving the increasing use of cable by political campaigns. Rapidly improving cable technology and the growing penetration of cable systems, which now serve 56 million homes, or about 61 percent of the country, including 75 percent of the homes in major metropolitan areas, suggest that this form of advertising is likely to increase in the near future.[57]

Cable campaigning facilitates two types of targeting for political advertisers. First, it facilitates more precise geographic targeting. For example, in his 1992 reelection campaign, New York Senator Alfonse D'Amato ran endorsement advertisements on the upstate cable systems featuring Jack Kemp, an enormously popular figure in the Buffalo area where he had been repeatedly elected to Congress and at one time quarterbacked the Buffalo Bills professional football team. Simultaneously, D'Amato ran endorsement advertisements on downstate cable systems in the New York City metropolitan area featuring former New York City Mayor Ed Koch. To use the same advertisements over normal channels might have caused D'Amato to pay for audiences in Canada or New Jersey that would be totally useless to him.[58] Second, cable stations segment the audience by interest and background. Stations such as ESPN, CNN, Arts and Entertainment, Lifetime, the History Channel, USA, the Nashville Network, and many others each appeal to a unique segment of the population.

In sum, the enormous costs of television advertising are driving political campaigners to seek the most bang for their buck. Consequently, political campaigns, seeking to harness the power of television with better ability to target and reduce costs have, by the late 1990s, begun to heavily utilize alternatives to the traditional over-the-air television advertisements—most notably, customized videocassettes and cable.

The Internet

During the 1996 elections some studies suggest that as much as 20 percent of the public utilized the Internet for politically related activities.[59] Virtually all observers feel that within the next few years the Internet is destined to play a much more prominent role in political campaigning. A survey of over 270 campaigns in late July and early August of the 1998 election cycle indicated that 63 percent of those campaigns already had web sites up and running and another 21 percent expected to have a web site shortly. Only 16 percent indicated that they had no plans for an Internet presence.[60] Moreover, a study by the Aspen Institute and the American Bar Association's Committee on Election Law suggests that, though political Internet usage is growing rapidly, "the full effects of the Internet on the electoral process will not be felt until 2000 and beyond."[61]

The principal effect of the Internet is to provide candidates a means of dispensing information directly to the public. The implications of this are considerable. The Internet is a high return, low cost means of dispensing information. As a consequence, it can be utilized by even poorly funded campaigns.

The minimal expenses in providing a campaign with an Internet presence can be seen in the costs born by campaigns in 1998. Fully 43 percent of 270 campaigns surveyed had already spent, or soon expected to spend, less than $500 "designing, building, and maintaining" their Internet site. An additional 38 percent had already spent, or soon expected to spend, between $500 and $2,000 to develop their Internet site, and an additional 17 percent had already spent, or soon expected to spend between $2,000–$10,000 to design, build and maintain their Internet site. Only 2 percent expect to spend in excess of $10,000 on their Internet site. Given that 62 percent of these campaigns had total budgets in excess of $50,000 and one-third were budgeted at $250,000 or more, the fact that over 80 percent of these campaigns were spending $2,000 or less on the Internet suggests that the Internet is a very low cost item in campaign budgets.[62] The low cost of an Internet presence means that in at least one advertising venue even third party or other poorly financed candidates can compete on a relatively even footing.

Currently, political Internet sites serve a variety of functions. In order of importance, campaigns rate the following as the principal functions of their Internet sites.

1. Provide information to voters about the candidate
2. Provide information to voters about candidate views on policy issues
3. Provide political information and news about the campaign
4. Communicate with supporters and endorsing groups
5. Provide election information, to voters (polling places, registration information, etc.)
6. Recruit campaign volunteers
7. Provide information and news about the community
8. Seek voter opinion on issues
9. Raise money
10. Attack the opposition[63]

The functions that Internet sites serve for candidates, as evidenced above, seem to coincide well with the purposes voters have in mind when they access political sites on the Internet. Researchers Marion Just, Ann Crigler, and Montague Kern have found that voters tend to use the Internet for what they term "surveillance" and "solidary" reasons. By surveillance, they refer to the desire of voters to survey or gain information about the campaign. By solidary, they refer to the desire of voters "to experience the gratifications of reinforced, shared political identification or orientation."[64]

Candidate sites are not the only places on the Internet where users can get political information. Virtually every major news organization in the nation has an Internet site. Moreover, there are political news sites that are not affiliated with any candidate or party. Many voters seeking to survey the campaign scene, Just, Crigler, and Kern claim, rely on these sites more than on candidate or party sites.[65] Nevertheless, candidate and party sites contribute to the surveillance function, and clearly serve the solidary function.

As with other media, the quality of political Internet sites varies. The best candidate Internet sites share several characteristics. First, the home page identifies the candidate, utilizes the candidate logo, and offers at least one clear indication of what the candidate is about. Frequently that indication may be a slogan or a a brief phrase or sentence synopsis of the candidate's position on a key issue.

Second, the home page clearly indicates what content is available throughout the candidate's site. Typically, the viewer can click on a series of icons that will take the viewer to such things as the candidate's biography, the candidate's issue positions, a message or story of the day, news of upcoming campaign events and information about key staff members. Moreover, again by clicking on an icon found on the home page, viewers can get involved in the campaign by indicating their willingness to volunteer on behalf of the candidate. Additional icons can offer viewers an opportunity to receive e-mail or make a contribution to the campaign.[66]

Third, a good site will be constantly updated by the campaign. Viewers who indicate strong interest in the campaign by volunteering should be contacted immediately. E-mail should be sent out regularly to voters who put themselves on receiver lists. The story or message of the day should be just that, and changed on a daily basis.

Finally, throughout the site large blocks of text should be broken up by frequent use of subheads, photos, links to other sites, or white space. Strong graphics should be used, but a good web site will also keep the graphics to a manageable size so that each area of the site can be accessed quickly and the viewer is not delayed, waiting for a large graphic.[67]

In sum, the use of the Internet as an advertising medium by political candidates has just begun. As the entire medium matures, no doubt political candidates will develop increasingly sophisticated ways of using it to communicate with voters. However, already it has become a source of information for many voters, and provides the campaign a means of interacting with voters, particularly supporters.

CAMPAIGN ADVERTISING STRATEGIES

The circumstances of the campaign normally dictate the use of one of four basic patterns in the purchase of radio and television time. Since radio and television constitute a major portion of the advertising of most campaigns, the strategies used for purchasing radio and television time typically characterize the entire campaign's advertising strategy. Time buyers aim at reaching targeted voters the maximum number of times the campaign budget allows. To do so they utilize the standard audience measure, gross rating points. A gross rating point represents 1 percent of the TV viewing audience. Theoretically a purchase of 100 points means that the entire TV audience will see the commercial once. Since most consultants estimate that a commercial needs to be seen at least three to five times before it makes an impression, a buy of 500 points is considered "saturation." However, by the 1996 and 1998 election cycles, many consultants were recommending that their clients buy even more TV time. They did so because of the growing "clutter" of political commercials. With soft money enabling many groups to utilize television, it was becoming harder and harder for the candidates' ads to register with the public. Moreover, the growing use of VCRs often meant that ads were skipped by many audience members.[68]

Buying backwards from election day, campaigns will seek purchases of at least 500 points. In markets where costs are low and perhaps where a large number of highly targeted voters can be expected to see the advertisements, or in exceedingly well-financed campaigns, it is not unheard of for a campaign to purchase 2,500 points in the last weeks of the campaign, thus providing that theoretically voters will see the commercial 25 times. Computerization of such things as program schedules, demographic audience data, and pricing information has facilitated more and more sophistication in the purchasing of air time.[69]

The purchase of commercial time reflects a campaign's overall strategy. With some differences that are reflected in the unique virtues of each form of media, the basic radio and television strategy is often commonly extended to the use of display graphics, direct mail, and print media. In this section we will briefly examine the four most common overall campaign advertising strategies.[70]

The Spurt Strategy

This strategy is often used by candidates who are not well known at the outset of the campaign. The strategy is to "spurt" early in the campaign, often four to six months before the election, purchasing a large amount of radio and television time for one to two weeks. The use of radio and television is often supplemented with an early round of newspaper advertisements and an early effort at distributing a large number of yard signs, bumper stickers, buttons and other display graphics. The point of this early spurt is to build name recognition and help establish the candidate as a credible contender for the office.

The campaign, having now utilized a reasonable amount of its resources early, then typically eliminates or drastically reduces its use of radio and television for a long period of time. During this period the campaign may well focus on direct mail efforts, often using direct mail both to target specific audiences for persuasive messages and to help raise funds to replenish the monies spent on the early spurt, deemed necessary to establish name recognition.

Finally, the campaign makes a final "spurt" purchasing considerable radio and television time from the morning of the election backwards as far as it can, hopefully at least a week or more. As with the original spurt, the final radio and television spurt is accompanied by the use of other media. The point of this strategy is to allow the candidate to open strongly and close strongly. While all candidates seek to close strongly, those who start at a disadvantage often utilize the spurt strategy to get them into the race. The candidate who starts out with little name recognition typically has many problems. The initial spurt in advertising spending will hopefully create a spurt in the candidate's standing in the polls, enhance the candidate's credibility, facilitate greater fund-raising, encourage more people to volunteer support, and in sum, simply get the campaign moving.

The Fast Finish Strategy

This strategy goes by a variety of names, including the Silky Sullivan Strategy, the Miracle Braves Strategy, or the '51 Giants Strategy. Just as Silky Sullivan, the famous California-bred race horse, and those famous baseball teams started very slowly, only to close with a rush and win, some candidates choose to start slowly, and close with a rush, expecting to win on election day.

Typically this strategy is implemented by buying a complete schedule of radio and television advertisements for the last portion of the election. Buying backwards from election day, the campaign purchases a complete schedule of radio and television time for as many days as it can afford, normally at least a week, and further back if it can afford it. Then, depending on what the campaign can afford, still buying backwards, the campaign gradually diminishes the amount of commercials it purchases each day. The effect of this type of purchase is that voters see the campaign starting very slowly, with a scattering of commercials. Gradually the advertising increases until voters are completely saturated in the week immediately preceding the election. Similarly, other media efforts are intensified as the election draws closer.

Most campaigns will use some variation of this strategy. Clearly candidates want their messages to have the greatest impact and feel that this is best achieved by surrounding the voter with their message in the days immediately preceding the election. Candidates who start from a position of strength find this strategy particularly appealing, since they often feel that their initial strength allows them to husband their resources until near the end of the campaign. By then, concentrating their advertising in a limited time, they can purchase so much air time in the last days of the campaign that they are confident their messages cannot be missed by voters.

The Really Big Show Strategy

This strategy is designed to capitalize on free news coverage. Named after the expression frequently used by 1950s and 1960s television variety show host Ed Sullivan to describe his show, this strategy is built around several major events that are scheduled periodically throughout the campaign. For example, in a congressional race the candidate holds a press conference and immediately follows it up with several speeches making a major accusation about the shortcomings of her opponent. Second, the candidate has a debate with her opponent. Third, a major national figure comes to town to speak on behalf of the candidate. Each of these three occurrences is a major event in the campaign. Moreover, the candidate has considerable control over their timing.

Using the "really big show" strategy, the candidate will focus her advertising around those events that are likely to receive considerable free media coverage on the news. She will increase her paid advertising at the time of the press conference and speeches, reinforcing through advertising what she is saying in the conference and speeches. She will increase her advertising at the time of the debate, reinforcing positions she takes in the debate or perhaps using cinema verité and testimonial commercials to emphasize how effective she was in the debate and reinforce the points she made during the debate. She will increase her advertising immediately preceding, during, and after the visit by the major national figure, better linking herself to that figure and basking in that figure's prominence and credibility.

By increasing her advertising at the time she is naturally receiving greater free coverage in the news, the candidate turns a campaign event into a "really big show." Often, because of the proximity in timing between the news coverage and the commercials, and depending on how her advertisements are handled, the paid media blends with the free news coverage in the mind of the voter. Candidates using this strategy will generally provide that at least one major event takes place within a few days of the election so that they can combine elements of this strategy with the fast finish strategy. Moreover, this strategy can also be blended with the "spurt" strategy by coordinating the early media effort with an important campaign event.

The Cruise Control Strategy

This strategy is particularly appealing for candidates who are clearly ahead and are striving to maintain their lead. Just as the cruise control of a car allows the driver to drive at a steady speed, this strategy calls for the campaign to advertise at a steady rate. The campaign makes what the media industry calls a "flat buy," purchasing a constant number of commercials each day during the stages of the campaign when media will be used.

Often this strategy is combined with the fast finish strategy, so that the campaign makes a flat buy for several weeks or even a month or more prior to the last week or two of the campaign, when it then increases its advertising. This strategy allows the candidate who is ahead to remain constantly visible for a long period of time and then finish strongly.

In sum, the overall advertising strategies of political campaigns can be characterized by the way they purchase radio and television time. Most campaigns utilize one of four strategies, or some combination of them. Though such factors such as the availability of funds, poll results, and the strategies of opponents may force modifications of strategy, part of the initial campaign plan should be to develop an overall advertising strategy.[71]

MEDIA AND OTHER TYPES OF POLITICAL CONSULTANTS

As part of the 1986 United States Senate race in Georgia, an Atlanta television station arranged a debate between Frank Greer and Mike Murphy. Yet, neither man was a candidate for the Senate. Rather, they were the respective media consultants for United States Senate candidates Wyche Fowler, Jr. and Mack Mattingly.[72] This debate dramatically illustrates the growing importance of political consultants, especially media consultants, in contemporary politics. While political consultants provide a variety of services to their candidates, most of those services are advertising and media related. Hence, we will conclude this chapter on the practices of political advertising by briefly examining the rise and growth of political consulting and the functions of political consultants.

History of Political Consulting

Virtually every political candidate, from Washington's day forward, has turned to a group of advisors for advice on getting elected, and often for advice on governing. Perhaps the most outstanding of America's early political consultants was John Beckley, a close personal friend and key political advisor to Thomas Jefferson. During Jefferson's bids for the presidency, Beckley wrote campaign material on his behalf, arranged for its distribution in key states, and organized a speaker's bureau on behalf of Jefferson.[73]

Throughout the nineteenth and early twentieth centuries, the growth of political parties, improvements in communication and transportation technology, and the need to deal with rapidly growing constituencies all contributed to the professionalization of political campaigning. The presidential campaigns of 1828, 1840, and 1896 were especially notable for advances in political campaigning and served as precursors to the consultant driven campaigns of today.[74]

However, it was not until the 1920s when Calvin Coolidge turned to Edward Bernays that political figures began to seek the advice of individuals with extensive backgrounds and expertise in advertising, public relations, and polling. Few political figures listened to Bernays, a public relations counselor who was far ahead of his time in advising candidates to make better use of the media and polling. Nevertheless, his ideas foreshadowed much of what political campaigning has become in the last decades of the twentieth century.[75]

In 1934 Californians Clem Whitaker and his wife Leona Baxter founded the public relations firm of Whitaker and Baxter, which from it's very inception took on political clients, normally California Republicans. In that year the firm helped defeat the popular writer Upton Sinclair, the Democratic candidate for governor. From that point forward political candidates sought their services. Whitaker and Baxter was a pioneer firm, and though they eventually diversified to handle a wide variety of accounts, they were still helping candidates as late as 1967 when they handled Shirley Temple's unsuccessful congressional race.[76] In 1952 television was first used as an advertising medium in a presidential campaign. The 1952 campaigns of both General Dwight David Eisenhower and Illinois Governor Adlai Stevenson made use of television. Although both candidates had reservations about television, both campaigns secured the services of advertising agencies to help produce television commercials and serve in a variety of other functions.[77]

The fact that media consultants, whether in the employ of political consulting firms or advertising agencies, were in politics to stay was evident in 1956 when Stevenson again challenged Eisenhower. Accepting the Democratic nomination, Stevenson decried the use of mass media advertising techniques, claiming that "the idea that you can merchandise candidates for high office like breakfast cereal—that you can gather votes like box tops—is, I think, the ultimate indignity in the democratic process." Yet, Stevenson made this very remark from a platform that had been redesigned by an advertising agency, to a national convention whose activities were being orchestrated in no small part by that same agency, for the benefit of the television audience.[78]

By the 1960s campaigns were being waged more and more in the media and political consultants were becoming more and more conspicuous in the conduct of those campaigns. Stuart Spencer, Bill Roberts, David

Garth, Tony Schwartz, and a host of other consultants began to bring high technology to political campaigning throughout the 1960s.

In recent years two factors have combined to make political consultants essential players in virtually every major political campaign. First, getting elected has become a perpetual job. Thus, helping candidates has become a perpetual job. In the past it was difficult to work as a political consultant, simply because during nonelection years the political consultant had no clients.

But the 1970s witnessed the advent of the perpetual candidate.[79] In the footsteps of the perpetual candidate has come the perpetual political consultant. As Burdett Loomis has incisively illustrated, since 1974 "new breed" politicians have encouraged the growth of administrative staffs, subcommittee and committtee staffs, campaign staffs, political action committees and their staffs, a variety of political caucuses and their staffs, a variety of task forces and their staffs, a host of party organizations and their staffs, as well as the expansion of lobby groups and the dramatic growth of political action committees. Though the surge of these enterprises is perhaps most evident in Washington, it is also apparent in virtually every state capital as well. These organizations allow candidates to "warehouse" consultants. That is, as Ken Kling, former executive director of the Virginia Republican party and a consultant to a wide variety of candidates, observes, candidates, especially incumbents, can find jobs for trusted political operatives that enable those operatives to maintain themselves during off-election periods yet allow those operatives to work on behalf of the candidate on a moment's notice during the election cycle.[80] In addition to the increased opportunities for employment of those with the skills of political consultants, political consulting itself is now a full-time job. In sum, since the 1970s political consulting has become a viable career for a large number of individuals.

Second, it has become financially feasible to engage in political consulting as a career. In 1980 there were 50 members of the American Association of Political Consultants, the principal professional organization. As of the summer of 1998, there were over 2,400 commercial firms and related organizations listed in the most widely used directory of political consultants, products, and services.[81]

The rapid growth of the political consulting profession is a consequence of a variety of changes in our political system during the last three decades. From the standpoint of candidates, political consultants provided two big advantages over a candidate's own campaign staff and the efforts of party professionals. First, they provided a bigger bang for the buck, a greater return on the money spent in the campaign. Consultants were specialists in designing media messages and insuring that those messages were transmitted most effectively. Whether it was the consultant who specialized in setting up phone banks, coaching political debaters, or producing television advertisements, consultants provided the campaign with a better return on its dollars. Second, political consultants could provide campaigns with public opinion polling designed and executed specifically to help the campaign locate voters and prepare messages for those voters. Hence, the consulting profession grew rapidly in the period 1960–1990 because it provided candidates with highly desired services.[82]

Moreover, during the last decades, the growth of political consulting services has made this field one in which growing numbers of people are able to make a living. Though fees vary from consultant to consultant, currently it is not unusual for media consultants to charge a straight fee of $25,000–$75,000 for a statewide race and receive a 15 percent cut of the money spent on media advertising time. With statewide races, as we have seen, now routinely running $3 million or more, and the majority of that money going into the purchase of media time, some media consultants may make $250,000–$500,000, or more, for a campaign.[83]

The "elite" political consultants, a group of about 40 firms, have focused most of their efforts on statewide races. Working for presidential candidates, while potentially bringing prestige to a firm, is risky from a business standpoint. Only two of perhaps 10 or more candidates will make it through the primaries. A consulting firm whose clients lose primaries has little to boast about when it seeks additional clients. Moreover, a presidential campaign is so demanding that a consulting firm handling a presidential campaign normally has to sacrifice other candidates, or neglect them. Hence, a firm that opts to work for a presidential candidate typically turns away business during the primary season and may find itself lacking clients for the general election if its candidate loses the primaries.[84]

The typical consulting fee for a variety of political services, such as setting up a precinct organization or a phone bank operation, had reached $1000 per day by the late 1980s and continues to rise.[85] An all-purpose consulting firm that will develop a campaign strategy and offer advice on implementing that strategy will typically charge base fees of approximately $5,000 for a congressional race and $10,000 for a statewide race. Additional fees will depend on the specific services provided. Most consultants or consulting firms are also available on a monthly retainer fee of $2,000–$6,000, which allows the candidate and his staff unlimited phone contact with the consultant and also provides that the consultant will be in the campaign several days a month. Though overhead and expenses for consulting are high, for a growing number of people, political consulting has become a viable way to make a living.[86]

It should be remembered, however, that as with the time of any professional—plumber, electrician, lawyer, or doctor—the time of political consultants is limited. Most shy away from taking on more than four or five races simultaneously.[87] Hence, political consulting is no longer the province of enthusiastic amateurs, perhaps occasionally taking leaves from their other positions to help the candidate of their choice. While this type of individual is still a feature of some campaigns and may provide valuable services, today political consulting is a fast-growing profession.

Though this discussion has focused on the economic aspects of consulting, because it was not until the field became an economically viable one that people could enter it on a full-time basis, virtually everyone involved in political consulting will note that monetary rewards are a secondary motivation. The primary motivation of most consultants is to have an impact on the political process. Most consultants have strong political beliefs. They work for like-minded candidates. And, invariably, consultants will claim that the most satisfying aspect of their job is to "win one you're not suppose to win."[88]

FUNCTIONS OF POLITICAL CONSULTANTS

Political consultants can provide candidates with virtually any service necessary in the conduct of a campaign, including help in targeting voters, setting up a precinct organization, setting up and utilizing phone banks, polling the electorate, preparing and utilizing direct mail, preparing and utilizing radio and television commercials, writing and preparing to deliver a speech, and preparing for a debate.[89] A full-service political consulting firm can provide clients with virtually all of these services, though it may well specialize in a more limited number. Smaller firms will limit their work to providing a group of related services. It would be impossible to discuss all of the services provided by consulting firms in the remainder of this chapter. Rather, we will briefly focus on four services that are directly related to the campaign's efforts to communicate through advertising.

Writers

The preparation and communication of messages is at the heart of any campaign. Hence, virtually all consultants are involved in some form of writing. In the chapter on public speaking we discussed political speechwriting. Consultants who specialize in writing can often handle virtually all of the advertising writing chores in the campaign: radio and television scripts, press releases, preparation of copy for all printed materials such as brochures, mailpieces, or newspaper and magazine advertisements. There are techniques unique to writing each of these types of advertisements well, and often in larger campaigns different individuals will handle each. In small and mid-sized campaigns the writer who often serves as the press secretary and speechwriter is generally involved in the preparation of scripts for commercials.

Speech Coaches

One of the basic services frequently provided to candidates at the schools for candidates run by the Republican and Democratic party organizations is speech coaching. Many consulting firms will provide candidates with coaching in public speaking, and if necessary, in debate. Most speech coaches would agree with Democratic consultant Michael Sheehan, who has worked with President Clinton and former Texas Governor Ann Richards among others, when he describes his job by claiming that "I bring out their [the client's] strengths, I try to bring out the best qualities in candidates that they already have."[90]

Although he is currently involved primarily in television production, Republican Roger Ailes, who coached both Ronald Reagan and George Bush for many of their major addresses and debates, is also among the best known consultants to have specialized in coaching candidates for speeches and debates. Based on his experiences, Ailes has identified what he calls the 10 most common commnication problems. Depending on the individual candidate's strengths and weaknesses, speech coaches will normally work to help the candidate overcome one or more of the 10 problems Ailes identifies.

1. Lack of initial rapport with listeners
2. Stiffness or woodenness in use of body
3. Presentation of material is intellectually oriented, forgetting to involve the audience emotionally
4. Speaker seems uncomfortable because of fear of failure
5. Poor use of eye contact and facial expression
6. Lack of humor
7. Speech direction and intent unclear due to improper preparation
8. Inability to use silence for impact
9. Lack of energy, causing inappropriate pitch pattern, speech rate, and volume
10. Use of boring language and a lack of interesting material[91]

Direct Mail Specialists

The preparation of direct mail pieces, and in many instances providing the lists of individuals to whom such pieces are sent, has become a critical political consulting speciality. Such firms are typically involved in utilizing direct mail both for voter persuasion and for for fund-raising. Perhaps the best known consultant to specialize in direct mail is Richard Viguerie, and his story is highly illustrative of how direct mail specialists operate.

In 1960–1961 Viguerie worked in the Houston campaign offices of Texas Senator John Tower. Soon after, he was employed by Young Americans for Freedom, a group of conservative young people, and was placed in charge of the organization's fund-raising. Recalling his early experiences, Viguerie states,

I'm basically a pretty shy person and I did not feel comfortable asking for money directly. So I began writing letters instead, and they seemed to work. So I wrote more and more letters and before many months, direct mail was my whole focus—for fundraising, subscriptions for *The New Guard* [Young Americans for Freedom publication], YAF membership, everything.[92]

Quickly recognizing the power of direct mail, Viguerie used the simplest of means to begin to develop a mailing list. After the 1964 election, he simply copied the names and addresses of those who had given $50 or more to the Goldwater campaign from the contributor records that, by law, were on file with the Clerk of the House of Representatives. This effort provided him with over 12,000 names, which became his first mailing list.[93]

Direct mail consultants like Viguerie are continually building their lists, adding new names after each campaign in which they are involved. The use of sophisticated computers and printers enables them to handle thousands of pieces of mail quickly and further enables them to tailor lists to the geographic and demographic needs of a client.

Political consultants who specialize in direct mail typically provide two services for their clients. First, they can provide help in designing and producing the actual mailpieces. Second, they can provide lists of individuals to whom such pieces should be sent. This second service is highly valuable for major national campaigns and other larger races.

However, in smaller races often the candidate and campaign staff can develop a good mailing list, based on their associates, the lists of other candidates who have run in the same area, or the lists of the local party. Candidates who contract to utilize the lists of consulting firms must be certain that the lists are likely to be of help to them and almost invariably will want to supplement those lists. One of the principal ways in which direct mail firms increase the size and value of their lists is by constantly adding names from the campaigns in which they work.

Specialists in Television Commercial Production and Placement

Because of the large expense involved and the technical expertise necessary, today few campaigns will attempt to produce and air television commercials without the advice of political consultants who specialize in such work. Some campaigns will supplement the efforts of such consultants by also utilizing local advertising agencies that are familiar with local media. But clearly, political media consultants have come to dominate the business of producing and buying time for televised campaign commercials.

Clearly, the candidate and campaign staff must make the final decision. Typically, the campaign staff, the polling firm, and the television consultants will all work closely together, with the campaign having the final authority. Aware of the issues in their particular campaign, they will certainly be receptive to the advice of consultants, but they must make the final decisions on what they want to accomplish with the commercials. The typical statewide campaign produces and airs about 20–30 advertisements.[94] Well-financed campaigns test ads in focus groups and never air the ones that don't work. The standard approach is to begin with biographical ads and continue with issue, endorsement, and attack ads before ending with inspirational commercials, in the belief that voters want something positive as they enter the voting booth.[95]

Political consultants can help in a variety of ways. They can suggest types of commercials that can implement the candidate's goals. They may be able to point out how other campaigns successfully, or unsuccessfully, handled similar problems. They are aware of what approaches are working or failing in other parts of the country and hence might or might not work in this region. Depending on their background, they will help script and produce the commercial, utilizing their skills in every phase of production including casting, shooting, and editing. In well-financed campaigns, using focus groups and electronic advertising testing techniques that facilitate monitoring voter responses to individual sentences, phrases, and split second visual images contained within the ad, some commercials are rejected; others are improved before they are finally accepted for broadcast.[96] In many campaigns the consultant takes personal control over creating the commercials.

The consulting firm will also purchase air time. A good firm knows the demographics of the local media market, is experienced in dealing with the local media, and is familiar with the candidate's strategy. Utilizing all of this information, it purchases air time to maximize the impact of the candidate's messages among those voters that the campaign has targeted.

Until very recently, most consultants would suggest that the campaign

purchase 300–500 rating points of time per week for television advertisements. If the campaign could not afford to do this, many consultants
would suggest that they consider dropping television from their advertising strategy. Rating points are the percentage of television sets tuned
to a specific show. If *60 Minutes* has a 25 rating in the Boston market, 25
percent of the television sets in Boston are tuned to *60 Minutes*. Most
consultants feel that the message of a political spot will not really register
until the audience has seen the message at least three to five times—
hence, the desirability of purchasing 300–500 rating points, which should
enable 100 percent of the audience to see the commercial three to five
times.[97]

By 1996 the 300–500 rating points guideline was being questioned, as
most consultants urged larger purchases than in prior years. They did
so largely because of the proliferation of remote controls, which facilitates channel surfing by viewers during ads, and the proliferation of
VCRs, which enable viewers to totally skip advertisements. In 1996, in
addition to these two technological changes, voter apathy and insensi-
tivity to political commercials was also frequently mentioned as yet another reason that political advertisers had to purchase larger quantities
of time than in past years.[98] While consultants are often paid a percentage
of the cost of the television time they purchase and hence have a self-
interest in purchasing larger quantities of time, by 1996 it was hard to
deny that traditional viewing habits had been changed by technology
and that voter indifference to the election was widespread.

Clearly, campaigns can make use of a wide variety of political consultants. In this section we have treated those consultants who we feel
impact most directly on political advertising. It is significant to note that
although we have not treated such consulting specialties as the public
opinion pollster, the fund-raising specialist, the precinct organizer, or the
database manager, it could well be argued that even these consultants
impact on political communication and political advertising. We would
not dispute that argument in the least, for it gives further credence to
the principal thesis of this book—that communication is at the heart of
political campaigning.

CONCLUSIONS

This chapter has illustrated some of the practical concerns that must
be confronted when using political advertising. We have first noted the
importance of advance planning in the development of the campaign's
use of political advertising. Second, we have examined the seven principal advertising mediums used in political campaigns: display graphics,
direct mail, telephone, print, radio, television, and the Internet. We have
illustrated the virtues and liabilities of each medium for political adver-

tising. Third, we have examined the four principal overall advertising strategies commonly utilized in political campaigns: spurt, fast finish, really big show, and cruise control. Fourth, we have examined political consultants who have, largely because of their mastery of advertising media, become key players in contemporary political campaigns. We have examined the history of poltical consulting, observing the rapid growth and professionalization of political consulting in the last three decades. Moreover, we have examined the functions of those political consultants who are most directly concerned with political communication and advertising: writers, speech coaches, direct mail specialists, and television specialists.

NOTES

1. The Bond vs. Woods race was commented upon in many national publications as it developed. However, by far the best work on that race, upon which this account relies heavily, is Deborah L. Chasteen, "The Effect of Television Advertising on the 1986 Harriet Woods U.S. Senate Campaign" (unpublished Ph.D. dissertation, University of Kansas, 1989). For background on Woods and Bond, including an analysis of Woods's decision to rely heavily on television advertising, see pp. 18–20.

2. The figures found in this paragraph are drawn from Chasteen, "Effect of Television Advertising," pp. 26–34. Chasteen was provided access to many of the internal working documents of the Woods campaign.

3. Ibid., pp. 125–26.

4. Ibid., p. 126.

5. Ibid., p. 48, 57. The "crying farmer" commercials consisted of a sequence of three commercials that showed Harriet Woods talking with a family whose farm had been foreclosed by Mutual Benefit Life, a company whose board of directors included Kit Bond.

6. Ibid., p. 57. For an excellent analysis of the consequences of these commercials that focuses on the inability of the Woods campaign to anticipate Bond's response to the "crying farmer" commercials, see pp. 48–64.

7. Ibid., p. 126.

8. Frank Luntz, "Preparing Your Campaign Playbook," *Campaigns and Elections* 12 (July 1991): 40–46.

9. Smithsonian Institution, National Museum of American History, "Campaign Buttons" (Washington D.C.: Smithsonian Institution, 1989). This small flyer on the history of campaign buttons is included with a variety of reproductions of campaign materials available through the Smithsonian.

10. Campaign materials, primarily buttons and bumper stickers, using all of these slogans are in the collection of one of the authors, Robert V. Friedenberg.

11. Ibid.

12. The price figures for buttons and bumper stickers, cited in this and the next few paragraphs are drawn from the 1998 catalogs of national distributors as well as the author's April 29, 1998 interview with Kirby Ralston of Ralston Advertising and Supply, a major national distributor. The prices offered by na-

tional suppliers who specialize in political display graphics are consistent with
those of local suppliers in the Cincinnati area, based on discussions with two of
the largest suppliers of display graphic advertising in the Cincinnati area. The
authors wish to thank Harry Pallas of A-1 Acme Advertising and David Horo-
witz and Lucy Chagares of Associated Premium Corporation for their helpful-
ness in providing price figures for a variety of display graphic items.

13. Ibid.

14. Ibid.

15. Ibid.

16. These figures were provided by Larry Steir of Norton Outdoor Advertising, Cincinnati, Ohio, in a phone interview with Robert V. Friedenberg, April 22,
1998. While there are a variety of ways to purchase billboards, costs reflect the
percent of the metropolitan area that will see the board on a daily basis and the
size of the board.

17. Billboard advertising firms much prefer to sell for longer periods of time.
Depending on the firm and the market, discounts for 3-month-, 6-month-, and
12-month-long purchases can sometimes be negotiated. These figures represent
the most common way that billboards are currently purchased by political figures
in the Cincinnati area. Due to limits on the locations of billboards, and the preference of billboard advertising firms to sell for longer periods of time, arrangements for billboard advertising should be made well in advance.

18. These figures are drawn from the price lists of national suppliers such as
Artype, Inc., of Fort Myers, Florida and Cross and Oberlie, of Neenah, Wisconsin.
They are consistent with the prices provided by local suppliers in the Cincinnati
area, such as those provided by Gary Littleton and Kathy Geiger of Berman
Printing, Cincinnati, Ohio, in a phone interview with Robert V. Friedenberg,
April 29, 1998 and subsequent correspondence.

19. Patriot Signage, Inc., 1998 price list. Current prices can be obtained by
contacting Patriot Signage, 1001 Second Avenue, Dayton, Kentucky 41074. The
durability of these signs, especially in bad weather areas, the ease of installation,
and the ease of storage are among the features that have attracted campaigns to
the usage of these signs, though their price is modestly higher than other forms
of yard signs.

20. Direct mail has often been called a "high interest, low backlash, communications vehicle" in campaign seminars conducted by the Republican National
Committee and in the literature that the Committee has produced for candidates
and their staffs. See, for example, Republican National Committee, *Campaign Seminars: Campaign Graphics, Direct Mail and Outdoor Advertising* (Washington, D.C.:
Republican National Committee, no date of publication), p. 5.

21. Richard Viguerie, *The New Right: We're Ready to Lead* (Falls Church, Va.:
The Viguerie Company, 1980), pp. 125–26. Viguerie, the principal direct mail
fund-raiser of the conservative movement throughout the 1960s and 1970s, cred-
its the McGovern campaign with making political figures aware of the enormous
potential of direct mail as a medium of political fund-raising.

22. Ron Kanfer, "Direct to the Bank," *Campaigns and Elections* (July 1991): 22.
Kanfer is president of Response Dynamics, Inc., a political direct mail fund-
raising firm.

23. See both Kanfer, "Direct to the Bank," p. 24 and Viguerie, "The New

Right," p. 124. Viguerie argues that direct mail fund-raising is exceptionally useful for underdog, nonestablishment candidates.

24. These figures are drawn from the 1998 price list of Picture Perfect Campaigns, Irving, California.

25. See Kate McKeown, Richard Schlackman, Jamie Douglas, Jason Ercole, Eric Jayne, Michael Terris, Eva M. Campbell, and Mark Campbell, "Direct Mail," *Campaigns and Elections* (May 1997): 22.

26. Jan Crawford of Crawford Communications made this observation at a session of the American Association of Political Consultants Annual Meeting, Washington, D.C., January 17, 1997.

27. Hal Malchow, "10 Ways to Design In-House Voter Mail That Works," *Campaigns and Elections* (June/July 1990): 50–51.

28. For good overviews of telephone contact services see Roger S. Conrad, "Winning Votes on the Information Super Highway," *Campaigns and Elections* (July 1994): 22–25 and 52–54; Robert V. Friedenberg, *Communication Consultants in Political Campaigns: Ballot Box Warriors* (Westport, Conn.: Praeger, 1997), pp. 112–18. On the cost of voter contact services, Friedenberg provides representative figures for the 1996 election cycle and the reader can obtain current costs by contacting the firms directly. Most major firms are listed in the *1998–1999 Political Pages*. (Washington D.C.: Congressional Quarterly Publications, 1998), pp. 100–106.

29. Newspaper advertisements played a role in the nation's earliest elections. See Robert J. Dinkin, *Campaigning in America: A History of Election Practices* (Westport, Conn.: Greenwood Press, 1989), pp. 3–4, 14–16. Also see Kathleen Hall Jamieson, *Packaging the Presidency* (New York: Oxford University Press, 1984), p. 5.

30. This information was provided by Sharon Katon of the *Cincinnati Enquirer* advertising sales department. Phone interview with Robert V. Friedenberg, April 17, 1998.

31. Typical of many major market stations, in the Cincinnati market most television stations must be provided the television commercial by noon of the work day prior to when it will first air.

32. Studies have repeatedly indicated that Americans usually speak at a rate of between 120 and 150 words per minute. See Stephen E. Lucas, *The Art of Public Speaking* (New York: Random House, 1998), p. 298.

33. This figure is drawn from "Bush, Governors Set Goals," *Facts on File: World News Digest With Index*, March 2, 1990, p. 141.

34. The cost figures used throughout this paragraph were provided by Sharon Katon of the *Cincinnati Enquirer* advertising sales staff. See note 30.

35. Republican National Committee, *Campaign Seminars: Media Advertising* (Washington, D.C.: Republican National Committee, no date of publication), p. 12.

36. Dinkin, *Campaigning in America* p. 167.

37. Mitchell is quoted in Dan Nimmo, *The Political Persuaders* (Englewood Cliffs, N.J.: Prentice-Hall, 1970), p. 134.

38. Radio consistently seems to be more popular among Republican campaign professionals than among Democrats. There is no clear explanation for why Republicans tend to like radio to a greater degree than Democratic campaign professionals. Nevertheless, Republican political advisors will, more commonly

than their Democratic counterparts, claim that radio is an "important" campaign communications vehicle and also laud it as especially cost effective. See Republican National Committee, *Campaign Seminars: Media Advertising*, p. 12.

39. These figures were provided by Gerry Wildebor, who handled political sales for several of the Jacor stations in Cincinnati during the 1998 election cycle. Interview with Robert V. Friedenberg, April 20, 1998. These figures are all for nonpreemptable purchases, which are typically utilized by political figures advertising on Cincinnati radio.

40. Ibid. Wildebor also provided the author with the political rates for both WKRC and WSAI.

41. These figures were provided by Wildebor in the phone interview and were confirmed by subsequent written correspondence.

42. This is the practice of many Cincinnati stations and according to members of their sales departments, similar practices are widespread in most larger media markets. For example, the 1998 schedules of political rates for Cincinnati stations WKRC and WSAI explicitly reserve this right.

43. While figures such as these have long been commonplace for major national and statewide races, David Wells's article on campaign expenses in one metropolitan area during the 1988 elections, "If You Run, Bring Money," indicates that in the last 10 years figures such as these are becoming commonplace even in many lower ballot races. Examining a wide variety of 1988 Cincinnati-area races, including judicial contests, Wells found candidates consistently spending 70 to 80 percent of their money on television commercials.

44. See, for example, Charles Green, "Congress for Sale?" *Cincinnati Enquirer*, October 8, 1989, p. B1; Jeff Schear, "Weird Political Science: How Dwight Morris Cornered the Campaign Money Market," *Capitol Style* (September 1998): 25–27. The reader can check FEC figures on federal campaigns at any time through the FEC Internet home page.

45. Green, "Congress for Sale." While a variety of other factors including the greater use of polling services, the greater use of direct mail, and the general lengthening of campaigns have undeniably contributed to increasing campaign costs, no authority would deny that the increased use of television is a primary factor causing the dramatic increase in campaign expenses. Moreover, this increase has far exceeded increases in the consumer price index throughout the 1970s and 1980s. Nor does it seem to be leveling off in the 1990s. While inflation has risen at a modest 2–4 percent during most of the 1990s, the author's informal discussions with individuals in the advertising industry suggest that the costs of television advertising have increased by 30–50 percent during that same period.

Indeed, Montague Kern reports that as of 1984 media consultants testifying at congressional hearings reported that media costs in major markets doubled every four years. See Montague Kern, *30 Second Politics: Political Advertising in the 1980s*, (New York: Praeger, 1989), p. 17, note 8. On television expenses and their effects, also see Robert J. Dinkin, *Campaigning in America*, pp. 164–68 and Sig Mickelson, *From Whistle Stop to Sound Bite: Four Decades of Politics and Television* (New York: Praeger, 1989), pp. 3–5, 16–18.

46. Between April 18 and May 6, 1998, Robert V. Friedenberg held a series of phone interviews with the specialists in political advertising sales at three network affiliate stations in Cincinnati. In addition to these phone interviews, the

full political advertising disclosure statements and political rate cards were provided by several stations. The author is particularly grateful to Jerry Imsicke of WLWT, the NBC affiliate in Cincinnati, and Mike Anderson, of WKRC, the CBS affiliate in Cincinnati, for their help.

All of the television cost figures cited in the following paragraphs and notes reflect fixed rates, which guarantee that the commercial will air. Candidates may gamble and pay lower rates but they run the risk that they will be preempted. Typically, most candidates will not gamble during the last 10 days of the campaign, though some will place advertisements at lower rates earlier in the campaign and gamble that they will not be preempted by nonpolitical advertisers willing to pay more.

47. Because the demographics of the CBS afternoon soap operas—*The Young and the Restless, The Bold and the Beautiful, As the World Turns,* and *The Guiding Light*—were so similar in the Cincinnati market, advertisers simply bought time on this block of shows, rather than on a specific show.

48. Although *Seinfeld* was the top-rated showed nationally in 1998, in Cincinnati it was only the second most expensive show on which to advertise. For much of the 1997–1998 television season, *E.R.* commanded $17,000, $3,000 more than *Seinfeld* for a 30-second political spot in Cincinnati. Though *E.R.* was not as popular as *Seinfeld* in most markets, in Cincinnati it often drew stronger ratings than *Seinfeld*. *E.R.'s* popularity in Cincinnati may stem from the fact that its star, George Clooney, was a Cincinnati native whose father, Nick, had hosted a popular local talk and entertainment show for many years and then anchored the city's most highly rated local news show during much of the 1980s. Moreover, his aunt, singer Rosemary Clooney, had gotten her start on the city's local radio stations. In the Cincinnati area, George Clooney is an enormously popular figure, literally the local boy-made-good.

49. These figures are drawn from the second quarter (March–May) political broadcast rate disclosure statements of WLWT-TV, the Cincinnati NBC affiliate, and WKRC, the Cincinnati CBS affiliate.

50. The calculation of political advertising rates is highly complex because in addition to the normal variety of rate options, political advertising is also governed by a variety of federal and often state or local laws. The complexity is such that at each of the network affiliate stations Friedenberg contacted, only one salesperson was allowed to handle political advertising. That individual was clearly designated as the station's specialist but, as one of them indicated, the station's attorney was frequently consulted. For a sense of the complexities involved, see the sections on discounted rates and other regulations in Paul S. Hoff, *Beyond the 30-Second Spot: Enhancing the Media's Role in Congressional Campaigns* (Washington D.C.: Center for Responsive Politics, 1988), pp. 69–92.

51. See Robert V. Friedenberg, *Communication Consultants in Political Campaigns,* pp. 158–60, for an examination of political television production costs. It should be noted that the production of political commercials is typically accomplished at a small fraction of the cost of product commercials. As of 1997, the average 30 second product spot cost producers $278,000, according to a survey conducted by the American Association of Advertising Agencies. See "Production Costs Rise for TV Ads," *Cincinnati Enquirer-TV Week,* September 21, 1997, p. 2.

52. Typically the change will be to a form of commercial that does not require

the candidate to be on the camera. One of the most successful such adjustments was engineered by New York Governor Nelson Rockefeller's 1966 reelection campaign managers. At the outset of the campaign Rockefeller had several major political liabilities, moreover his deep gravelly bass voice was not appealing. These factors caused his management team to conclude that putting him on television was counterproductive. Instead they produced a series of advertisements featuring a puppet fish that focused on his many accomplishments as governor. Later in the campaign, when his standing had increased, Rockefeller appeared in his own advertisements. See Edwin Diamond and Stephen Bates, *The Spot: The Rise of Political Advertising on Television* (Cambridge, Mass.: MIT Press, 1984), pp. 318–19, for an account of this campaign.

53. These figures are from "Push Play to Win," a promotion video available through West Coast Video Duplicating, Inc., the largest American video duplicator. They may be contacted at 11755 Wilshire Boulevard, Suite 2400, Los Angles, California 90025.

54. This is the benchmark figure cited by both West Coast Video Duplicating and Promotional Video Duplicators, the two largest players in the political cassette market. Both firms use this figure in their promotional videos. West Coast Video can be reached at the address cited in note 53. Promotional Video Duplicators can be reached at 900 Second Street, NE, Washington, D.C. 20002. Among the lowest prices advertised is that of Video Duplication Service, which claims that for mailings of 100,000, it charges $1.38 per cassette, a price that includes duplication, labels on the cassette itself, a color printed sleeve, shrinkwrap, addressing, and postage. See their advertisement in *Campaigns and Elections* (June 1994): 19.

55. Paula Tait, "Eight Myths of Video Cassette Campaigning," *Campaigns and Elections* (December/January 1994): 34.

56. The 3–6 percent estimate was made by Robin Roberts, of National Media Inc., one of the largest Republican media consulting firms, interview with the author, Alexandria, Va., January 17, 1997. The 80% estimate was made by Ondine Fortune of Creative Cable TV, interview with the author, Washington D.C., January 16, 1997.

57. The information utilized in this paragraph is drawn primarily from Michael Labriola, "Campaigning on Cable," *Campaigns and Elections* (August 1993): 34–35, and Jerry Hagstrom, *Political Consulting: A Guide for Reporters and Citizens* (New York: The Freedom Forum, 1992), pp. 25–26.

58. Ibid., p. 35.

59. James Katz, Philip Aspden, and Warren Reich, "Elections and Electrons: A National Opinion Survey on the Role of Cyberspace and Mass Media in Political Opinion Formation during the 1996 General Election," paper prepared for the Telecommunications Policy Research Conference, Washington, D.C., October 1997, cited in Marion Just, Ann Crigler, and Montague Kern, "Citizens and the Internet: Diversifying Information Sources in Cyberspace," paper prepared for the annual meeting of the National Speech Communication Association, Chicago, Ill., November 1997, p. 2.

60. Ron Faucheux, "How Campaigns Are Using the Internet: An Exclusive Nationwide Survey," *Campaigns and Elections* (September 1998): 23. This was a comprehensive survey. Approximately 45 percent of the campaigns studied were

for the United States Senate, House of Representatives, and other major statewide offices such as governors or state judicial races. The remaining 55 percent were for state Senate or statehouse seats and a variety of local and municipal offices. Approximately 28 percent of those campaigns studied were incumbents, approximately 37 percent were challengers running against incumbents, and the remaining campaigns studied involved open seats. These campaigns were drawn from all sectors of the country. Approximately 85 percent involved candidates of the two major parties and 15 percent involved third party candidates.

61. Rachel Van Dongen, "2000 Election Will Be First of Digital Era, New Study Predicts," found on April 25, 1997 at http://www.rollcall.com/election/cyber-politics.html.

62. All of the figures in this paragraph are drawn from Faucheux, "How Campaigns Are Using the Internet," p. 23.

63. Ibid.

64. Just, Crigler, and Kern, "Citizens and the Internet," pp. 17–19.

65. Ibid., pp. 12–21.

66. Mike Connell, "Internet Survival Guide: Designing Lively Web Sites," *Campaigns and Elections* (September 1998): 29–32 and 41. Connell offers an analysis of the characteristics of good web sites based on his examination of a wide variety of 1998 sites.

67. Ibid. Also see Michael Cornfield, Shabbir Safdar, and Jonah Seigler, "The Top 10 Things We're Tired of Seeing in Candidate Web Sites," *Campaigns and Elections* (September 1998): 26.

68. See Robert V. Friedenberg, *Communication Consultants in Political Campaigns*, pp. 173–83, for a detailed analysis of political time-buying practices.

69. The explanation of purchasing found in this pargraph is drawn from Hagstrom, *Political Consulting: A Guide for Reporters and Citizens*, pp. 22–23.

70. These strategies are adapted and in some cases renamed from those presented in Republican National Committee, *Campaign Seminars: Media Advertising*, pp. 21–22.

71. Once that strategy has been agreed upon, campaigns should be hesitant to deviate, particularly in a spur-of-the-moment response to an opponent. The Harriet Woods example at the outset of this chapter indicates some of the potential problems that can be created. Moreover, as David Hill indicates in "The Preemptive Strike," *Campaigns and Elections* (January 1993): 38, often an opponent might be deliberately baiting your candidate, hoping your candidate will make hasty decisions for short-term gains, and in the process make decisions that have negative long-term consequences.

72. "What's in a Name? For Consultants, Much Cash," *Congressional Quarterly Guide to Current American Government* (Fall 1988): 28.

73. The best readily available source of information on Beckley is Nobel E. Cunningham, Jr., "John Beckley: An Early American Party Manager," *William and Mary Quarterly* 13 (January 1956): 40–52.

74. See Robert V. Friedenberg, *Communication Consultants in Political Campaigns*, pp. 2–15, for an overview of the growth of political consulting during the nineteenth and early twentieth centuries.

75. On Bernays, see Robert V. Friedenberg, *Communication Consultants in Political Campaigns*, pp. 16–17; Sidney Blumenthal, *The Permanent Campaign: Inside*

The World of Elite Political Operatives (Boston: Beacon Press, 1980), pp. 11–26; and for the last interview Bernays gave prior to his death, see Chapter 1 of Stuart Ewen, *PR! The Social History of Spin* (New York: Basic Books, 1996).

76. Ibid., pp. 143–47.

77. On Eisenhower's and Stevenson's television consultants in 1952, see Friedenberg, *Communication Consultants in Political Campaigns*, p. 153–56, and Chapter 2 of Kathleen Hall Jamieson, *Packaging the Presidency*.

78. For a brief discussion of the rise of political advertising and media influence on the 1956 campaign, which includes the quotation from Stevenson, see Stan Le Roy Wilson, *Mass Media/Mass Culture* (New York: Random House, 1989), p. 309.

79. In his remarkably incisive study, Burdett Loomis claims that the huge freshman class of "Watergate" congressmen elected in 1974 changed the face of American politics by combining ambition and entrepreneurship to perpetually work at acquiring resources to guarantee their reelection and to push their favorite policies. Since 1974 the "new breed" politician, Loomis argues, approaches Congress as an enterprise and seeks to develop a group of personnel resources, such as those discussed in this paragraph, that can be relied upon to further their own election and policy aspirations. See Burdett Loomis, *The New American Politician: Ambition, Entrepreneurship, and the Changing Face of Political Life* (New York: Basic Books, 1988), pp. 1–52 and 181–208.

Ironically, in the early days of political consulting, campaigns drew on the expertise of outside experts who frequently learned their craft working in product advertising and corporate public relations. Today, the process is frequently reversed. Firms established to do political consulting, such as those established by Matt Reese or Eddie Mahe, have taken the skills they perfected working for candidates and now use them primarily on behalf of issues and corporations. See, for example, Michael Clark, "Selling Issues," *Campaigns and Elections* (April/May 1993): 27–28.

80. Ken Kling, interview with Robert Friedenberg, June 11, 1990, Washington, D.C.

81. Chris Meyer, "Ten Years in the Making," *Campaigns and Elections* (April/May 1990): 39, discusses the early history of the American Association of Political Consultants. For an indication of the full scope of the industry, readers are advised to examine *The Political Pages*, the yearly directory issued by *Campaigns and Elections*.

82. This paragraph is based largely on the analysis of Charles Press and Kenneth Verburg, *American Politics and Journalists* (Glenview, Ill.: Scott, Foresman and Company, 1988), pp. 155–56.

83. The figures used in this paragraph are drawn from "What's in a Name? For Consultants, Much Cash," p. 25.

84. Jerry Hagstrom, *Political Consulting: A Guide for Reporters and Citizens,"* p. 6.

85. These figures are based on interviews with a wide variety of political consultants. Among them, Ken Kling of S.K.C. and Associates, a lobbying and consulting firm, Jim Weber, of Eddie Mahe and Associates, an all-purpose consulting firm, and Gary Koops, press secretary and campaign manager in a variety of Republican congressional races.

86. Larger political consulting firms that contract to handle a variety of races

during a single election period are normally headed by one or more individuals with exceptional reputations. These individuals serve as "magnets" to attract clients. Often they are heavily involved in the formulation of basic strategies and subsequently turn much of the work over to their associates and/or the local campaign staff to implement, returning on a periodic basis to help the candidate with major events such as the filming of commercials or preparing for a debate. Like any business, the consulting firm must judge the often considerable costs of doing business: labor, materials, travel, and so on, when establishing fees.

87. Most consultant's recognize that if they spread themselves too thin they run the risk of being involved in losing races and hence jeopardizing future employment. Additionally, today most candidates, expecting their consultants to provide them with considerable time and service, shy away from those who have already committed to a large number of other races. The exceptions to this rule are polling consultants who can deal with many campaigns at once.

88. This sentiment is constantly voiced when consultants are asked about the satisfaction of their job. It came up in every interview conducted for this chapter.

89. Perhaps the best way to get a feel for the wide variety of services provided by political consulting firms is to simply examine the advertisements found in trade publications such as *Campaigns and Elections* and *The Political Pages*. The latter divides consulting firms into 38 categories, based upon the service provided.

90. Morgan Stewart, "Michael Sheehan: Coaching Clinton," *Campaigns and Elections* (June/July 1993): 54.

91. Roger Ailes, *You Are the Message: Secrets of the Master Communicators* (Homewood, Ill.: Dow Jones–Irwin, 1988), p. 9.

92. Viguerie, *The New Right*, p. 26.

93. Ibid., pp. 26–27.

94. Hagstrom, *Political Consulting*, p. 14. Moreover, if anything, this number has grown in the last election cycle.

95. Ibid.

96. For an informative explanation of contemporary ad testing in political settings, see "Allan Rivlin, Lisa Grove, Mark Mellman, Ed Lazarus, and Steve Hopkins, "Dial a Soundbite," *Campaigns and Elections* (January 1993): 45.

97. The explanation of rating points in this paragraph is based on Pat Beall, "Buy Your Own Time," *Campaigns and Elections* (July 1991): 48. Also see Chris Meyer and Phil Porado, "Hit or Miss: Your Guide to Effective Media Buying," *Campaigns and Elections* (August/September 1990): 37–41.

98. These reasons were remarked upon by a variety of political television consultants interviewed by Robert Friedenberg in December of 1996 and January of 1997, shortly after the 1996 elections. Among those citing the growing need for time were Robert Tannenbaum of HMS Associates, Columbus, Ohio, Joseph Mercurio, of National Political Services, Inc., New York, New York, John Franzen, of John Franzen Multimedia, Washington, D.C., and Robin Roberts of National Media Inc., Alexandria, Virginia.

Chapter 11

Political Campaign Communication: An Epilogue

The central thesis of this book has been that communication is the heart of the modern political campaign. It is, as we argued in Chapter 1, the epistemological base. Without it, there would be no campaign. With this as our premise, we explored many principles of contemporary political campaigning including the communicative functions, styles, and media channels. We have also examined a number of the communicative practices in the contemporary campaign including speechmaking, debating, and interpersonal communication. Moreover, as we analyzed technological advancements in the modern campaign, we were talking about techniques of communication. While we have not denied the importance of such variables as political parties, voter demographics, philosophical questions, or even economic considerations, we have consistently maintained that understanding the principles and practices of campaign communication is the only way to come to grips with the reality of the modern campaign.

We have striven to present a realistic picture of the way in which candidates and their consultants go about their tasks, implementing the techniques of communication. In so doing, we have attempted to be descriptive. We have not attempted to make judgments, to cast praise or blame on candidates or their methods. We do not intend to do so now. However, we would be remiss (or at the least not very observant) if we failed to acknowledge some of the most important questions or concerns that have been raised regarding modern political campaigning.

In 1983, when the first edition of this book appeared, we raised six questions or concerns about political campaigning. Those concerns still remain, and in some instances have grown alarmingly more disturbing than they were 17 years ago. Moreover, those six questions or concerns have, we believe, in the past 17 years given rise to an overarching question that both subsumes and transcends our original six concerns. In this epiloque we wish to review our original six questions, examining them in light of recent developments. Moreover, we wish to address a final and substantially more meaningful question that Americans of all walks of life have been asking with increasing frequency in the past 16 years. Finally, while we scarcely presume to be able to resolve many of the questions and concerns generated by contemporary political campaigning, we wish to conclude by examining some of the many proposals that thoughtful citizens, academicians, and practitioners have offered in response to the questions and concerns being raised by contemporary political campaigns.

The first question we and others were asking in 1983 about political communication was simply: Will these trends continue? Will the new techniques of communication continue to play a dominant role in the campaigns of the future? While we do not have the benefit of a political crystal ball, our answer is yes. Seventeen years ago we observed that it seemed unlikely that the methods of campaigning would revert to those of an earlier day. Since 1983 the technological changes in campaigning have been as far reaching as any in any period in our history. This is unlikely to change. People have consistently embraced technology and there is every reason to believe that they will continue doing so. This is especially true of political candidates and consultants. As new methods of transportation and communication were developed, they were incorporated into political campaigns, often before they were widely employed in other situations. We see little prospect that candidates or their staffs will shun current technology or turn their backs on the future. However, the very fact that new tools of communication have changed the nature and methods of campaigning has resulted in more calls to alter campaigns. After every election, political parties, political scientists, candidates, and legislators call for such things as shorter primary seasons, national primaries, more stringent finance reforms (particularly in regard to the use of soft money), providing candidates with free television time, significantly altering the negative tone of campaigns, term limits, and a host of other changes. Moreover, as we have detailed earlier, changes often take place. But, in the largest sense, the trends we have indicated throughout the book, trends that have made communication the preeminent factor in the waging of contemporary political campaigns, will continue.

A second question that has been raised by many is basic to the thrust of this book. And that is: Does campaigning make a difference? Apparently those who ask the question do so because they see such trends as low voter turnout, diminished party affiliation, and the growth of citizen distrust and apathy as clear signs that political campaigns have little or nothing to do with election results. Obviously, we disagree with this point of view. Any number of examples illustrate that campaigns have indeed made a difference in winning and losing elections. If we cite only a few contemporary instances, we would have to include the 1992 election of Bill Clinton; the 1994 elections of a host of congresspeople, most noticeably George Nethercutt of Washington, Steve Stockman of Texas, and Michael Flanagan of Illinois, the 1994 Senate elections of Rick Santorum of Pennsylvania, Bill Frist of Tennessee, and Olympia Snowe of Maine; and the 1998 elections of Senators Jim Bunning of Kentucky and Peter Fitzgerald of Illinois and Governors Jesse Ventura of Minnesota and Gray Davis of California. Indeed, if campaigning makes no difference to election returns, why then are there more and more candidates, including those on state and local levels, who spend enormous amounts of time and energy, to say nothing of money, planning and implementing campaigns? Political campaigning has become a growth industry. It is difficult to believe this would have happened if the contenders doubted its worth. Finally, and from our point of view, most importantly, we believe that beyond helping to determine winners and losers, political campaigns serve many useful functions for voters and candidates. While some of these functions are important symbolically, others have instrumental value. Taken collectively, what all of this suggests is that campaigning does make a difference to citizens and candidates alike.

The third question raised by the growing emphasis on political campaigns as communication phenomena is related to the whole area of ethics. This book has dealt with several ethical questions that are conspicuous in contemporary campaigns, including the appropriate use of speechwriters, public opinion polls, and media advertising. Throughout this study we have chosen to describe, not evaluate. But anyone interested in political campaign communication cannot fail to be concerned with its ethical dimensions. "Dirty politics" has been around long before the advent of "unfair" or "unethical" television spot commercials. In fact, it was a part of political life in our nation's first political campaigns. Though campaign principles and practices may change from election to election, practitioners do not. Office seekers and their advisors are human beings. They remain subject to the foibles and temptations that have always confronted people. We see no evidence that contemporary candidates and their advisors are inherently less ethical than those of prior generations. The new communication-oriented politics, in which candidate and media have focused on the negative, have doubtlessly brought questions regarding political ethics into sharper focus.

The fourth question raised by the growing emphasis on communication in political campaigns is that of cost. Many have expressed concern, if not outrage, about the high costs of political campaigning. In recent years the expenses associated with effective campaigning have increased dramatically. In 1996 the total cost of political campaigns in the United States exceeded 2.2 billion dollars.[1] As costs escalate, there are those who feel that we have reached, or are fast reaching, the point where access to money will become the chief determinant of a candidate's success. This is a principal advantage of candidates who are incumbents.

In the 1998 races for the House of Representatives the fund-raising gap between the incumbents and challengers grew to almost ridiculous levels. Of the 435 races, 260 incumbents had a 10 to 1 advantage in money. As Larry Makinson of the Center for Responsive Politics said, "It's becoming more and more impossible to defeat an incumbent in the U.S. House because there is no money out there for challengers." In 1998 approximately three-quarters of the money raised by all House candidates was raised by incumbents.[2]

Moreover, the inherent financial advantages of incumbency mean that as campaign costs increase, the advantages of incumbency increase. As Lawrence K. Klemens, a high school principal in western Pennsylvania who sought the congressional seat of incumbent Representative Phil English said, "If you don't have money you don't get money. It's not only the national party committee, but from all standpoints. Money begets money and it's difficult to break that chain. That's how the game is played. The first question asked me these days is not about my views, but how much money I have."[3]

Similarly, campaigns are becoming more expensive in terms of human resources. Candidates and their associates are spending enormous amounts of time and effort to win office. Three of our last four presidents, George Bush, Ronald Reagan, and Jimmy Carter, have made running for president into full-time jobs lasting several years, as have many of their competitors such as Pat Buchanan, Lamar Alexander, and Bill Bradley. Others, such as Vice President Albert Gore, Senators Bob Kerry and John McCain, Congressmen Richard Gephardt, Jack Kemp, and John Kasich, and Governors Bill Clinton and George W. Bush, find it difficult to campaign and simultaneously hold responsible positions. In 1996 Senator Bob Dole gave up his seat in the Senate to campaign for the presidency. Though the demands of presidental campaigning are unusually high, these same demands are often placed on those who seek lesser offices. Members of Congress or members of many of the state legislatures, for example, take extended recesses during the election period. Challengers find it necessary to temporarily abandon their professions, often taking leaves of absence. Because time demands are high, it grows increasingly difficult for many citizens to seriously consider running for public office, particularly those who are not financially secure.

Moreover, as we have seen, candidates are not the only individuals who face high costs in money and time when they choose to run. Often responsibilities must be borne by their spouses, children, business associates, and close friends. The use of family and friends as surrogates, fund-raisers, and in other campaign-related activities places heavy burdens on all. In sum, the length of current campaigns and the demands they make on the financial and time resources of candidates and associates are costs that have grown so dramatically in recent years that many concerned individuals are calling for change.

The fifth question raised by the growing emphasis on communication in political campaigns involves the extent to which public expectations are being affected. Many political observers have commented on the growing cynicism of voters. Voters feel that their opinions do not count, that the government in Washington does not understand either their problems or their aspirations, and that candidates do not keep their campaign promises. One manifestation of these feelings is low voter turnout. Americans are staying home on election day in record numbers. The average voter turnout in the 1998 midterm elections was 16.8 percent, which was down from the previous historic low of 19.6 percent in the 1994 midterm elections.[4]

At least two campaign phenomena contribute to unfulfilled public expectations. The first is the pervasiveness and ugliness of negative advertisements. As Charles Krauthammer has observed:

Delta Airlines, you might have noticed, does *not* run negative TV ads about USAir. It does not show pictures of the crash of USAir flight 427 with a voice-over saying: "USAir, airline of death. Going to Pittsburgh? Fly Delta instead."

And McDonald's you might also have noticed, does not run ads reminding viewers that Jack in the Box hamburgers once killed two customers. Why? Because Delta and McDonald's know that if the airline and fast food industries put on that kind of advertising, America would soon be riding trains and eating box-lunch tuna sandwiches.

Yet every two years the American politics industry fills the airwaves with the most virulent, scurrilous, wall-to-wall character assassination of nearly every political practitioner in the country—and then declares itself puzzled that America has lost trust in its politicians.

Voters declare a burning desire to throw the bums out. Polls show an aversion to politicians that can only be called malignant. And the sages pull on their beards stumped.

Why? No need for exotic theories. The simplest explanation is always the best. Politics is the only American industry whose participants devote their advertising budgets to regular, public savage undermining of one another. It is the only American industry whose participants devote prodigious sums to destroying whatever shred of allegiance any of them might once have with customers.[5]

Thus, as Krauthammer illustrates, negative advertising has had a deleterious effect on public perception of the process, the candidates, and the institutions of government. This perception has been reflected in a retreat from political activities—"precinct work, communication with Congress and federal agencies—and from voting itself."[6]

The second campaign phenomenon contributing to unfilled public expectations is voter belief that they are being manipulated by political consultants, pollsters, and advertising wizards. Voters believe that the purpose of campaign consultants is to elect candidates by using words and images that manipulate with "inflammatory messages and insinuations that often are totally false or grotesquely misleading."[7]

The sixth issue raised by contemporary campaigns focuses on the candidates. The skills of advocacy necessary for election are not necessarily the skills of compromise and deliberation necessary for effective governing. Moreover, today the closest advisors of many elected officials are their pollsters and other communication specialists, not issue experts or party liaisons. Can a nation, even a county, be adequately, much less skillfully, governed by officials and advisors whose skills reflect the demands of successful political campaigning?

Since we first expressed these concerns 17 years ago, none have been remedied. Indeed, many of our concerns have grown more serious. Like many Americans we sometimes grow exasperated by the effectiveness of modern campaign methods, repeated revelations about campaign and campaigner ethics, the skyrocketing costs of campaigning, which consistently works to the advantage of the incumbent, growing evidence of the public's disillusionment with our political process, and similar evidence of our citizenry's dissatisfaction with the caliber of our national, regional, and local political leaders. These growing concerns all contribute to a fundamental question that both subsumes and transcends the six concerns we expressed in 1983. Put bluntly: Is contemporary political campaigning failing the nation?

The very fact that a question such as this must be asked, and is being asked, not simply by us, but by countless Americans, both politically sophisticated and politically naive, is disturbing. We would not have asked it 25 years ago, nor would other Americans. Yet, today it cannot be escaped. Virtually every retiring officeholder laments the election process and celebrates that they will no longer be subject to it. Columnists from across the political spectrum bemoan our election system. Two recent retirees from Congress, Indiana Democratic Representative Lee Hamilton and Wyoming Republican Senator Alan Simpson, agreed on few things other than the need to reform our election system.

If contemporary political campaigning is failing our nation, what might be done? The list of suggested reforms is lengthly. Among the most frequent suggestions are limiting the number of terms that officeholders such as congresspeople and senators can serve, providing candidates for major statewide and federal offices free television time, providing additional public financing for candidates, and limiting PAC contributions.

We have reservations about all of these suggestions. This is not to say that they may not have merit. But it is to say that they do not strike to the heart of the question. If contemporary political campaigning is failing the nation, it does so because it does not enable the nation to select its best leaders.

Most of the concerns being expressed about our election systems and about contemporary campaigning center on congressional, senatorial, and presidential elections. Several observations are in order. First, we have no evidence that the losing candidates in recent years would have been better officeholders than the winning candidates. Obviously judgments such as this often reflect the highly subjective and partisan feelings of the individuals making judgment. Second, we have no compelling evidence to suggest that hordes of extraordinary candidates and office holders are out "there," refusing to run because of the demands of political campaigning. If contemporary political campaigning is failing our nation, presumably it is doing so by providing us with a lesser quality of leadership. It strikes us as virtually impossible to prove such a contention.

Third, the indictments of contemporary political campaigning often seem to miss the point. In one fashion or another most of the complaints about current campaigning hinge on the charge that campaigns cost too much money. It is this charge that gives rise to most major suggestions for reform: public financing, shorter election periods, or free television. But the problem is not that campaigning costs too much money. It is that incumbents have blatant financial advantages over challengers. The monies spent on campaigning are not excessive given the significance of campaigning. Each year more money is spent on advertising snack food and soft drinks than on political advertising. What is excessive is the disproportionate share of money that flows to the coffers of incumbent officeholders. Although voter desire for change propelled the 1992 Clinton defeat of an incumbent president and the 1994 Republican victories over a host of incumbent Democratic officeholders, in 1998 incumbents were once again consistently winning elections. And, frankly, we are not optimistic that incumbents will approve legislation that will diminish their chances of winning. However, any serious attempt at reforming our system of electing public officials must come to grips with this problem.

Questioning political campaign principles and practices is not unique to Americans of our generation. Dissatisfaction has always existed and our system has evolved to accommodate those dissatisfactions that seemed warranted. Dissatisfaction with methods of campaigning and electing officials has prompted a host of changes over the years, many of which we chronicled earlier in this book. Presumably current questions about political campaigning will prompt changes as well.

Contemporary political campaigning is by no means perfect. It has never been perfect in the past and we see no reason to expect perfection in the future. Critics will always have questions about our election procedures and practices. And they should. Surely no activity is more central to our way of life than the establishment, maintenance, and transfer of leadership through free elections. Political campaign communication is the apotheosis of the democratic experience. It warrants our constant reexamination and reappraisal.

NOTES

1. *Cincinnati Enquirer*, November, 25, 1997, p. A2.

2. The information in this paragraph is all drawn from Leslie Wayne, "Challengers to Incumbents Are Fighting Uphill Battle," *New York Times*, November 1, 1998, p. 26.

3. Ibid.

4. William Greider, *Who Will Tell the People: The Betrayal of American Democracy* (New York: Simon and Schuster, 1992), p. 21.

5. Charles Krauthammer, "Either Way, We Get Brand X," *Cincinnati Enquirer*, October 30, 1994, p. E2.

6. Richard Harwood, "The Ugly Elections of '94," *Washington Post National Weekly Edition*, November 14–20, 1994, p. 29.

7. Ibid.

Selected Bibliography

Bennett, W. Lance. *The Governing Crisis: Media, Money, and Marketing in American Elections*. New York: St. Martin's Press, 1992.

Brareton, Charles. *First in the Nation: New Hampshire and the Premier Presidential Operatives*. Portsmouth, N.H.: Peter E. Randall, 1987.

Campbell, Karlyn Kohrs, and Kathleen Hall Jamieson, eds. *Form and Genre: Shaping Rhetorical Action*. Falls Church, Va.: Speech Communication Association, 1977.

Cook, Elizabeth Adell, Sue Thomas, and Clyde Wilcox, eds. *The Year of the Woman: Myths and Realities*. Boulder, Colo.: Westview Press, 1994.

Darcy, R., Susan Welch, and Janet Clark. *Women, Elections, and Representation*. 2d ed. Lincoln: University of Nebraska Press, 1994.

Davis, Richard, ed. *The Press and American Politics: The New Mediator*. New York: Longman, 1992.

Denton, Robert E., Jr., ed. *The 1992 Presidential Campaign: A Communication Perspective*. Westport, Conn.: Praeger, 1994.

———. *The 1996 Presidential Campaign: A Communication Perspective*. Westport, Conn.: Praeger, 1998.

Denton, Robert E., Jr., and Dan F. Hahn, eds. *Presidential Communication*. New York: Praeger, 1986.

Devlin, L. Patrick. *Political Persuasion in Presidential Campaigns*. New Brunswick, N.J.: Transaction, 1987.

Diamond, Edwin, and Stephen Bates. *The Spot: The Rise of Political Advertising on Television*. 3d ed. Cambridge: MIT Press, 1992.

Edelman, Murray. *The Symbolic Uses of Politics: With a New Afterword*. Urbana and Chicago: University of Illinois Press, 1985.

Elder, Charles D., and Roger W. Cobb. *The Political Uses of Symbols*. New York: Longman, 1983.

Foote, Joe S. *Television Access and Political Power: The Networks, the Presidency, and the Loyal Opposition.* New York: Praeger, 1990.

Friedenberg, Robert V. *Communication Consultants in Political Campaigns: Ballot Box Warriors.* Westport, Conn.: Praeger, 1997.

————, ed. *Rhetorical Studies of National Political Debates: 1960–1992.* Westport, Conn.: Praeger, 1994.

————, ed. *Rhetorical Studies of National Political Debates—1996.* Westport, Conn.: Praeger, 1997.

Garment, Suzanne. *Scandal: The Culture of Mistrust in American Politics.* New York: Doubleday, 1991.

Hahn, Dan F. *Political Communication: Rhetoric, Government, and Citizens.* State College, Pa.: Strata Publishing, 1998.

Hoff, Paul S. *Beyond the 30-Second Spot: Enhancing the Media's Role in Congressional Campaigns.* Washington, D.C.: Center for Responsive Politics, 1988.

Iyengar, Shanto, and Richard Reeves, eds. *Do the Media Govern? Politicians, Voters, and Reporters in America.* Thousand Oaks, Calif.: Sage Publications, 1997.

Jamieson, Kathleen Hall. *Packaging the Presidency: A History and Criticism of Presidential Campaign Advertising.* New York: Oxford University Press, 1984.

Jamieson, Kathleen Hall, and David S. Birdsell. *Presidential Debates: The Challenge of Creating an Informed Electorate.* New York: Oxford University Press, 1988.

Kaid, Lynda Lee, Dan D. Nimmo, and Keith R. Sanders. *New Perspectives on Political Advertising.* Carbondale and Edwardsville: Southern Illinois University Press, 1986.

Kern, Montague. *30-Second Politics: Political Advertising in the 1980s.* New York: Praeger, 1989.

Kraus, Sidney. *Televised Presidential Debates and Public Policy.* Hillsdale, N.J.: Lawrence Erlbaum, 1988.

Loomis, Burdett. *The New American Politician: Ambition, Entrepreneurship, and the Changing Face of Political Life.* New York: Basic Books, 1988.

Mandel, Ruth B. *In the Running: The New Woman Candidate.* New Haven, Conn. and New York: Ticknor and Fields, 1981.

Martel, Myles. *Political Campaign Debates: Images, Strategies, and Tactics.* New York: Longman, 1983.

Mayer, Jane, and Doyle McManus. *Landslide: The Unmaking of the President, 1984–1988.* Boston: Houghton Mifflin, 1988.

McQuail, Denis. *Audience Analysis.* Thousand Oaks, Calif.: Sage Publications, 1997.

Mickelson, Sig. *From Whistle Stop to Sound Bite: Four Decades of Politics and Television.* New York: Praeger, 1989.

Miller, Arthur H., and Bruce E. Gronbeck, eds. *Presidential Campaigns and American Self Images.* Boulder, Colo.: Westview Press, 1994.

Morris, Dick. *Behind the Oval Office: Winning the Presidency in the Nineties.* New York: Random House, 1997.

Nimmo, Dan D., and James E. Combs. *Mediated Political Realities.* 2d ed. New York: Longman, 1990.

Noonan, Peggy. *What I Saw at the Revolution.* New York: Random House, 1990.

Paletz, David L. *The Media in American Politics: Contents and Consequences.* New York: Longman, 1999.

————, ed. *Political Communication Research: Approaches, Studies, Assessments.* Norwood, N.J.: Ablex Publishing, 1987.

Payne, Gregory J., ed. *American Behavioral Scientist* (March/April 1989; November/December 1993; August 1997).

Pfau, Michael, and Henry C. Kenski. *Attack Politics: Strategy and Defense.* New York: Praeger, 1990.

Press, Charles, and Kenneth Verburg. *American Politics and Journalists.* Glenview, Ill.: Scott, Foresman and Company, 1988.

Reichley, A. James, ed. *Elections American Style.* Washington, D.C.: Brookings Institution, 1987.

Sabato, Larry J. *Feeding Frenzy: How Attack Journalism Has Transformed American Politics.* New York: Free Press, 1993.

Sabato, Larry J., and Glenn R. Simpson. *Dirty Little Secrets: The Persistence of Corruption in American Politics.* New York: Random House, 1996.

Sanders, Keith R., Lynda Lee Kaid, and Dan D. Nimmo. *Political Communication Yearbook 1984.* Carbondale and Edwardsville: Southern Illinois University Press, 1985.

Scher, Richard K. *The Modern Political Campaign: Mudslinging, Bombast and the Vitality of American Politics.* Armonk, N.Y.: M. E. Sharpe, 1997.

Selnow, Gary. *High-Tech Campaigns: Computer Technology in Political Communication.* Westport, Conn.: Praeger, 1994.

Simons, Herbert W., and Aram Aghazarian, eds. *Form, Genre, and the Study of Political Discourse.* Columbia: University of South Carolina Press, 1986.

Swanson, David L., and Dan D. Nimmo. *New Directions in Political Communication: A Resource Book.* Newbury Park, Calif.: Sage Publications, 1990.

Swerdlow, Joel L., ed. *Presidential Debates: 1988 and Beyond.* Washington, D.C.: Congressional Quarterly Books, 1987.

————. *Media Technology and the Vote: A Source Book.* Boulder, Colo.: Westview Press, 1988.

Thurber, James A., and Candice J. Nelson. *Campaigns and Elections American Style.* Boulder, Colo.: Westview Press, 1995.

Valley, David B. *A History and Analysis of Democratic Presidential Nomination Acceptance Speeches to 1968.* Lanham, Md.: University Press of America, 1988.

White, Theodore H. *The Making of the President 1960.* New York: Pocket Books, 1961.

————. *The Making of the President 1964.* New York: Atheneum, 1965.

————. *The Making of the President 1968.* New York: Atheneum, 1969.

————. *The Making of the President 1972.* New York: Bantam, 1973.

Williams, Frederick. *The New Communications.* 2d ed. Belmont, Calif.: Wadsworth Publishing Company, 1989.

Windt, Theodore Otto, Jr. *Presidents and Protesters: Political Rhetoric in the 1960s.* Tuscaloosa: University of Alabama Press, 1990.

Woodward, Bob. *The Choice.* New York: Simon and Schuster, 1996.

Index

acceptance addresses, 216–25
Adams, John Quincy, 170
Aden, Roger, 160
advertising in political campaigns, 319–57; basic considerations, 326–45; consultants and, 349–57; developing a master plan for, 322–26; direct mail and, 329–32; display graphics and, 326–29; Internet and, 343–45; print and, 333–35; radio and, 335–38; strategies of, 345–49; telephones and, 332–33; television and, 338–43
agenda setting, 126–29
Agnew, Spiro, 118
Ailes, Roger, 154, 233, 354
Alexander, Lamar, 13, 23, 27, 38, 40, 41, 210, 370
Allen, Cathy, 307–8
Anderson, John, 330
announcement speeches, 23–34, 208–16
apologias, 235–42
Aspen decision, 256
Atwood, Erwin L., 311–12
audiences, 174–79
Auer, J. Jeffery, 249

Babbitt, Bruce, 28
Baker, Howard, 42
Bancroft, George, 189
Baxter, Leona, 350
Bayh, Birch, 10, 42
Becker, Samuel L., 38–39, 282
Beckley, John, 349
Benoit, William L., 220–21, 224
Bentsen, Lloyd, 275
Benze, James G., 160
Berelson, Bernard, 114–17, 129–31
Berger, Josef, 192
Bernays, Edward, 350
Berquist, Goodwin F., 265
Biden, Joseph, 75
Birdsell, David S., 249
Bitzer, Lloyd, 207
Blaine, James G., 71
Blumenthal, Sidney, 12
Blumler, Jay G., 120–21, 123–25
Bond, Christopher (Kit), 320, 323
Bono, Sonny, 28
Boosalis, Helen, 160
Bormann, Ernest, 191
Boschwitz, Rudy, 308, 310
Boulding, Kenneth E., 66
Boxer, Barbara, 157
Bradley, Bill, 20, 28, 370

Brady, James, 54
Brady, Sarah, 54
Brinkley, David, 72
Broder, David, 151–52
Brown, Edmund G. (Jerry), 12, 28, 36, 52, 92, 211–12
Brown, Ronald, 52
Bruce, Lenny, 276
Bryan, William Jennings, 70, 91, 216, 218, 326
Buchanan, Frank, 260
Buchanan, Patrick J., 27–29, 32, 40, 43, 53, 326, 370
Bunning, Jim, 369
Burgoon, Michael, 157–58
Bush, George, 11; acceptance address (1992), 219–20; debate strategies of, 268–72, 277, 326, 370; and news conferences, 227–28, 232, 235–41, 250; and nominating conventions, 52, 54, 75, 81, 85–87, 96, 98–101, 145, 148, 151–52, 184–85, 187, 192, 195, 198, 201; and primary campaigns, 35, 37, 42; surfacing in campaigns of, 20–22, 28–29
Bush, George W., 21, 27
Byrne, Jane, 84–85

Campbell, Carroll, Jr., 21, 264
Carter, Jimmy, 11–12; acceptance address (1980), 222–23, 227–28, 234, 250, 255; use of challenger strategies, 96–97, 99; use of merged campaign styles, 102–4, 141, 143, 190, 195, 199; and nominating conventions, 50–51, 54, 81, 84–85; and political debates, 265–66, 271, 275, 278, 326, 370; strategies of announcement address (1976), 211–13; surfacing and, 11–12, 22, 29, 30, 42
Carvey, Dana, 192
Chabot, Steve, 155
Chaffee, Steven H., 122, 276–77, 280, 282
challenger campaign style and strategies, 93–101
Chasteen, Deborah, 320–21
Chavez, Linda, 164

Church, Frank, 10, 211
Clay, Henry, 70
Cleveland, Grover, 71, 216
Clinton, Bill, 7, 9, 12, 13; announcement addresses of, 212, 214, 217, 220; apologias and, 235–41, 250, 266; debate strategies and, 268–72, 278, 326, 329, 354, 369, 370, 373; and nominating conventions, 43, 50, 52–54, 74–75; political ads of, 145, 149, 151, 153, 155; and political debates of, 183–85, 187–90, 195, 198–99, 201; and primary stage, 31, 36–38, 40–41; styles and strategies in campaigns of, 77, 81, 83, 85, 87–88, 95–101; and surfacing stage, 21, 27, 29
Clinton–Bush–Perot debate (1992), 260–63
Clinton–Dole debate (1996), 263–65
Clinton, Hillary Rodham, 200–201
coffees, 298–300
Cohen, Bernard C., 126
Collins, Catherine, 232
Collins, Thomas, 330
Combs, James, 109
Commission on Presidential Debates, 260, 262–63
Commission on Presidential Nominations, 5
Connally, John, 7, 42
Coolidge, Calvin, 189, 350
Coughlin, Father Charles, 113
Cox, James, 91
Crane, Phillip, 330
Crigler, Ann, 344–45
Cronkite, Walter, 46, 72
Culver, John, 10
Cuomo, Mario, 28

D'Amato, Alfonse, 53, 77, 151, 303, 343
Dance, Frank E. X., 11
Danforth, Jack, 319
Davis, Dennis, 122, 282
Davis, Gray, 369
Davis, John, 44, 71
debates in political campaigns, 249–92; conditions required for, 259–65; de-

ciding whether to debate, 256–59; effects of, 274–82; history of, 249–56; strategies of, 265–74

Declercq, Eugene, 160

Dees, Morris, 330

Denton, Robert E., Jr., 231

Devlin, L. Patrick, 146, 148–49

Dewey, Thomas, 254

DeWine, Michael, 326–27

Diamond, Edwin, 146

diffusion of information theory, 121–23

DiNicola, Ron, 303–4

Dionne, E. J., Jr., 31

direct mail, 329–32

DiSalle, Michael, 213

display graphics, 326–29

Dole, Robert, 7, 9, 12–13; acceptance address of, 217, 220–21, 223–25; announcement speech (1996), 210, 213–14; and nominating conventions, 43, 53–55, 75, 83, 95, 98, 100–101; and political debates, 266, 270, 278, 280–81, 329, 370; and surfacing, 21, 23–24, 28–29, 30, 32, 37, 40–41; and television ads of, 140, 145, 149, 151, 153, 188, 190, 199, 201

Dole, Elizabeth, 76, 159, 198–200

door-to-door canvass, 300–302

Douglas, Stephen, 89

Drew, Elizabeth, 277

Dreyfus, Lee, 34

Dukakis, Michael, 29, 42; and nominating convention, 49–52, 54, 97, 100–101; use of political ads, 148, 151–52, 195, 211, 227–28, 232; and political debate (1984), 261, 268–69, 271

Eagleton, Thomas, 122

Eastwood, Clint, 28

Edelman, Murray, 23, 80

Edley, Paige, 162

Eisenhower, Dwight David, 12, 81, 96, 122, 140, 189, 254, 259, 336, 350

EMILY'S LIST (Early Money Is Like Yeast), 10

Engler, John, 95–96

English, Phil, 303–4, 370

Fabrizio, Tony, 53

Faircloth, Lauch, 77

Faucheux, Ron, 186–89

Feiger, Geoffrey, 95–96

Feinstein, Dianne, 155, 157

Feldman, Jacob, 277

Fenno, R. F., 78

Ferraro, Geraldine, 50, 67–68, 159, 164, 303, 326

Fields, Wayne, 223

Fitzgerald, Peter, 78, 369

Fitzpatrick, Mary Anne, 157

Flanagan, Michael, 369

Flowers, Gennifer, 36, 235–41

Forbes, Malcolm S., Jr. (Steve), 7; and surfacing, 21–23, 27, 29–30, 76, 86

Ford, Gerald, 22, 47, 54; campaign strategies of, 90–91, 94, 141, 143, 149, 190, 195, 255, 258; and political debate (1976), 271, 275, 278

Fowler, Wyche, Jr., 349

Freeman, Orville, 190, 194–95

Frist, Bill, 369

fund-raising, interpersonally, 302–11

Funkhouser, G. Ray, 127

Gallup, George, Jr., 276

Garth, David, 350

Gaudet, Hazel, 114–16

Gavin, William F., 192

general election stage of campaigns, 55–57

Gephardt, Richard, 20–21, 42, 370

Gingrich, Newt, 21, 37, 53

Glenn, John, 28, 34, 97, 175, 326–27

Gold, Ellen Reid, 236

Golden, James L., 265

Goldwater, Barry, 50–51, 97, 99–100, 141–42, 313, 355

Gore, Albert, Jr., 20–21, 42, 53–54, 76, 184, 198; and political debates, 264, 266, 269, 281, 326, 370

Gosnell, Harold F., 113

Gramm, Phil, 13, 22–23, 26–27, 32, 38, 210, 215

Greer, Frank, 349
Gronbeck, Bruce E., 24, 56, 64, 147
Gross, Bert, 211–12
Gumpert, Gary, 46

Haase, Karen, 163
Hagner, Paul R., 280
Hahn, Dan F., 231, 281
Haig, Alexander, 28
Haldeman, H. R., 72
Hamilton, Alexander, 189
Hamilton, Lee, 370
Hanna, Mike, 301
Harding, Warren, 43, 71, 91
Harkin, Tom, 22, 32, 42, 212
Harkness, William, 253
Harrison, Benjamin, 90–91
Harrison, William Henry, 65–66
Hart, Gary, 28, 42, 67
Hayakawa, S. I., 34
Helms, Jesse, 193, 341
Hill, Anita, 95
Hitler, Adolf, 100, 112–13
Hoffa, Jimmy, 87
Holtzman, Elizabeth, 25, 164
Hooker, John J., Jr., 255
Hoover, Herbert, 71, 81, 189
Huddleston, Walter (Dee), 154
Humphrey, Hubert, 51, 127, 142, 195,
    224, 255, 268
Hyatt, Joel, 175, 178
hypodermic effect, 112–14

Iacocca, Lee, 28
imagery and campaigning, 65–69
incumbent campaign style and strate-
    gies, 77–93
Internet, 4, 12–13, 343–45
interpersonal communication and po-
    litical campaigns, 293–314; between
    candidates and financial contribu-
    tors, 302–11; between candidates
    and voters, 294–302; between vot-
    ers, 311–14
Iyengar, Shanto, 128–29

Jackson, Andrew, 70, 189
Jackson, Henry (Scoop), 42

Jackson, Jesse, 28, 51–52, 235, 241,
    326, 338
Jamieson, Kathleen Hall, 140–41, 143,
    147
Japp, Phyllis, 160
Javits, Jacob, 174
Jefferson, Thomas, 349
Johnson, Lyndon, 81, 91, 142, 233
Jones, Paula, 74, 241
Joslyn, Richard, 146
Just, Marion, 344–45

Kaid, Lynda Lee, 145, 153, 295–96
Kaplan, Robert, 310
Kasich, John R., 76, 370
Katz, Elihu, 116, 124, 277
Kefauver, Estes, 47, 254
Kemp, Jack, 46, 53, 220, 266, 343, 370
Kendell, Amos, 189
Kennedy, Edward (Ted): announce-
    ment speech (1980), 211, 213, 222,
    236; campaign styles and strategies
    of, 84–85, 92, 97, 101; and surfacing,
    25–26, 28, 42, 53
Kennedy, John, 12, 54; campaign
    styles and strategies of, 70, 87, 96–
    98, 122, 190, 195, 213–14, 234; politi-
    cal debates and, 249–50, 254–55,
    268, 275, 277, 280, 326
Kennedy, Robert, 260
Kenski, Henry, 156
Kern, Montague, 145–46, 150, 162, 344–
    45
Kerry, Robert (Bob), 42, 212, 370
Kessler, Frank, 86
Kessler, Martha Stout, 201
Khrushchev, Nikita, 259
Kimsey, William D., 312
King, Martin Luther, Jr., 51
King, Martin Luther, Sr., 61
kingmakers, 5–6
Kinnock, Neil, 75
Kissinger, Henry, 232
Klapper, Joseph, 114
Klemens, Lawrence, 370
Kling, Ken, 351
Koch, Edward I., 83, 95, 343
Kraus, Sidney, 122, 282

Krauthhammer, Charles, 371
Kroft, Steve, 235–41

Lake, James, 104
Landon, Alfred, 253
Lang, Gladys Engel, 128
Lazarsfeld, Paul F., 114, 118, 129–31
League of Women Voters, 256
Lehrer, Jim, 280
Lenart, Silvo, 315
Leno, Jay, 22
Letterman, David, 22
Lewinsky, Monica, 241
Limbaugh, Rush, 337
Lincoln, Abraham, 43
Lincoln–Douglas debates, 249–52
Linkugel, Will, 238–39
Lodge, Henry Cabot, 254, 260
Loomis, Burdett, 351
Louden, Allan, 67
Lucier, James, 193
Lugar, Richard, 29, 38, 210

MacArthur, Douglas, 189
Magnuson, Warren, 10
Makinson, Larry, 370
Malchow, Hal, 332
Mandel, Ruth, 158–59
Manhattan Project, 36
mass media and political campaigns,
    109–34; agenda setting and, 126–29;
    diffusion of information and, 121–
    23; hypodermic effect and, 112–14;
    social influence model and, 114–19;
    uses and gratifications and, 123–26
Matalin, Mary, 201
Mattingly, Mack, 349
McAdoo, William, 71
McCain, John, 370
McCarthy, Eugene, 25, 40
McCombs, Maxwell, 127
McConnell, Mitch, 154
McGovern, George, 10, 12, 45, 51;
    communicative styles and strategies
    of, 90, 97, 99–101, 142, 297
McKinley, William, 90–91
McLeod, Jack, 126
McPhee, William, 116

McQuail, Dennis, 120–21, 124–26
Melcher, John, 154
Michel, Robert, 192, 195
Mikulski, Barbara, 164
Miller, Gerald R., 157
Mitchell, George, 20
Mitchell, John, 336
Molinari, Susan, 53, 341
Mondale, Walter: campaign styles and
    strategies, 100–104, 149, 227–28; and
    political debates, 266, 275, 277, 280,
    326
Mongeau, Paul, 68–69
Moody, Blair, 254
Morris, Dwight, 305
Morris, Richard, 37
Mosely-Braun, Carol, 71, 77–78
Murphy, Michael, 349
Muskie, Edmund, 326
Mussolini, Benito, 113

National Communication Association,
    261
Nethercutt, George, 369
Neustadt, Richard, 264
news conferences, 225–35
Nickles, Don, 21
Nimmo, Dan, 48, 109, 270
Nixon, Richard, 54; campaign styles
    and strategies, 70, 72–73, 86–87, 90,
    96, 99, 127–28, 142–43, 186, 189,
    195, 236; and political debates, 250,
    255, 268, 275, 277, 327, 336
nominating conventions, 43–57
Noonan, Peggy, 198
Nunn, Sam, 20

O'Donnell, Kenneth, 260
Olson, Kathryn M., 239–40
Orr, C. Jack, 231
Orr, Kay, 160–61

PACs (political action committees), 8–
    11
Patterson, Thomas, 38–39, 41, 129–31
Peck, Laura, 299–301
Perot, H. Ross, 7, 12–13, 28, 37, 73,
    110, 149, 198, 220; and political de-

bates, 263–64, 266, 270, 278, 326, 329
Perry, James, 71
Pfau, Michael, 156, 279
Pier, P. M., 220–21, 224
Pierce, Franklin, 43
Plumb, J. H., 4
political action committees, 8–11
political advertising. *See* television
political campaigns: advertising strategies of, 345–49; changes in, 5–12; communicative functions of, 19–57; communicative styles and, 64–104; importance of, 3–5; primaries and, 31–43; stages of, 19–57; technology and, 12–14, 69–76
political consultants, 349–57; functions and types, 353–57; history of, 349–53
political parties, 5–6
Portman, Rob, 201
Powell, Colin, 53
primaries, 31–43
print media, 333–35
Procter, David E., 160, 163
public speaking in political campaigns, 171–202; audiences and, 174–79; competency and format, 180–81; decision to speak, 173–81; political speechwriting and, 189–98; use of polls and, 179–80; speech modules and, 182–86; stock speeches, 181–82, 186–89; surrogate speakers and, 198–201

Qualls, Roxanne, 155
Quayle, J. Danforth (Dan), 22–23, 187, 198
Quayle, Marilyn, 53

radio, 335–38
Rather, Dan, 22
Reagan, Ronald, 12, 28; and political debates, 250, 265–66, 271, 275, 277, 326, 341, 370; in primary campaigns, 35–37, 42, 46–47, 79, 81; styles and strategies in campaigns of, 96–100, 102–4, 110, 123, 128, 143, 148, 195, 198
recurring forms of political campaign communication, 207–42; acceptance addresses, 216–25; announcement speeches, 208–16; apologias, 235–42; news conferences, 225–35
Reeve, Christopher, 54
Reston, James, 118
Rice, Donna, 42
Richards, Ann, 164, 354
Rieselbach, Leroy N., 280
Ritter, Kurt, 219–23
Roberts, Bill, 350
Robertson, Marion G. (Pat), 7, 24, 28, 45, 53
Robinson, John P., 312
Rockefeller, John (Jay), 20
Rockefeller, Nelson, 51, 190, 194–95, 326
Rogers, Everett, 121–22
Roosevelt, Franklin Delano, 54; campaign styles and strategies, 70–71, 84, 91, 96, 98, 102, 115; public speaking practices of, 189–90, 194–95, 198, 216, 236, 253–54
Roper, Elmo, 174, 277
Rosenstiel, Tom, 272–73
Ryan, Nolan, 180

Sabourin, Teresa, 160–62
Sanchez, Loretta, 157
Sanders, Keith R., 311
Santorum, Rick, 369
Sauter, Kevin, 280
Savage, Robert L., 122
Schenck-Hamlin, William J., 163
Schlesinger, Laura (Dr. Laura), 337
Schroeder, Patricia, 159
Schwartz, Tony, 351
Scott, Dred, 250
Sears, David O., 277–80
Sears, John, 35–36
Shadegg, Stephen, 313–14
Sharp, Stephen A., 255–56
Shaw, Donald L., 127
Sheckels, Theodore, Jr., 164

Sheehan, Michael, 354
Sherwood, Robert, 189
Shoemaker, Floyd, 121–22
Short-Thompson, Cady, 68, 163
Sigal, Leon V., 227
Simpson, Alan, 370
Sinclair, Upton, 350
Sirica, John, 128
Smith, Alfred, 44
Smith, Carolyn, 232
Smith, Craig Allen, 195, 266–67
Smith, Kathy B., 266–67
Smith, Larry David, 48
Snowe, Olympia, 369
social influence model, 114–19
Soirauf, Frank, 304
Specter, Arlen, 27, 95, 210
speechwriting, 189–98; job demands
    of, 192–94; justification for, 190–92;
    methods of, 196–98; use of teams
    in, 194–96
Spencer, Stuart, 350
Springer, Gerald (Jerry), 339–40
Squier, Robert, 321
Stassen, Harold, 254
Steeper, Frederick T., 272
Steinbeck, John, 189
Stern, Bobbi, 212
Stevenson, Adlai, 140, 194–95, 254,
    336, 350
Stockdale, James, 281
Stockman, Steve, 369
Stone, Richard, 215
strategies of political campaigns. See
    styles of political campaigns
Strauss, Robert, 51
styles of political campaigns, 64–69;
    challenger style, 93–101; incum-
    bency style, 77–93; merger of chal-
    lenger and incumbency styles, 101–
    4; technology and, 69–76
Sullivan, Ed, 348
surfacing, 19–31
surrogate speakers, 198–202; benefits
    of, 200–202; selection of, 198–99;
    utilization of, 199–201
Swanson, David L., 278
Swanson, Linda L., 278

Swerdlow, Joel L., 71
Swift, Jane, 159

Taft, Robert, 122
Taft, William Howard, 212
Tannen, Deborah, 158
Taylor, Maurice (Mory), 7
Taylor, Zachary, 70
Teasdale, Joseph (Walking Joe), 174,
    215
technology and campaigns, 5–14, 69–
    76. See also Internet
telephones, 332–33
television, 139–70; advantages/disad-
    vantages as political media, 319–22,
    338–43; effectiveness of in political
    campaigns, 164–65; historical use of
    in politics, 140–45; history of politi-
    cal debates and, 252–56; types and
    functions of political ads, 145–56;
    women candidates and, 156–64
Temple, Shirley, 350
Thatcher, Margaret, 86
Third Millennium, 10–11
Thomas, Clarence, 95
Thompson, Fred, 21
Tower, John, 355
Trent, Jimmie D., 68–69
Trent, Judith S., 68–69, 160–62
Truman, Harry, 54, 81, 94, 180, 190,
    194–95, 234, 254
Tsongas, Paul, 36, 43, 212

Udall, Morris, 45
uses and gratifications model, 123–26

Valley, David, 218, 222
Van Buren, Martin, 65
Vandenberg, Arthur, 253
Ventura, Jesse, 110, 369
Viguerie, Richard, 355

Walkosz, Barbara, 163
Wallace, George, 127
Ware, B. L., 238–39
Washburn, Wilcomb E., 66
Washington, George, 69, 77, 89, 189

Waters, Maxine, 127
Weiss, Robert O., 269
Wells, William J., 220–21, 224
Wellstone, Paul, 153
Whitaker, Clem, 350
White, Theodore H., 6, 12, 72, 78
Wilder, Douglas, 212
Williams, Frederick, 70
Wilkie, Wendell, 115, 253

Wilson, Pete, 30, 155, 210, 212–13
Wilson, Woodrow, 43–44, 89, 91
Winburn, Charles, 7
women candidates and advertising,
    156–64
Woods, Harriet, 319–23, 341

Yeakel, Lynn, 95
Yeltsin, Boris, 85

About the Authors

JUDITH S. TRENT is Professor of Communication and Associate Vice President for Research and Advanced Studies at the University of Cincinnati. She is the author of numerous books and book chapters including "The Beginning and the Early End" in *The 1996 Presidential Campaign: A Communication Perspective* (Robert E. Denton, Jr., ed.) (Praeger, 1998) and "The Early Campaign of 1992: The Reluctant Candidates" in *The 1992 Presidential Campaign: A Communication Perspective* (Robert E. Denton, Jr., ed.) (Praeger, 1994). She also served as editor of the book *Communication: Views from the Helm for the 21st Century* (1998). She has written and spoken widely on the subject of political campaign communication and is a frequent commentator and analyst on political campaigns and candidates for the ABC, NBC, and CBS television affiliates in Cincinnati as well as Ohio/Cincinnati newspapers. In 1997 she served as President of the National Communication Association.

ROBERT V. FRIEDENBERG is Professor of Communication at Miami (Ohio) University. He is the author of *Communication Consultants in Political Campaigns: Ballot Box Warriors* (Praeger, 1997). He is the editor of *Rhetorical Studies of National Political Debates—1996* (Praeger, 1997) and *Rhetorical Studies of National Political Debates: 1960–1992* (Praeger, 1994), and is the author of *Theodore Roosevelt and the Rhetoric of Militant Decency* (Greenwood, 1989). In 1989 he received the "Outstanding Book of the Year Award" from the Religious Speech Communication Association for *"Hear O Israel": The History of American Jewish Preaching 1654–1970*. He has served as a communication consultant for the Republican National Committee and has been involved in over 70 political campaigns.

ISBN 0-275-96404-3

90000>

EAN

9 780275 964047

HARDCOVER BAR CODE